# Classroom
# Teaching
# Skills

**JAMES M. COOPER, GENERAL EDITOR**
University of Virginia

**SANDRA SOKOLOVE GARRETT**
Medifacts, Ltd.

**TOM LOUGH**
Piedmont Virginia Community College

**PETER H. MARTORELLA**
North Carolina State University, Raleigh

**GRETA G. MORINE-DERSHIMER**
Syracuse University

**JEANNE PFEIFER**
California State University, Sacramento

**DAVID SADKER**
American University

**MYRA SADKER**
American University

**JERRY SHORT**
University of Virginia

**ROBERT SHOSTAK**
Florida International University

**TERRY D. TENBRINK**
University of Missouri

**WILFORD A. WEBER**
University of Houston

D. C. HEATH AND COMPANY
Lexington, Massachusetts    Toronto

# Classroom
# Teaching
# Skills Third Edition

TO OUR STUDENTS
*because those who can, teach;*
*and those who teach, learn.*

**Cover:**   Stock, Boston: (*left*) Jean-Claude Lejeune; (*right*) Richard Sobol

**Interior Photos:**   Stock, Boston: Paul Fortin, p. iii; Owen Franken, p. 1; George Bel-
lerose, pp. 19, 359; Norman Hurst, p. 67; Jean-Claude Lejeune,
pp. 111, 181; Bohdan Hrynewych, p. 225; Peter Southwick, p. 271

Jean-Claude Lejeune, pp. 139, 401

Published simultaneously in Canada.

Printed in the United States of America.

International Standard Book Number: 0-669-07574-4

Library of Congress Catalog Card Number: 85-81022

# Preface

Margaret Mead once said, "No man will ever again die in the same world in which he was born." Her theme of change certainly applies to the field of teacher education. At one time in the not-too-distant past, teacher education consisted of a few courses on education theory, some courses on methods, and a topping of student teaching. Except for the student teaching, and maybe a little observation experience, the program consisted of campus-based courses.

Teacher education today differs considerably from the preceding description. Programs are much more field-oriented than ever before, requiring prospective teachers to spend more time working with students in schools. The present emphasis on practical experience with students should not be interpreted as a movement away from theory. Rather, educational theory is being integrated with practice. This integration recognizes that theory, to be internalized, must be learned in the context in which it is to be applied. In the past, prospective teachers were expected to translate theory into practice with little help. Usually they were unsuccessful. Today, with the help of newly developed curriculum materials, teacher educators help trainees apply the theory in field contexts and give them feedback on their efforts.

The third edition of *Classroom Teaching Skills* will help prospective teachers meld theory with practice. The book conceptualizes the teacher as a decision maker — one who makes planning, implementing, evaluation, and management decisions as part of the instructional role. To make and carry out these decisions the teacher needs certain teaching skills. The conceptual framework of the teacher as a decision maker is presented in Chapter 1. Each subsequent chapter addresses a particular skill by first discussing the theory behind the skill and then giving the reader practice situations in which the skill can be applied and feedback received. Because each chapter presents specific learning objectives as well as mastery tests, the reader receives immediate feedback on this learning.

After students have completed the chapters, the instructor may want to set up microteaching experiences that will enable the students to practice the skills with actual learners. Ultimate acquisition of the skill must, of course, take place in actual classroom situations.

From the outset our goal was to produce instructional materials that are (1) important, (2) flexible, (3) readable, and (4) scholarly. A word about each of these features follows.

First, the *importance* of the teaching skills contained in this book has been dramatically demonstrated during the last several years by the millions of dollars spent on researching the skills and the multitude of publications on each skill. Our experience indicates that students emphatically want to master practical teaching skills that will enable them to cope successfully with their classroom responsibilities. Consequently, it is our belief that these instructional materials, dedicated as they are to the mastery of basic teaching skills, will be retained and used by most students as an ongoing, self-evaluation tool — to be referred to both during and after their field experiences.

Our second goal, to produce a highly *flexible* text, has been met in two ways. First, the content itself — the skills — is ubiquitous, reaching into virtually every course in the teacher-training curriculum. Second, the book has been designed as a self-contained teacher-education

v

learning package, thus permitting use in a variety of capacities in all parts of the curriculum. Instructors may choose to focus on particular chapters for one course and different chapters for another course. How the book is used will depend on the structure and organization of a given teacher-education program.

Our third goal, *readability,* has been achieved through editing the manuscripts of the various authors. While each author's unique writing style has been consciously preserved, the level and structure of writing has been adjusted to conform to preplanned standards. In each chapter we have tried to present a relatively simple, jargon-free presentation within a four-step, self-teaching format: (1) a statement of objectives, (2) a presentation of written information, (3) practice exercises with answers, and (4) a mastery test with answer key.

Our fourth goal, developing materials representative of the best current *scholarship,* has been met by experienced authors, each a recognized authority regarding the particular skill about which he or she has written. Further information on each author is presented following the Contents.

Before revising *Classroom Teaching Skills,* questionnaires were mailed to professors who had used the books in their classes, asking them to evaluate the various chapters and to suggest changes for improvement. These evaluations and comments were mailed to each author, along with my suggestions for revision. The resulting product is a third edition that addresses specific concerns and suggestions made by users of the second edition. We believe that the third edition is an even more readable book than the second edition, that it reflects recent research in the respective skill areas, and that it is based on extensive field testing.

In addition, previous users of the book will recognize that we have added a new chapter on the use of microcomputers in the classroom. Since our second edition was published in 1982, there has been a tremendous burgeoning of microcomputers in schools and classrooms. Preservice and inservice teacher education programs are incorporating training in the use of microcomputers as requirements or options for teachers. More so than any other technological advance, microcomputers have the capacity to transform much of our classroom teaching processes. While many courses exist on the technical operations of microcomputers, the new chapter addresses the issue of how microcomputers can be used to improve student learning and improve instruction.

*James M. Cooper*

# Contents

# 4. Lesson Presentation Skills

ROBERT SHOSTAK

# 5. Questioning Skills

MYRA SADKER AND DAVID SADKER

# 6. Teaching Concepts

PETER H. MARTORELLA

# 7. Interpersonal Communication Skills    225

SANDRA SOKOLOVE GARRETT, MYRA SADKER, AND DAVID SADKER

# 8. Classroom Management    271

WILFORD A. WEBER

# 9.    Evaluation    359

TERRY D. TENBRINK

# 10.    Using Microcomputers in the Classroom    401

JERRY SHORT AND TOM LOUGH

# About the Authors

**James M. Cooper** is Commonwealth Professor and Dean of the Curry School of Education at the University of Virginia. He received four degrees from Stanford University — two in history and two in education, including his Ph.D. in 1967. He has written or edited nine books, including *Those Who Can, Teach* and *Kaleidoscope: Readings in Education*, coauthored and coedited with Kevin Ryan; and *Developing Skills for Instructional Supervision*. His books and articles address the areas of teacher education, supervision of teachers, microteaching, and teacher education program evaluation. His articles have appeared in such journals as *Phi Delta Kappan, Journal of Teacher Education, Educational Leadership, Elementary School Journal, Elementary English, Journal of Research and Development in Education*, and *Education and Urban Society*. He was Director of one of the USOE Model Elementary Teacher Education Programs at the University of Massachusetts and later was Associate Dean for Graduate Studies in the College of Education at the University of Houston.

**Sandra Sokolove Garrett** is President of Medifacts, Ltd., a company that provides medical support service to a variety of health-care settings. Dr. Garrett is involved in ongoing research related to physician-patient interpersonal communications and the effects of such interaction on issues such as health maintenance, rehabilitation, and compliance. She is the author of several articles related to this and other humanistic health care issues. She received her Ed.D. from the University of Massachusetts and has been on the faculties of Lesley College, Wheaton College, University of Texas Health Science Center at Dallas, and Georgetown University School of Medicine.

**Tom Lough** is an Assistant Professor of Physics at Piedmont Virginia Community College and is editor of *The National Logo Exchange* newsletter. He also instructs computer courses for teachers in the University of Virginia's Curry School of Education, and is a doctoral candidate in Educational Psychology. He coordinates a writing team that produces computer books for Holt, Rinehart and Winston. His professional interests include exploring methods of integrating computers into physics instruction and exploiting the potential of the Logo computer language. His work with computers began in earnest when his wife, Posy, bought him a personal computer for Christmas several years ago with money she had earned from her part-time craft business. Since then he has enjoyed introducing their young son, Kyser, to the computer.

**Peter H. Martorella** is Professor and Head of the Department of Curriculum and Instruction, North Carolina State University, Raleigh. He received his Ph.D. from The Ohio State University and later completed a postdoctoral fellowship at the University of Washington. The author of two books on concept learning, Professor Martorella also has written a number of articles and books in social studies and computer education. His latest book is *Elementary Social Studies: Developing Reflective, Competent, and Concerned Citizens* (Little, Brown, 1985). In 1977 he was selected as a Senior Fulbright-Hays consultant by the Ministry of Education of Portugal to make recommendations for that country's social studies and teacher education programs. He has been Director of the Education Program of the Rockefeller Family Fund. Formerly Professor of Elementary and Secondary Education at Temple University, where he directed the Graduate Program in General Education, Professor Martorella has also taught at the elementary, junior high, and senior high levels.

**Greta G. Morine-Dershimer** is a Professor in the Division for the Study of Teaching at Syracuse University. She received her Ed.D. from Teachers College, Columbia University, in 1965. She taught in elementary and junior high schools for ten years, worked in preservice and inservice teacher training for fifteen years, and most recently was involved in research on teacher and pupil information processing. Her earlier publications include *Discovering Your Language* (Holt, Rinehart and Winston), *Discovery: A Challenge to Teachers* (Prentice-Hall), and *Creating the School: An Introduction to Education* (Little, Brown). She has contributed chapters to many books, including "Teaching" in the 1974 N.S.S.E. Yearbook, entitled *The Elementary School in the United States*. She has also written articles for several journals, including *Teachers College Record, Theory into Practice, The Journal of Teacher Education, Social Education, Elementary School Journal*, and *American Educational Research Journal*. Her most recent publication is *Talking, Listening, and Learning in Elementary Classrooms* (Longman).

**Jeanne Pfeifer,** Associate Professor at California State University, Sacramento, received her Ph.D. from University of California, Riverside. She is interested in the development of thinking skills for both preservice teachers and elementary school students. She has conducted several studies with elementary students in recognizing and generating different types of questions and responses. She has worked extensively with elementary and secondary teachers to create a model for thinking processes. That model has served as a focus for developing and adapting curricula that highlight and emphasize thinking.

**David Sadker** is Professor of Education at American University in Washington, D.C. He received his B.A. from CCNY, his M.A.T. from Harvard University, and his Ed.D. from the University of Massachusetts. He has conducted training programs concerned with teacher effectiveness, supervision, and educational equity for teachers and supervisors in over forty states. As director of a number of projects funded by the National Institute of Education, The Fund for the Improvement of Postsecondary Education, Title IV of the 1964 Civil Rights Act and The Women's Educational Equity Act, he has conducted and managed numerous training and research efforts. His articles have appeared in *Psychology Today, Phi Delta Kappan, Harvard Educational Review, Journal of Teacher Education*, and many others. Three books, including *Teachers Make the Difference: An Introduction to Education* (Harper & Row, 1980), *Sex Equity Handbook for Schools* (Longman, 1982) and *Now Upon a Time: A Contemporary View of Children's Literature* (Harper & Row, 1977) were coauthored by David and Myra Sadker. His current research and writing activities are concerned with the nature and distribution of student-teacher interaction, computer literacy, and educational equity.

**Myra Sadker** is Professor of Education at American University in Washington, D.C. She received her B.A. from Boston University, her M.A.T. from Harvard University, and her Ed.D. from the University of Massachusetts. She is coauthor of *Sex Equity Handbook for Teachers* (Longman, 1982) and *Teachers Make the Difference: An Introduction to Education* (Harper & Row, 1980), among other education texts. She has been published in many journals, including *Phi Delta Kappan, National Elementary Principal, Instructor, Educational Leadership, Social Education, Harvard Educational Review, Elementary English, Journal of Teacher Education*, and *Psychology Today*. She has codirected several projects funded under The Women's Educational Equity Act, Title IV of the 1964 Civil Rights Act, The National Institute of Education, and The Fund for the Improvement of Postsecondary Education. In 1980 the American Educational Research Association (AERA) awarded David and Myra Sadker the Women Educator's Award for research making the greatest contribution to women in education. The research conducted with David Sadker on equity and excellence in classroom interaction has been highlighted in popular media such as the *Today Show* and *Parade* magazine.

**Jerry Short** is a Professor at the University of Virginia, where he is Chairman of the Department of Educational Studies and Associate Dean of the School of Medicine. His interests include system design, instructional technology, and educational and industrial psychology. He is one of the authors of a series of computer books for students, teachers, and parents including *Nudges: IBM Logo Projects* and *Beyond Mindstorms: Teaching With IBM Logo*. His work with computers has been encouraged by his wife, Zan, and his children, Cathy, Carol and John, and by their interest in personal computers.

**Robert Shostak** is Coordinator of the English Education program and Administrative Director of the International Institute for Creative Communication at Florida International University. He received his bachelor's degree in humanities from Colgate University, a master's degree in teaching English from the State University of New York at Albany, and a Ph.D. in curriculum and instruction from the University of Connecticut. He taught high school English for six years before focusing his professional career on higher education and teacher training. He has written and edited numerous books and articles, and presently writes a monthly column for THE COMPUTING TEACHER in which he discusses and publishes articles by practitioners who use computers in the teaching of English.

**Terry TenBrink** is Professor of Educational and Counseling Psychology as well as Professor of Medicine, at the University of Missouri. He is the Director of Education for the Multipurpose Arthritis Center on the Columbia Campus. He received his Ph.D. in educational psychology from Michigan State University in 1968, where his studies emphasized learning theory, evaluation, measurement, and research design. His teaching experience spans elementary, junior high school, high school, and college students, and he has been principal of an elementary school. He stays in touch with the classroom through numerous consulting activities in public schools and in adult education, and by teaching courses in evaluation, learning, human development, and general educational psychology at the University of Missouri. He has published numerous journal articles and is engaged in continuing research on the conditions under which learning occurs efficiently. In 1974 his textbook *Evaluation: A Practical Guide for Teachers* was published by McGraw-Hill.

**Wilford A. Weber** is Professor of Education in the Department of Curriculum and Instruction of the College of Education of the University of Houston — University Park. He holds a bachelor's degree in psychology from Muhlenberg College and a doctorate in educational psychology from Temple University. Dr. Weber has taught at Temple University, Villanova University, and Syracuse University and has been at the University of Houston since 1971. He presently serves as a member of the Committee of Examiners for the National Teacher Examinations Core Battery Test of Professional Knowledge. Dr. Weber has directed numerous funded research projects and has authored more than one hundred papers, articles, chapters, monographs, and books concerned with teacher education, teacher effectiveness, classroom management, and school discipline. During his career Dr. Weber has conducted scores of seminars and workshops on the subject of classroom management and school discipline; his audiences have included teachers, administrators, and teacher educators throughout the United States and in Germany, Italy, and Mexico. Dr. Weber stays in touch with the realities of the classroom and the school through consulting and research activities that take him into the schools, by doing substitute teaching, by teaching graduate courses for inservice teachers, and through his wife—an elementary school principal—and his two school-age children. His interest in classroom management and school discipline stems from his experience as a teacher of court-committed juvenile delinquents.

James M. Cooper

# 1. The Teacher as a Decision Maker

## What Is a Teacher?

At first glance such a question seems obvious. A teacher is a person charged with the responsibility of helping others to learn and to behave in new and different ways. But who is excluded from this definition? Parents? Band directors? Drill sergeants? Boy scout leaders? At some time or another we all teach and, in turn, are taught.

We generally reserve the term "teacher," however, for persons whose primary professional or occupational function is to help others learn and develop in new ways. While education, learning, and teaching can, and do, take place in many different settings, most societies realize that education is too important to be left to chance. Consequently, they establish schools to facilitate learning and to help people live better and happier lives. Schools are created to provide a certain type of educational experience, which can be called the curriculum. Teachers are trained and hired by societies to help fulfill the purposes of the curriculum. Teachers, in the formal educative process of schooling, are social agents hired by society to help facilitate the intellectual, personal, and social development of those members of society who attend schools.

Until modern times teachers themselves had very little formal schooling; often they knew barely more than their students. As late as 1864 an Illinois teacher described the image of the teacher as "someone who can parse and cypher; has little brains and less money; is feeble minded, unable to grapple with real men and women in the stirring employments of life, but on that account admirably fitted to associate with childish intellects." [1] Needless to say, this early-day image of the teacher has changed considerably for the better. Today teachers are better educated, earn more money, and are more highly respected members of society than their nineteenth century counterparts. Society requires its teachers to obtain a college education and specific training as teachers. This increase in the educational level of teachers is recognition that if teachers are to facilitate the intellectual, personal, and social development of their students, then they must be much better educated than ever before.

## Effective Teaching

Possession of a college degree does not in any way ensure that teachers will be effective. But what is an effective teacher? What is a good teacher? Are they the same?

Good teaching is very difficult to define because the term "good" is so value-laden. What appears to be good teaching to one person may be considered poor teaching by another, because each one values different outcomes or methods. One teacher may run the classroom in a very organized, highly structured manner, emphasizing the intellectual content of the academic disciplines. Another may run the class in a less structured environment, allowing the students much more freedom to choose subject matter and activities that interest them personally. One observer, because of his value system, may identify the first teacher as a "good" teacher, while he criticizes the second teacher for running "too loose a ship." Another observer may come to the opposite conclusion with respect to which teacher is better, again, because of a different set of values.

While it remains difficult to agree on what "good" teaching is, "effective" teaching can be demonstrated. *The effective teacher is one who is able to bring about intended learning outcomes.* The nature of the learning is still most important, but two different teachers, as in the example above, may strive for and achieve very different outcomes and both be judged effective. The two critical dimensions of effective teaching are *intent* and *achievement*.

Without intent student achievement becomes random and accidental, rather than controlled and predictable. However, intent is not enough by itself. If students do not achieve their intended learning goals (even if the failure is due to variables beyond the control of their teacher), the teacher cannot truly be called effective.

While effective teachers are defined as teachers who can demonstrate the ability to bring about intended learning outcomes, what enables them to achieve desired results with students? Have you ever stopped to think about what, if anything, makes teachers different from other well-educated adults? What should effective, professional teachers know, believe, or be able to do that distinguishes them from other people? Think about these questions seriously because they are central questions, the answers to which should be at the heart of your teacher education program.

Some people will state that the crucial dimension is the teacher's personality. Teachers, they will say, should be friendly, cheerful, sympathetic, morally virtuous, enthusiastic, and humorous. In a massive study, David Ryans concluded that effective teachers are fair, democratic, responsive, understanding, kindly, stimulating, original, alert, attractive, responsible, steady, poised, and confident. Ineffective teachers were described as partial, autocratic, aloof, restricted, harsh, dull, stereotyped, apathetic, unimpressive, evasive, erratic, excitable, and uncertain.[2] But as two educational researchers once remarked, ". . . what conceivable human interaction is not the better if the people involved are friendly, cheerful, sympathetic, and virtuous rather than the opposite?"[3] These characteristics, then, while desirable in teachers, are not uniquely desirable to that group alone.

It might be difficult to reach a consensus on exactly what knowledge and skills are unique to the teaching profession, but most educators would agree that special skills and knowledge are necessary and do exist. Certainly teachers must be familiar with children and their developmental stages. They must know something about events and happenings outside the classroom and school. They must possess enough command of the subject they are going to teach to be able to differentiate what is important and central from what is incidental and peripheral. They must have a philosophy of education to help guide them in their role as teachers. They must know how human beings learn and how to create environments which facilitate learning.

### General Areas of Teacher Competence

B. O. Smith has suggested that a well-trained teacher should be prepared in four areas of teacher competence to be effective in bringing about intended learning outcomes.

1. Command of theoretical knowledge about learning and human behavior.
2. Display of attitudes that foster learning and genuine human relationships.
3. Command of knowledge in the subject matter to be taught.
4. Control of technical skills of teaching that facilitate student learning.

**1. Command of Theoretical Knowledge About Learning and Human Behavior.**   For years education has been criticized for its "folkways" practices. Educational recipes and standardized procedures were formally and informally passed on to new teachers to help them survive in classrooms. While this practice still exists, many scientific concepts from psychology, anthropology, sociology, linguistics, cybernetics, and related disciplines are now available to help teachers interpret the complex reality of their classrooms. Those teachers who lack the theoretical background and understanding provided by such scientifically derived concepts can only interpret the events of their classrooms according to popularly held beliefs or common sense. Although common sense often serves us well, there is ample evidence that teachers who habitually rely on it will too often misinterpret the events in their classrooms.

Beginning teachers frequently face the difficult situation of receiving different, contradictory messages from their professors and from the teachers with whom they work. While their professors are apt to focus on theoretical knowledge, the experienced teacher may often advise them, "Forget the fancy theoretical stuff and listen to me. I'll tell you what works in real life." This "folkways" approach to education may be in conflict with what the new teacher has learned and create a dilemma about how to handle an actual situation.

The problem confronting new teachers is not that the theories put before them are unworkable, but that they simply haven't internalized those theories to the point where they can be used to interpret and solve practical problems. They have not been provided with sufficient opportunities to apply the knowledge, to translate it from theory into practice and thereby master it.

An example of a theoretical concept that is derived from psychology and that has enormous implications for teachers is the concept of "reinforcement." From their educational psychology courses most teachers know that a behavior that is reinforced will be strengthened and is likely to be repeated. Nevertheless, these same teachers often respond to a disruptive pupil by calling his or her actions to the attention of the class. If the pupil is misbehaving because of a need to be recognized, the teacher, by publicly acknowledging the misbehavior, is actually reinforcing it. When the pupil continues to act up periodically, the teacher doesn't understand why. Although the teacher may have intellectually grasped a concept such as "reinforcement," this understanding is not synonymous with internalizing or mastering the concept. Mastery requires practical application to concrete situations.

Because theoretical knowledge can be used to interpret situations and solve problems, many classroom events that might otherwise go unnoticed or remain inexplicable can be recognized and resolved by applying theories and concepts of human behavior. This is not an easy task. It requires understanding, insight, practice, and feedback from colleagues and professors. Proficiency will not be achieved as a result of formal training alone; it is a lifelong process involving both formal training and an unending program of on-the-job self-improvement.

**2.  Display of Attitudes that Foster Learning and Genuine Human Relationships.**   The second area of competence identified as essential for effective teaching has to do with attitudes. An attitude is a predisposition to act in a positive or negative way toward persons, ideas, or events. Most educators are convinced that teacher attitudes are a very important dimension in the teaching process. Attitudes have a direct effect on our behavior; they determine how we view ourselves and interact with others.

The major categories of attitudes that affect teaching behavior are: (a) teachers' attitudes toward themselves; (b) teachers' attitudes toward children; (c) teachers' attitudes toward peers and parents; and (d) teachers' attitudes toward the subject matter.

(a) *Teachers' attitudes toward themselves.*   There is evidence from psychology that persons who deny or cannot cope with their own emotions are likely to be incapable of respecting and coping with the feelings of others. If teachers are to understand and sympathize with their students' feelings, they must recognize and understand their own feelings. Many colleges are responding to this need by including counseling sessions, sensitivity training, and awareness experiences as part of their teacher education programs. These experiences emphasize introspection, self-evaluation, and feedback from other participants. The goal is to help prospective teachers learn more about themselves, their attitudes, and how others perceive them.

(b) *Teachers' attitudes toward children.*   Most teachers occasionally harbor attitudes or feelings toward students that are detrimental to their teaching effectiveness. Strong likes and dislikes of particular pupils, biases toward or against particular ethnic groups, low learning expectations for poverty-level children, and biases toward or against certain kinds of student behavior, all can reduce teaching effectiveness. Self-awareness of such attitudes toward individual pupils or classes of children is necessary if teachers are to cope with their own feelings and beliefs. If teachers possess empathy for their students and value them as unique individuals, they will be more effective and will derive more satisfaction from their teaching.

(c) *Teachers' attitudes toward peers and parents.*   Teachers do not exist in isolated classrooms. They interact with fellow teachers and administrators and often have sensitive dealings with parents. Sometimes they can be very effective in dealing with children, but because of negative attitudes toward the adults they encounter, their professional life is unsuccessful. This is a rare instance, however, for most people have similar attitudes toward all persons, adult and child, possessing similar characteristics. Many of the comments already made regarding teachers' attitudes toward themselves and children also apply to their attitudes toward peers and parents.

(d) *Teachers' attitudes toward subject matter.*   The message, in one word, is ENTHUSIASM! Just as students are very perceptive in discovering the teacher's attitude toward them, they are also sensitive to the teacher's attitude toward the subject matter. Teachers who are not enthusiastic about what they teach can hardly hope to instill enthusiastic responses in their pupils. The best way to ensure such enthusiasm is for teachers to plan their instruction around subject matter that is of high interest to them. From whom do you think you would learn more — an enthusiastic teacher dealing with an esoteric topic, such as cave paintings of primitive man, or an uninspired teacher dealing with contemporary political history? As a teacher, you should not allow yourself to be pressured into teaching something that you care little about. After all, if you don't care about the subject matter, how can you ever hope to motivate your students into learning about it?

**3. Command of Knowledge in the Subject Matter To Be Taught.** Command of the subject matter to be taught is an obvious necessity for any teacher. But taking courses in biology or history or mathematics is not sufficient. A teacher's subject matter preparation really has two aspects: (1) a study of the subject matter itself, and (2) a judicious selection of the material that can be transmitted successfully to the student.

College courses taken in disciplines like mathematics or English help teachers acquire an understanding of the disciplines, their basic concepts, and their modes of inquiry; but college courses are not directed toward what should be taught to elementary or secondary school students. What should be taught is obviously much less extensive and advanced than the content of the college courses and requires that teachers know the school curriculum as well.

Teachers must, therefore, rethink much of the content of a particular discipline as it relates to the lives of their pupils. To be effective communicators, teachers need an understanding of both children and subject matter and, beyond that, special training in linking the two.

As B. O. Smith states:

. . . the teacher should know the content he is to teach as well as that of the disciplines from which his instructional subject matter may be taken. The first is necessary for teaching anything at all. The second applies a depth of knowledge essential to the teacher's feelings of intellectual security and his ability to handle instructional content with greater understanding.[4]

**4. Control of Technical Skills of Teaching that Facilitate Student Learning.** The fourth area of competence required of effective teachers is possession of a repertoire of teaching skills. Such a repertoire is necessary if teachers are to be effective with students who have varied backgrounds and learning aptitudes. Teacher education programs must, therefore, include a training component focusing on the acquisition of specific teaching skills. No program can afford to concentrate so exclusively on the acquisition of knowledge that it ignores or slights the "practice" dimension of teaching. Whereas the knowledge components involved in teacher preparation focus on the contexts or situations that confront teachers, the skills component focuses directly on the trainees — on the observation, analysis, and modification of their teaching behavior.

**THE TEACHER AS DECISION MAKER**

We have examined briefly four general areas of competence in which teachers must develop proficiency to be effective. While this examination is useful for obtaining an overview of the basic components of a well-designed teacher education program, it does not provide any guidelines on what a teacher actually does when teaching. A model of the teacher and of the instructional process can provide some guidelines to help teachers better understand what they should be doing when they teach. For this purpose, we shall examine the model of the teacher as a decision maker.

First consider the following situation: You are a middle school social studies teacher. You want to teach your students what a protective tariff is. What decisions must you make before this can be accomplished? First, *you have to decide exactly what you want them to know about protective tariffs.* You probably will want them to know how protective tariffs differ from revenue tariffs, why countries impose protective tariffs, how other countries are likely to respond, and who benefits and who suffers when protective tariffs are imposed.

Second, *you must decide what student behavior you will accept as evidence that the students understand protective tariffs and their ramifications.* Will they have to repeat a definition from memory? Will they have to give examples? Will they have to analyze a hypothetical situation and describe the pros and cons of imposing a protective tariff?

Third, *you will have to plan a strategy for obtaining the desired pupil learning.* Will you have the students do some reading? Will you lecture to them? Will you show them some audiovisual materials? How many examples will you need to show them? What provisions will you make for those students who don't understand? How much time will you allot for this learning activity?

Fourth, *as you teach the lesson, you will have to decide, based on student reactions, which parts of your strategy to adjust.* Are the students responding in the manner you thought? Are there any new classroom developments that will force you to change your tactics or the decisions you had previously made?

Fifth, *you will need to evaluate the impact and outcomes of your teaching.* Have the students satisfactorily demonstrated that they understand what protective tariffs are? If not, what is the deficiency in their understanding? What can you do about it? How effective were the strategies you used to teach the concept?

All these questions require decisions from alternative choices. Even the initial decision to teach the concept of protective tariffs required a choice from other social studies concepts. As this example demonstrates, the teacher is constantly making decisions with regard to student learning and appropriate instructional strategies.

What kinds of decisions? In the example of the protective tariff, you would have to decide how the students would best learn the characteristics of protective tariffs, based on their previous learning experiences. If you had decided to lecture, you would be predicting that, given the particular students and the available material, they would learn best through a lecture method.

Suppose that midway through the lecture you pick up cues from the students that they are not really understanding the concept of a protective tariff. It may be that they weren't ready to understand the concept, or it might be that your lecture was ineffective. Now you have to decide whether to continue, try a different strategy, or reintroduce the concept later.

The various steps of this decision-making model are depicted in Figure 1.1.

Within the instructional role teachers must make decisions related to the three basic teaching functions shown in Figure 1.1: (1) planning, (2) implementation, and (3) evaluation.

The *planning* function requires that teachers make decisions about their students' needs, the most appropriate goals and objectives to help meet those needs, the motivation necessary to attain their goals and objectives, and the instructional modes and teaching strategies most suited to the attainment of those goals and objectives. The planning function usually occurs when teachers are alone and have time to consider long- and short-range plans, the students' progress toward achieving objectives, the availability of materials, the time requirements of particular activities, and other such issues. Some teaching skills that support the planning function include observing pupil behavior, diagnosing pupil needs, setting goals and objectives, sequencing goals and objectives, and determining appropriate learning activities related to the objectives.

The *implementation* function requires that teachers implement the decisions that were made in the planning stage, particularly those related to instructional modes, teaching strategies, and learning activities. While much of the planning function is accomplished when teachers are alone, the implementation function occurs when teachers are interacting with students. Teaching skills that support the implementation function include presenting and explaining, listening, introducing, demonstrating, eliciting student responses, and achieving closure.

The *evaluation* function requires decisions about the suitability of chosen objectives as well as the teaching strategies keyed to those objectives and, ultimately, whether or not the students are achieving what the teacher intended. To make the necessary decisions, teachers must determine what kind of information they need and then gather it. Teaching skills that support the evaluation function include specifying the learning objectives to be evaluated; describing the information needed to make such evaluation; obtaining, analyzing, and recording that information; and forming judgments.

The *feedback* dimension of the decision-making model simply means that you examine the results of your teaching and then decide how adequately you handled each of these three teaching functions. On the basis of this examination you determine whether you have succeeded in attaining your objectives or whether you need to make new plans or try different implementation strategies. Feedback, then, is the new information you process into your decision making in order to adjust your planning, implementation, or evaluation functions or to continue on the same basis. It is the decision-making system's way of correcting itself.

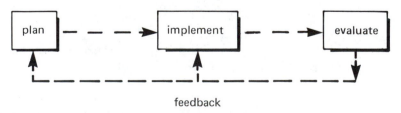

**FIGURE 1.1**  Model of the teacher as decision maker.

The model of the teacher as a decision maker has been introduced as a way of conceptualizing the instructional role of the teacher. Admittedly, this conceptualization is a simplification of what actually occurs in teaching, but that is why models are useful. They allow us to see the forest without being confused by the trees.

This particular model represents a theory of teaching and makes several basic assumptions. First, the model assumes that teaching is goal directed, that is, that some change in the students' thinking or behavior is sought. Second, the model assumes that teachers are active shapers of their own behavior. They make plans, implement them, and continually adjust to new information concerning the effects of their actions. Third, the model assumes that teaching is basically a rational process that can be improved by examining its components in an analytical manner. It assumes teachers can control the feedback process by selecting both the amount and kind of feedback to use. Fourth, the model assumes that teachers, by their actions, can influence students to change their own behavior in desired ways. Stated another way, the model assumes that teaching behavior can affect student behavior and learning.

There are other models that depict the teacher's role differently and are based on different assumptions about effective teaching. However, this model was selected as the organizing rubric of this book because of the model's simplicity and its power to capture the essence of what teachers do in the instructional process. Teachers are professionals who are educated and trained to make and implement decisions.

The four general areas of teacher competence, identified by Smith and discussed earlier, represent the broad categories of preparation that teachers need in order to make intelligent, effective decisions. Thus, competence in theoretical knowledge about learning, attitudes that foster learning and positive human relationships, knowledge in the subject matter to be taught, and a repertoire of teaching skills provide teachers with the tools necessary to make and implement professional judgments and decisions. Figure 1.2 on p. 10 depicts this relationship.

As you think about Figure 1.2, it should become obvious to you that people may strive toward mastery of the decision-making model without ever achieving it. To achieve mastery would require total command of the four general areas of competence and the ability to apply expertly the knowledge, attitudes, and skills acquired in each instructional decision. But, even if decision making cannot be mastered, teachers can become increasingly competent at it and, consequently, become increasingly effective with their students.

## How Are Teaching Skills Acquired?

*Classroom Teaching Skills* is designed to equip you with a repertoire of teaching skills crucial to the decision-making process. Without such a repertoire of skills, your decision-making alternatives are severely reduced.

What teaching skills have had the most beneficial impact on student learning? To answer that question conclusively is impossible. While much educational research has been directed toward answering this question, the results to date are either too tentative, varied, or of little practical value to help educators design training programs. Re-

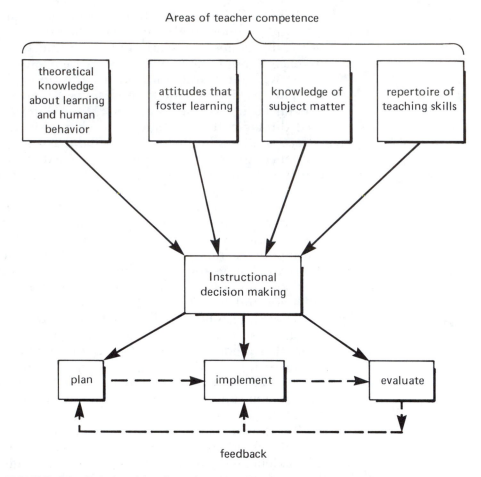

Areas of teacher competence

theoretical knowledge about learning and human behavior

attitudes that foster learning

knowledge of subject matter

repertoire of teaching skills

Instructional decision making

plan

implement

evaluate

feedback

**FIGURE 1.2**  Relationship of teacher-competence areas to process of instructional decision making.

search studies may soon prove helpful in the design of such programs, but at present their value is limited.

The skills chosen for this book are skills supported by many teacher educators on the basis of their own teaching experience and their diagnosis of the teacher's role as a decision maker. These skills are complex, not simple, ones. Their acquisition requires both careful study and diligent practice. This book is designed to get you thinking about the skills, to understand their purposes and how they fit into the instructional act, and to start you practicing their application in analytical, simulated, or classroom situations. It will be up to you and your instructors to provide opportunities where you can practice the skills in more complex and realistic situations, eventually practicing them in a classroom context with actual students.

How does one go about learning complex teaching skills so that they become part of one's "natural" teaching style? Bryce Hudgins has described very well a three-stage process of complex skill acquisition.[5] The first phase is a *cognitive* one. The learner must form a cognitive map of the skill he is to learn. He should know the purpose of the skill and how it will benefit him. Further, this cognitive phase helps the learner to isolate the various skill elements, their sequencing, and the nature of the final performance. As Hudgins says, ". . . this is a time when the learning of the student can be facilitated by assisting him to form a concept of what is contained in the skill, how its elements fit together, and how his present knowledge and experience can contribute (that is, transfer positively) to what he is to learn." [6]

The second phase for complex skill acquisition is *practice*. We have all heard the old saying, "Practice makes perfect." While this statement may not take into account many other requisites, it is certainly true that complex skills cannot be learned without a good deal of practice. The seemingly effortless motion of an Olympic swimmer is not acquired without thousands of miles of practice swimming. Similarly, the skill of driving a car is not learned without a lot of practice. So too, with complex teaching skills. Both Hudgins and B. O. Smith agree that the amount of practice devoted to the acquisition of teaching skills in most teacher education programs is so small that it is ridiculous to expect teachers to demonstrate these skills at even passable levels.

The third phase for acquiring a complex skill is *knowledge of results*. Practice will not really make perfect unless the persons trying to acquire the skill receive feedback regarding their performance. This point has been repeatedly demonstrated in psychological experiments where subjects are given great amounts of practice in a given skill but are deprived of any feedback regarding their performance. Without such feedback their performance does not improve, while other subjects, whose practice of the same skill includes feedback, do improve upon their initial performance.

Since learning complex teaching skills requires (1) *cognitive understanding*, (2) *practice*, and (3) *knowledge of performance* (feedback), any teacher-training materials aimed at developing such skills should incorporate these three conditions into their design. This book has such a design. *Classroom Teaching Skills* is also self-contained; that is, you can acquire conceptual aspects of a particular skill without reliance on outside instructors, materials, or the availability of a group of students to teach. There will be times, however, when you will be asked to work with some of your peers and provide feedback to one another.

You might be asking yourself the question, "Can complex teaching skills really be mastered in the absence of pupils to be taught?" Ultimately, no, but there are various intermediate stages that are helpful to go through as you acquire skills. Hudgins has presented these stages in Figure 1.3* (p. 12). Stage 1 involves a conceptual understanding of the skill, its elements, their sequence, and the nature of the final performance. Usually this first stage is accomplished by reading about the skill and its elements and/or by seeing the skill demonstrated and having its various elements explained. It does not normally involve practice.

Stage 2 is accomplished through self-contained training materials directed at each of the major elements comprising a model of the skill. Appropriate feedback must also be provided for each of the elements within the model. The training materials should themselves be prepared in accordance with the elements of the model.

---

* From Bryce B. Hudgins, "Self-Contained Training Materials for Teacher Education: A Derivation from Research on the Learning of Complex Skills," Report 5, National Center for the Development of Training Materials in Teacher Education (Bloomington, Indiana: School of Education, Indiana University), 1974, p. 23. Reprinted by permission.

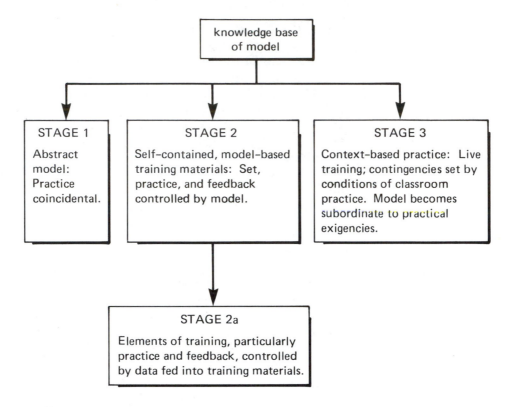

**FIGURE 1.3**  Self-contained training materials in a teacher-training sequence. Figure shows (1) the dependence of training materials upon an adequate knowledge base for the model and (2) the position of the materials as the reality dimension of training is varied.

Stage 2a requires that the practice exercises contained in the training materials be developed around actual data obtained from studies of real children. In other words, practice situations, drawn from actual data, should be used in order to make them as realistic as possible and, hopefully, highly transferable to actual classrooms.

Stage 3 represents actual classroom situations where the skill can be practiced with actual students. This is the context where the teacher tries to "put it all together" and receives feedback on his or her performance. The importance of Stages 2 and 2a becomes apparent when one thinks of moving directly from Stage 1 to Stage 3. Reading about the skill and then immediately practicing it in a real classroom is analogous to reading a manual on how to operate an automobile and then taking it out into heavy traffic to practice. Obviously, no responsible driver educator would use this procedure. Instead, the learners would be required to practice various elements in simulated or controlled situations before allowing them to take a car out alone.

Because teacher education has lacked the training materials needed to develop basic teaching skills, beginning teachers have traditionally been asked to move directly from Stage 1 to Stage 3. Sometimes the teacher has succeeded in spite of these circumstances, but in many instances the results have been disastrous. Although ultimately you must exercise these skills with actual students in real teaching situations, your probability of success will be greatly increased if you first develop a thorough understanding of the skill and its elements, if you have controlled practice situations which are reality-based, and if you receive feedback in order to adjust your performance in necessary ways.

**THE BOOK'S DESIGN**

The purpose of *Classroom Teaching Skills* is to help you develop competence in selected teaching skills that are basic to implementing the decision-making model. To acquire these complex teaching skills, you will need to follow Hudgins's three-stage model. Accordingly, *Classroom Teaching Skills* incorporates Hudgins's model of complex skill acquisition in its design.

Each chapter in the book focuses on a particular teaching skill. Within each chapter a cognitive map of the skill you are to acquire is provided. This cognitive map includes the purpose of the skill, its various elements and their sequencing, and the nature of the final performance.

Each chapter consists of self-contained materials that require practice and provide you with feedback on your efforts. If circumstances permit it, your instructor may also provide you with opportunities to practice these skills in classroom contexts.

To develop a smoothness and a high level of competence in teaching skills, far more practice is necessary than can be provided in this book. Further, if you are an elementary school teacher, many of these skills must be practiced within the context of different subject matter areas. Your competence in questioning skills, for example, is partially a product of your knowledge of the subject about which you are asking questions. Using our previous example, if you know little about protective tariffs, you are not likely to ask stimulating and provocative questions about that topic.

### Format of Each Chapter

Each chapter is written with a common format that contains (1) a set of objectives, (2) a rationale, (3) learning materials and activities, and (4) mastery tests.

**1. Objectives.** The objectives, stated in terms of learner outcomes, specify the competency or competencies you will be expected to demonstrate. Wherever it is appropriate, the objectives will be arranged in a learning hierarchy, leading you from relatively simple objectives to more complex ones.

**2. Rationale.** The rationale describes the purpose and importance of the objectives within the chapter. It attempts to explain why you should want to spend your time acquiring the competencies the chapter is designed to produce. The rationale is considered very important because if you are not convinced that the particular skill you are being asked to develop is important to effective teaching, then it is unlikely that you will be willing to spend the time and effort needed to acquire competence in that skill.

**3. Reading Materials and Activities.** Each objective has an accompanying set of reading materials written specifically for that objective. In addition, some of the authors have provided backup activities for those who want additional work on a particular objective. The nature of the reading materials and activities varies depending on the specific objective for which they were constructed.

**4. Mastery Tests.**   Each chapter contains mastery tests with answer keys to enable you to assess whether or not you have achieved the objectives. These mastery tests assess your learning after you have completed the reading and backup activities related to each objective. This technique allows you to discover immediately after completing each section whether or not you have met the objective satisfactorily. In addition, at the end of some of the chapters there are final mastery tests that serve as a last check on your achievement.

This format (objectives, rationale, learning activities, and mastery tests) has been successfully tested in hundreds of teacher education programs. It is a very efficient design because all the materials are geared to help students achieve the stated objectives. Extraneous and inconsequential materials are eliminated, allowing students to make best use of their time. If used properly, the format increases the probability that you will be able to acquire a beginning level of competency in these basic teaching skills.

## Description of the Skills

Skills were included in this book on the basis of their importance in implementing the decision-making model of instruction. While other skills might have been included, those that were selected are among the most crucial to the model.

As you will recall, the three basic elements of the decision-making model are *to plan*, *to implement*, and *to evaluate*. Each skill is important in carrying out at least one of these three functions. Some skills are useful for more than one function. The nine skills that comprise this book are:

| | | |
|---|---|---|
| Plan | 1. | Planning |
| | 2. | Writing instructional objectives |
| Implement | 3. | Presentation skills |
| | 4. | Questioning |
| | 5. | Teaching concepts |
| | 6. | Interpersonal communication |
| | 7. | Classroom management |
| | 8. | Evaluation |
| Evaluate | 9. | Use of microcomputers |

1. Planning is perhaps the most important function a teacher performs since the whole decision-making model is based on this skill. In Chapter 2 Greta Morine-Dershimer and Jeanne Pfeifer emphasize the need to generate alternatives in the planning process. On the basis of research studies, Morine-Dershimer and Pfeifer conclude that a con-

sideration of alternatives is *the* basic skill to be learned in instructional planning. Unless alternatives have been considered, no decision has truly been made.

The chapter focuses on four basic questions to be asked in planning:

1. What are some alternative objectives or purposes to be achieved through this instruction?
2. What are some alternative ways of determining where pupils stand in relation to a given objective?
3. What are some alternative procedures for helping pupils to achieve a stated objective?
4. What are some alternative methods for determining whether a given procedure was effective?

These four questions are the major focus in the chapter by Morine-Dershimer and Pfeifer, but each of the other chapters in the book addresses one or more of these questions as well.

2. Writing instructional objectives is a basic planning skill. By specifying instructional objectives, teachers define their purposes in terms that are clear and understandable. In Chapter 3 Terry TenBrink makes the distinction between well-written and poorly written objectives. Furthermore, opportunities are provided within the chapter (1) to rewrite poorly written objectives and (2) to write objectives for a specified unit of instruction. Well-written instructional objectives enable teachers to plan and implement their instructional strategies. The success of teachers' implementation skills greatly depends on the thoughtfulness and clarity of their instructional objectives.

3. In Chapter 4 Robert Shostak presents three basic presentation skills — set induction, explaining, and closure — which research studies have demonstrated to be important components of effective presentations. Set induction refers to teacher-initiated actions or statements that are designed to establish a communicative link between the experiences of students and the objectives of the lesson. Explaining refers to planned teacher talk designed to clarify any idea, procedure, or process not understood by a student. Closure refers to those teacher actions or statements designed to bring a lesson presentation to an appropriate conclusion. The effective use of these three skills will help establish and maintain student interest in the lesson and will ensure that the main parts of the lesson have been learned.

4. Probably no teaching behavior has been studied as much as questioning. This is not surprising since most educators agree that questioning strategies and techniques are key tools in the teacher's repertoire of interactive teaching skills. In Chapter 5 Myra and David Sadker chose Bloom's *Taxonomy of Educational Objectives: Cognitive Domain* as their system for classifying questions, since Bloom's *Taxonomy* is the most widely used cognitive classification system in education. They designed their chapter (1) to classify and construct questions according to the six levels of Bloom's *Taxonomy* and (2) to describe the nature and dynamics of four teaching techniques (wait time, probing questions, reinforcement, and equity in interaction) that can increase the quantity and quality of student responses. If the skills

presented in this chapter are utilized in teaching, the net effect will be students who are more active participants in the learning process.

5. How people learn concepts and how teachers can facilitate student acquisition of concepts are the focus of Chapter 6. Concepts, as used in the chapter, are: (1) categories into which our experiences are organized and (2) the larger network of intellectual relationships brought about as a result of the categorization process. As Peter Martorella points out, our view of reality depends on our conceptual network. A primary task of every teacher is to help students gain an understanding of the world both by teaching new concepts and by fitting new phenomena into already existing concepts. Without mutual understanding of concepts and their meanings, communication with one another would be impossible.

6. "He knows his subject matter, but he just can't seem to relate to his students." At one time or another most of us have had a teacher who would fit this description. While much of a teacher's success in relating to students is difficult to explain and even more difficult to teach, some specific behaviors that stimulate personal inquiry can be taught and should contribute positively to the affective climate of the classroom. In Chapter 7 Sandra Sokolove Garrett, Myra Sadker, and David Sadker define interpersonal communication skills as a series of specific behaviors that stimulate personal inquiry — inquiry that leads to greater self-knowledge and eventually to more precise and meaningful communication. Teachers who successfully employ the skills of *attending behavior, active listening, reflection, inventory questioning,* and *encouraging alternative behaviors* will help their students to gain greater self-knowledge and become more effective communicators — two vital steps toward better human relations.

7. No problem concerns beginning teachers more than the problem of classroom management. Most new teachers are afraid of not being able to control their students and are aware that lack of control will impede effective instruction. Furthermore, few areas in teacher education curriculums have been neglected as much as classroom management. The major reason for this neglect has been that, until recently, educators had a poor systematic understanding of classroom dynamics. Recently, however, our knowledge in this area has expanded to the point where systematic instruction in classroom management is now possible.

In Chapter 8 Will Weber emphasizes that teachers need to establish and maintain proper learning environments. While the purpose of teaching is to stimulate desired student learning, the purpose of classroom management is to establish the conditions that best promote student learning. Classroom management skills are necessary for effective teaching to occur, but they do not guarantee such behavior. Weber examines three different philosophical positions regarding classroom management — behavior modification, establishing a proper socioemotional climate, and group processes — and provides numerous opportunities for diagnosing classroom situations according to each of these three viewpoints.

8. Evaluation and knowledge of results are essential if teachers are to improve their teaching effectiveness. The critical nature of evaluation is rarely disputed; nevertheless, few teachers receive adequate training in evaluation concepts and procedures. Terry TenBrink's chapter on evaluation focuses on critical components of the evaluation process. His basic position is that educational evaluation is useful only

to the extent that it helps educators make decisions. (Again, the emphasis is on the teacher as a decision maker.)

TenBrink perceives evaluation as a four-stage process: (1) preparing for evaluation, (2) obtaining needed information, (3) forming judgments, and (4) using judgments in making decisions and preparing evaluation reports. Throughout the chapter examples of problems and decisions that teachers are likely to face are used. Developing good test items, checklists, and ratings scales for evaluating student knowledge, products, and performance is a major focus of the chapter. This practical emphasis should make evaluation concepts and procedures for making better instructional decisions easier to understand and apply.

9. Over the years many technological innovations have been touted as being revolutionary in their potential impact on schooling and teaching. Up until now none of these innovations has lived up to expectations. With the advent of microcomputers we have at last a technological advance that is significantly affecting teaching and learning in the schools. As the authors of Chapter 10, Jerry Short and Tom Lough, point out, the percentage of U.S. high schools with at least one computer increased from 43 percent to 86 percent from 1981 to 1983. A similar growth rate is occurring in elementary schools. If this trend continues — and we think it will — many classrooms will have computers in the next decade, and many teachers will be using computers in their own instruction as well as teaching their students to use them. Knowing how to use microcomputers will become an essential teaching skill for many teachers.

In Chapter 10 Jerry Short and Tom Lough attempt to familiarize the reader with the use of microcomputers in the classroom. They recognize that "hands-on" training with computers will be necessary after reading this chapter, but they believe that knowing how microcomputers can be used in classrooms to enhance instruction and learning is as important as the technical knowledge of how microcomputers are operated. The focus of their chapter, therefore, is on the instructional applications of microcomputers, including such aspects as how to help students overcome computer fear or anxiety; how to use computers to individualize instruction; and how to use computers for class presentations, demonstrations, and simulations.

NOTES

1. Myron Brenton, *What's Happened to Teacher?* (New York: Coward-McCann, 1970), p. 71.

2. David Ryans, *Characteristics of Teachers* (Washington, D.C.: American Council on Education, 1960).

3. J. W. Getzels and P. W. Jackson, "The Teacher's Personality and Characteristics," in *Handbook of Research on Teaching*, ed. N. L. Gage (Chicago: Rand McNally, 1963), p. 574.

4. B. O. Smith, *Teachers for the Real World* (Washington, D.C.: American Association of Colleges for Teacher Education, 1969), p. 122.

5. Bryce B. Hudgins, "Self-Contained Training Materials for Teacher Education: A Derivation from Research on the Learning of Complex Skills," Report 5, National Center for the Development of Training Materials in Teacher Education (Bloomington, Indiana: School of Education, Indiana University), 1974.

6. *Ibid.*, pp. 5–6.

ADDITIONAL READINGS   Hudgins, Bryce B. *The Instructional Process.* Chicago: Rand McNally, 1971.

McDonald, Frederick J. *Educational Psychology*, 2nd ed. Belmont, California: Wadsworth Publishing Co., 1965, pp. 48–69.

Mosston, Muska. *Teaching: From Command to Discovery.* Belmont, California: Wadsworth Publishing Co., 1972.

Shavelson, Richard J. "What Is *The* Basic Teaching Skill?" *Journal of Teacher Education* 24 (Summer 1973): 144–149.

Smith, B. O., et al. *Teachers for the Real World.* Washington, D.C.: American Association of Colleges for Teacher Education, 1969.

Greta Morine-Dershimer
and Jeanne Pfeifer

# 2. Instructional Planning

# Objectives

**1** Given a set of instructional procedures, to identify in each case the skills practiced, the materials used, and the provisions for pupil ideas, individual differences, and evaluative feedback.

**2** Given two alternative lesson plans for teaching the same content, to identify the differences and similarities between the two plans in terms of their: (a) instructional materials, (b) skills to be practiced, (c) provision for group or individual skill practice, (d) provision for pupil ideas, (e) provision for individual differences, and (f) provision for written feedback.

**3** Given several possible topics for long-range planning, to select a topic; to plan two alternative sequences of activities, ideas, and/or skills; and to compare the sequences, identifying the criteria used in organizing each.

Planning is a central skill for teachers because it incorporates so many other teaching skills. Teachers build their instructional plans around goals or purposes, but, in order to make these goals specific, they must develop skill in writing instructional objectives (see Chapter 3). The instructional procedures they formulate to pursue their objectives should be keyed to their diagnoses of student needs, which, in turn, are keyed to their classroom observation abilities. In order to provide instructional variety within an appropriate learning environment, they must decide how to present information (see Chapter 4), when and how to question students (see Chapter 5), and how to manage their classrooms (see Chapter 8). Finally, they must decide how to evaluate the effectiveness of their instruction (see Chapter 9).

Many people believe that planning is one of the most important skills a teacher can have and that teachers who plan better must also teach better. Some people think that planning is something teachers do in the quiet of their classrooms — before pupils arrive for the day or after they leave for the night. Others may suspect that many teachers never really plan at all, except to write down the page numbers of the textbook to be covered each day. The truth, of course, is that none of these views is completely accurate.

The myths about teacher planning are legion. Unfortunately, they are influential in determining what prospective teachers learn about the process of planning. Which of the following statements are myths, and which are probably accurate descriptions of the reality of teacher planning?

Everybody's doing it.

A little goes a long way.

A plan a day keeps disaster away.

Plans are made to be broken.

Don't look back!

Try it — you'll like it.

Ten years ago it would have been difficult to determine which of these statements were myths and which were realities. Little was known about how teachers actually went about planning in their classrooms. In recent years, however, a number of researchers have observed and interviewed teachers as they were engaged in instructional planning. While there is still much to be learned, a useful base of knowledge has been established.

## Everybody's Doing It — in a Variety of Ways

Teachers do plan, and they plan in a variety of ways. There are five basic types of planning in which teachers regularly engage: yearly planning, term-long planning, unit planning, weekly planning, and daily planning.[1] All of these types of planning are important for effective instruction.

While all teachers plan, they do not all plan in exactly the same way.[2] Some may jot a few notes down in a lesson plan book. Others may write outlines detailing lessons or units they intend to teach. Many teachers write more detailed daily plans for their substitutes than they do for themselves, wanting to ensure that established routines are understood and maintained. Teachers who have embraced the computer age may keep a file of lesson or unit plans stored on disks, and update or revise these each year to fit new circumstances.

Studies have shown that few experienced teachers plan precisely according to the procedures recommended by curriculum experts for many years.[3] Rather than beginning by stating instructional objectives, and then selecting and organizing instructional activities to meet those objectives, many teachers seem to begin by considering the context in which teaching will occur (e.g., the instructional materials and time available), then think about activities that will interest and involve their pupils, and finally note the purposes that these activities will serve. This does not mean that teachers have no real goals, but it does suggest that a basic consideration for most teachers is maintaining the interest and involvement of their pupils. Since research has shown that pupil attention and on-task behavior is associated with achievement,[4] pupil involvement is an important thing for teachers to keep in mind when planning for instruction.

## A Little Goes a Long Way — Especially at the Beginning

The tricky thing about teacher planning is that one kind of plan is "nested" within another. This means that plans made at the beginning of the year have important effects on the weekly and daily plans that will be made throughout the year. Before the students ever enter the room, most teachers have planned the physical arrangement of the classroom, determining where and how students will be seated, where materials will be kept, what areas will be set up as centers for particular types of activities, and how bulletin board or wall space will be utilized. Decisions about daily and weekly scheduling of subjects are usually completed by the end of the first week of school. Within the first few weeks, student abilities are assessed and plans are made for instructional grouping. Classroom rules or management procedures are also established during these early weeks. Not all of these plans are made by individual teachers in isolation. A grade level or subject area team may work together to schedule classes or group pupils. General time schedules and rules for student behavior may be determined by school administrators. Wherever these plans originate, however, they will set the framework within which later plans will develop.

Many teachers identify unit planning as their most important type of planning.[5] Weekly and daily plans are nested within unit plans. Since teachers tend to focus on activities in their planning, unit plans serve to organize a flow of activities related to a general topic, for an extended period of time (two weeks to a month, typically).

### A Plan a Day Keeps Disaster Away — for Novice Teachers

Experienced teachers report that unit planning, weekly planning, and daily planning are the most important types of planning that they do during the year.[6] Few of them write out complete lesson plans on a regular basis, though they will make lesson plans when they are dealing with new content or curriculum materials. They do recommend that student teachers and beginning teachers write lesson plans, however.[7] This suggests that lesson plans are particularly useful tools in less familiar teaching situations, such as working with new students, new subject matter, or new procedures. For novice teachers all these aspects of teaching are new and unfamiliar, and lesson plans can be very helpful.

In their daily planning, as well as in their yearly planning, experienced teachers rely heavily on curriculum guides and textbook materials to determine the content and pace of their lessons.[8] Plans for lessons may consist of selecting and adapting activities suggested in the textbook's teacher's guide so that these are particularly interesting or suitable for the instructional needs of their particular pupils. These teachers have established instructional routines over the years, and they fit these suggested activities into their routines; therefore, extensive planning of procedures does not seem as necessary. Novice teachers are in the process of developing routines, experimenting to see what procedures will work for them. More detailed planning of lessons is an essential activity at this stage in their professional development.

### Plans Are Not Made to be Broken — Just Bent

Lesson plans serve several important functions, and teachers say that one of the most important of these is the plan as a guide for their interactions with students.[9] A written plan can ensure that directions are structured in exactly the right way when an activity is begun. A plan can operate like a secretary's "tickler file," reminding the teacher about what to do next, if the rapid-fire interaction of the lesson causes a sudden lapse of memory. A plan can also provide a framework for later evaluation of a lesson, assisting the teacher in identifying productive learning activities.

Because a lesson plan can be such a useful guide, teachers rarely change their plans drastically in the middle of a lesson.[10] They do make adjustments in their plans as they are teaching, and effective teachers seem to be particularly capable at noting how certain pupils are reacting, and "fine-tuning" their procedures accordingly.[11] Some teachers seem to have a "steering group" of pupils who are in the low-average range of achievement, and they adjust the pace of their lessons depending on how well these students are doing.[12] Thus, lesson plans are not made to be "broken," but good plans are flexible enough to bend a little when adjustments are needed.

### Do Look Back — It Helps in Planning Ahead

Experienced teachers report that, soon after a lesson has been taught, they do rethink it and consider how it might be improved or varied another time.[13] This helps them in planning future lessons. Looking back can be especially helpful in long-term planning, such as unit planning or yearly planning. Teachers who have kept records of their plans from prior years can start by considering what activities or procedures worked well and what revisions might be made in sequencing or selection of topics and activities. This is more efficient than starting from scratch every year, and it is an effective aid to teachers who want to improve by learning systematically from their own experience.

### Try It — You'll Like It

Teachers report that besides serving as a guide for interactions with students and as an organizational tool (assisting them to organize time, activities, and materials for a lesson), a lesson plan can provide them with a sense of security.[14] Security is a valuable commodity for a beginning teacher to have. A well constructed lesson plan or unit plan can provide a strong foundation for a novice teacher, who may be more than a little shaky about those first few days and weeks with a new group of students.

Research has not demonstrated that teachers who write behavioral objectives or detailed lesson plans are more effective than those who state general goals or write sketchy lesson plans. But an early study of teacher planning did show that teachers whose pupils learned more made fewer broad, general statements in their plans than teachers whose pupils learned less.[15] While we still have much to learn about teacher planning, we do know that teachers think ahead, that they consider planning to be an essential activity, and that designing lessons and units is, for many teachers, one of the most interesting parts of teaching, providing them with an opportunity to use their imagination and ingenuity. We also know that a great deal of variety exists in the way that different teachers approach planning. One important aspect of developing skill in planning is discovering what kind of planning works best for you. This chapter is designed to assist you in that process.

WHAT'S IN A PLAN?   One of the primary tasks of the teacher is to make planning decisions. These decisions range from such seemingly simple matters as organizing the seating arrangement of the classroom to more complex problems such as determining what it is that children need to learn. Planning decisions are of two basic types: long-range decisions that may stand relatively unchanged for several months or a full year, and short-term decisions that determine what will go on for a given day or just a given hour. Both simple and complex planning decisions, and both short-term and long-range planning decisions, involve essentially the same process.

### Specific Steps in Planning

The basic planning process involves (1) having some goal or purpose in mind, (2) finding out where pupils are in relation to this goal, (3) devising some instructional procedures to move pupils toward the goal, and (4) determining how to tell whether or not the procedures work. All teachers use this simple four-step process when they plan, but they do not always take the steps in this precise order. Nor do they always emphasize every step equally. The goal or purpose may be rather vague at times. A very general description of pupil background or needs may be considered sufficient. The instructional procedures to be used may be just barely sketched in. The method for evaluating the procedures may not be stated at all; it may exist only in the teacher's head.

The reason that many teachers skim over certain steps in the planning process is that planning has become a habit with them. Although good habits are essential to orderly functioning and achievement, if all teacher actions were habitual, the job would become unbearably dull and routine. It is important, therefore, not to let the instructional planning process become too routine. One thing that early educational research demonstrated is that teachers who *vary* their instruction have students who learn more and like school better.[16]

### Generating Alternatives

One good way to keep planning from becoming too habitual is to consider alternatives continually. The teachers in various studies of planning demonstrated in several ways that, as they planned, they worked at generating alternatives. New ideas for lessons were thought of while shaving or driving to work. Ideas were solicited from colleagues. These are all examples of teachers actively seeking alternatives.

Consideration of alternatives is *the* basic skill to be learned in instructional planning, for unless alternatives have been considered, no decision has truly been made. Furthermore, thinking of alternatives helps teachers to be more specific about their actual plans, for each alternative provides a comparison and defines more precisely what the final plan will be. But what kinds of alternatives should teachers consider when planning? A good starting point is provided by the four steps of the planning process itself. The basic questions to be asked are:

1. What are some alternative objectives to be achieved through this instruction?
2. What are some alternative ways of finding out where pupils stand in relation to a given objective?

3. What are some alternative procedures for helping pupils to achieve a stated objective?

4. What are some alternative methods for determining whether a given procedure was effective?

## Making Choices

At some point in the planning process the teacher must settle on one of several alternatives and move to implement the plan. Teachers are always making choices, but the choices are only explicit if the alternatives have been stated. A teacher who never considers existing alternatives has chosen to follow an established routine, even though that choice was not made consciously.

An interesting by-product of choosing among alternatives is that it can help the teacher to clarify his or her own preferences. Suppose that every time you chose between two alternatives you had to explain your choice. Over a period of time the reasons you gave for certain choices would begin to form patterns.

Some teachers may consistently pick the same instructional procedures, because they can predict pupil responses, while others may vary their procedures, because variety appeals to them and helps them stay interested and alert. Some teachers may regularly decide to use the method that requires the least preparation, because there is never enough time to get all the work done, while others may spend a great deal of extra time in preparation, simply because they enjoy this aspect of teaching.

The choices that you make stem from your concerns and interests, and by studying your choice patterns you can gain needed insight into your own style of instructional planning. As you work through this chapter, you will be asked to reflect on these choices at several points.

The procedures for using this chapter are fairly simple. A series of tasks will be presented, corresponding to the three objectives stated at the opening of the chapter.

For each task there are some open-ended response forms that invite you to develop your own ideas and to practice using the concepts presented. These response forms are meant to be learning activities, not tests. At the end of each task there is a mastery test.

When you have completed the three tasks, you will be asked to select a new topic and subject area and to plan two alternative lessons on that topic. You may then decide to teach these two lessons to two different groups of children and to study the responses of pupils to each plan. The final test of competency in planning, as with all teaching competencies, is based on what children learn as a result of the teacher's efforts.

188685

# Objective 1

Given a set of instructional procedures, to identify in each case the skills practiced, the materials used, and the provisions for pupil ideas, individual differences, and evaluative feedback.

## LEARNING ACTIVITY 1

Teachers write lesson plans in many different ways. Some plans are highly organized and detailed. Others are very sketchy. But one thing almost all written plans have in common is a list of steps or procedures that the lesson will follow. Almost all teachers find that notes on the sequence of lesson activities serve as useful reminders to them while they are actually teaching the lesson.

A fairly common format for writing a lesson plan is (1) to state the objective of the lesson, (2) to list the instructional materials to be used, and (3) to indicate the steps to be followed in the lesson. Many teachers add detail to this type of plan by designing a worksheet to use with children during a lesson. Others list specific questions to be asked at each step in the lesson; some even write in expected pupil responses to these questions. Teachers who plan to elicit and use pupil ideas as a major source of information in a lesson will frequently make notes about how they plan to write these ideas down on the chalkboard.

Lesson plans serve three basic functions for the teacher, and these should be kept in mind when choosing a format for writing plans. First, the act of writing down both the purpose and the planned procedures for a given lesson can help the teacher to clarify them in his or her own mind. Thus, a plan can be an *organizer of ideas*.

Second, a written lesson plan can function as a *record* of teacher ideas and classroom activities. Teachers must keep so many details in mind as they engage in their daily work with students that their memory banks sometimes become overloaded. Written notes can be referred to while a lesson is in progress to remind the teacher of the next step. The same notes can be used later to remind the teacher of what ideas or skills were actually covered in a given lesson. This can also be useful in planning later lessons.

Third, a lesson plan can be used as a guide for classroom observers. This function is probably more important for novice teachers than for experienced teachers, since the former are apt to be observed more frequently. However, all teachers are observed at times, and it is not always easy for the observer to tell what the teacher is trying to accomplish. A written lesson plan helps the observer to focus on the lesson being taught. Thus, a lesson plan can function to *direct the observation* of someone who is watching a lesson in progress.

Because the first function of a lesson plan (organizing teacher ideas) is the most important, teachers should make notes about instructional procedures they have planned in whatever way is useful for them. If a plan is also to serve the third function (directing observation), it should be written in a form that is useful or comprehensible to others as well. Many different formats can accomplish both these goals simultaneously. As you work through this learning task, one of your personal goals might be to discover the format that is most useful to you.

## The Task

A group of teachers was presented with the following suggestions for developing a plan for a lesson on the topic of expanded sentences. Read the suggestions carefully and then study the examples of several different lesson plans developed by these teachers. When you have studied this information, fill out Response Form I, which follows.

LESSON TOPIC: EXPANDED SENTENCES

In this lesson you will be teaching one aspect of language comprehension, the skills of understanding and constructing expanded sentences. How you teach the principle of expanded sentences is left to your judgment. The following paragraphs describe what is meant by "expanded sentences," suggest some possible objectives for a lesson, and give some examples of how this principle can be communicated to children.

When a sentence is expanded, the meaning of the sentence (statement, question, or command) in its simple form is altered by adding any one of a variety of modifiers. Expansions can be made on any sentence, although the simplest illustrations begin with basic noun–verb constructions. The expansions of a sentence can be either further expanded or gradually "contracted" in order to demonstrate the effect of additional words. For example, the sentence "She climbed the tree" may be expanded to "She climbed the big apple tree" or contracted to "She climbed." Both modifications illustrate the effect of expansion.

The expanded-sentences material is drawn from work in the area of structural linguistics, which focuses on the "transformation" of sentences, that is, the ways in which changes in sentence structure affect changes in meaning. These principles of transformation are somewhat atypical of the subject matter covered in the regular curriculum. You should feel free, therefore, to experiment using any material and examples you wish.

Some rules of sentence expansion which may emerge in the course of a lesson include:

1. Adding words to a sentence is one way to change the meaning of a sentence (or, adding more information changes the meaning of a sentence).
2. All sentences can be expanded; no sentence is too long to be expanded.
3. You can expand (change the meaning of) a sentence by describing each thing in more detail (use of adjectives and adverbs).
4. You can expand a sentence by talking about more kinds of actions (additions of verbs).
5. You can expand a sentence by saying *when* (or *where*) something happened.
6. You can expand a sentence by saying *what* (addition of direct or indirect objects).

7. You can expand a sentence by adding phrases as well as single adjectives or adverbs.
8. You can expand a sentence by adding clauses.

You may select one or more or any combination of the above rules as objectives for the lesson, or you may think up your own. Other kinds of objectives, not built around rule identification, might be:

1. Pupils can identify expanded sentences from a list containing both simple and expanded sentences.
2. Given a set of simple sentences, pupils can expand them in at least one (or two, or three) way(s).
3. Given an expanded sentence, pupils can reduce it to a simple sentence by removing the appropriate words.

Different objectives may be appropriate to different groups of pupils, depending on grade level and general ability. You should select objectives you feel comfortable with for your class and arrange the lesson accordingly.

Some examples of expanded sentences which you might want to use in your lesson are given below. You may use these and/or others that you may think up; the only real restriction on use is that the vocabulary be appropriate to the grade level of the pupils for whom you are planning the lesson.

### Examples of Expanded Sentences

The snow covers the streets.
The *dirty* snow covers the streets. (adjective expansion)
The dirty snow covers the *cold*, *dark* streets. (adjective expansion)

The birds fly.
The *green* birds fly. (adjective expansion)
The *big*, *mean*, green birds fly *south today*. (adjective and adverb expansion — where, when)

The children ran.
The children ran *to school*. (adverb expansion — where)
The children ran *and skipped* to school. (verb expansion)

The monkey ate.
The monkey ate *a sandwich*. (direct object expansion — what)
The *big*, *hairy* monkey ate a *turkey* sandwich *very fast*. (adjective and adverb expansion)

The robin sang.
The *red* robin sang *in the tree*. (adjective and adverbial phrase expansion — where)
*Yesterday* the red robin sang *happily* in the tree. (adverb expansion — when and how)

Danny cooked.
Danny cooked *dinner*. (direct object expansion — what)

Danny cooked dinner *because his mother was sick*. (clause expansion)

These sample sentence expansions suggest the kinds of changes that can be made using the sentence expansion rules. Others should be easy to think up. You might plan to ask the pupils to suggest other simple or expanded sentences to work on.

**PLANNED PROCEDURES FOR TEACHING SENTENCE EXPANSION**

## Plan A (Elementary)

1. Review what a sentence is.
2. Define *expand*; describe how and why sentences can be expanded.
3. Go over charts on adjectives, adverbs, and prepositional phrases.
4. Show them the process you want them to use in expanding sentences, for example:
   (a) The child laughs. (Subject and predicate)
   (b) The happy child laughs. (Add an adjective)
   (c) The happy child laughs loudly. (Add an adverb)
   (d) The happy child laughs loudly at the clown. (Add a prepositional phrase)
   (e) The happy child laughs loudly at the silly clown. (Add anything you like)
5. Pass out worksheets.
   Do the first exercise together, if necessary; then have children work by themselves. (See worksheet which follows.)

## WORKSHEET FOR PLAN A

Name _____

Expanding Sentences

1. Subject and predicate.
2. Add an adjective.
3. Add an adverb.
4. Add a prepositional phrase.
5. Add anything you like to expand the sentence further.

1. The cat plays.

2. _____

3. _____

4. _____

   _____

5. _____

   _____

1. The boy walks.

2. _____

3. _____

4. _____
   _____

5. _____
   _____


1. The motorcycle races.

2. _____

3. _____

4. _____
   _____

5. _____
   _____


1. The birds fly.

2. _____

3. _____

4. _____
   _____

5. _____
   _____


*Try some on your own:*

1. _____

2. _____

3. _____

4. _____
   _____

5. _____
   _____


1. _____

2. _____

3. _____

4. _____

_____

5. _____

_____

## Plan B (Elementary)

*Any simple sentence can be expanded by adding phrases, clauses, or descriptive words.*

*Objective:* Children learn they can expand a sentence by adding descriptive words or words that tell when or where something happened.
(The class has just completed "The Gulls," a story of the Mormons in their first year in Utah. Sentences using information from the story will be used.)

1. Discuss with class the meaning of *expand*.

2. Write on the board:

   The                     corn     grew.

   Ask: What kinds of corn? (for example, green)
   Ask: Where is it? (for example, in the garden)
   The sentence might look something like:

   $$\begin{bmatrix} \text{green} \\ \text{fresh} \\ \text{graceful} \end{bmatrix} \qquad \begin{bmatrix} \text{in the garden} \\ \text{in the field} \\ \text{in the summer (when)} \end{bmatrix}$$

   The                     corn     grew

3. Ask volunteers to read the sentence using one or more of the additions.

4. Continue in the same manner with the following sentences:

   $$\begin{bmatrix} \text{Suddenly} \\ \text{All at once} \\ \text{All of a sudden} \end{bmatrix} \quad \begin{bmatrix} \text{blue} \\ \text{gray} \\ \text{cloudy} \end{bmatrix} \qquad \begin{bmatrix} \text{white} \\ \text{graceful} \\ \text{large} \end{bmatrix}$$

   the                 sky was filled with            gulls.

   The cornstalks were covered with insects.
   The gulls ate.

5. If children seem interested, have them copy the following sentence on paper:

   The     snow     covers     the     street.

   Ask:  Can you expand or change the sentence by
       (a) describing the snow?
       (b) describing the street?
       (c) telling where?
   Encourage the students to read their sentences.

## Plan C (Elementary)

*Objective:* Most of the children will be able to add words to a simple two-word sentence that will change the meaning of the original sentence in at least two ways.

*Materials:*
1. Wooden chart for sentence strips
2. Sample strips of two-word sentences with companion expanded sentences
3. Two-word sentence suggestions for the children in the group

*Introduction:*
Place a simple two-word sentence on the chart with the expanded sentence under it. Children will be asked to find *similarities* and *differences*.
Sample:
Birds fly.
The graceful birds fly swiftly in the sky.
(Have another sample ready if children seem to need it.)

*Lesson for Children:* Each child will be provided a two-word sentence to expand. (Option for children — to originate their own if sample doesn't "appeal.") Since these will be prepared in advance, reading levels and interests of the children will be considered.

| | |
|---|---|
| David C. | Airplanes fly. |
| Mike D. | Firemen work. |
| Rebecca F. | Scientists experiment. |
| Keith E. | Dogs bark. |
| Chris E. | Cars race. |
| Larry G. | Planets rotate. |
| Judith H. | Flowers bloom. |
| Billy M. | Astronauts prepare. |
| Anne-Marie M. | Children play. |
| Guy McC. | Monsters hide. |
| Decio R. | Doctors help. |
| Jamie S. | Spring appears. |

*Summary:*
Lead children to discuss which sentences "tell more" and to think about opportunities they have to use expanded sentences.

## Plan D (Secondary)

*Objective:* Given a set of simple sentences and a group of logical connectives, students will expand a sentence in at least four different ways, while maintaining logical sense.

*Materials:* overhead projector
chalkboard

*Procedure:*
1. Have each student write a simple sentence on his/her paper by completing the sentence frame, The _____ _____.

2. Have several students read their sentences aloud. Record these sentences on chalkboard.

3. On overhead projector, write "The helicopter landed *because . . .*" Have students suggest ways to end the sentence. Write these on transparency.

4. Ask pupils to expand their own simple sentences by adding "because" and an appropriate clause. Have several examples read aloud.

5. Proceed in same manner for "but," "therefore," "whenever," "since," "then," and "so."

6. On the overhead projector write *"Although* the helicopter landed, . . ." Have students suggest ways to end the sentence. Write a few on the transparency.

7. Ask students which of the logical connectives already discussed could be used at the beginning of their sentence. Have them write one or two and have some read aloud.

*Evaluation:*

Ask each pupil to take any three of the sentences written on the board at the beginning of the lesson and to expand each sentence in four different ways, using the logical connectives listed on the transparency.

## Plan E (Secondary)

List the logical connectives on board. Divide the class into eight groups. Each group will be given one logical connective (because, but, etc.) and must expand the sentence "The man stumbled," using the connective they have been given. Members of the group will act out the sentence thus constructed, while the rest of the class tries to figure out what logical connective is being demonstrated and how the sentence ends. When each group has performed, list four simple sentences on board, and ask each pupil to expand each of the four sentences in four different ways, using the logical connectives.

# RESPONSE FORM I

1. What specific skill in expanding sentences would you expect pupils to develop by participating in the activities described on the preceding pages?

*Plan A.* Pupils would be able to . . . _____

_____

_____

_____

*Plan B.* Pupils would be able to . . . _____

_____

_____

*Plan C.* Pupils would be able to . . . _____

_____

_____

*Plan D.* Pupils would be able to . . . _____

_____

_____

*Plan E.* Pupils would be able to . . . _____

_____

_____

2. Select one or two alternative instructional procedures from among the teacher plans reported here. Which plan(s) do you prefer? What grade level are you planning for?

_____

3. Think of another possible procedure for helping students attain the objective of expanding a simple sentence in at least two ways, or the objective of using logical connectives to expand sentences in four different ways.

_____

_____

_____

_____

_____

_____

_____

_____

_____

_____

_____

_____

_____

_____

_____

_____

_____

_____

4. Compare the three alternative sets of instructional procedures that you have chosen/generated. How are they similar to each other?

_____

_____

_____

How are they different from each other?

_____

_____

_____

## Identifying Procedural Differences

One important consequence of different instructional procedures is that they involve children in different kinds of learning activities. The skills that are learned may vary according to the instructional procedure used. For example, in the five lesson plans presented earlier, all the teachers had a similar goal in mind — they were working with pupils who expanded sentences in limited ways, and they wanted to teach these pupils to expand a sentence in more extensive ways. Nevertheless, the activities that these teachers included in their lesson plans varied widely.

The skills actually practiced in each lesson are generally related to the learning outcome of the lesson. The lesson activities are described below. (Compare this presentation with your answers to question 1 on Response Form I.)

*Plan A.* Pupils individually write several expanded sentences of different, specified types.

*Plan B.* Pupils as a group suggest words and phrases to be added at several specified points in a lesson. Pupils individually construct one expanded sentence, adding specified types of content.

*Plan C.* Pupils individually write one expanded sentence after seeing one example of an expanded sentence. The types of expansions used are specified.

*Plan D.* Pupils individually write a simple sentence, then expand it through the addition of several different logical connectives, both at the end and beginning of the sentence.

*Plan E.* Pupils as a group expand a simple sentence through use of a single, given, logical connective. Then they act out the sentence, while others try to guess it.

One procedural difference that probably affects learning outcomes involves *group versus individual activity*. In a group activity not every pupil may have an opportunity to practice the skill to be learned. Some teachers deal with this by trying to call on every student at some point in the group lesson. Other teachers use a group activity to demonstrate the skill and then have individual pupils practice the skill on their own.

Another difference that affects learning is the *amount of skill practice* given a child. The child who writes three or four expanded sentences will probably remember the concept longer than the child who only writes one. The child who writes twenty may become so weary of the process that he or she learns to *dislike* expanded sentences instead of learning to write them well.

A third procedural difference that can affect learning is the *specificity of the skill* being practiced. A child who writes three or four different types (adjective, adverb, phrase, clause) of expanded sentences probably develops a clearer concept of sentence expansion than the child who writes several unspecified types of expansions, all of which may turn out to duplicate one another.

In planning a lesson, these procedural differences should be kept in mind. A teacher must think carefully about the *skills being practiced*, whether they involve *group or individual practice*, the *amount of practice*, and the *specificity of the practice*. The teacher who can describe instructional procedures in these terms will be better equipped to predict the learning outcome of a given lesson.

The five planned procedures presented here can also be compared on a number of other interesting bases. They vary in the *instructional materials* to be used and in their provision for *independent pupil ideas, individual differences,* and *feedback on pupil learning.* It is important for a teacher to be alert to these types of differences in instructional procedure, as well as to differences in the type of skill practice provided pupils.

Reexamine the five plans, paying particular attention to these four types of variation, and compare the lessons, using Response Form II.

# RESPONSE FORM II

1. Which plan(s) use the most typical or traditional instructional materials?

_____

_____

Which plan(s) use the least typical or traditional materials?

_____

_____

What additional alternative instructional materials might be used for a lesson?

_____

_____

_____

_____

2. Which plan(s) make the most provision for development of independent pupil ideas?

_____

_____

Which plan(s) make the least provision for development of independent pupil ideas?

_____

_____

What are some additional alternative procedures that might be used to encourage independent pupil ideas in a lesson?

_____

_____

_____

_____

3. Which plan(s) provide for individual differences of pupils?

_____

_____

Which plan(s) have no provision for individual differences of pupils?

_____

_____

What are some additional alternative procedures that might be used to provide for individual differences in a lesson?

_____

_____

_____

_____

4. Which plan(s) provide for written feedback to the teacher regarding what pupils learned?

_____

_____

Which plan(s) do not provide for written feedback to the teacher?

_____

_____

What are some additional alternative procedures that might be used to provide a teacher with feedback on pupil learning?

_____

_____

_____

_____

## Comparison of Instructional Procedures

**1. Most Typical Instructional Materials.**  Plans A and B.
*Least typical instructional materials:* Plans C and E.
(Plans A, B, and E all use the chalkboard as the basic medium for recording information. In Plan A this is supplemented with worksheets, while Plan E uses student demonstration as an additional source of information. Plan D uses an overhead projector, the chalkboard becoming supplemental. Plan C uses a chart and sentence strips to present examples of simple and expanded sentences and follows up with individual worksheets. This plan requires much more prelesson time for preparation of materials than do the others, because the sentence strips and worksheets must be made in advance.)
*Additional alternative materials:* Use word cubes (like dice) or word cards to form sentences; examples of students' own creative writing; etc.

**2. Most Use of Independent Pupil Ideas.**  Plans A and E.
*Least use of independent pupil ideas:* Plans B and C.
(Plan A is probably the most open to pupil ideas, with its worksheet saying "Add anything you like" and "Try writing some sentences of your own." Plan E provides for another type of pupil independence by organizing small groups of pupils who must cooperate to expand and act out sentences. Plans B and C provide little opportunity for independent pupil thinking. In Plan B pupils merely generate words or phrases to fit in spaces the teacher specifies. In Plan C pupils are only given the option to write their own simple sentences if the ones they are given don't appeal to them. Plan D provides a moderate opportunity for independent thinking. Pupils generate their own individual simple sentences, make up their own clauses to follow the given connectives, and test to see which connectives can be used at the beginning of their sentences.)
*Additional alternative provisions for independent pupil ideas:* Ask pupils to design a game for expanding sentences, developing their own rules and point system; (and others).

**3. Provision for Individual Differences.**  Plans A, C, and D.
*Little or no provision for individual differences:* Plans B and E.
(Plan A provides for individual differences by the worksheet section that says "Try writing some sentences of your own." Pupils can write sentences of varying complexity here. Thus, children with more advanced language skills can practice expanding with more complex sentences. Plan C provides for individual differences by giving indi-

vidually assigned sentences based on pupil interest. Plan D invites pupils to write their own simple sentences. The other two plans make no real provision for individual differences. They are geared to the group. None of the plans seem to make provision for differences in time individual pupils or groups may require to complete the task assigned. What will pupils do if they finish their work early?)

*Additional alternative provisions for individual differences:* Provide pupils with options, for example, write your own sentence or choose one of these, work with a partner or work alone; divide students into groups on the basis of early responses (or pretest) and use tasks of varying difficulty with the different groups; (and others).

**4. Provision for Written Feedback to Teacher.** Plans A, B, C, D. *No provision for written feedback:* Plan E.

(All but one of these five plans have made provision for written feedback to the teacher, so that he or she can examine pupils' papers at the end of the lesson to determine whether pupils were able to achieve the instructional goal. Plan E involves pupils physically acting out sentences, but they do not do any written work.)

*Additional alternative provisions for feedback on pupil learning:* Have each child give an oral example of an expanded sentence at end of lesson; have children identify examples of simple and expanded sentences (various types) read by teacher, by holding up small card of red (simple sentence) or blue (expanded sentence); (and others).

## Advantages and Disadvantages

Each of the planned procedures presented here has some advantages and some disadvantages. Each one accomplishes some goals and fails to accomplish others. That is true of all lesson plans ever written or carried out by a teacher. Furthermore, the advantages of a given plan will vary according to the pupils with whom it will be used.

One aspect of the procedures that has not been discussed so far is the grade level for which they were planned. Think back over the plans. Which ones would you expect to be most effective with first or second graders? Which ones would you expect to be most effective with fifth or sixth graders, or with eighth or ninth graders? It is highly unlikely that you would pick the same plan for use with all age levels.

Designing appropriate procedures for instruction involves thinking about a number of aspects of the lesson. Only the most important have been discussed here. They are shown below.

*Aspects of the Lesson*

1. Skills to be practiced
2. Group vs. individual practice
3. Amount of practice
4. Specificity of practice
5. Materials to be used
6. Provision for independent pupil ideas
7. Provision for individual differences
8. Provision for feedback on pupil learning

Probably no single plan will ever be perfect with respect to all of these aspects. As we have seen in the five plans reviewed here, certain aspects will be emphasized in one lesson, while others take the fore in the next lesson. But a teacher needs to be aware of the decisions he or she is making with regard to instructional procedures.

As you plan lessons, you might find it helpful to ask yourself questions based on the preceding points, for example:

What skills will students practice in this lesson?

Will students receive group practice or individual practice?

How much practice will each individual student actually get?

How specific will the practice be?

What alternative instructional materials can be used?

What provisions can be made for development of independent pupil ideas?

What are some ways to provide for individual differences in pupils?

What kind of feedback can be obtained regarding what pupils learned?

The answers to these questions will differ from lesson to lesson, for there is no one best procedure that can achieve all objectives.

These are good questions to keep in mind as you work through Response Form III, which follows.

# RESPONSE FORM III

1. Review the instructional procedures you selected or invented on Response Form I. Select *one* of these that you would like to try out. Indicate your reasons for selecting it below.

_____

_____

_____

_____

_____

_____

_____

2. If possible, compare the instructional plan you have chosen with those chosen by other students who are reading this chapter. Discuss your reasons for selection. What aspects of instruction does the group tend to emphasize?

_____

_____

_____

_____

Are there any aspects of instruction that the group tends to ignore?

_____

_____

_____

_____

3. After reading and hearing more about various instructional procedures, can you think of additional ways of teaching sentence expansion? If so, describe your new plan below.

_____

_____

_____

_____

_____

_____

_____

_____

_____

_____

_____

_____

4. While working through the task, what new ideas have you developed on identifying alternative procedures for achieving an instructional goal? List them below.

_____

_____

_____

_____

_____

5. What questions do you still want to have answered about planning instructional procedures?

_____

_____

_____

_____

Your planning skills will grow as you learn more about alternative instructional strategies and work through the other chapters in this book. The questions you raise now will help you focus your attention in studying later topics. It is time now to assess your understanding of the ideas presented in this section.

# Mastery Test

**OBJECTIVE 1**    Given a set of instructional procedures, to identify in each case the skills practiced, the materials used, and the provisions for pupil ideas, individual differences, and evaluative feedback.

Read each of the following two lesson procedures and answer the questions which follow them.

PROCEDURE A

*Objective:* Students will identify similarities and differences in roles of family members.

1. Ask each student to list the tasks or jobs his or her mother performs.
2. Have students tell class the jobs they have listed. Write these on chalkboard.
3. Follow same procedure for tasks or jobs fathers do.
4. Compare lists for fathers and mothers. What tasks are on both? What tasks are only on one?
5. Discuss tasks that appear on both lists. Do *all* mothers and fathers perform these tasks?
6. Discuss tasks that appear on only one list. Are they unique to fathers or mothers? Do any fathers cook dinner, for example? Do any mothers wash the car? Are there big differences between what mothers do and fathers do?
7. Have each student study both lists and write down any tasks on the lists that he or she helps with at home. Collect the papers.

*Questions*

1. What skill is practiced in this lesson?

   _____

   _____

   _____

2. Do students receive group or individual practice in use of this skill?

   _____

   _____

3. What instructional materials are used?

   _____

   _____

   _____

4. Is there any provision for pupil ideas? If so, what?

_____

_____

_____

5. Is there any provision for individual differences? If so, what?

_____

_____

_____

6. Is there provision for written feedback to the teacher on what pupils learned? If so, what?

_____

_____

_____

PROCEDURE B

*Objective:* Given a film that depicts a different culture ("The Hunters," a film about the Kalihari Bushmen), pupils will identify at least three differences from and two similarities to their own culture.

1. Explain the task to students. Tell them that as they view the film they are to take notes about events they see that are different from or similar to their own experiences.
2. Show the film.
3. Have each pupil use notes to list three differences and two similarities.
4. Discuss the differences and similarities noted. Ask students how they felt as they watched certain events, for example, boys shooting tiny arrows into cricket; a father kissing his baby; a hunter spearing a giraffe.
5. After a discussion, have the students draw a line under their initial lists and add as many items as possible to each list. Collect the papers.

*Questions*

1. What skill is practiced in this lesson?

_____

_____

2. Do students receive group or individual practice in use of this skill?

_____

_____

3. What instructional materials are used?

_____

_____

4. Is there any provision for pupil ideas? If so, what?

_____

_____

_____

5. Is there any provision for individual differences? If so, what?

_____

_____

_____

6. Is there provision for written feedback to the teacher on what pupils learned? If so, what?

_____

_____

_____

# ANSWER KEY

## Mastery Test, Objective 1

(Your written responses need not be worded in exactly the same way as the answers given below.)

*Procedure A*

1. The skill of comparing or noting similarities and differences.
2. Group practice.
3. Paper, pencil, chalkboard.
4. Yes. In discussion, pupils can form their own ideas about the norms of family tasks and share these with each other.
5. Some. In listing tasks and in discussion, students can identify facts of their individual home situations and note how these differ from other homes. (However, there is no provision noted for pupils who have no mother or father in the home.)
6. No. Student's final writing assignment does not relate to identifying similarities and differences. It gives the teacher information on students' home backgrounds, but not on what was learned in this lesson.

*Procedure B*

1. The skill of comparing or noting similarities and differences.

2. Individual practice, supplemented by group practice.
3. Film, paper, and pencil.
4. Yes. Pupil ideas about similarities and differences in cultures form the basis of the whole discussion.
5. Yes. Pupils are encouraged to talk about their individual emotional reactions to various events in the film.
6. Yes. The teacher gets written feedback concerning each student's initial identification of similarities and differences and also concerning the information that was picked up during the discussion (additions to lists).

If you answered eight or more of the twelve questions accurately, you have demonstrated understanding of the ideas presented in this section. Proceed to Learning Activity 2.

If you answered less than eight questions correctly, you need to review the ideas in this section. Reread one of the lesson procedures described at the beginning of Learning Activity 1 and try to answer the eight questions in the section called "Advantages and Disadvantages" preceding Response Form III. Then check your answers by rereading the sections following Response Forms I and II.

# Objective 2

Given two alternative lesson plans for teaching the same content, to identify the differences and similarities in the two plans in terms of their: (a) instructional materials, (b) skills to be practiced, (c) group or individual skill practice, (d) provision for pupil ideas, (e) provision for individual differences, and (f) provision for written feedback.

## LEARNING ACTIVITY 2

Planning and teaching two alternative lessons on the same topic is a procedure that has been used with both experienced teachers and teachers-in-training to introduce them to the process of self-evaluation. The teachers who have used this procedure have generally found it to be an interesting experience. They have noted that pupils respond differently to the alternative procedures and that they themselves act and feel differently.

For our purposes here, planning two alternative lessons serves to emphasize the importance of thinking of alternatives, and it also provides an opportunity to double the practice of the planning skills developed so far in this chapter.

Alternative lessons can vary in several different ways. They might utilize different instructional materials, ask pupils to engage in different types of activities (that is, practice different skills), or provide different roles for the teacher (as lecturer vs. discussion leader). They may even vary in all of these ways at once. But alternative lessons always have one basic similarity: They both deal with the same topic and expect pupils to learn the same general content.

An example of alternative lessons is given below. These two lessons were planned by an eighth grade teacher and taught to two different groups of eighth grade students. (Both groups of students attended a storefront school, were public school "dropouts," and had difficulty with both reading and mathematics.)

---

*Subject matter:* Mathematics

*Topic:* Introduction to Topology

*Lesson objective:* To have students develop a new awareness of lines and the various relationships they can have to each other in space and to indicate an interest in further study of the topic.

*Materials:* Chalkboard

---

| *Procedure for Lesson One* | *Procedure for Lesson Two* |
|---|---|
| 1. Write letters of the alphabet on the board in capitals. | 1. Ask students if someone can write the alphabet on the board in capital letters. |
| 2. Say: "Some of these letters are similar to other letters in certain ways. I have one kind of similarity in mind, and I want to see if you can figure out what my idea is. Here are some of the letters that I think belong together." Write on the board:<br>Yes  A, H, I | 2. Say: "Some of the letters of the alphabet are like each other in certain ways. Can you find some letters that you think are alike?" (Students will raise hands.) "Okay, come up and write down the letters that you think belong together" (maybe E, F, L or B, D, P). |

| *Procedure for Lesson One (cont'd)* | *Procedure for Lesson Two (cont'd)* |
|---|---|

3. Say: "A lot of the letters in the alphabet can't fit in my group. They don't have the characteristic I have in mind. Here are some letters that don't fit." Write on the board:

   No  B, G, Z

4. Say: "Look at the letters that are left and pick some that you think might fit in my group. I'll tell you if you're right." As letters are suggested, write them down in the Yes or No group (that is, add M, O, T, U, V, W, X, Y to Yes group, all others to No ).

5. When all letters are written in Yes or No group, ask: "Can anyone see the rule I'm using to tell what letters fit in my group? Can you see how all these letters are alike?" (They are all "mirror-letters" when divided on the vertical axis, e.g., A.)

6. Ask students to think of another grouping that could be made. Have each student write examples of letters that fit his/her group and also write down the common characteristics of the letters in the group. Collect the papers.

7. Ask who would like to try this again with some other kinds of shapes. Note the responses.

3. Say: "Great. Does anyone else have a group of letters that they think belong together because they are alike somehow?" (Another student comes to the board.)

4. Continue asking students to suggest groups until all letters are included in a group and/or all students have suggested a group.

5. Say: "We have a lot of groups now, so let's look back and decide why the letters in a group belong together. Let's give our groups names that tell how they are alike." (For example, E, F, L could be called "sidelines.")

6. Ask students to think of another way that letters could be grouped, different from the groupings on the board. Have each student write down his new group and give it a name. Collect the papers.

7. Ask who would like to try this again with some other kinds of shapes. Note the responses.

One way to compare these two alternative lessons is to review the aspects of planning that have been dealt with so far in this chapter. The following chart presents a comparison based on the types of characteristics that have been discussed.

| | *Lesson One* | *Lesson Two* |
|---|---|---|
| Skills to be practiced | Noting similarities and differences in shape. Discovering someone else's "rule" for grouping. | Noting similarities and differences in shape. Forming your own "rule" for grouping. |
| Type of skill practice | Group. Students help each other with their "guesses" and their discussion of possible reasons. | Individual. Each pupil can form his/her own group. |
| Materials | Chalkboard, letters of the alphabet. | Same as One |
| Provision for pupil ideas | Pupils hypothesize about basis for teacher's group and test their hypotheses by suggesting other letters to be added. | Pupils invent their own groupings and their own names for groups. |
| Provision for individual differences | Some pupils may guess the rule earlier than others. They can test their guess by adding new letters to group, while others are still trying to figure out the rule. | Pupils may perceive letters differently and focus on different characteristics. |

|  | Lesson One | Lesson Two |
|---|---|---|
| Provision for feedback | Written check on whether pupils can get another fresh perspective on similarities in letters. | Same as One |

The basic difference in these two alternative lessons is that the pupils' mental activity is different, that is, pupils have to think in different ways in the two lessons. But other variations could be easily developed. For example, open and closed shapes could be used rather than letters of the alphabet (alternative materials). Or pupils could be given a worksheet of logical problems to work on alone or in pairs, problems such as: If O, Q, and G belong together because they are alike in some way, which of the following letters would belong in the same group: J, C, T? (alternative with less provision for independent pupil ideas).

## RESPONSE FORM IV

1. Decide on a subject matter area, topic, and grade level and plan two alternative lessons, using the form given below.

*Subject matter:* _____

*Topic:* _____

*Grade level:* _____


PLAN ONE

*Objective:*

*Materials:*

*Procedures:*

PLAN TWO

*Objective:*

*Materials:*

*Procedures:*

2. Compare your two plans by filling in the following form, noting where they are similar (write "S" in blank) and different (explain the differences you see).

| | Plan One | Plan Two |
|---|---|---|
| Content/Topic | | |
| Specific objective | | |
| Instructional materials | | |
| Skills to be practiced | | |
| Group or individual skill practice | | |
| Provision for pupil ideas | | |
| Provision for individual differences | | |
| Provision for feedback | | |

| | Plan One (cont'd) | Plan Two (cont'd) |
|---|---|---|
| Other (_____) | | |

3. Exchange both your plans and analysis forms with another student; study each other's papers to decide whether you agree on the similarities and differences between the two alternative plans. Check your agreements and disagreements below.

Partner's Name _____

| | Agreed | Disagreed |
|---|---|---|
| Content/Topic | | |
| Specific objective | | |
| Instructional materials | | |
| Skills to be practiced | | |
| Group or individual skill practice | | |
| Provision for pupil ideas | | |
| Provision for individual differences | | |
| Provision for feedback | | |
| Other | | |

# Mastery Test

**OBJECTIVE 2**    Given two alternative lesson plans for teaching the same content, to identify the differences and similarities in the two plans in terms of their: (a) instructional materials, (b) skills to be practiced, (c) group or individual skill practice, (d) provision for pupil ideas, (e) provision for individual differences, and (f) provision for written feedback.

To determine whether you have understood the concepts presented in this section, review your record sheets for Response Form IV.

In response to question 3, were you and your partner able to agree on the similarities and differences between your plans in at least six of the eight basic areas listed for analysis? If so, you have demonstrated accuracy in your analysis of the two plans.

In response to question 2, were you able to note differences in your two plans in at least four of the eight basic areas? If so, you have demonstrated an ability to plan lessons that are really varied. You are beginning to develop the competencies that are the ultimate goals of this chapter.

**Testing Alternatives**

The real purpose of thinking in terms of alternatives when you plan lessons is that this enables you to vary your teaching and to learn more about what procedures work or don't work for you. The only real way to test the alternatives you have planned is to see how pupils react to them. The ultimate mastery test for Objective 2, therefore, is a test that you must create for yourself. Here are the steps to follow.

1. Find two groups of students of about the same age level and ability and make arrangements to meet with each group for about half an hour to teach your lessons, one lesson to each group.

2. As you teach the lessons, have a fellow student observe the lessons or make an audiotape to listen to later. The lessons should be observed so that the differences in pupil responses can be noted (comments made, questions asked, interest displayed, amount learned).

3. When the lessons are over and you have the results of the observation, decide whether the two lessons were more or less different than you originally thought. Did you prefer one lesson over the other? Why? Can you think of additional alternative lessons for the same topic? What are they?

   (*An alternative:* If no elementary or secondary pupils are available to you, form a group of your fellow students who are studying this chapter and teach your two alternative lessons to them. When the lessons are over, you can ask them what differences they noted and whether they [as pupils] felt differently in the two lessons.)

The "ultimate mastery test" may take time for you to arrange, but you will find it to be of great value.

# Objective 3

Given several possible topics for long-range planning, to select a topic; to plan two sequences of activities, ideas, and/or skills; and to compare the sequences, identifying the criteria used in organizing each.

## LEARNING ACTIVITY 3

Thus far you have learned about individual lesson plans that have specific objectives, procedures, materials, and methods of evaluation. Teachers plan not only one lesson at a time, but also sequences of lessons. Sequential, or long-range, planning may include unit, mastery, semester, or annual planning.

The purpose of long-range planning is to tie ideas together. The goals, or objectives, expressed in long-range plans are usually larger, more general, or more complex than the objectives of a single lesson plan. Because of the characteristics of such objectives, students need more than one lesson in order to understand the complexities. If students have more than one encounter with a concept, they need to understand how the encounters are related to one another. Therefore, when creating long-range plans, teachers must be concerned with the *sequence* of the plans, i.e., the various types of relationships that exist between parts of the plan.

Sequences may be created based on different characteristics, such as time, complexity, or order. For instance, you might plan a list of errands by beginning with the earliest that you plan to accomplish and continuing to the latest. You could also plan your errands beginning with the simplest or easiest and proceeding to the most difficult or most complex. Or, you might look at a map and create an order based on the physical proximity, the first errand being the closest to your starting point and the last errand being farthest from your home.

When creating long-range plans, teachers often sequence activities, ideas, or skills. The following section will present examples of each type of sequencing, using examples from everyday life. Then each type of sequencing will be investigated with specific reference to lesson planning.

## Sequencing Activities

Gardening has several activities that must be completed in order to be successful. What order would you follow for these gardening activities? (Number each, to indicate your preferred sequence.)

_____ plant

_____ harvest

_____ fertilize

_____ weed

_____ rake

_____ turn ground

_____ water

_____ buy seed, supplies

_____ plan

Although not everyone would use exactly the same order, the activities of planning, buying, and turning the ground would most likely be first in a sequence, whereas weeding and harvesting would be toward the end of the sequence. Using practical order as the criterion for creating a garden, one might produce the following list:

1. plan
2. buy seeds, supplies
3. turn ground

4. rake
5. plant
6. fertilize
7. water
8. weed
9. harvest

## Sequencing Ideas

We often order events based on when they occur or occurred, and we usually order ideas based on some relationship that they have to one another. If one were planning a story, the plot would be considered the order of ideas. Directions and historical accounts are also examples of ordered ideas.

You may have experienced a conversation in which someone brought up what appeared to be an unrelated idea. However, quizzical looks on people's faces may have cued the speaker that the relationship was unclear, and she or he then explained that something said in the conversation had triggered a series of ideas which led finally to her or his remark. For instance:

the football game
yellow chrysanthemum
tulip bulbs
mail order
catalog
blouse/shirt order
blouse/shirt has not arrived

Use each of the following words to trigger a series of ideas. Compare your idea associations or idea sequence with someone else's lists.

| *Children* | *Expensive* | *Television* |
| --- | --- | --- |
| | | |
| | | |
| | | |
| | | |
| | | |
| | | |
| | | |

## Sequencing Skills

Skills such as swimming, handwriting, or categorizing can be organized on the basis of complexity. A skill might first be separated into component parts and then the part ordered from simple to complex. For instance, swimming involves the ability to:

> float
>
> kick feet
>
> stroke arms
>
> breathe rhythmically

To learn the skill of swimming, a learner must learn each of the subskills above separately. Then several subskills might be combined:

> float and kick
>
> kick and stroke arms
>
> kick and breathe rhythmically
>
> stroke arms and breathe rhythmically

Finally, all subskills are combined. As the subskills and combination of skills are practiced, continual refinement occurs to create coordinated body movement.

Name a skill you have learned recently: _____
In the spaces below, list the components of one skill. (*Note*: Use the short lines to indicate the order you would follow in teaching the skill (e.g., write "1" by the first subskill, "2" by the second, etc.).

_____    _____

_____    _____

_____    _____

_____    _____

_____    _____

_____    _____

_____    _____

## Unit Plan

The following outline represents the brief, initial plans for a unit in which the teacher wishes to introduce *propaganda*.

### Unit Outline for Propaganda

A. Define propaganda

B. Describe and show examples of different types of propaganda

    1. Glittering generalities
        "The better soap . . ."
        "More doctors recommend . . ."

     2. Testimonial (famous people recommending or advertising products, ideas, or laws)

     3. Card stacking (telling only positive points of one candidate and negative points of another candidate)

  C. Students locate examples of each type of propaganda

  D. Compare propaganda (types and methods) in

     1. Magazines

     2. Newspaper

     3. Television

  E. Students create and test propaganda. Determine how it affects people.

## RESPONSE FORM V

1. Suppose that the teacher began the propaganda unit plan by selecting and sequencing activities. Explain what you think the teacher's reasoning might have been for this sequencing of activities.

_____

_____

_____

_____

_____

_____

_____

_____

_____

_____

*Feedback:* The selection of activities may have been planned beginning from *shorter, discrete activities to longer, more involved activities*. First, students learn about specific propaganda examples. Choosing examples of propaganda from a set of materials requires greater involvement and more time than the first exercise does. Each of the following activities requires an increase in time and student involvement.

    The activities may also have been planned to change gradually the *degree of structure or direction given the student*. Activities may be specifically structured by the teacher, or activities may allow for student self-direction. The propaganda unit begins with teacher-directed activities of defining and providing examples of propaganda. The activities that follow involve less teacher direction and a greater degree of student direction. The final activity, creating and testing propaganda, requires a high degree of student self-direction.

2. Suppose that the teacher began the propaganda unit plan by selecting and sequencing ideas. Explain what you think the teacher's reasoning might have been for this sequencing of ideas.

_____

_____

_____

_____

_____

_____

_____

_____

_____

*Feedback:* The sequence of ideas in the propaganda unit might be described as moving from *abstract ideas to concrete ideas:* (a) there is a thing called propaganda, (b) there are different types of propaganda, (c) you can find propaganda in a lot of places, and (d) in fact, you can create it yourself. The ideas are first described and discussed; then students locate and generate actual examples of propaganda.

   Another way of organizing ideas might be to move from the *unfamiliar to the familiar.* Beginning with a definition implies that the idea is unfamiliar to the learners. Students then encounter examples from materials that are familiar to them. Finally, students develop their own examples, probably the most familiar type of ideas.

3. Suppose that the teacher began the propaganda unit by selecting and sequencing skills. Explain what you think the teacher's reasoning might have been for this sequencing of skills.

_____

_____

_____

_____

_____

_____

_____

_____

*Feedback:* A unit organized around skills might proceed *from simple, discrete skills to complex, integrated skills.* The propaganda unit begins with observing, then combines that skill to have students make applications. Finally, students perform the most complex skill, that of creating, which incorporates both observing and making applications.

   A second means of skill organization might emphasize the movement *from developing common conclusions or results, called convergent thinking, to developing different, branching conclusions or results, called divergent thinking.* For instance, in the propaganda unit students should be able to identify specific types of propaganda correctly. However, all the final propaganda creations should be unique and divergent, compared not only to the first exercises, but also to one another.

4. Can you change one of the sequences without changing the other sequences?

_____

_____

_____

_____

_____

_____

5. Describe a new sequence for the unit. You may add activities if you would like.

_____

_____

_____

_____

_____

_____

_____

_____

_____

_____

_____

_____

_____

_____

_____

6. How does your reorganization differ from the original unit organization?

_____

_____

_____

_____

_____

_____

_Feedback:_ One idea may have occurred to you: You cannot sequence activities without also sequencing ideas and/or skills, because each activity incorporates an idea and/or skill. The three are integrally related; therefore, if you change your sequence of activities, you will want to question what effect this has had on your sequences of ideas and skills. Review your response to question 6. Have you discussed the different types of sequences that are involved in your reorganization?

In analyzing your new sequence, did you identify what your primary organizer is? _____Which of the following criteria have you used in organizing your sequences?

From shorter to longer activities

From skills of observing, to applying, to creating

From familiar to unfamiliar ideas

From easy-to-organize to difficult-to-organize activities

From simple to complex ideas or skills or activities

From convergent to divergent thinking skills

From teacher-directed to student-directed activity structure

From abstract ideas to concrete ideas

7. What might be some strengths and weaknesses of using each type of sequence as a primary organizer?

| Activities | | Ideas | | Skills | |
|---|---|---|---|---|---|
| *Strengths* | *Weaknesses* | *Strengths* | *Weaknesses* | *Strengths* | *Weaknesses* |
| | | | | | |

*Feedback:* Following are some possible strengths and weaknesses of each type of sequencing. You may have noted some additional strengths and weaknesses.

| Activity | | Ideas | | Skills | |
|---|---|---|---|---|---|
| *Strengths* | *Weaknesses* | *Strengths* | *Weaknesses* | *Strengths* | *Weaknesses* |
| A variety of activities may be planned, thus increasing chances of reaching individuals with different learning styles | May be difficult to generate a variety of activities for some topics | Ideas related to one another have a greater probability of being remembered | May result in "covering the content" and exclude other types of learning | Helps to learn prerequisite skills, enhancing probability of learning large skill | Not all types of learning involve overt skills |

## Practice Sequencing

Listed below are several topics with illustrative questions. Choose one of the following topics and develop a brief sample unit. The questions following each topic unit may help you generate ideas. Record your ideas on Response Form VI, giving two alternative sequences for development of this unit.

### Television programing

What types of programs are available?

How is audience considered?

How do time of day and day of week affect programing?

How does programing affect commercials?

*Salesmanship*

What are the qualities of a "good" salesman?

What are the possible targets for sales? — (product, political candidate, self)

What are techniques of sales?

*Categorizing*

What types of things might people categorize?

What criteria might people use to classify? (description, composition, function)

What happens when someone uses more than one attribute as a basis for classification?

*Your own:* _____

---

# RESPONSE FORM VI

Grade level: _____          Subject area: _____

Alternative Sequences

| Sequence 1 | Sequence 2 |
|---|---|
|  |  |

1. Analyze your sequences, using the following outline:

|  | *Plan One* | *Plan Two* |
|---|---|---|
| Criteria used for organizing your activity sequence |  |  |
| Criteria used for organizing your idea sequence |  |  |
| Criteria used for organizing your skill sequence |  |  |

2. Star whichever one of these three was your primary organizer. Explain what made you choose this as your primary organizer.

_____

_____

_____

3. If you had to teach this tomorrow, how might your sequence change?

_____

_____

_____

_____

_____

4. Exchange your unit sequences and analysis form with another student. Study each other's papers to decide whether you agree in identifying the criteria that have been used in organizing each type of sequence and in perceiving these sequences as different. Check your agreements and disagreements below.

_____

| *Partner's name:* _____ | | *Agreed* | *Disagreed* |
|---|---|---|---|
| *Criteria used for organizing your activity sequence* | Plan 1 | | |
| | Plan 2 | | |
| *Criteria used for organizing your idea sequence* | Plan 1 | | |
| | Plan 2 | | |
| *Criteria used for organizing your skill sequence* | Plan 1 | | |
| | Plan 2 | | |
| *Two plans (are/are not) different in activity sequence* | | | |
| *Two plans (are/are not) different in idea sequence* | | | |
| *Two plans (are/are not) different in skill sequence* | | | |

# Mastery Test

## Objective 3

Given several possible topics for long-range planning, to select a topic; to plan two sequences of activities, ideas, and/or skills; and to compare the sequences, identifying the criteria used in organizing each.

In response to question 4 on Response Form VI, were you and your partner able to agree in four out of six instances on the criteria used in organizing the various types of sequences? Did you agree that the plans were or were not different in sequence in two out of three instances? If so, you have demonstrated some ability to plan and to analyze alternative sequences in long-range planning.

# Final Mastery Test

*Directions:* Study the two alternative lesson plans presented here. Then answer each of the questions which follow.

*Subject matter:* Social studies

*Topic:* Inventions

*General goal:* To introduce the topic of inventions and provide opportunity for creative thinking.

PLAN ONE

*Objective:* Given an everyday object, each pupil will invent at least one new use for it.

*Diagnostic procedure:* Ask each pupil to list at least three different things they might do with a deck of cards. Collect the papers. Identify the number of common uses (e.g., play card games, build a cardhouse, do a magic trick) and the number of uncommon uses (e.g., make a mobile) listed by each pupil.

*Instructional materials:* Chalkboard, a chain of paper clips, a newspaper, several decks of cards, general art supplies.

*Procedures:*
1. Introduce the topic of inventions. Ask pupils what inventions they have heard of. Explain that an invention can be something very new, but it can also be a new use for a familiar thing.
2. Show pupils a paper clip. Ask why it was invented — what it is used for. Ask if they can think of any other uses. Show them a chain of paper clips. Does that help them think of additional uses?
3. Show pupils a newspaper. Identify its normal use. Ask for inventive uses. List these on chalkboard. Note that changing the form of an object can help us think of other uses. Roll the newspaper up. Tear off a piece and crumple it up. What additional uses do these forms suggest?
4. Bring out a deck of cards. Ask pupils to think of a new way to use a deck of cards. They can work alone or with a partner. Tomorrow they will be asked to explain or show their invention to the rest of the class. Remind them that changing the form of the object can help them to be inventive. If they need any supplies like pens, scissors, paper, paste, etc., let them help themselves.

*Evaluation:* At the end of the "reporting" period next day, pupils will again be asked to list at least three different things they might do with a deck of cards. Compare each pupil's first and second lists. Are there more total items? Are there more uncommon uses?

PLAN TWO

*Objective:* Given an example of one humorous account of an early invention, pupils will write an imaginative explanation of how something else might have been first invented.

*Diagnostic procedure:* Ask each pupil to pick an invention that he or she is familiar with (e.g., has seen or used it) and in a brief paragraph tell how or why they think it was invented. Collect the papers. Note how many pupils pick machines to discuss. What other types of things are seen as inventions? How realistic or accurate are the explanations of how or why things were invented?

*Instructional materials:* Charles Lamb's essay on the origin of roast pork, chalkboard, paper and pencils for pupils, several common objects such as a cup, a bowl, a spoon.

*Procedures:*
1. Introduce the topic of inventions. Ask pupils what things they think of when the word "invention" is used. Ask why people invent things. Do inventions ever occur by accident?
2. Explain that almost everything we use today was once invented. Most things are so familiar that we don't think of them as having been invented. It can be fun to imagine how some of the earliest things were invented.

3. Read (or tell) Charles Lamb's account of the origin (invention) of roast pork. (This is a funny story about a Chinese boy who accidentally burns down his hut and discovers that a pig has been burned inside it. He burns his hand on the pig and licks his fingers. The burned pig tastes so good, he begins to burn down the hut regularly, in order to eat a roasted pig each time. The practice spreads until everyone in the village is burning down their house once a week.)

4. Ask pupils what other common things they can think of that were once invented. List their ideas on the board. Display common objects like a cup, a bowl, or a spoon if they need help to get started.

5. Pick one or two things from the list to discuss. What might this have been made from originally? How might people have gotten the idea? Why did they need something like this? Can they think of a funny explanation? Write ideas on the board.

6. Ask pupils to write an explanation of how or why something was invented. They can choose something from the list or think of something else. Papers will be read aloud to the class the next day.

*Evaluation:* Compare papers at the end of the lesson to those written before the lesson. Are more common objects or procedures (that are not machines) listed the second time? Are the explanations of how or why things were invented more humorous or imaginative the second time?

*Questions*

1. For each of the two instructional procedures described, identify its characteristics by answering the questions below.

    (a) What skill is practiced in the lesson?

    Plan One _____

    _____

    Plan Two _____

    _____

    (b) Do students receive individual or group practice in use of this skill?

    Plan One _____

    Plan Two _____

    (c) What instructional materials are used?

    Plan One _____

    _____

    Plan Two _____

    _____

    (d) Is there any provision for pupil ideas? If so, what?

    Plan One _____

    _____

    _____

    Plan Two _____

    _____

    _____

(e) Is there provision for individual differences? If so, what?

Plan One _____

_____

_____

Plan Two _____

_____

_____

(f) Is there provision for written feedback to the teacher on what pupils learned? If so, what?

Plan One _____

_____

_____

Plan Two _____

_____

_____

2. Compare the two lesson plans by noting whether they are basically similar or basically different in each of the following six areas. (Circle "similar" or "different" for each area.)

| | | |
|---|---|---|
| *Instructional materials* | Similar | Different |
| *Skills to be practiced* | Similar | Different |
| *Group or individual skill practice* | Similar | Different |
| *Provision for pupil ideas* | Similar | Different |
| *Provision for individual differences* | Similar | Different |
| *Provision for written feedback* | Similar | Different |

3. Suppose that a teacher used Plan One as a follow-up for a lesson in which students read together a textbook chapter on the Industrial Revolution (which mentioned inventions like the sewing machine and the cotton gin) and discussed the answers to the questions presented at the end of the chapter. Identify the types of sequences that would be involved in moving from this textbook lesson to the lesson described in Plan One.

*Types of sequence:*

From shorter to longer activities _____

From skills of observing or recalling or comprehending to skills of creating _____

From familiar to unfamiliar ideas _____

From easy-to-organize to difficult-to-organize activities _____

From simple to complex ideas _____

From simple to complex skills _____

From simple to complex activities _____

From convergent to divergent thinking skills _____

From teacher-directed to student-directed activity structure _____

From abstract ideas to concrete ideas _____

# ANSWER KEY

## Final Mastery Test

1  (a) *Plan One*   The skill of generating new or uncommon uses for everyday objects.
    *Plan Two*   The skill of imagining possible explanations for how or why familiar things were first invented.

  (b) *Plan One*   Both group and individual practice.
    *Plan Two*   Both group and individual practice.

  (c) *Plan One*   Paper clips, newspaper, decks of cards, art supplies.
    *Plan Two*   Story by Charles Lamb, some common objects such as a cup or a spoon.

  (d) *Plan One*   Yes. In several instances pupils are asked their ideas (about new uses for objects), and these are listed on the board.
    *Plan Two*   Yes. Pupils are asked for their ideas (about how familiar objects might originally have been invented), and these are listed on the board.

  (e) *Plan One*   Yes. Pupils can opt to work alone or with a partner. They can select the kind of materials they want to work with in inventing a new use for cards.
    *Plan Two*   Some. Pupils can select the object they want to write about, but all of them are asked to write a paper. This may not be the best form of communication for all pupils.

  (f) *Plan One*   Yes. Each pupil's list of three different uses for cards can be compared to the original papers to inform the teacher if additional ideas have been developed. (In addition, there will be oral feedback as pupils report on their inventions.)
    *Plan Two*   Yes. Each pupil's final paper can be compared to the original paper to determine whether imaginative ideas were developed.

2. 

| | |
|---|---|
| Instructional materials: | Different |
| Skills to be practiced: | Different |
| Group or individual skill practice: | Similar |
| Provision for pupil ideas: | Similar |
| Provision for individual differences: | Different |
| Provision for written feedback: | Similar |

3. *Types of sequence:*

| | |
|---|---|
| From shorter to longer activities | X |
| From skills of observing or recalling or comprehending to skills of creating | X |
| From familiar to unfamiliar ideas | |
| From easy-to-organize to difficult-to-organize activities | |
| From simple to complex ideas | |
| From simple to complex skills | |
| From simple to complex activities | X |
| From convergent to divergent thinking skills | X |
| From teacher-directed to student-directed activity structure | X |
| From abstract ideas to concrete ideas | X |

NOTES      1. Robert Yinger, *A Study of Teacher Planning: Description and Theory Development Using Ethnographic and Information Processing Methods* (unpublished doctoral dissertation, Michigan State University, 1977).

2. Greta Morine and Elizabeth Vallance, *Teacher Planning*, Beginning Teacher Evaluation Studies Technical Report, Special Study C (San Francisco: Far West Laboratory, 1976).

3. Philip Taylor, *How Teachers Plan Their Courses* (Slough, England: National Foundation for Education Research in England and Wales, 1970). See also John Zahorik, "Teacher's Planning Models," *Educational Leadership* 33, no. 2 (1975): 134–139.

4. Charles Fisher, David Berliner, Nicola Filby, Richard Marliave, Leonard Cahen and Marilyn Dishaw, "Teaching Behaviors, Academic Learning Time, and Student Achievement: An Overview," in Carolyn Denham and Ann Lieberman, eds., *Time To Learn* (Washington, D.C.: National Institute of Education, 1980).

5. Christopher Clark and Robert Yinger, *Three Studies of Teacher Planning*, Research Series No. 55 (East Lansing, Michigan: Institute for Research on Teaching, Michigan State University, 1979).

6. *Ibid.*

7. Morine and Vallance, *op. cit.*

8. Christopher Clark and Janis Elmore, *Teacher Planning in the First Weeks of School*, Research Series No. 56 (East Lansing, Michigan: Institute for Research on Teaching, Michigan State University, 1981).

9. Clark and Yinger, *op. cit.*

10. Greta Morine-Dershimer, *Teacher Plan and Classroom Reality: The South Bay Study*, Part IV, Research Series No. 60 (East Lansing, Michigan: Institute for Research on Teaching, Michigan State University, 1979).

11. Bruce Joyce, "Toward a Theory of Information Processing in Teaching," *Educational Research Quarterly* 3, no. 4 (1978–79): 66–77.

12. V. Dahllof and Ulf Lundgren, *Macro- and Micro-Approaches Combined for Curriculum Process Analysis: A Swedish Educational Field Project* (Goteborg, Sweden: Institute of Education, University of Goteborg, 1970).

13. Morine and Vallance, *op. cit.*

14. Clark and Yinger, *op. cit.*

15. Morine and Vallance, *op. cit.*

16. Barak Rosenshine and Norma Furst, "Research in Teacher Performance Criteria," in B. Othanael Smith, ed., *Research in Teacher Education* (Englewood Cliffs, New Jersey: Prentice-Hall, 1971).

Terry D. TenBrink

# 3. Writing Instructional Objectives

# Objectives

**1** To list the sources of instructional objectives and to describe the kind of objectives to be found for each source.

**2** To select instructional objectives that will be useful to you and your students.

**3** To rewrite poorly written objectives.

**4** To write well-defined and useful objectives of your own.

You are probably well aware of the controversy that has continued for several years over the value of instructional objectives. Before you begin to develop your skills in selecting, writing, and using instructional objectives, you should understand their value to you as a teacher. The first few pages of this chapter will be devoted to the value of instructional objectives; the remainder of the chapter will show you *how* to use them.

Think for a moment about what teachers do. Sit back and try to remember the *one* teacher who you felt had the most influence upon you. In the space provided below, write down the characteristics of that teacher as well as you can remember them.

*Characteristics of a Favorite Teacher*

_____

_____

_____

_____

_____

_____

Chances are that among the characteristics of your favorite teacher was the fact that the teacher knew you as an individual and knew what he or she wanted for you. This favorite teacher probably had a significant influence on your life, playing a part in the development of your attitudes, the formation of your habits, and the acquisition of information that was new and exciting to you. This teacher may have guided you subtly or may have directly "pushed" you toward these behavior changes. The teacher may have used a great many visual aids or none at all; or may have given multiple choice tests, essay tests, or no tests at all. What effective teachers have in common is *not* their techniques, their teaching styles, or the kinds of tests they use. It is *what* they accomplish, not how they accomplish it, that makes the difference.

If teachers are going to make a significant difference in the lives of their students, they must know what they want their students to accomplish. Having formulated such goals, teachers can share them with their students so that the students will *also* know where they are going and what is expected of them.

There is considerable evidence[1] to support the contention that when teachers have clearly defined instructional objectives and have shared them with their students, a number of things happen:

1. Better instruction occurs.
2. More efficient learning results.
3. Better evaluation occurs.
4. The students become better self-evaluators.

Furthermore, it is important to note that the most successful instructional-design and systems-design approaches to education rely heavily upon well-defined objectives.

However, objections have been raised about the use of instructional objectives. The major objections to their use are summarized as follows:

1. Writing good instructional objectives requires a lot of work and expertise.
2. Using instructional objectives hampers the process of individualizing and humanizing education.
3. The use of instructional objectives curtails spontaneity and decreases the teacher's flexibility.
4. Using instructional objectives leads to trivial learning outcomes.

If you examine each of these objections carefully, you will see that the objectives themselves are not at fault, but the way they are used. If a teacher becomes a slave to the writing and making use of instructional objectives instead of skillfully using them as an important teaching aid, then the above objections become valid. However, when objectives are viewed in proper perspective and used appropriately, there emerges a positive side to each of these objections. Let us briefly examine the positive counterparts to the above objections.

**1. Writing Instructional Objectives Is Well Worth the Effort Involved.**  There is no denying the fact that writing good instructional objectives can be time-consuming and difficult. However, if instructional objectives can improve instruction and produce more efficient learning, then surely the effort involved in writing and in using them is worth it.

One of the things that you should keep in mind is that writing instructional objectives is a task that need not be accomplished by a single teacher. Teachers can work together in teams, writing objectives for a common unit of study. Likewise, much time and effort can be saved by learning to rework objectives prepared by others.

Also keep in mind that teachers usually can develop their instructional materials over a period of time. It is not always possible to begin the year with a comprehensive list of objectives for each subject you are teaching. As you teach, you are continually updating and upgrading old objectives and writing appropriate new ones as needed. Thus, it is not only permissible, but valuable, to be working on objectives while the instructional process is in progress. This allows you to alter the objectives you discover are inappropriate for your students.

**2. Instructional Objectives Can Be Helpful in Individualizing and Humanizing Education.**    In order to individualize instruction successfully, teachers need to know each individual student's abilities, strengths and weaknesses, and likes and dislikes. Furthermore, they need to be able to monitor each student's progress as he or she moves toward individually assigned goals. The more clearly and precisely those goals are stated, the easier it will be to determine when an individual student reaches them.

Of course, not all students will reach the same educational goals at the same time. Therefore, well-defined subgoals, specified in observable terms, serve as important "landmarks" along the way. As a given student progresses toward a goal, these "landmarks" help in pinpointing exactly what the student has learned so far and what he or she needs to learn next. This kind of diagnostic information is invaluable in planning appropriate learning experiences for each student.

**3. Instructional Objectives Help the Teacher To Be Flexible.** There is a phenomenon in education which occurs regularly in most classrooms. The students call it "getting the teacher sidetracked." The teachers call it "capitalizing on the interests of the moment." In any dynamic classroom, unplanned but potentially powerful learning situations sometimes arise spontaneously from the classroom activities. Teachers who have clearly defined instructional objectives will be more able to capitalize on those spontaneous activities, seeing them as alternate ways to reach their objectives. If there are no well-defined objectives, these same spontaneous activities are likely to sidetrack instruction rather than move the class toward desired goals. In short, objectives can help teachers harness spontaneity instead of being derailed by it. Having clearly defined instructional objectives will not only help the teacher capitalize on spur-of-the-moment situations but will also help in planning a variety of activities specifically designed to help the students reach their objectives.

It is not uncommon to find teachers who depend on textbooks and other classroom materials for a definition of what their students should accomplish. In these situations the student or the teacher often finds the materials uninteresting or inappropriate, and the teacher may decide to switch to new materials. Chances are that the newly acquired materials were *not* designed to help the students toward the same educational objectives as the materials they replaced. Consequently, switching materials often means switching goals, which can become frustrating and confusing to students. On the other hand, teachers who have clearly specified their *own* instructional objectives can be more flexible in the selection and use of instructional materials. Because they know precisely what they want their students to accomplish, they can select and use materials on the basis of their own objectives. In this situation, a midstream change of materials does not automatically produce a change of objectives.

**4. Well-Written Instructional Objectives Help Produce Important Learning Outcomes.**   A common misuse of instructional objectives is to write trivial ones that emphasize the memorization of unimportant facts. The result is that the instructional objectives are blamed for trivia being taught in the schools. An examination of the classroom tests does reveal that much purely factual, trivial information is being taught. Whether or not teachers write instructional objectives, they are subject to the common error of emphasizing the memorization of trivia. However, if instructional objectives are drawn up *before* instruction begins, they can be evaluated to see if there is a proper balance of memory versus the higher levels of learning. Once a good balance is achieved, the objectives can serve as a guide in lesson planning as well as in test construction. Well-written objectives, rather than causing the teaching of trivia, can help teachers avoid that error by reviewing their objectives to see if a proper balance of learning levels has been achieved prior to teaching.

Instructional objectives fulfill a number of useful functions. Primary among these are the following:

1. Lesson planning.
2. Selection of learning aids such as textbooks, films, etc.
3. Determining appropriate assignments for individual students.
4. Selecting and/or constructing classroom tests.
5. Determining when to gather evaluative data.
6. Summarizing and reporting evaluation results.
7. Helping learners determine where they are and where they have to go as they strive toward becoming independent learners.

# Objective 1

To list the sources of instructional objectives and to describe the kind of objectives to be found for each source.

## LEARNING ACTIVITY 1.1

In developing a set of objectives for your own class, you may find it useful to begin with objectives that have already been written by others. Some of these objectives may be usable in their original form, whereas others may have to be rewritten to suit your needs and the needs of your students. Among the major sources of objectives available to you, these should be particularly useful:

1. Published learning materials
2. Course syllabi
3. Other teachers
4. Professional journals
5. Instructional objectives exchange

**1. Published Learning Materials.**   One important source of instructional objectives is the material that you use in teaching your students. Textbooks, educational games, workbooks, slide-tape programs, films, and so on are all potential sources for instructional objectives. The objectives they contain will vary greatly in terms of how well they are written. Some objectives may be clearly stated in observable terms, while others may be vague and somewhat ambiguous. Some may state specific short-term objectives; others may include only long-term goals. Sometimes there may be no observable objectives stated at all. However, by carefully examining the content of the materials, you should perceive what the student is expected to learn and, consequently, have a valuable source of ideas for designing your own objectives.

The objectives (or goals) that accompany published materials are usually appropriate for the grade level specified by the materials themselves. However, make certain there is a "match" between the objectives and the lessons. Sometimes a publisher's claims about what students will accomplish when using the materials are unrealistic. Always examine educational materials carefully and ask yourself this important question:

> If the students use these materials as they were designed to be used, what will they likely be able to do that they couldn't do before using them?

If your answer to the above question resembles the publisher's claims, then those claims may indeed serve as realistic objectives for your students.

If published materials do not include learning objectives per se, then use the materials as a source of ideas when you construct your own set of objectives. Examine the following items in particular:

*Sources of Ideas from Published Materials*

1. General goals
2. Statements of purpose
3. Publisher's claims of success
4. Test items
5. Exercises and suggested assignments
6. Preface

**2. Course Syllabi.**   Sometimes the objectives published by the local school district in a course syllabus are quite clear. When this is so, you can use them as written. However, the course syllabus objectives are often vague and represent long-term goals rather than the specific, short-term goals that make good instructional objectives.

There are a couple of very important advantages to using objectives found in a course syllabus. First, the objectives are usually a part of a larger set of goals (e.g., objectives for a ninth grade English class are part of the objectives for the total English curriculum in the school). Seeing your instructional objectives as part of a much larger set may help you better understand what to expect of your students when they enter your class and when they leave it.

A second advantage of objectives found in course syllabi is that they are not usually tied to particular instructional materials. Thus, you can exercise your academic freedom, possibly using a variety of materials, to help your students attain the goals set by your school.

**3. Other Teachers.** Teachers teaching the same subject matter and/or grade level can be a great deal of help to each other. Often what one will not think of, another will; so, when writing objectives for a given course, it is helpful for the teachers of that course to work as a team. This procedure not only will lighten the load on individual teachers but will also broaden their perspective and probably ensure a more appropriate set of objectives.

Since many teachers have not been trained to specify their instructional goals clearly, don't be surprised if some of those you borrow are poorly conceived and written. Instead of being critical, accept whatever statements of expected outcomes you can get. If the intent of the borrowed objectives seems appropriate, you can always rewrite them so that they will be more useful to you and your students. Later in this chapter you will learn how to do this.

**4. Professional Journals.** Professional journals frequently carry articles describing successful units of instruction or helpful approaches to teaching certain topics. Sometimes, these articles will include a list of objectives the authors used to measure the learning outcomes of their students. Although these objectives are frequently well written and at an appropriate level, they are usually highly specific, related to one small aspect of a given course or tied to a particular instructional methodology. Do not expect to find a well-balanced set of objectives for an entire course in a single journal article. If the specific objectives detailed in a given article fit well into your overall objectives, then use them accordingly.

**5. Instructional Objectives Exchange.** A particularly valuable source of instructional objectives is the behavioral objective exchange directed by W. James Popham. By contributing instructional objectives to the exchange, you become eligible to withdraw objectives which may suit your own needs. The exchange has objectives available for virtually all subject matter areas at many different grade levels.

The objectives received from this exchange have been checked for clarity and are likely to be well written and stated in observable terms. You can read more about this instructional objective exchange in an article which appeared in the *Phi Delta Kappan* in 1970.[2]

## LEARNING ACTIVITY 1.2

Most colleges and universities and many public school systems have a library of classroom materials including textbooks, learning kits, films, recordings, educational games, etc. Go to one of these libraries near you and browse through the offerings of the various publishers. Check for learning objectives accompanying the materials. What similarities and differences do you find from one publisher to the next? Does the kind and quality of the learning objectives vary from textbooks to other kinds of materials from the same publisher? Do the tests accompanying the materials reflect the goals or objectives of those materials?

# Mastery Test

### OBJECTIVE 1

To list the sources of instructional objectives and to describe the kind of objectives to be found for each source.

There are five major sources of instructional objectives. List each source and briefly describe the kind of objective you would likely find there.

_____

_____

_____

_____

_____

_____

_____

_____

_____

_____

_____

_____

_____

_____

_____

_____

_____

_____

_____

_____

_____

_____

# ANSWER KEY

## Mastery Test, Objective 1

1. *Published materials.* A variety of objectives will be found here. They will usually be appropriate for the grade level specified, but they might not be very clearly written. Besides objectives per se, published materials will often contain general goals, statements of purpose, claims of success, test items, exercises and assignments, and a preface, all of which may help you formulate your own objectives.

2. *Course syllabi.* Here one can find general goals and objectives appropriate for the grade level specified and related to a larger set of goals for the total curriculum. These objectives will not usually be tied to a particular set of instructional materials.

3. *Other teachers.* Objectives from other teachers will vary in quality but will probably be appropriate for the grade level specified. Those obtained from a single teacher may be narrow in scope, reflecting the interests and skills of that teacher only.

4. *Professional journals.* Here one can find highly specific objectives related to a small aspect of a given course or to a particular instructional methodology. They will usually be quite well written.

5. *Instructional objectives exchange.* This source will provide you with the widest variety of objectives. They will include cognitive, affective, and psychomotor objectives for virtually all subject matter areas and grade levels. They will be well written and observable.

# Objective 2

To select instructional objectives that will be useful to you and your students.

## LEARNING ACTIVITY 2.1

Instructional objectives that are useful in the classroom must meet certain criteria* below. Look them over carefully, and then we will discuss each of them in turn.

*A Useful Instructional Objective Must Be:*

1. Student-oriented
2. Descriptive of a learning *outcome*
3. Clear and understandable
4. Observable

**1. Good Instructional Objectives Are Student-Oriented.** An instructional objective which is student-oriented places the emphasis upon what the *student* is expected to do, not upon what the teacher will do. Look at the following examples; notice that they all describe student behavior and not teacher behavior.

*Examples of Student-Oriented Objectives*

1. Students should be able to solve long-division problems using at least two different methods.

* List taken from *Evaluation: A Practical Guide for Teachers*, by T. D. TenBrink. Copyright © 1974 by McGraw-Hill Book Company. Used with permission.

2. Students should be able to list the five punctuation rules discussed in the textbook.

3. Students should be able to write down their observations of a simple experiment, stating what was done and what happened.

4. When given the description of a form of government, the student should be able to classify that form of government and list its probable strengths and weaknesses.

Sometimes teachers use instructional goals which emphasize what they are expected to do rather than what they expect of their students. Such teacher-oriented objectives only have value to the extent that they direct the teacher to do something which ultimately leads to student learning. A teacher attempting to help his or her students attain the goal of solving long-division problems may work out some of the problems on the blackboard, explaining each of the steps involved. A teacher-oriented objective associated with this behavior might read something like: "To explain the steps in long division on the blackboard." Notice that this might be a helpful teacher activity, but it is only *one* of many possible activities that could help the students reach the goal of solving long division.

# Your Turn

## SELECT STUDENT-ORIENTED OBJECTIVES

The following exercise will give you practice in distinguishing between student-oriented and teacher-oriented objectives. Place an *S* before each student-oriented and a *T* before each teacher-oriented objective.

_____ 1. To read at least 250 words per minute with no less than 80 percent comprehension.

_____ 2. To show students proper eye movements for scanning material.

_____ 3. To outline my lecture on the board before class begins.

_____ 4. When given the description of a complex machine, to identify the simple machines contained within it.

_____ 5. To help the students appreciate classical music.

_____ 6. To lecture on the basic steps in the scientific method.

_____ 7. To carry out an investigation using the scientific method.

_____ 8. To maintain discipline in my class.

_____ 9. To write a unified paragraph on a single topic.

_____ 10. To evaluate a poem on the basis of the criteria for good poetry as discussed in class.

Now check your answers with the Answer Key. If you missed more than three, you may wish to reread this section before going on.

## ANSWER KEY

### Your Turn: Select Student-Oriented Objectives

1. *S.* A desirable learning outcome.
2. *T.* Students will need to learn proper eye movements, but it is likely that the teacher will have to demonstrate them to the students.
3. *T.* Probably helpful to students, but not an expected student outcome.
4. *S.* A student who can do this has learned well.
5. *T.* How would a teacher do this?
6. *T.* Lecturing is only important if it helps the students reach a desirable learning outcome.
7. *S.* A learning outcome requiring several prerequisite skills.
8. *T.* Of course, maintaining good self-discipline may be an important student-oriented objective.
9. *S.* A goal most English teachers hope their students will eventually attain.
10. *S.* A student-oriented objective. However, the teacher might work through such an evaluation with his or her students as one activity designed to help them reach this goal.

**2. Good Instructional Objectives Describe Learning Outcomes.** The important thing to keep in mind here is that we are interested in what the students will learn to do. In other words, it is the learning *outcome* that is important, not the learning activities that should lead to that outcome. To say that students will practice long-division problems using two different methods is not to specify a learning outcome. It specifies an activity designed to help the students reach some outcome. As such, it is a student-oriented activity, *not* an outcome.

It may be valuable for you as a teacher to determine what kind of learning activities you may want your students to carry out. However, determining which learning experiences and activities are most appropriate for your students can only be made *after* you have decided what it is you want your students to accomplish. Once learning outcomes are identified and described, then activities which are appropriate for attaining those outcomes can be determined. In the table that follows you will find a number of learning outcomes listed in the left-hand column and the corresponding learning activities in the right-hand column. Look these examples over carefully, noting how each learning outcome dictates the kind of learning activity which might help the students reach it. Note, too, that many learning activities may be needed for students to successfully reach a single learning outcome.[3]

### RELATIONSHIP BETWEEN LEARNING OUTCOMES AND LEARNING ACTIVITIES

| Learning Outcomes | Learning Activities |
|---|---|
| 1. To label the parts of a flower. | (a) Read pp. 17–22 in your science book. |
| | (b) Study the diagram of a flower in your book. |
| | (c) Use the unlabeled diagrams on the study table. Practice filling in the blanks. Check your labels with those in the book. |

| *Learning Outcomes (cont'd)* | *Learning Activities (cont'd)* |
|---|---|
| 2. To identify the four main parts of speech in simple and complex sentences. | (a) Complete Workbook pp. 75–78. <br> (b) Listen to the teacher's explanation of nouns, verbs, adjectives, and adverbs. <br> (c) Play the grammar game (part 5) with some of your classmates. <br> (d) Pick a paragraph from your reading book. List the nouns and verbs. Have your teacher check your work. |
| 3. To reduce fractions to the lowest common denominator. | (a) Watch the teacher reduce fractions. <br> (b) Practice at the blackboard with the teacher's help. |
| 4. To compute the area of a circle. | Read p. 78 and do Exercise 15. |
| 5. To choose to listen to classical music during free time. | Listen to classical music and to the teacher's explanation of it. |
| 6. To make a correct introduction of a friend to your teacher. | Listen to the record, "Introducing Friends." |

# Your Turn

## SELECT OUTCOMES, NOT ACTIVITIES

Now it's your turn to practice distinguishing learning activities from learning outcomes. For each statement below, mark an *A* next to each learning activity and an *O* next to each outcome. *Remember:* Activities are necessary for the attainment of outcomes, but outcomes specify what students should ultimately be able to do.

_____  1. To review the notes taken during yesterday's lecture.

_____  2. To explain the function of the carburetor.

_____  3. To practice multiplication with flash cards.

_____  4. To read Chapters 17 and 18.

_____  5. To distinguish between learning outcomes and learning activities.

_____  6. To identify the parts of speech in a prose passage.

_____  7. To identify correctly the types of trees found in this part of the country.

_____  8. To locate on a topographical map the most likely place for the development of a large metropolitan area.

———— 9. To study the diagram of the structure of an atom.

———— 10. To listen to the "Nutcracker Suite."

———— 11. To identify the instruments being played in the "Nutcracker Suite."

———— 12. To identify the instruments being featured in a particular musical performance.

———— 13. To practice hearing the difference between a French horn and a trombone.

———— 14. To watch the film "How Your Brain Works."

———— 15. To describe briefly the two-party system, listing its strengths and weaknesses.

Now compare your answers with those given in the Answer Key that follows. It is possible that you may have misinterpreted one or two statements. If this happened, don't worry about a couple of "wrong" answers. However, if you missed many of the items in this exercise, you may have read this section too rapidly. Go back and reread it, thinking carefully about what is being said. As you read, try to think of further examples taken from your own school experiences.

## ANSWER KEY
### Your Turn: Select Outcomes, Not Activities

1. *A*  2. *O*  3. *A*  4. *A*  5. *O*  6. *O*  7. *O*  8. *O*  9. *A*  10. *A*  11. *O (although this could be a practice exercise for the outcome specified in 12)* 12. *O* 13. *A*  14. *A*  15. *O*.

*Note:* Some of the above outcomes (such as 5, 6, 7, and 8) might best be learned by trying to do them and then getting feedback on how successful you were. This kind of practice, using a learning outcome as a learning activity, can be highly successful if (1) the student has reached a high enough level of understanding of the task and (2) good feedback is provided.

**3. Instructional Objectives Are Clear and Understandable.** The first prerequisite for a clear and understandable objective is explicitness. It should contain a clearly stated verb that describes a definite action or behavior and, in most cases, should refer to an object of that action. Examine the examples below. In each case the verb and its object have been italicized. As you read these examples, try to see if there is more than one possible meaning for any of them. If they are well stated and explicit, only one meaning should be possible.

### Examples of Clearly Stated Objectives

1. The student should be able to *label* the *parts of the heart* correctly on a diagram of the heart similar to the one on p. 27 of the text.

2. When given words from the list in the back of the spelling book, the student should be able to *identify words that are incorrectly spelled* and make any necessary corrections.

3. The pupils should be able to use a yardstick to *measure* the *length, width, and height* of any piece of furniture in the room. The measurements should be accurate to within half an inch.

4. To be able to *identify* correctly the *ingredients in a mixture of chemicals prepared in advance* by the teacher.

5. When given a *contemporary poem*, the student should be able to *evaluate* it according to the criteria discussed in class.

6. To *list* the *major parts of a friendly letter*, briefly *describing* the *function of each part.*

7. Given several occasions to listen to different types of music, the student will *select* at least *three different types of music* that he or she likes.

8. To *read out loud* a *prose passage of approximately 300 words*, making no more than three errors. The reading level of the passage will be at the 5.5 grade level.

Notice that in each of the above examples, not only are there a clearly defined verb and its accompanying object, but there is only one possible meaning for each of the statements. Furthermore, it is important to note that most people observing someone engaged in the behaviors described above, or observing the products of those behaviors, would agree in their judgments about whether the behavior had occurred as stated. In other words, the above objectives are not only explicitly stated but are also observable. This characteristic (observability) will be described in the next section.

### A Word of Caution

Let me digress from the present discussion to caution you against something which occurs frequently when teachers are first learning to write instructional objectives. It is very easy to confuse the notion that an objective must be explicit with the idea that it must be highly specific. Objectives should be explicit, that is, unambiguous and understandable. However, being explicit does not mean they have to be highly specific, written down to the very minutest of details and the lowest level of a given behavior. Below is an example* of an instructional objective that has been written in very general terms and then rewritten several times, each time becoming a bit more specific.[4]

1. Students should be able to read with understanding.

2. When given a story to read, the student should be able to answer questions about the content of the story.

3. When given a short story, the student should be able to identify the passages which describe the traits of the main characters.

4. Students should be able to identify the passages which describe the personality traits of the main characters in *Catcher in the Rye.*

5. Students should be able to identify at least five passages from *Catcher in the Rye* that illustrate Holden's confidence in himself.

6. Students should be able to recognize five passages cited in Handout 3 which illustrate Holden's lack of confidence in himself.[5]

Notice that the most useful instructional objectives in the above examples are those which fall somewhere in the middle of the continuum from very general to very specific. When instructional objectives become too specific, they lose much of their value as a guide to study and become

---

* Examples taken from *Evaluation: A Practical Guide for Teachers*, by T. D. Ten-Brink. Copyright © 1974 by McGraw-Hill Book Company. Used with permission.

little more than test questions to be answered. Instructional objectives that are too specific might very well encourage poor study habits. Students may tend to learn just enough to meet the specific objectives but not enough to meet the more general end-of-the-course objectives. The value of getting students to identify the passages from *Catcher in the Rye* which illustrate descriptions of personality traits is that this ability will transfer to other short stories as well. Transferability makes the objective more valuable than one which asks the student to recognize those passages from *Catcher in the Rye* which had previously been discussed and identified (like objective 6).

# Your Turn

## SELECT CLEAR AND UNAMBIGUOUS OBJECTIVES

For each of the following objectives, determine whether it has a single meaning (mark it with a "1") or two or more meanings (mark it with a "2"). The first three items have been done for you. The first is ambiguous. In fact it could be interpreted to mean the same thing as items 2 and 3. The problem with item 1, of course, is the fact that the verb is not explicit. Using a more explicit verb (as in item 2 or item 3) clears up the ambiguity.

___2___    1. To know the Presidents of the United States.

___1___    2. To list in writing the Presidents of the United States.

___1___    3. To recognize and call by name each President of the United States upon seeing his picture.

_____    4. To see the connection between well-written sentences and good short stories.

_____    5. To identify the vanishing points in a three-point perspective drawing.

_____    6. To establish eye contact with at least five different persons during a three-minute persuasive speech.

_____    7. To develop a roll of 35-mm black-and-white film.

_____    8. To run a 10-minute mile.

_____    9. To appreciate good music.

_____    10. To mold a lump of clay into the shape of an animal which can be recognized and correctly named by the rest of the class.

_____    11. Not to show favoritism to any given child in the preschool.

_____    12. To understand the workings of an atomic energy plant.

_____    13. To plant a miniature garden according to the criteria for such a garden as described in the article "Apartment Gardening."

_____    14. To enlarge your concept of realism.

**4. Good Instructional Objectives Are Observable.** The evaluation of learning outcomes hinges on the observability of those outcomes. The key to an observable objective is an observable verb. Consequently, when selecting instructional objectives for use in your teaching, *watch the verbs!* As discussed earlier, a good objective contains an explicit verb and (usually) a well-defined object of the verb. Both these requirements help make an objective clear and unambiguous. Now we add another requirement: the verb must describe an observable action or an action that results in an observable product.

The verbs in the box* are vague and unobservable. Avoid them.

| *Vague, unobservable verbs that should be avoided* | |
|---|---|
| to know | to enjoy |
| to understand | to familiarize |
| to comprehend | to value |
| to grasp | to realize |
| to believe | to like |
| to appreciate | to cope with |
| to think | to love |

If you do select an objective which contains a verb like those in the list, be certain to rewrite the objective, substituting a verb that describes a more observable action.

The kind of verb you hope to find in instructional objectives is also exemplified below. When you write objectives, use these kinds of verbs.

| *Verbs describing observable actions or actions which yield observable products** | |
|---|---|
| to identify | to analyze |
| to speak | to predict |
| to list | to locate |
| to select | to explain |
| to choose | to isolate |
| to compute | to divide |
| to add | to separate |
| to draw | to infer |

\* For a more complete list of these kinds of verbs see Appendix 3 in N. E. Gronlund's *Stating Behavioral Objectives* (London: Collier-Macmillan Ltd., 1970).

* The verbs in the boxed material on this page were taken from *Evaluation: A Practical Guide for Teachers,* by T. D. TenBrink. Copyright © 1974, by McGraw-Hill Book Company. Used with permission.

There are many processes and skills which cannot be directly observed but which produce observable products. It is not possible for us to observe the thinking process of a student as he strives to solve an algebraic equation. However, we can examine the solution he arrives at and decide whether or not it is correct. Furthermore, we may be able to look at each of the steps he takes to arrive at that solution if he writes them down for us (displaying his thinking as a product). On the other hand, a well-written prose paragraph, a poem, and an oil painting can all be observed and analyzed. These end products and others like them can serve as "observables," which may help to indicate whether or not an expected learning outcome has occurred.

When selecting or writing instructional objectives, it is helpful to distinguish between those that specify observable behaviors and those that specify end products of behaviors.

The use of strong, active verbs, such as those in the second box, will yield objectives which are either observable or whose end products are observable. However, if the object of any of these verbs does not describe an observable end product, the resulting objective would be vague and nonobservable. For example, examine the following objective: "To explain the Middle East Crisis."

What is supposed to be explained? The *causes* of the Middle East Crisis? The *positions taken by each side* in the Middle East Crisis? The *political ideologies* involved in the Middle East Crisis? All of these, and more, are possible explanations. The problem is not in the verb, but in the object of the verb. Make certain that both the verb and its object are clearly defined, pointing to observable actions or observable end products.

# Your Turn

## SELECT OBSERVABLE OBJECTIVES

Mark each observable objective with an *O* and each nonobservable objective with an *N*. Keep in mind that to be an observable objective, either the action *or* the end product of that action must be visible, audible, touchable, etc.

_____  1. To reduce fractions to their lowest denominator.

_____  2. To locate the fulcrum on a balance beam weighted in a variety of ways.

_____  3. To grasp the significance of the Monroe Doctrine.

_____  4. To separate the incomplete sentences from the complete ones in a list containing both types.

_____  5. To familiarize oneself with the rules of basketball before beginning to play the game.

_____  6. When given a limited amount of time, to learn the Morse code.

_____  7. To translate a passage from Plato's *Republic*.

## LEARNING ACTIVITY 2.2

Obtain copies of teacher's manuals for a subject matter area of interest to you. Find the statements of objectives listed in these manuals and evaluate them. Are they well written, meeting the criteria for good objectives specified earlier in this chapter? If not, what is wrong with them? You may wish to keep a tally of the type of error you find most frequently.

|  *Type of Error (if any)* | *Tally* |
|---|---|
| 1. No errors; well defined | _____ |
| 2. Not student-oriented | _____ |
| 3. Not descriptive of a learning outcome | _____ |
| 4. Not clear and understandable | _____ |
| 5. Not observable | _____ |

# Mastery Test

**OBJECTIVE 2**   To select instructional objectives that will be useful to you and your students.

For each of the following pairs, check the objective which best meets the requirements for useful objectives.

1. _____(a)  To be able to develop a roll of black-and-white film.
   _____(b)  To understand how a developing agent works.

2. _____(a)  To select useful objectives.
   _____(b)  To know what makes an objective useful.

3. _____(a)  To select from alternative definitions the one which best defines the terms provided on Handout 10.
   _____(b)  To know the meaning of the terms on Handout 10.

4. _____(a)  To solve math problems requiring an understanding of the place holder.
   _____(b)  To understand problem-solving techniques.

5. _____(a)  To recognize the pictures of men in the news.

   _____(b)  To match the names of men in the news with their pictures.

6. _____(a)  To select the good poems from good and bad examples.

   _____(b)  To evaluate a set of poems.

7. _____(a)  To remember the life cycle of the butterfly.

   _____(b)  To label, from memory, a diagram of the life cycle of a butterfly.

8. _____(a)  To hear clearly short and long vowel sounds.

   _____(b)  To distinguish between short and long vowel sounds.

9. _____(a)  To know the phonetic rules and their application in reading.

   _____(b)  To sound out nonsense words.

10. _____(a)  To punctuate a prose paragraph correctly.

    _____(b)  To list the punctuation rules.

In the space provided, list four criteria for judging the quality of an instructional objective.

11. _____

12. _____

13. _____

14. _____

For each of the following objectives, determine the primary fault:

15. To grasp the meaning of conservation.
    (a)  affectively oriented
    (b)  teacher-oriented
    (c)  vague and unobservable

16. To demonstrate to the students the need for cleanliness.
    (a)  teacher-oriented
    (b)  unobservable
    (c)  student-oriented

17. To paint.
    (a)  poorly defined product
    (b)  vague
    (c)  teacher-oriented

18. To do workbook, pp. 18–20.
    (a)  vague
    (b)  poorly defined product
    (c)  a learning activity

19. To listen to the guest speaker from the narcotics division.
    (a)  teacher-oriented
    (b)  a learning activity
    (c)  vague

# Objective 3

To rewrite poorly written objectives.

## LEARNING ACTIVITY 3.1

In order to correct poorly written objectives, you must first know what is wrong — what it is about the objective that makes it unacceptable. That shouldn't be too difficult if you remember what makes an objective acceptable. Review the criteria for well-written objectives in the list that follows.

*A Well-Written Objective:*

1. Is student-oriented.
2. Defines a learning outcome.
3. Is clear and explicit.
4. Describes an observable performance (or end product).

There are three major problems with poorly written objectives:

*The Major Problems of Poorly Written Objectives*

1. An emphasis on learning activities.
2. A vague description of student performance.
3. Poorly defined products of student performance.

Each of these problems is discussed in turn and practice is provided for correcting each.

### Correcting Problem 1

**An Emphasis on Learning Activities.** A common problem with instructional objectives is that they are stated in terms of learning activities, not in terms of learning outcomes. Sometimes objectives are stated as the teacher's objectives. For example, "Discuss with the student the relationship between good writing and the use of active rather than passive verbs." Notice that this describes what the teacher will do in guiding learning but does not describe the outcome expected of the students.

Another kind of error frequently made is one where the objective is stated in terms of a student activity. For example, "The students will work in groups, finding the passive verbs in a passage supplied by the teacher. Then they will change the passive verbs to active wherever possible." This may be a very worthwhile activity for the students and may lead them to some outcome, but it is not the outcome itself and, therefore, it is not useful as an instructional objective. What is really needed to guide both the students and teacher is a student-oriented learning outcome such as the following: "When given a passage containing passive verbs, the student should be able to improve that passage by changing those verbs to appropriate active verbs." This objective is stated so that it is clear what the students should be able to do *after* they have learned.

Once you realize that there is a close connection between any learning activity and its corresponding learning outcome, it becomes easier to correct this first problem of instructional objectives. Any learning activity, whether teacher-oriented or student-oriented, is designed to help the student reach some learning outcome. Consequently, whenever you have an objective stated as a learning activity instead of a learning outcome, you can convert it into an acceptable objective simply by answering the following question:

What will this learning activity help the student be able to do?

Take some examples of objectives specified in terms of activities instead of outcomes and try to answer the above question about each activity. In each case, the answer to the question should yield a learning outcome that will be usable as an instructional objective.

Suppose, for example, the teacher's manual accompanying a reading text suggests that the teacher place the new sight words on the blackboard, read them to the pupils, and offer assistance in saying them aloud. What will this series of teacher activities help the pupils to be able to do? It is fairly obvious that the idea behind the activities is to get the students to the point where they can recognize and pronounce each of the new sight vocabulary words. We might state this as a learning outcome as follows: "Upon seeing any one of the new sight vocabulary words found in the teacher's manual, the student should be able to pronounce that word correctly."

As another example, a seventh grade social studies teacher has students bring in news items which illustrate conflicts among nations. As the items are brought in, the students discuss them and attempt to identify the source of each conflict. Although several possible learning outcomes might result from this set of activities, a likely one would be: "When given enough information about a conflict among nations, students should be able to identify the source of that conflict."

In another case, suppose that a high school speech teacher decides to have the students listen to the Gettysburg Address. What will the student-oriented learning activity help the students be able to do? What learning outcome does this teacher have in mind? High school students could learn something about the type of sentence structure utilized by President Lincoln, or they might try to remember the major points being made in the address. Because it is a speech class, the teacher probably would not want them to be able to recall from memory the content of the Gettysburg Address. However, it is possible that the speech teacher would want the students to be able to pick out the point at which the introduction to the address stops and the main body of the address begins. That would lead them one step closer to the longer-range objective of being able to identify the transition points in a given speech.

Many good learning activities (lectures, assignments, projects, etc.) are *potentially* useful for helping students reach any one of a number of learning outcomes. Consequently, you should specify precisely what it is you want *your* students to learn from any given activity. If you do not do this, your students might approach the learning tasks inappropriately, looking for the wrong kinds of things and coming away with the wrong information or with incomplete skills. All too frequently students are asked to read material, listen to tapes, watch films, etc., but are never told *why* they are to do these things and precisely what is expected of them upon completion.

# Your Turn

## CORRECTING PROBLEM 1

Listed below are a number of teacher- and student-oriented learning activities. For each activity listed, answer the question, "What will this activity help the students be able to do?" Write your answer in the form of a clearly stated learning outcome. When you have completed this exercise, check your answers with the Answer Key that follows.

1. A class discussion about the effect of inflation on the economy.

   _____

   _____

   _____

   _____

2. The students will work out long-division problems on the blackboard. Their answers will be checked by the teacher and discussed with the class.

   _____

   _____

   _____

   _____

3. The students will watch a film on the use of the reference section in the library.

   _____

   _____

   _____

   _____

4. A spelling workbook includes the following instructions for the students: "Fill in the blanks in the following sentences. Use the words found in this week's review list."

_____

_____

_____

5. The students will try to write down the learning outcomes associated with given learning activities. They will check their answers with those of the instructor.

_____

_____

_____

# ANSWER KEY

## Your Turn: Correcting Problem 1

As you know, any given learning activity can be used to help the students attain a number of possible outcomes. Compare your answers with those given below and also with those written by your peers.

1. (a) To be able to describe in two to three pages the effect of inflation on the economy.
   (b) To be able to predict economic trends, given information about the rate of inflation.
   (c) To be able to define _inflation_.
   (d) To be able to cite examples (from news stories) of inflation's effect upon our economy.

2. (a) To be able to solve long-division problems.
   (b) To be able to identify errors made in an attempted solution to a long-division problem.

3. (a) To be able to locate specified reference works in the library.
   (b) To list the major types of reference works found in the library.
   (c) When given the reference works discussed in the film, to be able to describe the kind of information each one contains.

4. (a) To be able to spell review words correctly, when using those words in a sentence.
   (b) To be able to spell words correctly long after they were first learned in spelling class.

5. When given a learning activity, to be able to identify correctly what learning outcomes the activity would be likely to serve.

## Correcting Problem 2

**A Vague Description of Student Performance.** Whenever the performance expected of the students is not clearly stated, the problem lies in the verb selected to describe that performance. The solution to this problem is relatively simple: Replace any vague, ambiguous verbs with strong, active verbs that describe observable actions. The objective "To know the multiplication tables" is obviously not clearly stated. Teachers undoubtedly want their students to be able to do more than simply recognize the multiplication tables, but how much more — to recite them, to write them, or both?

Examine the following objective: "To know how to shift a manual transmission." Does this objective mean that the student has "head-knowledge" or that the student has actually learned a skill? The verb used will make the difference. Suppose we replace the verb phrase "to know how to shift" with the phrase "to list the steps to take when shifting." The objective, as originally written, calls for "head-knowledge." But, if we delete the words "to know" and simply say "to shift a manual transmission," we are then specifying the skill of actually doing the shifting.

Suppose a teacher decides that it is important for his or her students "to comprehend what they read." Does this mean *recalling* the facts, or does it mean listing the main points made by the author? Perhaps it means having students explain what they read to someone else, using their own words. Then it would read, "To explain to someone else, in your own words, what you have read."

Now let's try correcting an affective objective, one that deals primarily with emotion and feeling. Suppose a teacher thinks it is important for his or her students "to enjoy science projects." It is difficult to decide what any given teacher might accept as evidence of enjoyment. This objective becomes much clearer when better verbs are selected. Any one of the following alterations could be made, each changing what enjoyment means slightly:

To choose to work on a science project when given other possible choices.

To ask for extra science projects to do.

To check out books from the library explaining various science projects.

Now study the following examples, noting how changing the verb clarifies the description of the expected performance.

***Examples:*** *How to Correct Vague Descriptions of Student Performance*

Vague:    To understand long division.
Clarified:    To solve long-division problems.

Vague:    To grasp the importance of good gestures.
Clarified:    To use good gestures in each speech given.

Vague:    To be familiar with recent research findings on the effects of smoking pot.
Clarified:    To recall from memory the findings of recent research on the effects of smoking pot.

Vague:    To realize the importance of warming up properly before each session.
Clarified:    To warm up properly before each session.

Vague:    To understand the weather.
Clarified:    To predict the weather.

Notice that in some of the preceding examples it was necessary not only to change the verb but also to clarify the object of that verb (the whole verb phrase needed changing). You will get some practice doing that in the next section.

# Your Turn

## CORRECTING PROBLEM 2

Before you begin this exercise you may wish to look over the list of verbs found on p. 90. These are the kinds of verbs you will need to use in order to clarify the descriptions of student performances found in this exercise.

Correct each of the following objectives by changing the vague verbs (or verb phrases) to more observable ones.

1. To know the causes of the Civil War.

_____

_____

_____

2. To learn this week's French vocabulary words.

_____

_____

_____

3. To *really* know Chapter 3 in your chemistry book.

_____

_____

_____

4. To understand the difference between hard and soft woods.

_____

_____

_____

5. To know the rules for correct punctuation.

_____

_____

_____

# ANSWER KEY
## Your Turn: Correcting Problem 2

Suggested corrections are given below. Other corrections are possible. What is important is to use verbs that describe observable action (or end products of that action).

1. (a) To list the causes of the Civil War in writing.
   (b) To arrange the events causing (leading up to the beginning of) the Civil War in sequential order.

2. (a) To write the English equivalent of each French word in this week's vocabulary.
   (b) To use correctly each word in this week's French vocabulary in a conversation with the teacher.
   (c) To spell correctly each of the words in this week's French vocabulary.

3. (a) To recall the major facts in Chapter 3 and list them from memory.
   (b) To explain the contents of Chapter 3 to the teacher, using your own words.

4. (a) To sort a pile of wood into hard woods and soft woods.
   (b) To explain the difference between hard and soft woods in one page or less.
   (c) To list the names of the hard woods and the soft woods.

5. (a) To list the rules for correct punctuation.
   (b) To punctuate a paragraph correctly.
   (c) To correct the improper punctuation in a given paragraph.
   (d) To explain each punctuation rule and write a sentence illustrating the proper application of each rule.

## Correcting Problem 3

**Poorly Defined Products of Student Performance.** To use a strong, active verb is to produce an observable objective — most of the time. However, there are times when more is needed. If the objective specifies an end product, something the student is expected to produce, then that product must also be clearly defined. Take, for example, the following objective: "To be able to solve problems in math." There is nothing wrong with the verb, "to solve." However, the object of that verb, "problems in math," is not well defined. What kind of problems? Addition? Subtraction? Multiplication? Division? Straight computation? Story problems?

Sometimes a good verb alone is not enough to produce a good objective. Study the following examples. Note, in each case, how a vague objective was clarified by specifying the object of the verb more precisely (thus more clearly defining the *product* of student performance).

*Examples: How to Correct Poorly Defined Products of Student Performance*

Poorly defined:   To write well.
Specified:   To write a paragraph containing a topic sentence and several supporting sentences.

*or*

To write all your letters with proper shape and form.

Poorly defined:   To calculate area.
Specified:   To calculate the area of any geometric plane which is defined by straight lines.

Poorly defined:  To make introductions.
Specified:  To introduce a person to another person (or group of persons).
To write an introductory paragraph to an expository theme.

# Your Turn

## CORRECTING PROBLEM 3

In the following, mark well-defined products of student performance with a "+" and poorly defined products with a "−".

_____ 1. poetry

_____ 2. poems written in iambic pentameter

_____ 3. multiplication tables through 12 × 12

_____ 4. arithmetic facts

_____ 5. concepts listed in the summary of p. 17

_____ 6. major concepts of psychology

_____ 7. drawings

_____ 8. line drawings in two-point perspective

Correct the following objectives by specifying the products of student performance.

9. To recall the important history dates.

_____

_____

10. To explain ecology.

_____

_____

11. To interpret literature.

_____

_____

12. To describe democracy.

_____

_____

## ANSWER KEY

**Your Turn:   Correcting Problem 3**

1.–   2.+   3.+   4.–   5.+   6.+   7.–   8.+

9. To recall the dates of the events listed on Handout 2.

10. To explain how nature maintains a proper balance and how man can disrupt that balance.

11. To interpret a short story by describing the author's purpose and illustrating how he or she accomplishes that purpose.

12. To describe the primary characteristics of a democratic form of government.

## LEARNING ACTIVITY 3.2

Get together with a small group of your peers. Each person in the group should write four to five objectives. At least three of those should be poorly written to illustrate the three problems discussed in this chapter. Exchange objectives and correct each other's poorly written objectives. Discuss the results.

Were any problem objectives "undiscovered"?

Were any improperly corrected?

Were any correct objectives made worse by attempts to correct them?

Was the original intent of the author left intact when a given objective was corrected?

What do you need to know about well-written objectives before you can purposely write one with a specific kind of error "built in"?

# Mastery Test

**OBJECTIVE 3**   To rewrite poorly written objectives.

Each of the following objectives is poorly written. Identify the major problem and rewrite the objective to correct that problem.

1. To listen to the lecture carefully.

Problem _____

_____

Correction _____

_____

2. To see the value of learning how to compute percentage.

Problem _____

_____

Correction _____

_____

3. To show the class how to clean and oil a sewing machine.

   Problem _____

   _____

   Correction _____

   _____

4. To be organized.

   Problem _____

   _____

   Correction _____

   _____

5. To understand the problems of small, struggling nations.

   Problem _____

   _____

   Correction _____

   _____

6. To capture the students' interest.

   Problem _____

   _____

   Correction _____

   _____

7. To grasp the significance of Watergate.

   Problem _____

   _____

   Correction _____

   _____

8. To collect newspaper clippings about détente.

   Problem _____

   _____

   Correction _____

   _____

# ANSWER KEY

## Mastery Test, Objective 3

1. *Problem:*    Learning *activity* rather than outcome.
   *Correction:*   To recall the major points being made in the lecture or to explain in your own words the major concepts presented in the lecture.

2. *Problem:*    Vague verb.
   *Correction:*   To list actual situations in which it is necessary to be able to compute percentage.

3. *Problem:*    Teacher-oriented learning activity.
   *Correction:*   To be able to clean and oil one of the sewing machines in class.

4. *Problem:*    Vague; no product of student performance.
   *Correction:*   To organize your desk so that everything has its place and can be easily located; to organize a class project, assigning jobs in an equitable way; or . . . .

5. *Problem:*    Vague; unobservable.
   *Correction:*   To describe the problems a small, struggling nation is likely to encounter; to present the pros and cons of solutions to the typical problems of small, struggling nations; or . . . .

6. *Problem:*    Teacher-oriented; vague.
   *Correction:*   During a given lecture, students will ask many questions, take accurate notes, and contribute information they might have to the discussion.

7. *Problem:*    Vague; unobservable.
   *Correction:*   To be able to predict future trends in American government which are likely to occur as a result of Watergate or to speculate about the future of America (economically, politically, etc.) if Watergate had gone unnoticed.

8. *Problem:*    Learning *activity* rather than outcome.
   *Correction:*   To list the major political agreements coming out of the détente with the Soviet Union.

# Objective 4

To write well-defined and useful objectives of your own.

## LEARNING ACTIVITY 4.1

There are four simple steps* for writing good instructional objectives. Although these steps should normally follow the given order, you may occasionally wish to go back and rework a step before moving on. This constant monitoring of your own work, always checking against the criteria for well-defined objectives, will help you produce a clear list of objectives for your own use. The four steps are shown below. Each step will be discussed in turn.

---

* From *Evaluation: A Practical Guide for Teachers*, by T. D. TenBrink. Copyright © 1974 by McGraw-Hill Book Company. Used with permission.

*Four Steps for Writing Instructional Objectives*

1. Describe the subject matter content.
2. Specify the general goals.
3. Break down the general goals into more specific, observable objectives.
4. Check objectives for clarity and appropriateness.

Although these four steps can be applied to course planning as well as lesson planning, it is important to remember that you will not be able to write a set of objectives for an entire course in a short time. You will find it useful, therefore, to work on small units of instruction, one at a time. Eventually, you will have a set of objectives that will cover the full course you are teaching. However, your unit objectives and daily objectives should fit into the overall plan for your course. Consequently, the first two steps listed above should be fairly well completed before you begin working on the objectives for specific units of instruction or for daily lesson plans.

So that you will be able to see the interrelationship of all four steps, we will now proceed to develop a set of objectives for a complete course. We will develop objectives for a high school psychology course, because this is a subject area with which all teachers should be familiar. Examples from other subject matter areas at various grade levels will also be used as each step is explained. The four steps discussed here can be used for the development of objectives for any course at any grade level.

## Step 1

**Describe the Subject Matter Content.**   Many things have to be considered when describing the content of a given course or unit of instruction. There are the major concepts to be covered, the relationship the material has to a broader base of knowledge, and the value of the content for the student. Perhaps the easiest way to get a good description of the content of a course is to answer the following questions:

In general, what is the course about?

How does this course fit into the total curriculum?

What would be included in an outline of the course?

What value does this course have for the student?

*What is the course all about?* The answer should be very general. All you need to do is describe the kinds of things the course will cover in a paragraph or two. Suppose you were writing a friend about what you will be teaching. This friend would probably not be interested in a long, detailed discourse of the subject matter; a general description of the kinds of concepts to be covered in the course would be sufficient. Such a summary could serve as the basis for a more detailed course outline. The summary, along with the main topics included in a course outline, will provide the basis for the selection of a textbook and other learning materials.

A summary for a high school psychology course is shown in Exhibit A. Read it carefully. Later you will see how the summary leads to a course outline and to the general goals of the course.

**EXHIBIT A**    Subject Matter Content of High School Psychology Course

This introductory psychology course is designed to acquaint students with psychology as a science and as a potential area for further study, leading to a specialized career in psychology. Psychology will be discussed both as a research-oriented science, which is in the process of theory building, and as a science of practical application. The content of the course will center on the study of human behavior, seeking answers to such questions as "Why does man act the way he does, and what causes him to be the kind of being he is?" and "How does he function as an individual and as a group member?"

The aspects of human behavior that are most important to high school students will be stressed, such as problems dealing with the psychological, physical, and social development of man; personality; learning; motivation; mental health; and social psychology. The emphasis throughout the course will be on major psychological research findings and how these findings have been, and can be, applied to the solution of everyday problems.

If you had been asked to write a summary like the one in Exhibit A, what would you have included? Does a summary statement like this one help you to begin thinking about what the students might learn from such a course?

*How does this course fit into the total curriculum?* Once the general content of the course has been described, the next task is to write a short statement describing how the course fits into the total curriculum. In order to do this, you must know something about what else is being taught in the school system. You should know what kinds of courses your students have had and are likely to have after they finish your own course. Likewise, you will want to know what the other teachers of your course expect of their students.

Obviously, what is expected of students at various levels of a curriculum will vary considerably in terms of both skills and attitudes.

Suppose the high school psychology course is the first course of this type the students will be exposed to. It will lead some of them into more advanced courses in college and eventually to degrees in that field. For others, it will be the only course in psychology they will ever take. Think about what this means to the development of such a course. A "statement of fit" for this course is presented in Exhibit B. Read it carefully. How does it differ from one you might have written? Would such a statement differ considerably from one school system to the next?

**EXHIBIT B**    Statement of Fit into Curriculum

This course is to be taught at the senior level and has no prerequisites. The only other area where students might encounter similar information is in home economics or one of the family-living courses. While most senior-level courses culminate a series of courses, this one really begins a sequence that will fit into the college curriculum. It is felt, however, that this course not only must serve the needs of students who will continue their studies in psychology but must also serve the needs of students about to go out into the working world. A greater understanding of what man is like, how he developed, how he thinks, what his emotional reactions are like, how he learns, and how he works with other men may be useful information for maintaining mental health and in learning to live with a variety of personalities.

What instructional goals came to mind as you read Exhibit A? Are there any goals that will not be appropriate because of limitations suggested by the statement in Exhibit B?

*What would be included in an outline of the course?* This third question involves specifying the major topics to be covered in the course in more detail. It should also determine a logical and defensible sequence for teaching those topics. Given a relatively complete course outline, one should be able to work on the development of instructional objectives for one part of the outline at a time. This will help make the task of writing objectives a manageable one. The outline for the high school psychology course is presented in Exhibit C.

**EXHIBIT C**  Suggested Course Outline

UNIT I.  Psychology as a Science
    A.  History of psychology
    B.  Psychological theory
    C.  Methodology of psychological research
    D.  Applicability of psychological concepts and principles

UNIT II.  How Humans Develop
    A.  General theory
    B.  Physical development
    C.  Intellectual and emotional development
    D.  Social development

UNIT III.  Personality
    A.  Theory of personality
    B.  Measuring personality
    C.  Individual differences in personality characteristics

UNIT IV.  The Learning Process
    A.  Learning theory
    B.  Kinds of learning
    C.  Measurement of performance
    D.  Intelligence
    E.  Learning to learn

UNIT V.  Motivation
    A.  Theories of motivation
    B.  Extrinsic motivation
    C.  Intrinsic motivation
    D.  Motivating yourself and others

UNIT VI.  Mental Health
    A.  Indicators of mental health
    B.  Factors accounting for mental health
    C.  Neuroses and psychoses
    D.  Maintaining mental health and preventing mental illness
    E.  Physiological causes of mental illness

UNIT VII.  Social Psychology
    A.  Theories of social psychology
    B.  Cultures and subcultures
    C.  Nationalism
    D.  The influence of the group

*What value does this course have for the student?* Notice that the topics in Exhibit C reflect the general content of the course as summarized in Exhibit A. What is *not* reflected in this course outline are the affective components of the course. Affective objectives are more likely to arise from a statement of the value of the course to the students. Such a statement for the high school psychology course is made in Exhibit D.

---

**EXHIBIT D**   List of the Values of this Course to the Students

1. Introduces the students to a new subject matter area.

2. Indicates to the students how psychology is a science which is important in all walks of life — in industry, in education, in business, in politics, in war, etc.

3. Helps the students to see the relationship between scientific research and the application of research findings to practical situations.

4. Gives the students information useful in helping them maintain their mental health.

5. Gives the students the basic tools with which to understand the behavior of people around them.

6. May help the students to understand the motives of others as well as their own motives.

7. Gives information about how we learn, which may be helpful in the improvement of their own learning strategies.

8. May make students more aware of the needs of others around them.

9. May help students understand the social pressures that operate within a society such as ours.

---

Most teachers hope to develop positive attitudes among their students toward the subject matter they are teaching. That is why the question "What value does this course have for the student?" is so important. A good way to answer this question is to imagine yourself having to defend your course to the students who must take it, to the parents of those students, and to the administrative staff of your school. Pretend, for a moment, that your course has just been introduced into the curriculum and you have been asked to write a defense of it for the school newspaper. Students, parents, and other people in the community are all interested in finding out why this course should be taught. The better you are able to tell them, the better base you will have for formulating the affective goals which you hope your students will accomplish.

The list of values found in Exhibit D not only suggests affective goals such as "becoming more aware of the needs of others" but also suggests cognitive ones such as "to understand the social pressures which operate within our society." These goals, you can see, could be readily translated into clear, observable objectives.

# Your Turn

## DESCRIBE THE SUBJECT MATTER CONTENT

Suppose you were asked to describe the subject matter content of a psychology course similar to the one described in Exhibits A through D. However, this time the students would be seventh and eighth graders.

1. How would the general course description differ from the one in Exhibit A?

2. How would the course outline differ from the one in Exhibit C?

3. Would the value of such a beginning psychology course be different for seventh and eighth graders than for high school seniors? How? Why?

4. Would there be differences that would not show up in a course description like the one found in Exhibits A through D? Where would these differences be made apparent?

Compare your own answers to these questions with the Answer Key that follows.

## ANSWER KEY
Your Turn: Describe the Subject Matter Content

1. There would probably be very little difference. The general topics to be covered could remain the same. The level of understanding expected might be different for seventh and eighth graders, but that would not show up in a general description of course content. Because the course will not serve as a precursor to a college-level course in this case, less emphasis might be placed on research and more on how-to-do-it techniques.

2. Seventh and eighth graders might take a little longer to learn the concepts involved in these topics, so one might shorten the outline slightly. Also, one could replace some of the terms with more common-usage words which would appeal more to seventh and eighth graders.

3. Probably not.

4. Yes, the primary differences would probably be in the level of understanding expected and the kinds of learning activities that would be assigned. These differences would only show up in the specific, behavioral objectives at the unit level and in the assignments designed to help the students reach those objectives.

### Step 2

**Specify the General Goals.**  In this step you will be determining in a general way what you would expect the students to be able to do. It is usually best to carry out this step in two parts. First, write down the general goals for the entire course. These will be most helpful (along with the course outline) when selecting textbooks, films, and other instructional materials. Second, specify general goals for each unit of instruction. These are intermediate goals and, therefore, should be somewhat more specific.

Look at the general end-of-course goals found in Exhibit E. These are some of the possible goals for the high school psychology course. Compare these goals to the summary of course content (Exhibit A) and the course outline (Exhibit C). The goals represent the first step in defining what the students should be able to do with the subject matter specified. Notice that the goals are not yet very observable. At this point that's not too serious. What's important is getting the general goals down on paper so that they can be rewritten according to our criteria.

---

**EXHIBIT E**   General Goals for High School Psychology Course

---

I. Terminal Goals

1. Students should understand what it means when we say that psychology is a science.

2. Students should know the major facts about the way in which men develop.

3. Students should know, in general, how man interacts with his environment, including his interaction with other humans.

4. Students will be aware of the various theories of personality, motivation, learning and mental health, and social psychology.

5. Students should be aware of the major research findings in the area of psychology.

6. Students should be able to apply major findings of psychology to the solutions of specific problems of human behavior and interaction.

7. Students should be more aware of their own typical behavior and the reasons for that behavior.

---

# Your Turn

## SPECIFYING GENERAL GOALS — PARTS 1 AND 2

Now try writing some general end-of-course goals for the psychology course. Do not duplicate those found in Exhibit E. You should be able to write at least five more general goals for this course. Examples of such additional goals are found in the Answer Key for Part 1. Compare what you have written with those examples.

Once the end-of-course goals have been determined, intermediate goals can be written for each unit of instruction. Again, do not worry about whether or not they are initially observable. First get them down in a general way, and then they can be rewritten.[6]

Exhibit F presents some possible goals for Unit I: Psychology as a Science. Three cognitive and three affective goals have been written. Read them carefully and then try writing some yourself. *Remember:* Unit-level goals should reflect the broader, end-of-course goals. Compare your work with the further examples of Unit I goals presented in the Answer Key for Part 2.

**EXHIBIT F**

II. The General Intermediate Goals for Unit I: Psychology as a Science

A. The Cognitive Goals

1. Students should know the major dates in the history of psychology.

2. Students should know the major avocations which have made psychology an important applied science.

3. Students should know the steps that are taken from the development of a theory to the research and testing of that theory to the final application of the research findings to practical situations.

B. Affective Goals

1. The student should appreciate the value of the science of psychology to a civilized country.

2. The student should show appreciation for the usefulness of various psychological theories.

3. The students should be sensitive to the problems of doing psychological research.

# ANSWER KEY

## Your Turn: Specifying General Goals

### PART 1

Here are further general goals for a high school psychology course. Your goals may not be identical to these, but there should be some similarity between these and the ones you have written. If there is not, have your instructor check your work.

1. Students should be aware of their major personality traits, usual learning strategies, the intrinsic and extrinsic motivating factors that influence their decisions and behavior, and the ways in which they respond under social pressure.

2. Students should have an appreciation for the value of psychological research.

3. Students should have an understanding of the importance of specialists in the area of psychology.

4. Students should have an appreciation for the intricacies of personality development.

5. Students should have developed better study habits based on the principles of learning.

6. Students should have a better understanding of why people act the way they do.

7. Students should have developed attitudes of concern and understanding toward the mentally ill.

8. Students should have developed an attitude toward mental illness that is positive.

### PART 2

Here are some further goals for Unit 1: Psychology as a Science. Many other goals could be written. They need not be written in observable terms, but they should be compatible with the end-of-course goals that have been specified.

*Cognitive Goals*

1. Students should know the major founders of psychological theory and the important points within their theories.

2. Students should be able to describe those aspects of psychology which make it a science.

3. The student should be able to list the methodological steps in psychological research.

4. The student should be able to define the major concepts and terms found in psychological science and research.

*Affective Goals*

1. The student should be able to accept differences that exist among the ideas of famous psychologists.

2. Students should enjoy doing simple psychological research.

3. Students should become interested in finding out more about specific aspects of psychology.

### Step 3

**Break Down the General Goals into More Specific, Observable Objectives.**   In this step each general goal is broken down into its two major parts: the subject matter content and the expected student response to that content. Look at one of the general goals from Unit I of the psychology course:

Students should know the major founders of psychological theory and the important concepts within their theories.

First of all, notice that the subject matter content is divided into: (1) the major founders of psychological theories and (2) the important concepts from each of these theories. When we finalize our list of objectives, these two areas should be kept separate, each serving as the basis for at least one objective. It is usually best to deal with only one area of the subject matter in a given objective.

Now we will take these descriptions of subject matter content and answer the following questions about each:

1. Is the subject matter content clearly defined and specific enough?
2. Precisely what response(s) do I want the students to make to that subject matter content?

In the above goal the subject matter content (the founders of psychological theory and concepts important to each theory) is fairly well defined. However, this goal could be made more specific by listing the major founders of theory. The most important concepts for each theory might also be listed.

Of course, the real problem with the above goal lies in the use of the vague, unobservable verb "to know." What observable student response could be accepted as evidence that a student "knows"? Would "to list in writing" be acceptable?

The following three objectives were derived from the above general goal. The subject matter content of that goal was clarified, and the expected student response to that content was more precisely specified.

1. Students should be able to list in writing all the founders of psychological theory discussed in the textbook.
2. Students should be able to match each important concept to the theory with which it is associated. (This goal is limited to the theories found in Unit I in the text.)
3. When given the name of an early psychological theorist, students should be able to identify the concept(s) which were central to the theory.

Try breaking down an affective goal:

Students should become interested in finding out more about the specific aspects of human behavior which have been studied by psychologists.

Sometimes teachers fail to plan for the teaching of affective goals because these goals seem difficult to define in observable terms. However, it is relatively easy if you clearly define the subject matter content and then specify the *behavior(s)* that are likely to accompany the desired attitude toward that content. The following objective was derived from the above goal in just that way.

> In an open discussion about the value of psychology, students should ask questions that would help them discover what aspects of human behavior psychologists have studied.

In this objective the content is "questions" that would help them discover what aspects of human behavior psychologists have studied. The behavior expected is "to ask." Notice, however, that something else has been added: "In an open discussion about the value of psychology." This phrase suggests a condition or type of situation under which we expect the desired student behavior to occur.

Although not necessary to the formation of a good objective, a statement describing the *condition* under which we expect the student to respond is often helpful. Here is another such objective, derived from the above goal (the condition is italicized):

> *When given the task of formulating questions to be sent to famous living psychologists*, the students will include questions like: "What aspects of human behavior have psychologists studied?"

Besides a statement specifying the condition under which the student response is expected to occur, there is one other useful (though not necessary) addition which can be made to most objectives. There are times when it may be useful to specify the *level of performance* expected of the students.[7] For example, we might derive the following objective from the above goal:

> When books and pamphlets describing the aspects of human behavior studied by psychologists are placed in the class library, the students will sign out *two or more* of these resources.

This objective has the criterion for success built in: two or more resources signed out.

Not only is it possible to set a standard (level of performance expected) for each student, but this can also be done for the class as a whole. By determining the level of performance of each student, each student's performance on that objective can be evaluated. By determining how well the class as a whole should learn, you assess your performance as a teacher. Suppose, for example, the above objective is written so it reads as follows:

> When books and pamphlets describing the aspects of human behavior studied by psychologists are placed in the class library, *at least 75 percent of the students* will sign out two or more of these resources.

Then, if less than 75 percent of the students reach the expected level of performance, the goal has not been reached (even though some of our students may have signed out two or more resources).

---

*A Review: Breaking down general goals
into specific, observable objectives*

1. Break the goal into two parts: (1) subject matter content and (2) student response to that content.
2. Clarify the subject matter content and, where necessary, make it more specific.
3. Determine the expected student response(s) to each statement of subject matter content.
4. As needed, identify the conditions under which the student response is expected to occur and/or any useful criteria for judging the level of performance expected.

---

# Your Turn

## BREAKING DOWN A GENERAL GOAL INTO SPECIFIC, OBSERVABLE OBJECTIVES

Write observable objectives for the following goal. Make certain you:

1. Identify the subject matter content and decide whether or not it is clearly enough defined. If not, describe what is needed to clarify it.
2. For each aspect of subject matter content identified above, describe at least one *observable* response the students might be expected to make to it.
3. If appropriate, specify the conditions under which the student response is expected to occur and specify a level of performance which would be acceptable.

    The students should understand the major concepts, terms, and principles used in psychological research.

_____

_____

_____

_____

_____

_____

_____

_____

_____

_____

_____

_____

## ANSWER KEY

### Your Turn: Breaking Down a General Goal into Specific, Observable Objectives

Below are three objectives that could have been derived from the goal you were given. Compare your objectives to these. Do your objectives contain the necessary elements to make them understandable and observable? Also, compare your objectives with those written by your classmates.

1. When given a major concept or term used in psychological research, the student should be able to select from among a number of alternatives the one definition or example that best illustrates that concept or term.

2. When asked to write a short paper explaining the methodologies of psychological research, the student should be able to use correctly 10 out of 15 major concepts that were presented in class lecture.

3. When given a description of psychological research problems, the student should be able to select from among a number of alternatives the principle(s) that would be most appropriate to the solution of the problem.

### Step 4

**Check Objectives for Clarity and Appropriateness.** To some extent this last step may be unnecessary. If you do a good job in the first three steps, your objectives should be ready to use. However, a final check on your work may save you the embarrassment of trying to explain to your students what it was that you "really meant to say."

A good way to check for the clarity of your objectives is to have a friend (preferably one teaching the subject matter under consideration) review them. If your friend will tell you in his/her own words what each objective means, you can usually tell whether or not the objective is understandable. If it isn't, that objective probably needs clarification.

Not only must an objective be clearly stated in observable terms, but it must also be appropriate for your students. Use the following checklist to help you determine whether or not an objective is appropriate:

*Criteria for Appropriate Objectives*

_____ 1. Attainable by the students within a reasonable time limit.

_____ 2. In proper sequence with other objectives (not to be accomplished prior to a prerequisite objective).

_____ 3. In harmony with the overall goals of the course (and curriculum).

_____ 4. In harmony with the goals and values of the institution.

If your objectives are clearly stated in observable terms and meet the above criteria, they should be useful to both you and your students. Now take the Mastery Test for this objective.

The following additional learning activities can be done individually or in small groups. In either case, the results should be shared with the other class members.

## LEARNING ACTIVITY 4.2

Select a unit of study from the psychology course outline found in Exhibit C. Develop a list of instructional objectives for one or more of the topics in the unit you selected. You will probably want to write general goals first and then break them down into more observable objectives.

## LEARNING ACTIVITY 4.3

Exchange your set of objectives (from the activity above) for a set that was developed by a classmate (or group of classmates). Analyze the set you received in the exchange. For each objective in the set, identify the following parts:

1. The subject matter content. (Is there only one? Is it clearly defined?)
2. The expected response to that content. (Is it observable? Is it reasonable to expect the students will reach it?)
3. Where appropriate, the conditions under which the response is expected and/or the level of performance expected.

# Mastery Test

## OBJECTIVE 4    To write well-defined and useful objectives of your own.

List the four steps involved in writing instructional objectives.

1. _____

2. _____

3. _____

4. _____

5. General, end-of-course goals do not need to be written in observable terms. (true or false)

Write at least two observable objectives for each of the following three goals.

6. Students should understand how people learn.

 (a) _____

 _____

 (b) _____

 _____

7. Students should know what motivates people to act.

 (a) _____

 _____

(b) _____

_____

8. Students should understand the value of the metric system.

(a) _____

_____

(b) _____

_____

9. What are the two parts needed in a well-written instructional objective?

(a) _____

_____

(b) _____

_____

10. What are the two useful (although not always needed) parts of a well-written objective?

(a) _____

_____

(b) _____

_____

## ANSWER KEY

### Mastery Test, Objective 4

1. Describe the subject matter content.
2. Specify the general goals.
3. Break down the general goals into more specific, observable objectives.
4. Check these objectives for clarity and appropriateness.
5. True. When broken down into more specific objectives, the end-of-course goals should be observable. However, the general goals are just a step along the way toward the development of usable, observable objectives.

Below are suggested answers for items 6–8. Other possibilities exist. Make certain each objective written specifies a clearly defined subject matter content, an observable response to that content, and, where necessary, a statement describing the conditions under which the response is expected to occur and/or the level of performance expected in the response.

6. (a) Given a description of a learning task, students should be able to describe the process utilized by the learner to accomplish that task.
   (b) Describe the major variables affecting the learning process — tell what makes a learning task easier and what makes it more difficult.

7. (a) Given several possible "motivators" and a description of a particular human behavior, students should be able to select the "motivator(s)" which would most likely stimulate that behavior.
   (b) To list the major motivators of human behavior.

8. (a) To list the advantages and disadvantages of the metric system.
   (b) When given the choice between using the metric system or some other system for solving a given problem, the student should be able to explain why the use of the metric system would be more appropriate.

9. (a) A description of subject matter content.
   (b) An observable, expected response to that content.

10. (a) The conditions under which the student response is expected to occur.
    (b) Level of performance expected or level of performance that would be acceptable as evidence that the objective was met satisfactorily.

NOTES

1. See the Additional Readings at the end of this chapter.

2. A discussion on how to rework poorly written objectives follows later on in this chapter.

3. W. J. Popham, "The Instructional Objectives Exchange: New Support for Criterion-Referenced Instruction," *Phi Delta Kappan* 52, 3 (1970): 174–175.

4. For further examples see Chapter 4 in T. D. TenBrink, *Evaluation: A Practical Guide for Teachers* (New York: McGraw-Hill Book Company, 1974).

5. This list was adapted from T. D. TenBrink, *Evaluation: A Practical Guide for Teachers* (New York: McGraw-Hill Book Company, 1974), p. 102.

6. Follow the suggestions for rewriting poorly written items when you rewrite your own objectives. These were discussed in objective 3 of this chapter.

7. Some authors use the term *performance* to refer to student outcome, the term *condition* to refer to conditions under which the performance is expected to occur, and the term *criteria* to refer to the level of performance expected.

ADDITIONAL READINGS

Burns, R. W. *New Approaches to Behavioral Objectives*. Dubuque, Iowa: Wm. G. Brown Company Publishers, 1972.

Gronlund, Norman E. *Stating Behavioral Objectives for Classroom Instruction*. Toronto: Macmillan Co., 1970.

Kibler, R. J., L. L. Barker, and D. T. Miles. *Behavioral Objectives and Instruction*. Boston: Allyn and Bacon, Inc., 1970.

Mager, Robert F. *Preparing Instructional Objectives*. Palo Alto, Calif.: Fearon, 1962.

Popham, W. James. "Probing the Validity Arguments Against Behavioral Goals." In R. C. Anderson, G. W. Faust, M. C. Roderick, D. J. Cunningham, and Thomas Andre, eds. *Current Research on Instruction*. Englewood Cliffs, New Jersey: Prentice-Hall, 1969.

Robert Shostak

# 4. Lesson Presentation Skills

# Objectives

**1** To define set induction, explain its purposes, and give examples of when it is used as a lesson presentation skill.

**2** To plan original sets for use in a series of hypothetical teaching situations.

**3** To identify the specific underlying purpose of four different types of explanations frequently used in lesson presentations.

**4** To plan original explanations, given a series of hypothetical teaching situations.

**5** To define closure, explain its purposes, and give examples of when it is used as a lesson presentation skill.

**6** To plan original closures for use in a series of hypothetical teaching situations.

It's been a rough day and you still have a lot to do. But you need a break. Anyway, it's just about time for your weekly weakness on the tube — whether it's a detective, doctor, lawyer, or family show — so you turn on the set, sit back, wait for the screen to light up, and relax. If you are lucky, you missed the last commercial spot before the program begins. Now, in brilliant color, with the musical theme throbbing through a quick series of tension-producing, emotion-grabbing, "teaser" scenes, the world of your favorite hero or heroine begins. You settle down for the drama of the next fifty minutes or so.

Even the occasional television viewer is familiar with this opening format. Every successful TV series uses it. Actually there is really nothing new each week. The plot follows a familiar pattern — one which you could block out with little effort. What keeps you turning it on each week is, in large part, the stimulation you experience in viewing the latest in chase scenes, shootouts, or lifesaving medical techniques. Once the show satisfies the viewer's appetite for thrills, excitement, or pathos, the story winds down, the heroes and heroines relax, the loose ends are all neatly tied together, and you can breathe easily once more, knowing that next week it will be back again.

It is no accident that TV uses this formula. Radio used it before TV, and before that dramatists practiced the art of teasing their audiences through a long list of weekly and monthly publications. Producers of popular television series meticulously plan, prepare, and direct their shows using audiovisual techniques designed *to get viewers "into" the show, to keep them glued to their sets, and to satisfy their needs for having participated in a complete experience.*

Learning theorists as well as practitioners interested in teacher training have known for some time how effective these techniques can be when skillfully employed by teachers in a classroom setting. Educators have developed elaborate schemes for classifying and analyzing the techniques and their underlying concepts. Although recent research[1] has identified 25 lesson presentation skills that are considered part of the classroom recitation process, the most frequently researched ones were found to be (1) introducing the lesson, or *set induction*;[2] (2) retaining student attention throughout the lesson, or *stimulus variation*;[3] (3) *explaining*; and (4) providing reinforcement through planned summarizing procedures, or *closure*.[4]

Gage and Berliner, in their research, describe the most common teaching method as a combination of lecture, discussion, and individual instruction.[5] This combination method requires that teachers do a considerable amount of verbal structuring and directing of the lesson. Other research on teachers' verbal classroom behavior gives additional support to the fact that teachers do tend to do most of the talking in their classrooms. Flanders states that almost 70 percent of the talk that goes on in the average classroom is teacher talk.[6]

This does not mean that teachers should always talk more than students. It simply emphasizes the fact that in many situations teachers must assume the important role of presenter. Regardless of the grade level one teaches, the necessity of exposing students to new facts, concepts, and principles, of explaining difficult procedures, of clarifying conflicting issues, and of exploring complicated relationships more frequently than not places the teacher in the position of having to do a great deal of presenting. Consequently, any prospective teacher ought to be interested in mastering those skills needed to become an effective presenter.

Think back for a moment to our opening description of the formula for the successful TV show. The technique used to gain the attention of viewers and to prepare them for the action which follows can be compared to that used by Aubertine in his teacher training experiments.[7] Aubertine, using what he called the process of *set induction*, found that instructional "sets" (special kinds of activities which precondition the learner) can have a significant positive effect on learning.

You can probably recall from your own experience many examples of how prior instructions ("sets") have influenced your responses in a new situation. If you have been told that a particular person you are going to meet is a "jerk," a "brain," "aggressive," or "sneaky," you prepare yourself to behave in a certain way when you come face to face with that person. Your entire behavior pattern, both verbal and nonverbal, is influenced by your prior information or "set."

Similarly, you can compare the kinds of techniques used to maintain a high level of audience attention in a TV production with teachers' efforts at varying their physical or verbal behavior during a classroom presentation. Gage and Berliner cite numerous studies to show that when teachers skillfully vary their verbal and physical behavior in the classroom, there is a strong positive effect on student learning.[8] Again, your own experience undoubtedly confirms that the lecturer who drones on and on in the same monotonous tone inevitably has a dulling effect on most listeners. Your mind tends to wander, your attention is easily diverted, or your eyelids grow too heavy to hold open.

Yet another analogy can be drawn between the ever present TV commercial that relies frequently on smooth-talking sales pitches to explain why one product is better than another and the skillful teacher whose clear, well-planned explanations are essential to effective lesson presentations. Researchers have found that of specific products produced for training teachers, one of the most frequently developed has dealt with improving teachers' explaining behavior.[9]

Last, consider the satisfaction of TV viewers when their hour of escape comes to a tidy end. There is a feeling of completeness, a sense that all is right with an orderly, regulated world. Similarly, learning theorists and teacher trainers have strong data to support the notion that skillful closing of a classroom presentation does enhance learning.

At the Stanford Center for Research and Development in Teaching, Margaret Bierly and others reported on the basis of survey research that most teachers are genuinely concerned with motivating and reinforcing their students.[10] In other words, they are interested in acquiring skills that will enable them both to initiate learning and to see that it is retained. Mastery of the three lesson-presentation skills which follow is aimed at assisting you toward the same goal.[11]

# Objective 1

To define set induction, explain its purposes, and give examples of when it is used as a lesson presentation skill.

## LEARNING ACTIVITY 1.1

**SET INDUCTION**

Set induction refers to those actions and statements by the teacher that are designed to relate the experiences of the students to the objectives of the lesson.[12] Effective teachers use set induction to put students in a receptive frame of mind that will facilitate learning — be it physical, mental, or emotional.

A story is told about a traveler who came upon an old man beating his donkey in an effort to make the animal rise. The animal sat placidly in the middle of the road refusing to get up, and the old man continued to whip the animal until a stranger stepped up and stopped his hand. "Why don't you tell the donkey to rise?" asked the stranger. "I will," replied the old man, "but first I have to get his attention."

Set induction has this as its first purpose — *to focus student attention on the lesson.* DeCecco, after reviewing the relevant theory and research on motivation, says that the first motivational function of the teacher is "to engage the student in learning."[13] Gagné and Briggs, in describing the events of instruction, echo the same notion.[14]

As its second purpose, set induction attempts *to create an organizing framework for the ideas, principles, or information which is to follow.* Gage and Berliner, in discussing the importance of lecture introductions, speak of *advance organizers* — "telling students in advance about the way in which a lecture is organized is likely to improve their comprehension and ability to recall and apply what they hear."[15] DeCecco calls attention to what he terms the expectancy function of teachers. He bases this notion on research which has shown that teachers can best shape student behavior when students have been told in advance what is expected of them.[16]

A very dramatic and certainly controversial study which demonstrates the power of set induction was reported by Robert Rosenthal and Lenore Jacobson in their book, *Pygmalion in the Classroom*. The authors conducted an experiment in which they tested all of the pupils from kindergarten through grade six in a particular school. Teachers were told that the test ". . . will allow us to predict which youngsters are most likely to show an academic spurt."[17] In September following this testing period, each teacher was given a list of students and was told that the students on their lists were the ones most likely to show a marked improvement in their school performance. Actually, the student names had been chosen at random.

However, after three successive testing periods the researchers claim that the test performance of these randomly identified students actually began to rise to meet the erroneous expectations of their teachers. In other words, the teachers, being told that their students were likely to do well academically, worked with the children in such a way that these expectations became a reality. By passing their expectations on to their students, the teachers were actually practicing a form of set induction, which, in this case, had a positive effect on learning.

A third purpose of set induction is *to extend the understanding and the application of abstract ideas through the use of example or analogy*. An idea or principle that is abstractly stated can be difficult for many students to comprehend. Moreover, many students who do understand an idea or principle have difficulty in applying their knowledge to new situations. The clever use of examples and analogies can do much to overcome such limitations. Novelists, dramatists, and poets are particularly good at using analogies to create expanded meaning in their works.

For example, read the following short poem:

### A Patch of Old Snow

There's a patch of old snow in a corner,
    That I should have guessed
Was a blow-away paper the rain
    Had brought to rest.

It is speckled with grime as if
    Small print overspread it,
The news of a day I've forgotten —
    If I ever read it.

        — Robert Frost[18]

Literally speaking, the poet is describing a patch of old snow which resembles an old newspaper. However, by use of metaphor (analogy) the poet creates a literary experience which enables the reader to extend his or her understanding far beyond the simple comparison of a patch of old snow to a discarded newspaper. At one level, the metaphor suggests that the snow, once fallen and now melted, has very little meaning in the grand scheme of things. Then, perhaps with tongue in cheek, Frost seems to suggest that what is recorded in the newspaper — today or yesterday — may not really be much more important than the remains of an old snowfall.

The fourth and last purpose of set induction is *to stimulate student interest and involvement in the lesson.* A great deal of research has been carried on over the years on student motivation and the need to increase the student's interest in learning. Maria Montessori observes how strong involvement in play activities can keep a young child motivated and interested in a single game over an extended period of time. The point here is that active involvement at the beginning of a lesson can increase curiosity and stimulate student interest in the lesson.[19] A good example is the teacher who wishes to teach the concept of categorizing and brings a collection of baseball player cards, record jackets, or even a basket of leaves to class. Then the students, divided into groups, are asked to categorize their collections and explain how and why they did what they did.

## LEARNING ACTIVITY 1.2

Now that set induction has been defined and its purposes explained, you are ready to focus on when teachers generally use set induction in the course of a lesson. To understand set usage better, think of a classroom lesson as a game. Bellack, in his research on the language used by teachers to direct classroom lessons, talks about "structuring moves [which] *set the context* for the entire classroom *game.*"[20] Furthermore, he views the lesson as containing several "subgames," each of which is identified primarily by the type of activity taking place during a given period of play.

For example, the teacher plans during the course of a lesson to carry on several different activities such as reading, writing, and discussion, each dealing with different subject matter. Each new activity can be seen as a subgame within the context of a larger game, the entire day's lessons. The teacher, then, must structure each situation so that students can participate (play) effectively in the lesson (game).

The kinds of classroom situations (subgames) for which it is necessary to employ a set are innumerable. To assist you in learning when to employ set induction in your own lessons, study carefully the list which follows.

### Examples of When to Use Set Induction

To begin a long unit of work in which the class might be studying plants, rockets, or local government.

To introduce a new concept or principle.

To initiate a discussion.

To begin a skill-building activity such as reading comprehension or visual discrimination.

To introduce a film, TV program, record, or tape.

To initiate a question-and-answer session.

To prepare for a field trip.

To present a guest speaker.

To introduce a homework assignment.

To begin a laboratory exercise.

To redirect a presentation when you see that students do not understand the content.

# Mastery Test

## OBJECTIVE 1

To define set induction, explain its purposes, and give examples of when it is used as a lesson presentation skill.

Questions 1 and 2 are designed to determine your knowledge and comprehension level. Successful completion of these questions meets the objective of the learning activity. Question 3 is designed to test a more advanced level of learning — analysis and application. It is a "bonus" and tests your ability to identify and analyze a set when it is being used in a teaching situation.

1. Define set induction as a teaching skill and explain three specific purposes it serves in lesson presentations.

_____

_____

_____

_____

_____

2. Describe briefly three different situations in which you would use set induction in making a classroom presentation.

_____

_____

_____

_____

3. Identify and explain how set induction has been employed in the presentation of this chapter.

_____

_____

_____

_____

_____

## ANSWER KEY

### Mastery Test, Objective 1

1. *General definition:* Should include the idea that a set is something a teacher does or says in order to relate the experiences of students to the objectives of the lesson.

   Any three of the following purposes could be listed: (1) to focus student attention on lesson, (2) to create an organizing framework for the information to be learned, (3) to extend the understanding and applications of the lesson content, and (4) to stimulate student interest in the lesson.

2. You may use any of the situations described in the examples or include situations of your own creation.

3. The author used previous TV viewing experiences of the reader and drew an extended analogy of what the TV director does in the presentation of a drama to what the teacher must do in the presentation of a classroom lesson.

# Objective 2

To plan original sets for use in a series of hypothetical teaching situations.

## LEARNING ACTIVITY 2

Now that you know what set induction is and the general purposes for which it is used, you are ready to begin practicing how to plan your own sets. Before you actually begin doing this, you should take time to familiarize yourself with some examples of how experienced teachers might use set induction in their lessons.

**USES OF SET INDUCTION**

Below is a list of specific uses of set induction employed by experienced teachers. Study these uses carefully. Then read each of the sample lessons that follow and the accompanying analysis. You should then be ready to plan your own sets for a given teaching situation.

1. To focus the student's attention on the presentation the teacher is about to make by employing an activity, event, object, or person that relates directly to student interest or previous experience.

2. To provide a structure or framework that enables the student to visualize the content or activities of the presentation.

3. To aid in clarifying the goals of the lesson presentation.

4. To provide a smooth transition from known or already covered material to new or unknown material by capitalizing on the use of examples (either verbal or nonverbal), analogies, and student activities which students have interest in or experience with.

5. To evaluate previously learned material before moving on to new material or skill-building activities by employing student-centered activities or student-developed examples and analogies that demonstrate understanding of previously learned content.

### Sample Lesson Number 1

The teacher has planned to get into the topic of percent and is aware of students' interest in local baseball fortunes. The teacher decides to introduce the unit with a brief discussion of the previous day's game. Talk is directed to batting averages, and the teacher demonstrates how they are calculated. Students are permitted to work out one or two of the averages for favorite players.

**Analysis.** This set is most appropriately used for introducing a unit on percent or the concept of percent itself. Referring to the list of uses for set induction mentioned above, note the following:

1. The set focuses students' attention on the concept of percent, which is the unit or topic being initiated by the teacher in this lesson.
2. It uses an event (like yesterday's baseball game) and an activity that is familiar to the students and in which they have considerable interest.
3. It provides a ready frame of reference (batting averages) for application of the percent concept to other situations.
4. Through teacher comment, the concept of batting averages and percent can be easily connected to help clarify the goals of the new unit or topic.

## Sample Lesson Number 2

The students working in a science unit have already demonstrated in the first part of their lesson some basic understanding of mixtures. The teacher has planned to conduct an experiment to demonstrate visually the concept of mixtures. He or she brings to class several bottles of different kinds of popular salad dressings. The students are directed to experiment with the various bottles and to observe differences in their appearance before and after they are vigorously mixed.

**Analysis.** This set is most appropriately used to begin a laboratory exercise. Referring to the list of uses for set induction mentioned above, note the following:

1. It is used specifically to provide smooth transition from what the students already know (knowledge of mixtures) to the new material to be covered in the lesson.
2. It relies on the use of an activity (experiment) that is familiar to all the students.

## Sample Lesson Number 3

The students have been reading short stories and examining the techniques authors use to create a mood through setting. The teacher begins the lesson by providing the class with a list of words that suggest different moods. Each student is asked to select one word and to tell how he or she, as an author, might create a setting appropriate to the suggested mood.

**Analysis.** This set is most appropriately used to initiate a discussion or question-and-answer session. Referring to the list of uses for set induction mentioned above, note the following:

1. It is being used to determine how well students understand the relationship of setting to mood.

2. It relies on student-developed examples that demonstrate their understanding of the relationship of setting to mood.

# Mastery Test

## OBJECTIVE 2    To plan original sets for use in a series of hypothetical teaching situations.

Following these directions are five hypothetical teaching situations. Read each one carefully and plan a set of your own which you feel would work effectively in that particular situation. You may refer to the list of uses for set induction on pages 116 and 117, and the example lessons which follow to help you generate ideas for your own sets.

*Situation 1.*   The class has been working on a unit in government. During the first part of the period, the students have been viewing a short filmstrip on the three branches of government. The filmstrip is not an in-depth experience, but gives a good overview. The teacher wishes to use the remainder of the period to promote a more thorough understanding of the role or function of each branch of the government, using a different kind of activity.

*Situation 2.*   You are introducing the study of pollution and the environment to your class. It is important that you "get off on the right foot."

*Situation 3.*   You are exploring the world of work with your class and have an excellent film you wish to show.

*Situation 4.*   Your class has been studying the letters of the alphabet. You wish to use part of the day to take up this subject matter again and to determine how far your students have come in being able to place the letters in order.

*Situation 5.*   Your class has been working on different techniques to put life into their writing. In this lesson you wish to present the idea of using descriptive words to paint verbal pictures.

# ANSWER KEY

## Mastery Test, Objective 2

Of course, no single response to any of the five situations described above will be the same. However, if you have read carefully each of the situations, each one suggests a general direction which you might follow.

*Situation 1.*   A set to determine how well the students understood the filmstrip or could apply what they learned in some new activity seems appropriate here.

*Situation 2.*   A set to orient students or focus their attention on the importance or significance of pollution and its effect on the environment would be helpful in this case.

*Situation 3.*   As in the previous lesson, student attention needs to be focused on the important concepts or ideas about to be presented in the film.

*Situation 4.*   The set in this situation should incorporate some kind of evaluation activity so that students are actively engaged in using previously learned knowledge and the teacher has an opportunity to see how much students have learned.

*Situation 5.*   The set should be transitional so that students have an opportunity to integrate previously learned material with new techniques.

**EXPLAINING BEHAVIOR**

One cold, dark night a fire broke out in a small, European, medieval town. After the townspeople had fought the destructive blaze for hours and successfully extinguished the flames, the mayor brought the people together for a few words. "Citizens," he began, "this fire was truly a blessing from God."

Noting the hostile glances from the crowd, the mayor hastily explained: "You must understand. If it were not for the light provided by the flames, how would we have been able to see how to fight the fire?"

The story never tells how the people accepted this explanation, but the lesson presentation skill that follows reveals a great deal about explaining behavior.

# Objective 3

To identify the specific underlying purpose of four different types of explanations frequently used in lesson presentations.

## LEARNING ACTIVITY 3

Explaining refers to planned teacher talk designed to clarify any idea, procedure, or process not understood by a student. Every teacher, as well as every student, knows the importance of being able to give clear explanations. Teachers rely heavily on this skill in lesson presentation; students know only too well the difficulty of learning from the teacher who lacks this critical skill.

The use and importance of explaining behavior extend far beyond the classroom. You encounter the use of explanations, both oral and written, in every aspect of your personal lives. You open cans, put furniture together, operate all kinds of devices which require simple training through directions, and frequently listen to experts explain what lies behind every contemporary problem imaginable. Unfortunately, the explanations you hear in these varied situations are frequently not very satisfying. Some time ago this writer bought a pair of snow chains for his automobile. I carefully unpacked them and read with great interest the directions for putting on the chains. The directions were simple and brief:

> Lay out the chains as illustrated in the diagram, and proceed to hook up in the usual manner.

You can imagine my frustration trying to follow a faded diagram that didn't really tell me anything and guessing wildly at what was meant by "the usual manner" — not ever having put on a set of tire chains in my life.

The importance of explaining in lesson presentation is well documented. Miltz cites a number of research studies that support the importance of explaining and its effect on student learning.[21] And in *A Catalogue of Concepts in the Pedagogical Domain of Teacher Education*, the authors include explanation as one of the critical skills in reception learning.[22]

A good way to begin to acquire skill in explaining is first to understand the underlying purpose of an explanation. Generally speaking, an explanation may have any of four different underlying purposes:

1. To show a direct cause-and-effect relationship.
2. To show that a particular action is governed by a general rule or law.
3. To illustrate a procedure or process.
4. To show the intent of an action or process.

Examples of ideas, procedures, and processes frequently requiring careful explanation are listed below. Note that although a wide range of subject matter is covered, the explanation of each idea, procedure, or process will have a particular underlying purpose. Study each group one at a time. Then complete the exercise and compare your results with other students.

1. Examples that require explanations whose underlying purpose is to show a cause-and-effect relationship.

   (a) The effect of heat in changing a liquid to gas.
   (b) The result of inaccurate measurement in constructing a woodworking project, baking a cake, etc.
   (c) The effect of an unclear communication.
   (d) The effects of pollutants in the air.

# Your Turn

Now that you have had a chance to study the examples above, write three of your own examples that require an explanation whose underlying purpose is to show a direct cause-and-effect relationship.

(1) _____

_____

(2) _____

_____

(3) _____

_____

2. Examples that require explanations whose underlying purpose is to show that a particular action is governed by a general rule or law.

   (a) The reason for sterilization procedures in a hospital operating room.
   (b) The need for a particular kind of clothing in varied weather conditions.
   (c) The need for protective glasses when using power tools.

# Your Turn

Now that you have had a chance to study the examples above, write three of your own examples that require an explanation whose underlying purpose is to show that a particular action is governed by a general rule or law.

(1) _____

_____

(2) _____

_____

(3) _____

_____

3. Examples that require explanations whose underlying purpose is to illustrate a procedure or process.

   (a) The preparation of vegetables for a salad.
   (b) Developing an outline for an essay.
   (c) The appropriate way to clean up after an art activity.
   (d) The proper care of a musical instrument.

# Your Turn

Now that you have had a chance to study the examples above, write three of your own examples that require an explanation whose underlying purpose is to illustrate a procedure or process.

(1) _____

_____

(2) _____

_____

(3) _____

_____

4. Examples that require explanations whose underlying purpose is to show the intent of an action or process.

   (a) The motivation for a character's behavior in a story.
   (b) Why we fire pottery.
   (c) The use of a particular defense in football, basketball, baseball, etc.
   (d) The function of a custom in a particular ethnic group.

# Your Turn

Now that you have had a chance to study the examples above, write three of your own examples that require an explanation whose underlying purpose is to show the intent of an action or process.

(1) _____

_____

(2) _____

_____

(3) _____

_____

# Mastery Test

## OBJECTIVE 3

To identify the specific underlying purpose of four different types of explanations frequently used in lesson presentations.

1. Identify what the underlying purpose would be for each of the following ideas, procedures, or processes that require an explanation. Use the letter preceding the definition of the underlying purpose to indicate your answer and write it in the space provided.

UNDERLYING PURPOSE

A. To show a direct cause-and-effect relationship.
B. To show that a particular action is governed by a general rule or law.
C. To illustrate a procedure or process.
D. To show the intent of an action or process.

IDEA, PROCEDURE, OR PROCESS TO BE EXPLAINED

(   ) a. Internal combustion

(   ) b. The purpose of a bat's "radar" system for "seeing."

(   ) c. The entrance of the United States into World War II.

(   ) d. The use of the question mark in written English.

(   ) e. The motivation for a character's behavior in a novel.

(   ) f. The ill effects of an improper diet.

(   ) g. How a bill is introduced in Congress.

(   ) h. The use of a sign or symbol, e.g., a red light to stop.

# ANSWER KEY

## Mastery Test, Objective 3

1. (C) a. The underlying purpose here is to illustrate the internal combustion process.

(D) b. The underlying purpose here is to show the intent or purpose of the bat's "radar" system, i.e., to enable it to "see."

(A) c. The underlying purpose here would be to show the causes that precipitated the entry of the United States into World War II.

(B) d. The underlying purpose here is to indicate that the use of a question mark is governed by certain linguistic rules.

(D) e. The underlying purpose here is to clarify the meaning behind a character's behavior.

(A) f. The underlying purpose here is to indicate how poor nutrition leads to poor health.

(C) g. The underlying purpose here is to illustrate the process that brings legislation before Congress.

(B) h. The underlying purpose here is to illustrate the general rule that a sign or symbol requires a particular kind of action.

# Objective 4

To plan original explanations, given a series of hypothetical teaching situations.

## LEARNING ACTIVITY 4

Now that you understand the importance of explaining behavior and the underlying purposes for which it is used, you need to know how to plan or structure an effective explanation. Explaining behavior is a teaching skill that depends a great deal on a teacher's knowledge and creativity. No two teachers utilize their skill in exactly the same way. However, beginning teachers can follow a simple procedure to help develop effective explaining behavior.

Once you have made a decision about what needs to be explained, the following four procedural steps will help you plan an effective explanation:

1. Identify the purpose of the explanation for yourself.
2. Prepare a definition for students of the key ideas (process or procedure) in the simplest terms possible.
3. Illustrate for students with examples or demonstrations.
4. Summarize for or with students.

Below are examples of how the procedure above can be used to help structure an effective explanation — each with a different underlying purpose. The material to be explained was chosen from the lists presented in the previous learning activity. Study them carefully. Then you should be ready to plan explanations in your particular teaching situation.

*Example 1:*  *You wish to explain to a general science class that the property of a liquid may be changed by raising its temperature.*

Step 1:  *Identify purpose for yourself.* The purpose of this explanation is to show *the direct cause-and-effect relationship* between the application of heat to a liquid and the consequent change of its property.

Step 2:  *Define key ideas.* Changing the property of a liquid in this instance simply means changing water from a liquid to a gas.

Step 3:  *Illustrate.* The simplest illustration of this change is to heat a tea kettle full of water until steam begins to come out of the spout.

Step 4:  *Summarize.* An oral or written summary of what occurred in the demonstration should be made by the teacher or a student.

*Example 2:*  *You need to explain the use of a question mark in written English to a group of elementary school children who have not yet been formally introduced to this mark of punctuation.*

Step 1:  *Identify purpose for yourself.* The purpose of this explanation is to indicate that there is a rule that governs the use of the question mark (?) in written English.

Step 2:  *Define key ideas.* A question mark (?) is a mark of punctuation that in the English language is used in writing to indicate that a question is being asked.

Step 3:  *Illustrate.* One of the simplest ways to illustrate this rule is to prepare handwritten examples of sentences, some of which are simple direct statements and others questions. Distribute the examples to the students and have them read the material aloud. The same procedure can be followed using examples from textbooks, newspapers, and magazines.

Step 4:  *Summarize.* An oral or written summary of the rule for the use of the punctuation mark should be given by either the teacher or a student.

*Example 3:*  *You need to explain the process known as internal combustion to a group of junior high school students beginning to study auto mechanics.*

Step 1:  *Identify purpose for yourself.* The purpose of this explanation is *to illustrate the process* of internal combustion as it takes place in a gasoline engine.

Step 2:  *Define key ideas.* Internal combustion is a process in which a mixture of gasoline vapor and air is burned inside a cylinder.

Step 3:  *Illustrate*. Depending on materials available, you may wish to demonstrate the process with a simple experiment, the use of photographs, slides, film, or a cut-away model.

Step 4:  *Summarize*. An oral restatement of the process itself, including the individual steps necessary for internal combustion to take place, should be made by the teacher or a student.

Example 4:  *You are teaching a pottery unit, and in the course of explaining each of the steps necessary to producing a finished product, you need to indicate the intent of the firing process.*

Step 1:  *Identify purpose for yourself*. The purpose of this explanation is *to show the intent* of the firing process in producing a finished piece of pottery.

Step 2:  *Define key ideas*. Firing is a drying process which removes water or moisture from clay in order to make the clay hard.

Step 3:  *Illustrate*. Allowing students to compare, by seeing, touching, and smelling samples of pottery that have not been fired with pottery that has been fired is a good way to illustrate the intent of the firing process.

Step 4:  *Summarize*. An oral restatement of the process, focusing on the intent of firing the unfinished pottery, should be made by the teacher or a student.

# Mastery Test

## OBJECTIVE 4   To plan original explanations, given a series of hypothetical teaching situations.

Following these directions are four hypothetical teaching situations. Read each carefully and plan an explanation of your own, using the step procedure outlined in the previous learning activity. If you are unfamiliar with any of these teaching situations, you may select one you are more familiar with to complete this exercise.

*Situation 1.*  You need to explain to a group of elementary school pupils what causes day and night.

*Situation 2.*  You are teaching a course or unit in economics and must explain why we pay federal income taxes.

*Situation 3.*  You are teaching in a woodworking shop and must instruct your students in the proper procedure for setting up the wood lathe.

*Situation 4.*  You are reading a story and wish to explain the reason why the main character behaved as he or she did.

## ANSWER KEY

### Mastery Test, Objective 4

Of course, no single response to any of the four situations described above will be the same. However, each plan you develop should follow the procedural steps listed in Learning Activity 6: identify purpose, define, illustrate, and summarize.

*Situation 1* was intended to show a direct cause-and-effect relationship.

*Situation 2* was intended to indicate that there is a law requiring the payment of income taxes.

*Situation 3* was intended to illustrate the procedure for setting up a wood lathe.

*Situation 4* was intended to show the motivation for a character's behavior in a story.

**CLOSURE**

In the introduction to this chapter the concept of closure was likened to the practice of TV directors who faithfully bring their weekly shows to a comfortable close. Think how uncomfortable the TV viewer would be not knowing what punishment the wrongdoer was to receive or how the detective actually solved the crime. Is there any reason that classroom learners should feel any differently regarding information being presented within a classroom context? With this in mind, let us proceed to our final lesson presentation skill, that of closure.

## Objective 5

To define closure, explain its purposes, and give examples of when it is used as a lesson presentation skill.

### LEARNING ACTIVITY 5.1

Closure refers to those actions or statements by teachers that are designed to bring a lesson presentation to an appropriate conclusion. Teachers use closure to help students bring things together in their own minds, to make sense out of what has been going on during the course of the presentation.

A good way to think about closure is to consider it the complement of set induction. If set induction is an initiating activity of the teacher, then closure is a culminating activity. Research into the psychology of learning indicates that learning increases when teachers make a conscious effort to help students organize the information presented to them and to perceive relationships based on that information.

Another good way to view closure is to compare it to the paper-and-pencil process of lesson planning. A good lesson plan will usually indicate where the students will be going, how they will get there, and how they will know when they have arrived. Making certain that students know *when they have arrived* is the result of the skillful teacher's use of closure. Gage and Berliner suggest that although research has not given us "assurances about the causal effectiveness (for learning) of these kinds of teacher behavior" (i.e., closure techniques), nevertheless, the most effective teachers seem to practice closure consistently.[23]

Closure, then, has as its first purpose *to draw attention to the end of a lesson or lesson segment.* Unfortunately, many teachers have neglected the development of this important skill.

Your own experience will tell you that typical closure procedure goes something like this:

*Teacher A:* "Okay. There's the bell! Get going — you'll be late for your next class!"

*Teacher B:* "Enough of this! Let's close our books and line up for recess."

*Teacher C:* "The bell? All right, we'll stop here and pick up at the same point tomorrow."

*Teacher D:* "Any questions? No? Good. Let's move on to the next chapter."

Certainly the students are aware that something has concluded in each case, but that is about all. These unsophisticated forms of closure completely ignore the fact that effective learning depends on the effective sequencing of lesson presentations. And one of the most important events in effective sequencing is providing opportunity for feedback and review.

The teacher who uses closure effectively understands the importance of cueing students in to the fact that they have reached an important point in the presentation and that the time has come to wrap things up. This activity must be planned just as carefully as its counterpart, set induction, and timing is critical. The teacher must be aware of the clock and must begin to initiate closure proceedings well before the activity is due to end.

Consequently, a second major purpose of closure is *to help organize student learning.* Simply calling attention to the lesson's conclusion is not enough. A great deal of information and a great many activities may have been covered, and it is the teacher's responsibility to tie it all together into a meaningful whole. The learner, just like the TV viewer, should not be left with a feeling of incompleteness and frustration. Like the TV detective who explains to the audience how the various pieces of the puzzle finally formed a coherent picture, so the skillful teacher should recapitulate the various bits and pieces of his or her lesson and make them into a coherent picture for the learner.

Finally, closure has as its third purpose *to consolidate or reinforce the major points to be learned.* Having signaled the end of the lesson and made an effort to organize what has occurred, the teacher should briefly refocus on the key ideas or processes presented in the lesson. The ultimate objective here is to help the student retain the important information presented in the lesson and thus increase the probability that he or she will be able to recall and use the information at a later time.

Gagné and Briggs, in discussing information storage and retrieval, have this to say: "When information or knowledge is to be recalled, . . . the *network of relationships* in which the newly learned material has been embedded provides a number of different possibilities as cues for its retrieval."[24]

Closure, then, is the skill of reviewing the key points of a lesson, of tying them together into a coherent whole, and finally, of ensuring their use by anchoring them in the student's larger conceptual network.

## LEARNING ACTIVITY 5.2

Now that closure has been defined and its purposes explained, you are ready to focus specifically on when the teacher uses closure in the course of the lesson. You should be able to understand more easily when closure is used if you completed the section on set induction. In that section a lesson was compared to a game containing several "subgames." In the classroom situation such "subgames" might involve a lesson introducing some new concept or skills or an activity with some combination of reading, writing, viewing, or discussing. Each of these activities can be viewed as a "subgame" within the context of a larger game — an entire class period for a particular subject or an entire day of nondepartmentalized instruction.

The role of the teacher is to structure each situation (subgame) so that it begins and ends in such a way as to promote student learning. This is the function of both set induction and closure technique. To assist you in learning when to use closure in a lesson presentation, study carefully the following list of situations:

### *Examples of When to Use Closure*

To end a long unit of work in which the class might be studying animals, or the family, or a country.

To consolidate learning of a new concept or principle.

To close a discussion.

To end a skill-building activity such as locating words in the dictionary or practicing basic functions in arithmetic.

To follow up a film, TV program, record, or tape.

To close a question-and-answer session.

To consolidate learning experiences on a field trip.

To reinforce the presentation of a guest speaker.

To follow up a homework assignment reviewed in class.

To end a laboratory exercise.

To organize thinking around a new concept or principle (e.g., all languages are not written, or different cultures reflect different values).

# Mastery Test

**OBJECTIVE 5**    To define closure, explain its purposes, and give examples of when it is used as a lesson presentation skill.

1. Define closure as a teaching skill and explain three specific purposes it serves in lesson presentations.

_____

_____

_____

_____

_____

_____

_____

_____

2. Try responding to the following statements by placing the letter *T* next to those which are true and the letter *F* next to those which are false.

_____ (a) Closure as a lesson presentation skill is a natural complement to set induction.

_____ (b) Closure is less important than set induction, because students can tell by the clock when the class period ends.

_____ (c) Closure helps students know when they have achieved lesson objectives.

_____ (d) One of the purposes of closure is to draw attention to the end of a presentation.

_____ (e) Good closure opens the opportunity for students to review what they are supposed to have learned.

_____ (f) Closure is a natural phenomenon and does not require planning.

_____ (g) One of the purposes of closure is to help organize student learning.

_____ (h) Timing is critical in using closure.

_____ (i) Closure helps to get your lesson off on the right foot.

_____ (j) One of the purposes of closure is to consolidate or reinforce the major points to be learned in a presentation.

3. Describe briefly ten different situations in which you could use closure in your lesson presentations.

_____

_____

_____

_____

_____

_____

_____

_____

_____

_____

# ANSWER KEY

Mastery Test, Objective 5

1. *General definition:* Should include the idea that closure is something a teacher says or does which brings a presentation to an appropriate close.

   *Purposes:*
   (1) To draw attention to the end of a lesson.
   (2) To help organize student learning.
   (3) To consolidate or reinforce major points to be learned.

2. (a) T. Whereas set induction *initiates* instruction, closure *terminates* it.
   (b) F. Clocks tell time, but only teachers can close a lesson.
   (c) T. Appropriate use of closure enables students to evaluate their own understanding of a lesson.
   (d) T. Closure signals the natural conclusion of a presentation sequence.
   (e) T. One purpose of closure is to recapitulate the important points in a lesson presentation.
   (f) F. Effective closure does not occur naturally but requires conscious control by the teacher.
   (g) T. Closure helps provide a coherence to learning through review.
   (h) T. Since closure is a part of a planned sequence of instructional events, it requires careful timing.
   (i) F. Closure *terminates* a lesson, whereas set induction *initiates* it.
   (j) T. Through review and evolution closure helps students organize and retain learning.

3. You may use any of the situations described in the examples or include situations of your own creation.

# Objective 6

To plan original closures for use in a series of hypothetical teaching situations.

## LEARNING ACTIVITY 6

Now that you know what closure is and the general purposes for which it is used, you are ready to begin practicing how to plan your own closures. Before you actually begin doing this, you should take time to familiarize yourself with some examples of how experienced teachers might use closure in their lessons.

USES OF CLOSURE    Below is a list of specific uses of closure employed by experienced teachers. Study them carefully. Then read each of the sample lessons which follow and the accompanying analysis. You should be ready then to plan your own closures for a given teaching situation.

1. Attempts to draw students' attention to a closing point in the lesson.
2. Reviews major points of teacher-centered presentation.
3. Reviews sequence used in learning material during the presentation.

4. Provides summary of important student-oriented discussion.
5. Relates lesson to original organizing principle or concept.
6. Attempts to lead students to extend or develop new knowledge from previously learned concepts.
7. Allows students to practice what they have learned.

### Sample Lesson Number 1

The lesson is in geography, and the teacher has planned to introduce two basic concepts: (1) man as the active shaper of his environment, and (2) environment as a limiting context within which man must operate. The teacher has reached the critical point in the lesson where he or she wishes to call students' attention to the fact that the presentation of the first concept is ready for closure.

*Teacher closure:* "Before moving to the next important idea, the restrictions which environment places on man, let's review the main points I've already covered on how man can play a critical role in shaping the environment." The teacher then proceeds to review the major points of the presentation, using either a prepared outline or one developed on the chalkboard during the lesson.

### Application Analysis

This closure is appropriate to use when you wish to help students organize their thinking around a new concept before moving on to a new idea. Referring to the list of uses for closure mentioned above, note the following:

(a) The closure draws attention to end of lesson with verbal cue — "before moving to the next important idea."
(b) It reviews important points of the teacher's presentation.
(c) It helps organize student thinking around the first concept presented by utilizing an outline on the chalkboard.

### Sample Lesson Number 2

The lesson is in language arts, social studies, science, etc., and the teacher is conducting a discussion around some specific issue which is important in the lesson plan for that particular day. The time has come to bring the discussion to a close.

*Teacher closure:* Teacher calls on specific student and says, "Elena, would you please summarize what has been said thus far and point out what you felt were the major points covered?"

### Application Analysis

This closure is appropriate to use when you wish to bring a classroom discussion to a close. Referring to the list of uses for closure mentioned above, note the following:

(a) The closure draws attention to the fact that teacher is calling for a temporary end to discussion by requesting a student summary.

(b) It summarizes what students have been discussing.

(c) It helps students to organize or rearrange their own ideas by specifically asking for students to point out major points made in the discussion.

### Sample Lesson Number 3

The lesson is in American history. The class has been given the homework assignment of recording the reaction in 1939–1941 of private citizens, the President, members of Congress, and the press to the idea of going to war. After reading student responses to that assignment, the teacher senses that the students seem to have the idea and wishes to close.

> *Teacher closure:* "Your responses to this homework assignment have been very good. Now let's turn to the present day and compare the responses of private citizens, the President, members of Congress, and the press to the current situation. How are they alike and how do they differ?"

### Application Analysis

This closure technique is appropriate to use when following up on a homework assignment being reviewed in class before moving on to application of ideas newly learned. Referring to the general characteristics for this closure listed above, you should note the following:

(a) It draws attention to the close of the assignment through teacher's comment or approval, "Your responses to this homework assignment have been very good!"

(b) It reviews material covered in the assignment by having students extend their knowledge of what they have already learned about the past to what is happening in the present.

### Sample Lesson 4

The lesson is in mathematics and the teacher is presenting a general reading skills approach to problem solving: (1) preview, (2) identify details or relationships, (3) restate problem in own words, (4) list computational steps to be taken. The time has come to see how well the students have understood the use of the new procedure.

> *Teacher closure:* "Before you try to use this new approach to problem solving by yourselves, let's list the steps on the chalkboard and try to apply them to the first problem in your textbooks on page 27. When you finish, I will ask some of you to share with the class your experience using this new technique."

### Application Analysis

This closure technique is a good one to use when ending a skill-building activity and you wish to help students consolidate what they have learned. You will have to refer to the characteristics above for *both review and transfer* in the analysis which follows:

(a) It draws attention to the close of the presentation by teacher's verbal signal, "Before you try to use this approach . . . let's list the steps . . .."

(b) It reviews the sequence used in learning new reading skills during the presentation.

(c) It permits students to practice immediately what they have learned.

# Mastery Test

## OBJECTIVE 6 To plan original closures for use in a series of hypothetical teaching situations.

Following these directions are five hypothetical teaching situations. Read each one carefully and plan a closure of your own which you feel would work effectively in that particular situation. You may refer to the list of uses for closure on page 138, and the sample lessons which follow to help you generate ideas for your own closures.

1. You have just completed a presentation on the steps one takes in preparing a green salad.
2. You have just completed a demonstration of parallel bar exercises.
3. You have reached a point in a class discussion at which it would be appropriate to close.
4. The teacher begins a lesson on theme in literature by comparing it to the threads running through a colorful tapestry and now wishes to close.
5. You have presented an important concept to the class and asked the students how the idea might be used in other situations.

## ANSWER KEY

### Mastery Test, Objective 6

Of course, no single response to any of the five situations described above will be the same as any other. However, if you have read carefully each of the situations, each suggests a general direction you might follow.

*Situation 1* A closure that reviewed the sequence demonstrated in the presentation would seem most appropriate in this lesson.

*Situation 2* A closure activity that would give students an opportunity to practice what they have observed seems appropriate in this instance.

*Situation 3* A review of the points, ideas, or concepts developed in the discussion would seem to be the most appropriate closure at this point in the lesson.

*Situation 4* As in the previous lesson, a review closure in which the teacher relates what has gone on to the original organizing principle introduced at the beginning of class seems most appropriate.

*Situation 5* A closure activity in which students can apply what they have learned in the lesson to a new situation seems most appropriate in this instance.

NOTES        1. Margaret Bierly et al., "Cataloguing Teacher Training Materials in a Computerized Retrieval System: Separating the Baby from the Bath Water" (Paper presented to the American Educational Research Association, Chicago, April 1974), p. 6.

2. H. E. Aubertine, "An Experiment in the Set Induction Process and Its Application in Training" (Ph.D. diss., Stanford University, 1964).

3. "Stimulus variation" as a lesson presentation skill was originally developed for use in a teacher training setting by Dr. D. C. Berliner for the Stanford Center for Research and Development in Teaching, Stanford University, Stanford, California.

4. "Closure" as a lesson presentation skill was originally developed for use in a teacher training setting by Dr. W. D. Johnson for the School of Education, Stanford University, Stanford, California.

5. N. L. Gage and David C. Berliner, *Educational Psychology* (Chicago: Rand McNally & Company, 1975), p. 482.

6. Ned A. Flanders, *Teacher Influence, Pupil Attitudes, and Achievement*, U.S. Department of Health, Education, and Welfare, Office of Education, Cooperative Research Monograph no. 12 (Washington, D.C.: U.S. Government Printing Office, 1965), p. 1.

7. Aubertine, *op. cit.*

8. Gage and Berliner, *op. cit.*, p. 516.

9. Margaret Bierly et al., *Teacher Training Products: The State of the Field*, Research and Development Memorandum no. 116 (Stanford University, California, Stanford Center for Research and Development in Teaching, January 1974), p. 25.

10. *Ibid.*, p. 22.

11. The prototype modules for these lesson presentation skills were developed and field tested by Dr. Francis T. Sobol for the School of Education at Florida International University, Miami, Florida, in 1972–1973.

12. "Set induction" as a lesson presentation skill was developed for use in teacher training by Dr. J. C. Fortune and Dr. V. B. Rosenshine for the School of Education, Stanford University, Stanford, California.

13. John P. DeCecco, *The Psychology of Learning and Instruction: Educational Psychology* (Englewood Cliffs, New Jersey: Prentice-Hall, 1968), p. 159.

14. Robert M. Gagné and Leslie J. Briggs, *Principles of Instructional Design* (New York: Holt, Rinehart & Winston, 1974), p. 123.

15. Gage and Berliner, *op. cit.*, p. 496.

16. DeCecco, *op. cit.*, p. 162.

17. Robert Rosenthal and Lenore Jacobson, *Pygmalion in the Classroom* (New York: Holt, Rinehart & Winston, 1968), p. 7.

18. From *The Poetry of Robert Frost,* ed. Edward Connery Lathem. Copyright 1916, © 1969 by Holt, Rinehart & Winston. Copyright 1944 by Robert Frost. Reprinted by permission of Holt, Rinehart & Winston, Publishers.

19. Maria Montessori, *The Montessori Method* (New York: Schocken Books, 1964), p. 170.

20. Arno A. Bellack et al., *The Language of the Classroom* (New York: Teachers College Press, Columbia University, 1966), p. 134.

21. Robert J. Miltz, *Development and Evaluation of a Manual for Improving Teachers' Explanations* (Stanford, Calif.: Stanford Center for Research and Development in Teaching, Stanford University, 1972).

22. *A Catalogue of Concepts in the Pedagogical Domain of Teacher Education* (Syracuse, New York: Syracuse University School of Education, 1974), p. 33.

23. Gage and Berliner, *op. cit.*, p. 524.

24. Gagné and Briggs, *op. cit.*, p. 132.

ADDITIONAL READINGS

Aubertine, H. E. "An Experiment in the Set Induction Process and Its Application in Training." Ph.D. dissertation, Stanford University, 1964.

Bellack, Arno A., et al. *The Language of the Classroom.* New York: Teachers College Press, Columbia University, 1966.

Bierly, Margaret, et al. "Cataloguing Teacher Training Materials in a Computerized Retrieval System: Separating the Baby from the Bath Water." Paper read at the American Educational Research Association, Chicago, April 1974.

Bierly, Margaret, et al. *Teacher Training Products: The State of the Field.* Research and Development Memorandum no. 116. Stanford Center for Research and Development in Teaching, Stanford University, Stanford, California, 1974.

DeCecco, John P. *The Psychology of Learning and Instruction: Educational Psychology.* Englewood Cliffs, New Jersey: Prentice-Hall, Inc., 1968.

Flanders, Ned A. *Teacher Influence, Pupil Attitudes, and Achievement.* U.S. Department of Health, Education, and Welfare, Office of Education, Cooperative Research Monograph no. 12. Washington, D.C.: U.S. Government Printing Office, 1965.

Gage, N. L., and David C. Berliner. *Educational Psychology.* Chicago: Rand McNally & Company, 1975.

Gagné, Robert M. *Conditions of Learning.* New York: Holt, Rinehart & Winston, 1959.

Gagné, Robert M., and Leslie J. Briggs. *Principles of Instructional Design.* New York: Holt, Rinehart & Winston, 1974.

Goldhober, Gerald M. "PAUSAL: A Computer Program to Identify and Measure Pauses." *Western Speech* 37 (Winter 1973): 23–26.

Montessori, Maria. *The Montessori Method.* New York: Schocken Books, 1964.

Rosenthal, Robert, and Lenore Jacobson. *Pygmalion in the Classroom.* New York: Holt, Rinehart & Winston, 1968.

Travers, Robert M. W. *Essentials of Learning: An Overview for Students of Education.* New York: Macmillan Co., 1967.

Myra Sadker and David Sadker

# 5. Questioning Skills

# Objectives

**1** To classify classroom questions according to Bloom's *Taxonomy of Educational Objectives: Cognitive Domain.*

**2** To construct classroom questions on all six levels of Bloom's *Taxonomy of Educational Objectives.*

**3** To describe additional teaching strategies for increasing the quantity and quality of student response.

The student teacher was attractive and composed. She quickly dispatched with the administrative details of classroom organization — attendance records and homework assignments. The classroom chatter about the Saturday night dance and the upcoming football game subsided as the tenth grade students settled into their seats. The students liked this teacher, for she had the knack of mixing businesslike attention to academic content with a genuine interest in her students. As the principal of Madison High walked by her room, he paused to watch the students settle into a discussion about *Hamlet.* Classroom operation appeared to be running smoothly, and he made a mental note to offer Ms. Ames a contract when her eight weeks of student teaching were over.

Had he stayed a little longer to hear the discussion, and had he been somewhat sophisticated in the quality of verbal interaction, he would not have been so satisfied.

*Ms. Ames:* I would like to discuss your reading assignment with you. As the scene begins, two clowns are on stage. What are they doing? Cheryl?

*Cheryl:* They are digging a grave.

*Ms. Ames:* Right. Who is about to be buried? Jim?

*Jim:* Ophelia.

*Ms. Ames:* Yes. One of the grave diggers uncovers the skull of Yorick. What occupation did Yorick once have? Donna?

*Donna:* He was the king's jester.

*Ms. Ames:* Good. A scuffle occurs by Ophelia's graveside. Who is fighting? Bill?

*Bill:* Laertes and Hamlet.

*Ms. Ames:* That's right. In what act and scene does Ophelia's burial occur? Tom?

*Tom:* Act V, Scene 1.

Throughout the forty-five minute English class, Ms. Ames asked a series of factual questions, received a series of one- and two-word replies

— and Shakespeare's play was transformed into a bad caricature of a television quiz show.

It is extremely important that teachers avoid ineffective questioning patterns such as the one above, for the questioning process has always been crucial to classroom instruction. The crucial role that questions play in the educational process has been stated by a number of educators.

> To question well is to teach well. In the skillful use of the question more than anything else lies the fine art of teaching; for in it we have the guide to clear and vivid ideas, and the quick spur to imagination, the stimulus to thought, the incentive to action.[1]

> What's in a question, you ask? Everything. It is the way of evoking stimulating response or stultifying inquiry. It is, in essence, the very core of teaching.[2]

> The art of questioning is . . . the art of guiding learning.[3]

It was John Dewey who pointed out that thinking itself is questioning. Unfortunately, research indicates that most student teachers, as well as experienced teachers, do not use effective questioning techniques. Think back to your own days in elementary and secondary school. You probably read your text and your class notes, studied (or, more accurately, memorized), and then waited in class for the teacher to call on you with a quick question, usually requiring only a brief reply. It did not seem to matter much whether the subject was language arts or social studies or science; questions revealed whether or not you remembered the material. But questions need not be used only in this way, and the appropriate use of questions can create an effective and powerful learning environment. Consider the following description of Mark Van Doren's use of questions:

> Mark would come into the room, and, without any fuss, would start talking about whatever was to be talked about. Most of the time he asked questions. His questions were very good, and if you tried to answer them intelligently, you found yourself saying excellent things that you did not know you knew, and that you had not, in fact, known before. He had "educed" them from you by his questions. His classes were literally "education" — they brought things out of you, they made your mind produce its own explicit ideas . . . . What he did have was the gift of communicating to them something of his own vital interest in things, something of his manner of approach; but the results were sometimes quite unexpected — and by that I mean good in a way that he had not anticipated, casting lights that he had not himself foreseen.[4]

It is all too easy to describe Van Doren as a gifted teacher and to dismiss his technique of questioning as an art to which most teachers can never aspire. It is our very strong belief that the teacher's effective use of questions is far too important to dismiss in this way. Unfortunately, research concerning the use of questions in the classroom suggests that most teachers do *not* use effective questioning techniques. If one were to review the research on questioning, the results would reveal both the importance of questioning in school and the need for teachers to improve their questioning technique. For example, did you know about any of the following facts or research that had been done about questioning techniques?

1. The first major study of classroom behavior was performed way back in 1912. The findings showed that 80 percent of classroom talk was devoted to asking, answering, or reacting to questions. Most of these questions were strictly memory, calling for only a superficial understanding of the material.[5]

2. Since 1912, the United States has seen several world wars, a depression, a dozen Presidents, the cure for several major diseases, the conquest of space, and tremendous social, economic, and political upheavals; but the state of questioning techniques in the classroom has remained basically unchanged. Studies into the 1970s show that most teachers still use questions as a major tool of learning, but the vast majority of these questions depend only on rote memory for a correct response.[6]

3. Teachers ask a tremendous number of questions. One study reveals that primary school teachers ask $3\frac{1}{2}$ to $6\frac{1}{2}$ questions per minute! Elementary school teachers average 348 questions a day. A recent study of student teachers found them asking 70 to 90 questions in several twenty-minute science lessons. Both at the elementary and secondary levels, there are an enormous number of questions asked by the typical teacher.[7]

4. Although teachers ask an incredible number of questions, they generally show little tolerance in waiting for student replies. Typically, only *one second* passes between the end of a question and the next verbal interaction! After the answer is given, only $\frac{9}{10}$ second passes before the teacher reacts to the answer. The tremendous number of questions asked and the brief amount of time provided before an answer is expected reinforce the finding that most questions do not require any substantive thought. Classroom questions simply call for the rapid recall of information.[8]

5. Although the research on the effect of questions on student achievement has accumulated slowly and at times is contradictory, in general findings do suggest that higher order questions, questions which require thought rather than memory, increase student achievement. In classes where higher order, thought-provoking questions are asked, students perform better on achievement tests.[9]

6. Studies also reveal that the quality and quantity of student answers increase when teachers provide students with time to think. If teachers can increase the one second of silence which usually follows a question to three seconds or more, student answers will reflect more thought, and more students will actively participate in the classroom.[10]

7. Although learning is designed to help students receive answers for their questions, become independent citizens, and understand their world, little provision is made in schools for student questions. The typical student asks approximately one question per month.[11]

The significant number of research findings related to classroom questions indicates that questions play a crucial role in the classroom and that teachers need to improve their questioning strategies. Other studies reveal that programs designed to improve this crucial skill have been effective.[12] A variety of self-instructional booklets have been published with the purpose of providing teachers with questioning skills. One that we have found to be particularly helpful as we developed this chapter was *Minicourse 9: Higher Cognitive Questioning* by Gall, Dunning, and Weathersby.[13] The activities in this chapter are designed to increase your mastery of questioning skills.

# Objective 1

To classify classroom questions according to Bloom's *Taxonomy of Educational Objectives: Cognitive Domain.*[14]

## LEARNING ACTIVITY 1.1

As the research in the introductory section reveals, questioning plays an important role in the classroom. Ever since Socrates, teaching and questioning have been viewed as integrally related activities. In order to be an effective teacher, one must be an effective questioner. The first step in effective questioning is to recognize that questions have distinct characteristics, serve various functions, and create different levels of thinking. Some questions require only factual recall; others cause students to go beyond memory and to use other thought processes in forming an answer. Both kinds of questions are useful, but the heavy reliance teachers place on the factual type of question does not provide the most effective learning environment. Learning the different kinds of questions and the different functions they serve is a crucial step in being able to use all types of questions effectively.

There are many terms and classifications for describing the different kinds of questions. Most of these classification systems are useful in that they provide a conceptual framework, a way of looking at questions. However, we have selected only one system, in order to simplify the process and eliminate repetitive terms. Bloom's *Taxonomy* is probably the best known system for classifying educational objectives as well as classroom questions. There are six levels of Bloom's *Taxonomy*, and questions at each level require the person responding to use a different kind of thought process. Teachers should be able to formulate questions on each of these six levels in order to encourage their students to engage in a variety of cognitive processes. Before teachers are able to formulate questions on each of these levels, they first must understand the definitions of the six categories, and they must be able to recognize questions written on each of these six levels. The six levels are:

1. Knowledge
2. Comprehension
3. Application
4. Analysis
5. Synthesis
6. Evaluation

The following definitions, examples, and exercises are designed to help you recognize and classify questions on the six cognitive levels of Bloom's *Taxonomy*. (By the way, taxonomy is another word for classification.)

### Level 1. Knowledge

The first level of the *Taxonomy*, knowledge, requires the student to recognize or recall information. The student is not asked to manipulate information, but merely to remember it just as it was learned. To answer a question on the knowledge level, the student must simply remember facts, observations, and definitions that have been learned previously.

### *Examples of Knowledge Questions*

What is the capital of Maine?

What color did the solution become when we added the second chemical?

Who is the secretary of state?

Who wrote *Hamlet*?

Recently, it has become fashionable to scoff at questions which ask the student to rely only on memory. For example, a common complaint about some college exams is that they ask students to "spit back" the information they have memorized from their text and class notes. However, memorization of material is important for several reasons. The knowledge, or memory, category is critical to all other levels of thinking. We cannot ask students to think at higher levels if they lack fundamental information. Some memorization of information is also required in order to perform a variety of tasks in our society, ranging from being an effective citizen to being a good parent. Our society expects that a good many things be memorized.

Although important, the knowledge category does have severe drawbacks, the main one being that teachers tend to overuse it. Most questions which teachers ask both in class discussions and on tests would be classified in the knowledge category. Another drawback to questions on this level is that much of what is memorized is rapidly forgotten. And a third drawback to memory questions is that they assess only a superficial and shallow understanding of an area. Parroting someone else's thoughts does not, in itself, demonstrate any real understanding. Further, use of knowledge questions promotes classroom participation and high success experiences for students. Students from lower socioeconomic backgrounds achieve more in classrooms characterized by a high frequency of knowledge questions. Recent studies show that effective teachers provide both low ability and high ability students with high success opportunities, and that in these successful classrooms students are responding correctly at least 70 to 80 percent of the time.[15] The use of knowledge questions plays a key role in establishing this high success rate.

Some words frequently found in knowledge questions are listed in the box that follows:

| *Words often found in knowledge questions* | |
|---|---|
| define | who? |
| recall | what? |
| recognize | where? |
| remember | when? |

# Your Turn

## KNOWLEDGE

The following questions will test your understanding of knowledge level questions and your ability to classify questions at the knowledge level of Bloom's *Taxonomy* correctly. Your answers will also provide you with a useful study guide when preparing for the Mastery Test.

In questions 1–5, mark a "T" for true and an "F" for false statements.

_____ 1. The first level of Bloom's *Taxonomy* requires higher order thinking.

_____ 2. Most classroom and test questions teachers ask are memory questions.

_____ 3. A drawback to knowledge, or memory, questions is that they are unimportant.

_____ 4. Knowledge, or memory, questions are important because they are necessary steps on the way to more complex, higher order questions.

_____ 5. All the questions asked so far in this activity (questions 1–4) are on the first level of the *Taxonomy* — Knowledge and Memory.

Mark a "K" in the space in front of those questions that are at the knowledge level and a "—" for those that are not.

_____ 6. Who discovered a cure for yellow fever?

_____ 7. Can you analyze the causes of World War I?

_____ 8. Where does the United States get most of its tin from?

_____ 9. What does this poem mean to you?

_____ 10. Who was the eighth President of the United States?

_____ 11. Define *antediluvian*. (The class has previously been given the definition of this word.)

_____ 12. Can you think of a title for this poem?

_____ 13. What do you predict would happen to teachers if this recession were to continue over the next several years?

_____ 14. When did the Spanish–American War end?

Check your answers with the answers and comments included in the Answer Key that follows. If you answered all correctly — terrific! One wrong is pretty good also. Two wrong suggests that you should check your answers again. If you got three or more wrong, perhaps you should reread this section to make sure that you understand it before you proceed to the next level.

## ANSWER KEY

### Your Turn: Knowledge

1. F. Knowledge, or memory, requires recall, a lower level activity.
2. T. Unfortunately.
3. F. Memory, or knowledge, questions are important. Learners must have mastery of a wide variety of information. Other levels of thought are not possible without such a base.
4. T.
5. T.
6. K.
7. —. Unless the student has just learned this material, and is remembering it, this is *not* a knowledge level question. It calls for analysis, a higher level thought process.
8. K.
9. —. Calls for higher order thinking.
10. K.
11. K.
12. —. Calls for a more creative thought process than recall or recognition.
13. —. Unless the student has been told what will happen if the recession continues, he or she must use a thought process at a higher level than memory to answer this question.
14. K.

### Level 2. Comprehension

Questions on the second level, comprehension, require the student to demonstrate that he or she has sufficient understanding to organize and arrange material mentally. The student must select those facts that are pertinent to answering the question. In order to answer a comprehension level question, the student must go beyond recall of information. The student must demonstrate a personal grasp of the material by being able to rephrase it, to give a description in his or her own words, and to use it in making comparisons.

For example, suppose a teacher asks, "What is the famous quote of Hamlet's that we memorized yesterday, the quotation in which he puzzles over the meaning and worth of existence?" By asking students to recall information, in this case a quotation, the teacher is asking a question on the knowledge level. However, if the teacher had asked instead, "What do you think Hamlet means when he asks, 'To be or not to be: that is the question'?", the teacher's question would have been on the comprehension level. With the second question, the student is required to rephrase information in his or her own words.

Frequently, comprehension questions ask students to interpret and translate material that is presented on charts, graphs, tables, and cartoons. For example, the following are comprehension questions:

### *Examples of Comprehension Questions*

What is the main idea that this chart presents?
Describe in your own words what Herblock is saying in this cartoon.

This use of the comprehension question requires the student to translate ideas from one medium to another.

It is important to remember that *the information necessary to answer comprehension questions should have been provided to the student.* For example, if a student has previously read or listened to material that discusses the causes of the Revolutionary War and then the student is asked to explain these causes in his own words, the student is being asked a comprehension question. However, if the student has *not* been given material explaining the causes of the

Revolutionary War and is asked to explain why the war started, he or she is *not* being asked a comprehension question, but, rather, a question on a different level of the *Taxonomy*.

> *Words often found in comprehension questions*
>
> describe              rephrase
> compare              put in your own words
> contrast              explain the main idea

# Your Turn

## COMPREHENSION

In questions 1–4, mark a "T" for true and an "F" for false statements.

_____  1. A comprehension question may require the student to use new information not previously provided.

_____  2. Comprehension questions may require students to rephrase information.

_____  3. It is possible to remember a definition without being able to put the definition in your own words.

_____  4. A comprehension question asks students to recall information exactly as they have learned it.

Some of the following questions are at the knowledge level and others are at the comprehension level. Write a "C" next to those questions on the comprehension level and a "K" next to those questions on the knowledge level.

_____  5. When did the American Revolution begin?

_____  6. Compare socialism and capitalism.

_____  7. How do whales differ from sharks?

_____  8. What is the meaning of this cartoon?

_____  9. Who is the author of "Stopping by Woods on a Snowy Evening"?

_____  10. What is the main idea of this poem?

_____  11. Describe what we saw on our visit to the planetarium.

_____  12. Compare Hemingway's style with that of Steinbeck.

_____  13. Where was the Declaration of Independence signed?

_____  14. Explain in your own words what the author suggests were the main reasons for the Civil War.

Check your answers with those in the Answer Key that follows. If you missed two or more, you had better reread the description of comprehension questions before going on to the next section.

## ANSWER KEY

### Your Turn: Comprehension

1. F. Although the student would use original phrasing, only previously provided information could be used.
2. T.
3. T. That's one reason why comprehension questions are important.
4. F. A comprehension question asks students to reorganize information and to phrase it in their own words.
5. K. Calls for recall of a fact.
6. C. Calls for a comparison.
7. C. Calls for a comparison.

8. C. Asks the student to translate from one medium to another.
9. K. Asks for the recall of a fact.
10. C. Asks students to reorganize information so that they can put the main idea in their own words.
11. C. Asks students to describe something in their own words.
12. C. Asks for a comparison.
13. K. Asks for the recall of a fact.
14. C. Again, placing information in "one's own words" is the key.

### Level 3. Application

It is not enough for students to be able to memorize information or even to rephrase and interpret what they have memorized. Students must also be able to apply information. A question that asks a student to apply previously learned information in order to reach an answer to a problem is at the application level of the *Taxonomy*.

Application questions require students to apply a rule or process to a problem and thereby determine the single right answer to that problem. In mathematics, application questions are quite common. For example,

$$\text{If} \quad X = 2 \text{ and } y = 5,$$
$$\text{then} \quad X^2 + 2y = \text{?}$$

But application questions are important in other subject areas as well. For example, in social studies, a teacher can provide the definitions of latitude and longitude and ask the student to repeat these definitions (knowledge). The teacher can then ask the student to compare the definitions of latitude and longitude (comprehension). At the application level, the teacher would ask the student to locate a point on a map by applying the definitions of latitude and longitude.

To ask a question at the application level in language arts, the following procedure might be used. After providing students with the definition of a haiku (a type of poem), a teacher would hand out a sheet with several different types of poems, then ask the students to select the poem which is a haiku, that is, the one which fits the definition of a haiku poem. To do this, the students must apply the definition to the various poems and select the poem which fits the definition.

In all the examples given, the student must apply knowledge in order to determine the single correct answer. Here are some other examples of questions at the application level.

### *Examples of Application Questions*

In each of the following cases, which of Newton's laws is being demonstrated?

According to our definition of socialism, which of the following nations would be considered socialist?

Write an example of the rule we have just discussed.

According to our criteria, which answer is correct?

If John works three hours to mow the lawn, and it takes Alice only two hours, how many hours would it take for them to mow the lawn together?

What is the rule that is appropriate in case 2?

| *Words often found in application questions* | |
|---|---|
| apply | write an example |
| classify | solve |
| use | how many? |
| choose | which? |
| employ | what is? |

# Your Turn

## APPLICATION

Indicate the level of the *Taxonomy* that each of the following questions represents. Use a "K" for those at the knowledge level, "C" for those at the comprehension level, and "Ap" for those at the application level.

_____ 1. What did I say we would do today?

_____ 2. What does "freedom" mean to you?

_____ 3. Using the rules we discussed, solve the following problems.

_____ 4. How are these two solutions similar?

_____ 5. Using the scientific method, solve this problem.

_____ 6. Who was the author of *The Great Gatsby*?

_____ 7. If these figures are correct, will the manager make a profit or suffer a loss?

_____ 8. Applying the rules of supply and demand, solve the following problem.

_____ 9. Classify the following plants according to the ten categories we reviewed.

Check your answers with those provided in the Answer Key that follows. If you missed two or more, reread this section and do the additional questions provided below. If you would like extra practice, the additional questions will provide you with that opportunity. When you feel ready, go on to the next level of the *Taxonomy*. At this point, you're half way through with the first learning activity.

*Additional Questions*

_____ 10. We have learned the definition of a noun. What are three examples of nouns?

_____ 11. Rephrase the definition of a noun in your own words.

_____ 12. Which of the following sentences has an error in punctuation?

_____ 13. State the three steps we have learned which must be followed before starting on a hike in the forest.

_____ 14. Solve this problem by using the procedure we discussed for quadratic equations.

_____ 15. According to our definition of a mammal, which of the five animals listed would be considered a mammal?

Check your answers in the Answer Key. If you still need help, you may want to check with your instructor, with some other students who are getting the exercises correct, or with the references listed at the end of the chapter. If you understand the application level, move on to the analysis level.

## ANSWER KEY
### Your Turn: Application

1. K. Calls for recall of teacher's words.
2. C. Interpret in your own words.
3. Ap. Learner must apply the rules to solve a problem.
4. C. Calls for a comparison.
5. Ap. Learner must apply the scientific method to solve the problem.
6. K. Recall of a name is needed.
7. Ap. Must apply information about profit and loss to determine if there will be a profit or a loss.
8. Ap. In this case, the rules of supply and demand must be applied. The verb "apply" is a giveaway.

9. Ap. To classify the plants, the definitions of the categories must be applied to each case.

*Additional Questions*

10. Ap. To write examples of the definition, the rules of the definition must be applied.
11. C. "In your own words" is the clue.
12. Ap. Applying the rules of punctuation to a specific example.
13. K. Recalling previous information.
14. Ap. To solve the problem, a certain procedure must be applied.
15. Ap. To choose the correct answer, the rules of the definition must be applied.

### Level 4. Analysis

Analysis questions are a higher order of questions that require students to think critically and in depth. Analysis questions ask students to engage in three kinds of cognitive processes.

1. To identify the motives, reasons, and/or causes for a specific occurrence.
2. To consider and analyze available information in order to reach a conclusion, an inference, or a generalization based on this information.
3. To analyze a conclusion, inference, or generalization to find evidence to support or refute it.

Following are examples of the three kinds of analysis questions:
1. To identify the motives, reasons, and/or causes for a specific occurrence.

What factors influenced the writings of Robert Frost?

Why did Senator Robert F. Kennedy decide to run for the Presidency?

Why was Israel selected as the site for the Jewish nation?

Why does our economy suffer from economic upswings and downturns?

In all these questions students are asked to discover the causes or reasons for certain events through analysis.

2. To consider and analyze available information in order to reach a conclusion, an inference, or a generalization based on this information.

After reading this textbook, how would you characterize the author's background, attitudes, and point of view?

Look at the diagram of this new invention. What do you think the purpose of this new invention is?

After studying the French, American, and Russian Revolutions, what can you conclude about the causes of revolution?

Now that your experiments are completed, what is your conclusion as to the name of the gas in the sample test tube?

This type of analysis question calls upon the learner to draw a conclusion, inference, or generalization based on evidence.

3. To analyze a conclusion, inference, or generalization to find evidence to support or refute it.

What information could you use to support the proposition that President Nixon was not a successful President?

What evidence can you cite to support the statement that Emily Dickinson was a more effective poet than Robert Frost?

Now that we have finished playing the simulation game, what did you experience that supports the idea of peaceful coexistence among nations?

These questions require students to analyze information to support a particular conclusion, inference, or generalization.

If you tried to answer any of these questions, you probably realized that several answers are possible. Furthermore, because it takes time to think and analyze, these questions cannot be answered quickly or without careful thought. The fact that several answers are possible and that sufficient time is needed to answer them is an indication that analysis questions are higher order ones. Unfortunately, teachers too often avoid higher order questions in favor of lower order ones, especially memory questions. But analysis questions are important because they foster critical thinking in students. Analysis questions not only help students learn what happened but also help them search for the reasons behind what happened.

A student cannot answer an analysis question by repeating information or by reorganizing material to put it into his or her own words. Students cannot rely directly on instructional materials when answering an analysis question.

Once again, analysis questions require students to analyze information in order to identify causes, to reach conclusions, or to find supporting evidence.

> *Words frequently found in analysis questions*
> identify motives or causes           why?
> draw conclusions
> determine evidence
> support
> analyze

*Review of the First Four Levels*

| | |
|---|---|
| 1. *Knowledge* | Requires memory only, repeating information exactly as memorized (define, recall, recognize, remember, who, what, where, when). |
| 2. *Comprehension* | Requires rephrasing and comparing information (describe, compare, contrast, rephrase, put in your own words, explain the main idea). |
| 3. *Application* | Requires application of knowledge to determine a single correct answer (apply, classify, use, choose, employ, write an example, solve, how many, which, what is). |
| 4. *Analysis* | Requires student to go beyond direct reliance on instructional materials to analyze a problem or situation.<br>1. Identify motives or causes<br>2. Draw conclusions<br>3. Determine evidence (support, analyze, conclude, why) |

# Your Turn

## ANALYSIS

_____ 1. Analysis questions call for higher order thinking. (true or false)

_____ 2. Which of the following processes is *not* required by analysis questions? (a) identifying evidence to support a statement (b) making a statement based on evidence (c) explaining motives or causes (d) making evaluations.

_____ 3. "Why" questions are often on the analysis level. (true or false)

_____ 4. Analysis questions require students only to rephrase information, to state it in their own words. (true or false)

_____ 5. Analysis questions require students to use or locate evidence in formulating their answers. (true or false)

Identify the levels of the following questions. (K = knowledge, C = comprehension, Ap = application, An = analysis)

_____ 6. Why didn't Hamlet act when he first learned of the treachery? (The student has not previously been given these reasons.)

_____ 7. What did Hamlet say?

_____ 8. What evidence can you find to support your statement that Hamlet was a coward? (The student has not previously been given this evidence.)

_____ 9. What was Hamlet's position or title in Denmark?

_____ 10. In your own words, how did we characterize Hamlet in yesterday's discussion?

_____ 11. After reading *Hamlet*, *Macbeth*, and *King Lear*, what can you conclude about Shakespeare's writing style? (These conclusions have not been given in previous reading or discussion.)

_____ 12. Using the definition of "climax," what part of *Hamlet* would you consider to be the climax?

Check your answers with the Answer Key that follows. Two or more wrong answers suggest you should review this section and answer the additional questions. If you made fewer than two errors, you may wish to solidify your expertise by answering the additional questions, anyway. If not, move on to the fifth level of the *Taxonomy*, Synthesis.

*Additional Questions*

_____ 13. When did Robert Kennedy campaign for the Democratic nomination for Presidency?

_____ 14. Why did R. F. Kennedy lose the Oregon primary? (The causes have not been given previously in reading or discussion.)

_____ 15. What can you conclude about the narrow victory for R. F. Kennedy over Eugene McCarthy in California? (The conclusions have not been given previously in reading or discussion.)

_____ 16. Can you analyze Kennedy's campaign strategy?

_____ 17. What evidence can you cite to support the contention that had Robert Kennedy lived, he would have won the Presidency?

_____ 18. How would you describe Kennedy's campaign style?

The answers are in the Answer Key. If you missed more than one of these additional questions, find out why. If the reading and examples aren't working for you, check with the references at the end of the chapter, with another student, or with your teacher. It is important that you understand the analysis level before you move on to the last two levels.

## ANSWER KEY

### Your Turn: Analysis

1. True.
2. (d) Making evaluations belongs at another level of the *Taxonomy*.
3. True. "Why" questions usually require the analysis of data to locate evidence or to determine causes, reasons, or motives.
4. False. Rephrasing information is required when a student answers a comprehension question.
5. True.
6. An. The student must analyze Hamlet's actions to identify a motivation.
7. K. Memory only is required.
8. An. Evidence to support a statement is sought.
9. K. Only memory is required.
10. C. Rephrasing a previous discussion.
11. An. A conclusion is called for.
12. Ap. Applying a definition to *Hamlet* to determine an answer.

## Level 5. Synthesis

Synthesis questions are higher order questions that ask students to perform original and creative thinking. These kinds of questions require students (1) to produce original communications, (2) to make predictions, or (3) to solve problems. Although application questions also require students to solve problems, synthesis questions differ in that they do not require a single correct answer but, instead, allow a variety of creative answers. Here are some examples of the different kinds of synthesis questions:

1. To produce original communications.

   Construct a collage of pictures and words that represent your values and feelings.

   What's a good name for this machine?

   Write a letter to the editor on a social issue of concern to you.

2. To make predictions.

   What would the United States be like if the South had won the Civil War?

   How would life be different if school were not mandatory?

   How would life be different if the courts did not exist?

3. To solve problems.

   How can we measure the height of a building without being able to go into it?

   How can we raise money for our ecology project?

Teachers can use synthesis questions to help develop the creative abilities of students. Unfortunately, as in the case of analysis questions, teachers too often avoid synthesis questions in favor of lower order questions, particularly knowledge questions. Synthesis questions rely on a thorough understanding of material. Students should not take wild guesses in order to answer synthesis questions. For example, one synthesis question that we suggested, "What would the United States be like if the South had won the Civil War?" requires the student to have a firm grasp of information before being able to offer a sound prediction.

To review, synthesis questions require predictions, original communications, or problem solving in which a number of answers are possible.

> *Words often found in synthesis questions*
>
> predict                   construct
> produce                   how can we improve?
> write                     what would happen if?
> design                    can you devise?
> develop                   how can we solve?
> synthesize

# Your Turn

## SYNTHESIS

In questions 1–10, identify the level of the questions by using the code provided (K = knowledge, C = comprehension, Ap = application, An = analysis, and S = synthesis).

_____ 1. What is the state capital?

_____ 2. Where is it located?

_____ 3. Point it out on the map.

_____ 4. If you could decide on a location for a new state capital, what location would you choose?

_____ 5. Why?

_____ 6. What would happen if we had two state capitals?

_____ 7. Draw a simple blueprint of your ideal state capital.

_____ 8. Quote what your textbook says about the primary function of a state capital.

_____ 9. Describe this primary function.

_____ 10. Given the categories of different kinds of state capitols, how would you classify the capitol of Maine?

_____ 11. Synthesis questions require students to do all the following *except*
   (a) make predictions
   (b) solve problems
   (c) rely primarily on memory
   (d) construct original communication

_____ 12. Synthesis questions require original and creative thought from students. (true or false)

   The Answer Key that follows will provide you with feedback on your progress in this section. If you want additional practice, then tackle these questions.

*Additional Questions*

_____ 13. How would you describe your school?

_____ 14. What would your ideal school be like?

_____ 15. Write a letter describing your ideal school.

_____ 16. What name would you give to this school?

_____ 17. Why?

# ANSWER KEY

## Your Turn: Synthesis

1. K.
2. K, C, or Ap. Depending on the student response, it could be at any of these levels. Pure repetition would be the knowledge level. Rephrasing the description of the location would place the answer at the comprehension level. Actually going to a map to point it out would place the response on the application level.
3. Ap. Calls for the student to demonstrate or apply the information.
4. S. Calls for problem solving with more than one answer possible.
5. An. Calls for evidence to support decision.
6. S. Calls for a prediction.
7. S. Original communication required.
8. K. Memorization of author's comments.
9. C. Rephrasing and description needed.
10. Ap. The student needs to apply rules in order to solve a problem.
11. (c). Synthesis is a higher order activity that calls for much more than memorizing.
12. True.

*Additional Questions*

13. C. Description is all that is necessary to answer this question. However, if the student responds to this question with a creative essay, it could be considered synthesis.
14. S. Response to this question calls for prediction, an original statement, and some problem solving.
15. S. Original communication.
16. S. Problem solving. Whenever an original name or title or main idea is called for, we are at the synthesis level.
17. An. Supporting evidence needed to explain the reason(s) for the name that was selected. To explain "why."

## Level 6. Evaluation

The last level of the *Taxonomy* is evaluation. Evaluation, like synthesis and analysis, is a higher order mental process. Evaluation questions do not have a single correct answer. They require the student to judge the merit of an idea, a solution to a problem, or an aesthetic work. They may also ask the student to offer an opinion on an issue. Following are some examples of different kinds of evaluation questions:

### Examples of Evaluation Questions

Do you think schools are too hard?

Should young children be allowed to read any book they want, no matter what it is about?

Which picture do you like best?

Which song do you prefer?

Is busing an appropriate remedy for desegregating schools?

Which approach offers the best method for attacking this problem?

Do you think that the statement "Americans never had it so good" is true?

Which U.S. Senator is the most effective?

In order to express your opinion on an issue or to make a judgment on the merit of an idea, solution, or aesthetic work, you must use some criteria. You must use either objective standards or a personal set of values to make an evaluation. For example, if you answer the last question above using a personal set of values, you might decide that the senator whose voting record is most congruent with your own political philosophy is the most effective senator. If you are strongly against defense spending or strongly in favor of civil rights legislation, these personal values would be reflected in your evaluation of the most effective senator.

Another way of evaluating senators would be through the use of objective criteria. Such criteria might include attendance records, campaign financing practices, influence on other senators, the number of sponsored bills that became law, etc. By comparing each senator to these criteria, a judgment can be made in relation to "the most effective senator."

Of course, many individuals use a combination of objective criteria and personal values when making an evaluation. The important thing to remember about evaluation questions is that some standard must be used. Differing standards are quite acceptable, and they naturally result in different answers. Evaluation questions are higher order questions, and different answers are expected.

| *Words  often  used  in  evaluation  questions* | |
|---|---|
| judge | give your opinion |
| argue | which is the better picture, solution, etc.? |
| decide | |
| evaluate | do you agree? |
| assess | would it be better? |

### *Review of the Taxonomy*

1. *Knowledge* — Requires memory only, repeating information exactly as memorized (define, recall, recognize, remember, who, what, where, when).

2. *Comprehension* — Requires rephrasing, rewording, and comparing information (describe, compare, contrast, rephrase, put in your own words, explain the main idea).

3. *Application* — Requires application of knowledge to determine a single correct answer (apply, classify, choose, employ, write an example, solve, how many, which, what is).

4. *Analysis* —
   1. identify motives or causes
   2. draw conclusions
   3. determine evidence
   (support, analyze, conclude, why)

5. *Synthesis* —
   1. make predictions
   2. produce original communications
   3. solve problems (more than one possible answer)

(predict, produce, write, design, develop, synthesize, construct, how can we improve?, what happens if?, how can we solve?, can you devise?)

6. *Evaluation*

1. make judgments
2. offer opinions
(judge, argue, decide, evaluate, assess, give your opinion, which is better?, do you agree?, would it be better?)

# Your Turn

## EVALUATION

Using all levels of the *Taxonomy*, classify the following questions (K = knowledge, C = comprehension, Ap = application, An = analysis, S = synthesis, and E = evaluation).

_____ 1. Who was the founder of the school of abstract art?

_____ 2. Describe the first attempts of the pioneers of abstract art.

_____ 3. What were some of the factors which motivated Picasso to join this new school?

_____ 4. We have read about the techniques of Picasso and Miro. Compare and contrast Picasso's techniques to those of Miro.

_____ 5. Which artist do you prefer, Miro or Picasso?

_____ 6. Paint your own abstract piece.

_____ 7. We have learned about the principle of balance. How is it used in this work?

_____ 8. Considering the different kinds of abstract paintings we have studied, what generalizations can you make about abstract art?

_____ 9. What do you predict is the future of abstract art?

_____ 10. What is your opinion of abstract art?

## ANSWER KEY

Your Turn: Evaluation

1. K. Recall required.
2. C. Description in one's own words needed.
3. K or An. Knowledge if the material was already learned. Analysis if the causes must be thought out.
4. C. Calls for comparison.
5. E. Calls for a judgment.
6. S. Original communicat on.
7. Ap. Calls for the applcation of a principle or rule to a given work.
8. An. Asks student to consider evidence and make a generalization.
9. S. Prediction called for.
10. E. Calls for a judgment.

At this point, we have reviewed all levels of the *Taxonomy*, and you should have a good idea of whether or not you are ready for the Mastery Test. In the Mastery Test you will be asked to identify the levels of a number of questions; all six levels of the *Taxonomy* will be represented. If, before taking the Mastery Test, you would like to have some more practice and also to compare your responses with those of another student, you might want to try Learning Activity 1.2, "The Question Master Game." You will find it in the perforated section at the back of the book. Two to six people can play at a time. The game should provide you with more practice in understanding the *Taxonomy* and in classifying questions. As a side benefit, you might enjoy it and, undoubtedly, you will be victorious over siblings, friends, relatives, and strangers who probably will not be able to use the *Taxonomy* with your facile abandon.

## LEARNING ACTIVITY 1.2

**THE QUESTION MASTER GAME**

The Question Master Game is designed to help you achieve competence in the first objective: "To classify questions on all six levels of Bloom's *Taxonomy*." In addition, we hope that you will enjoy playing the game.

To play the Question Master Game, you must be able to recall specific information about the characteristics of questions on the different levels of the *Taxonomy*; you must be able to classify questions on the various levels of the *Taxonomy*; and you should try to maintain your sense of humor. Having read Learning Activity 1.1 should help you to achieve the first two requirements. (Turn to Appendix A at back of the book to play.)

# Mastery Test

## OBJECTIVE 1   To classify classroom questions according to Bloom's *Taxonomy of Educational Objectives: Cognitive Domain.*

Read the paragraph below and then classify the following questions according to their appropriate level on Bloom's *Taxonomy*. Use the following abbreviations: (K = knowledge, C = comprehension, Ap = application, An = analysis, S = synthesis, and E = evaluation).

To pass the Mastery Test, you should classify 10 out of the 11 questions accurately. Good luck!

School reading texts were also studied. It was found that the major reading series used in almost all public and private schools across the country teach that being a girl means being inferior. In these texts, boys are portrayed as being able to do so many things: they play with bats and balls, they work with chemistry sets, they do magic tricks that amaze their sisters, and they show initiative and independence as they go on trips by themselves and get part-time jobs. Girls do things too: they help with the housework, bake cookies and sit and watch their brothers — that is assuming they are present. In 144 texts studied, there were 881 stories in which the main characters are boys and only 344 in which a girl is the central figure.

Nancy Frazier and Myra Sadker, *Sexism in School and Society*, New York: Harper and Row, 1973, pp. 103–104.

_____  1. In your own words, compare the portrayal of males and females in school texts.

_____  2. Why do you think feminists are concerned with the passive way in which girls are portrayed in textbooks?

_____  3. What do boys do in the school reading texts that were studied?

_____  4. What is the main idea of this paragraph?

_____  5. Considering the category descriptions that we have studied of sexist and nonsexist books, how would you classify *Miracles on Maple Hill*?

_____  6. What would your ideal nonsexist book be like?

_____  7. How many texts were analyzed for sexism?

_____  8. If all books became nonsexist during the next five years, what do you predict would be the effects on children?

_____  9. Why do you think that girls have been portrayed in such a stereotyped manner in school texts?

_____  10. What is your opinion on the issue of sexism in books?

_____  11. Do you think that sexist books should be banned from children's libraries?

## ANSWER KEY
Mastery Test, Objective 1

1. C   2. An   3. K   4. C   5. Ap   6. S   7. K   8. S   9. An   10. E   11. E

# Objective 2

To construct classroom questions on all six levels of Bloom's *Taxonomy of Educational Objectives*.

## LEARNING ACTIVITY 2.1

The first, and perhaps the most difficult, step in learning to ask effective classroom questions is that of gaining a thorough understanding of Bloom's *Taxonomy*. Now that you have demonstrated your ability to classify questions, you are ready to begin constructing them. Effective classroom questions make provision for student thinking on all levels of the *Taxonomy*. Although during a short period of time only one or two levels of the *Taxonomy* may be reflected in a teacher's questions, over the course of an entire semester students should have ample opportunity to answer questions phrased at all levels. The sample questions and the information in Learning Activity 1.1 provide you with useful information for constructing questions. The following review should provide you with a ready reference as you construct questions on the various levels of the *Taxonomy*.

**SUGGESTIONS FOR CONSTRUCTING QUESTIONS**

In the next few pages, we will review the nature of the cognitive processes and the verbs and key phrases that are frequently associated with specific levels of the *Taxonomy*. However, as you go over this review, remember that it is important to analyze each question you write, because inclusion of key phrases is not an unconditional guarantee of the taxonomic level of a particular question. After the brief review, you will get a chance to practice constructing questions that pertain to a specific reading selection.

1. *Knowledge:*

| | |
|---|---|
| recall | who? |
| define | what? |
| recognize | where? |
| identify | when? |

A knowledge question requires students to recall or recognize information.

2. *Comprehension:*

| | |
|---|---|
| describe | in your own words compare similarities and differences |
| compare | |
| illustrate | |
| interpret | derive main idea |
| rephrase | |
| reorder | |
| contrast | |
| differentiate | |
| explain | |

To answer a comprehension level question, the student must be able to organize previously learned material so that he or she can rephrase it, describe it in his or her own words, and use it for making comparisons.

3. *Application:*

| | |
|---|---|
| apply | select |
| solve (one answer only is correct) | use |
| | employ |
| classify | |
| choose | |

An application question asks students to use previously learned information in order to solve a problem.

4. *Analysis:*

| | |
|---|---|
| analyze | why? |
| identify motive, cause, or reason | determine the evidence |
| | determine a conclusion |
| conclude | |
| infer | |
| distinguish | |
| deduce | |
| detect | |

Analysis questions ask students (1) to identify reasons, causes, and motives; (2) to consider available evidence in order to reach a conclusion, inference, or generalization; and (3) to analyze a conclusion, inference, or generalization to find supporting evidence.

5. *Synthesis:*

solve (more than one answer correct)
predict
write

draw
construct
produce
originate
propose
plan
design
synthesize
combine
develop

Synthesis questions require students (1) to produce original communications, (2) to make predictions, or (3) to solve problems.

6. *Evaluation:*

| | |
|---|---|
| judge | what is your opinion? |
| argue | do you agree? |
| decide | which is better? |
| appraise | |
| evaluate | |

Evaluation questions ask students to judge the merit of an idea, a solution to a problem, or an aesthetic work.

Before proceeding into the exercises in this learning activity, you may find it helpful to keep in mind the following general comments about question construction.

It is important to phrase your questions carefully. You have probably been a student in more than one class where the teacher's questions were so cumbersome or so wordy that you lost the meaning of the question. In fact, one study indicates that 40 percent of teacher questions are ambiguous and poorly phrased. You should be explicit enough to ensure understanding of your questions, but, at the same time, you should avoid using too many words. When a question is too wordy, students become confused and unable to respond; frequently, the result is that the question has to be rephrased.

Now you are ready to construct questions at each of the six levels of Bloom's *Taxonomy*. Read the paragraph in the test that follows. Then construct at least 12 questions relating to it. When you are done, you should have two questions on each of the six levels of the *Taxonomy*. As you construct your questions, keep the following in mind. What facts are in the paragraph that you might want students to recognize or recall (knowledge level)? What are the main points in the reading selection that you would want students to comprehend and be able to rephrase in their own words (comprehension level)? What information is there in the paragraph that students could apply to solving problems, to classifying, or to giving examples (application level)? What questions can you ask about the reading selection that require students to consider reasons and motives, to examine the validity of a conclusion, or to seek evidence to support a conclusion (analysis level)? Using this paragraph as a springboard, how can you stimulate original student thought — creative problem solving, the making of predictions, and the production of original communication — in writing, music, dance, art, etc. (synthesis level)? Finally, what issues can you raise from the material in this paragraph that will cause students to judge the merit of an idea, the solution to a problem, or an aesthetic work (evaluation level)? As you develop your questions, it may be helpful to review the information in Learning Activities 1.1, 1.2, and 2.1.

After you have finished writing your questions, compare them with the sample questions in the Answer Key that follows. Obviously, a wide variety of questions could be written pertaining to this particular selection. The sample questions are simply meant to give you a basis for comparison and to indicate the kinds of questions that can be asked on each of the six levels of the *Taxonomy*.

Compare your questions with the information and examples in Learning Activities 1.1 and 2.1. Discuss the questions you develop with your instructor and with other members of your class. If 11 or 12 of your questions accurately reflect the appropriate level of the *Taxonomy*, you are doing very well. If you miss two or three, you will probably want to review the information in Learning Activity 2.1 and to study the sample questions very carefully, particularly those on the levels where you did not construct the questions accurately. If you miss more than three, a careful review of the Learning Activity 1.1 and additional practice in constructing questions may be necessary before you take the Mastery Test.

# Your Turn

## CONSTRUCTING QUESTIONS ON THE SIX LEVELS OF BLOOM'S TAXONOMY

In Des Moines, Iowa, two high school students and a junior high student, in defiance of a ban by school authorities, wore black armbands to class as a protest against the Vietnam War. As a result, they were suspended from school. But the U.S. Supreme Court later ruled the suspensions were illegal, holding that the first amendment to the Constitution protects the rights of public school children to express their political and social views during school hours.

. . .

This case illustrates a significant new trend in American life. Young people, particularly those under 21, are demanding that they be granted rights long denied them as a matter of course. And, with increasing frequency, they are winning those rights.

Michael Dorman, *Under 21* (New York: Delacorte, 1970) pp. 3 and 5.

1. Knowledge level questions

_____

_____

_____

_____

2. Comprehension level questions

_____

_____

_____

_____

3. Application level questions

_____

_____

_____

_____

4. Analysis level questions

_____

_____

_____

_____

5. Synthesis level questions

_____

_____

_____

_____

6. Evaluation level questions

_____

_____

_____

_____

_____

_____

## ANSWER KEY

### Your Turn: Constructing Questions on the Six Levels of Bloom's *Taxonomy*

Here are some questions on the six levels of the *Taxonomy* that you might have asked about the paragraphs. They are not the *only* questions that could have been asked but are simply meant to provide examples.

1. *Knowledge level questions*
   1. What action did the three students in Des Moines, Iowa, take that caused their suspension?

2. What was the ruling of the Supreme Court on their case?
3. What part of the Constitution did the Supreme Court refer to as a basis for its decision?

2. *Comprehension level questions*
   1. What is the main idea in this paragraph?
   2. In your own words, explain why the Supreme Court declared the suspensions illegal.

3. *Application level questions*
    1. Considering the ruling in the Des Moines case, what would the legal ruling be on a student who, despite a ban by school authorities, wore a yellow cloth star sewn on her jacket as a protest against the United Nations policy toward Israel?
    2. Considering the Supreme Court ruling in the Des Moines case, what do you think the legal ruling would be on a group of students who blockaded the entrance to a classroom as a protest against race discrimination?

4. *Analysis level questions*
    1. Why did the Supreme Court support the rights of students to express their political and social beliefs during school hours?
    2. What evidence, other than the specific case described in this paragraph, can you cite to support the conclusion that young people are now gaining long denied rights?

5. *Synthesis level questions*
    1. Develop a short story that portrays a young person seeking to attain a legal right denied to those under 21.
    2. If children gained the full legal rights enjoyed by adults in America, what implications would it have for family life?

6. *Evaluation level questions*
    1. What is your opinion on the issue of minors enjoying the full legal rights of adults?
    2. If you had been a judge on the Court in the case of the Des Moines students who protested the Vietnam War with black armbands despite a school ban, how would you have ruled?

## LEARNING ACTIVITY 2.2

If you feel that you need further practice in constructing questions or if you would like to improve your question construction skills, Learning Activity 2.2 provides that opportunity. This learning activity involves another way of playing the Question Master Game. All you need do is make one rule change. Instead of using the "Classification Cards" that have already been developed, you must construct a question of your own whenever you land on a square marked with a "C." The question must be at the same level of the *Taxonomy* as the number of spaces you move. Avoid using the same question more than once, and try to vary your question stems.

### *Example*

The die (or cards or spinner) indicates "6," and you move your piece six spaces. If you land on a "C" space, you must construct a question at level six of the *Taxonomy* (Evaluation). If you fail to do this, you must go back three spaces from your original space. If you are successful, you can remain on that space until your next turn.

The "C" spaces now represent *Construct* a question rather than *Classify* a question. All other rules remain the same. Any missed questions result in going backward three spaces.

| *If the die shows:* | *Question must be at:* |
| --- | --- |
| 1 | Knowledge |
| 2 | Comprehension |
| 3 | Application |

| | |
|---|---|
| 4 | Analysis |
| 5 | Synthesis |
| 6 | Evaluation |

Any disputes that cannot be resolved by referring to the explanations and examples in Learning Activity 1.1 will have to be arbitrated by your instructor.

Good luck!

# Mastery Test

**OBJECTIVE 2**  To construct classroom questions on all six levels of Bloom's *Taxonomy of Educational Objectives*.

Read the following paragraphs and then construct twelve questions based on this reading selection. Two of your questions must be at the knowledge level, two at the comprehension level, two at the application level, two at the analysis level, two at the synthesis level, and two at the evaluation level. To pass this Mastery Test successfully, 9 of the 12 questions should accurately reflect the level of the *Taxonomy* at which they are constructed.

Death may be an unwelcome terrifying enemy, a skeleton with an evil grin who clutches an ugly scythe in his bony hand. Or death may be a long awaited friend who waits quietly, invisibly, beside the bed of a dying patient to ease his pain, his loneliness, his weariness, his hopelessness.

Man alone among the things that live knows that death will come. Mice and trees and microbes do not. And man, knowing that he has to die, fears death, the great unknown, as a child fears the dark. "We fear to be we know not what, we know not where," said John Dryden. But what man dreads more is the dying, the relentless process in which he passes into extinction alone and helpless and despairing. So he puts death and dying out of his mind, denying that they exist, refusing to discuss them openly, trying desperately to control them. He coins phrases like "never say die," and somehow, when he says something is "good for life," he means forever. Unable to bear the thought of ceasing to be, he comforts himself with thoughts of a pleasant afterlife in which he is rewarded for his trials on earth, or he builds monuments to himself to perpetuate at least his memory if not his body.

John Langone, *Death Is A Noun* (Boston: Little-Brown, 1972) pp. 3–4.

Now that you have read the paragraphs, construct 12 questions in the appropriate spaces below. When you write the application level questions, you may find it helpful to consider that the following information has previously been given to the class: (1) definitions of various literary images including metaphor, simile, and personification; (2) a list of terms and definitions that characterize various psychological states; and (3) several novels that portray death as a central or minor theme.

*Knowledge questions*

1. _____

_____

2. _____

_____

*Comprehension questions*

1. _____

_____

2. _____
   _____

*Application questions*

1. _____
   _____

2. _____
   _____

*Analysis questions*

1. _____
   _____

2. _____
   _____

*Synthesis questions*

1. _____
   _____

2. _____
   _____

*Evaluation questions*

1. _____
   _____

2. _____
   _____

# ANSWER KEY

## Mastery Test, Objective 2

In order to pass the Mastery Test for objective 2, you must have constructed 12 questions relating to the given reading selection. There should be two questions on each level of the *Taxonomy*; at least 9 of the 12 questions you develop should be well constructed and should accurately reflect the appropriate taxonomic level.

Obviously there is a wide variety of questions that could be constructed on the given paragraphs. Below are three sample questions for each of the six levels of the *Taxonomy*.

### Knowledge questions

1. What are two somewhat contradictory images that man holds of death?
2. Who alone, among all things that live, realizes the eventual coming of death?
3. Who was the author who said, "We fear to be we know not what, we know not where"?

### Comprehension questions

1. In your own words, what did Dryden mean by his sentence "We fear to be we know not what, we know not where"?
2. People often hold different images of death. Compare two different conceptions of death that people hold.
3. What is the main idea of the second paragraph?

### Application questions

1. Considering our previous study of metaphor and simile, which of these two literary devices applies to the statement in the first paragraph: "Death may be an unwelcome, terrifying enemy, a skeleton with an evil grin who clutches an ugly scythe in his bony hand"?
2. You have previously been given a list of terms and definitions that characterize various psychological states. Which of these terms best applies to people's tendency to push the reality of death and dying out of their minds?
3. Give an example of a character from one of the novels we have read this semester who clearly exhibits this tendency to deny the reality of death.

### Analysis questions

1. Why do you think that people push the reality of death and dying out of their minds?
2. The author suggests that people are unable to face the notion of death. What evidence can you find to support this contention?
3. Considering the information you have in these paragraphs, how do you think the author feels people should react to death?

### Synthesis questions

1. Write a poem or a short story in which the main character must face his own or another's impending death.
2. What do you predict life would be like if there were no death?
3. What ideas can you propose to help people become more accepting of their own mortality?

### Evaluation questions

1. Do you think it would be better for people to ignore death, as many do now, or to be more aware and accepting of death in their daily living patterns?
2. What do you judge to be the finest literary or artistic expression which has the inevitability of death as its central theme?
3. In your opinion, is it a good idea for children to read books about death?

# Objective 3

To describe additional teaching strategies for increasing the quantity and quality of student response.

## LEARNING ACTIVITY 3

Much of this chapter has emphasized the need to ask questions on all levels of Bloom's *Taxonomy*. This is an important step in encouraging a variety of levels of student thought and discussion. But just asking thought-provoking questions isn't enough; in fact, one research study found that there was only a limited correspondence between the cognitive level of teachers' questions and the cognitive level of students' answers. When teachers asked application, analysis, or synthesis level questions, there was only a 50–50 chance that students would answer on the appropriate application, analysis, or synthesis level.[16]

So besides asking higher order questions, you will need to determine whether the student's response adequately matches the question you have asked. If the student's response is not accurate — or if it is inadequate in matching the level of your question — it's time to employ some new teaching strategies.

Recently a noted educator, John Goodlad, along with a team of researchers, conducted an in-depth observation study of over a thousand classrooms. As a result of this research he observed that

> there is a paucity of praise and correction of students' performance as well as of teacher guidance, in how to do better next time. Teachers tend not to respond in overtly positive or negative ways to the work students do. And our impression is that classes generally tend not to be strongly positive or strongly negative places to be. Enthusiasm and joy and anger are kept under control.[17]

Goodlad concluded that the emotional tone of schools is neither punitive nor joyful. Rather, he says, the school environment can best be characterized as "flat."

Part of the reason for this bland quality may lie in the way teachers deal with student answers to questions. Trained observers visited more than a hundred classrooms along the East Coast and analyzed teacher reactions to student answers and comments. They found that

- Teachers don't praise students very often. Approximately 10 percent of teacher reactions praise students. In approximately 25 percent of the classrooms observed, teachers never praised students.

- Teacher criticism is even more rare. (In this study, criticism was defined as an explicit statement that a student's behavior or work was wrong.) Approximately two-thirds of the hundred classrooms observed contained no criticism. In the approximately thirty-five classrooms where teachers did criticize students, it constituted only 5 percent of teacher interaction.

- Teacher remediation of student answers was quite frequent. It occurred in all classrooms and constituted approximately 30 percent of all teacher reactions. (Teacher remediation was defined as teacher comments or questions that would help students reach a more accurate or higher level response.)

- But neither praise, criticism nor remediation is the most frequent teacher response. Teachers most often simply *accept* student answers. Accept means that they say "Uh-huh" or "O.K." or that they don't say anything at all. Acceptance occurred in all of the classrooms and it constituted over 50 percent of teacher reactions. There was more acceptance than praise, remediation and criticism combined.[18]

The way the classroom question cycle most often goes is:

- Teacher asks a question.
- Student gives an answer.
- Teacher says "O.K."

The O.K. classroom is probably a bland, flat place in which to learn. Further, the O.K. classroom may not be O.K. in terms of encouraging student achievement. Research on teaching effectiveness indicates that students need specific feedback in order to understand what is expected of them, to correct errors, and to get help in improving their performance. However, if a student answers or questions, and the teacher reacts by saying "Uh-huh" or "O.K." the student is not getting the specific feedback he or she needs. Also these flat "acceptance" reactions to student comments are not likely to encourage high quality of student thought and discussion.

There are specific strategies you can use in reacting to student answers so you can avoid the trap of the O.K. classroom. The remainder of this learning activity is comprised of four brief sections. Each discusses a teaching technique that can help you increase the quantity and quality of student responses in your classroom.

### Wait Time[19]

If we were to stop and listen outside a classroom door, we might hear classroom interaction similar to this:

*Teacher:* Who wrote the poem "Stopping by Woods on a Snowy Evening"? Tom?

*Tom:* Robert Frost.

*Teacher:* Good. What action takes place in the poem? Sally?

*Sally:* A man stops his sleigh to watch the woods get filled with snow.

*Teacher:* Yes. Emma, what thoughts go through the man's mind?

*Emma:* He thinks how beautiful the woods are . . . . (She pauses for a second)

*Teacher:* What else does he think about? Joe?

*Joe:* He thinks how he would like to stay and watch. (Pauses for a second)

*Teacher:* Yes — and what else? Rita? (Waits half a second) Come on, Rita, you can get the answer to this. (Waits half a second) Well, why does he feel he can't stay there indefinitely and watch the woods and the snow?

*Rita:* He knows he's too busy. He's got too many things to do to stay there for so long.

*Teacher:* Good. In the poem's last line, the man says that he has miles to go before he sleeps. What might sleep be a symbol for? Sarah?

*Sarah:* Well, I think it might be — (Pauses a second)

*Teacher:* Think, Sarah. (Teacher waits for half a second) All right then — Mike? (She waits again for half a second) John? (Waits half a second) What's the matter with everyone today? Didn't you do the reading?

There are a number of comments we could make about this slice of classroom interaction. We could note the teacher's development from primarily lower order questions to those of a somewhat higher order nature. We could comment on the inability of the students to answer her later questions and on the teacher's increasing frustration. But, perhaps the most devastating thing we could say about this interaction segment is that it lasts for less than a single minute.

In less than one minute of dialogue this teacher manages to construct and ask six questions, some of them, at least, requiring a fairly high cognitive level of response. As discussed earlier, a very rapid questioning rate is not at all atypical of many classrooms across the country. The mean number of questions a teacher asks averages between two and three per minute, and it is not unusual to find as many as seven to ten questions asked by a teacher during a single minute of classroom instruction.

The effect of this incredibly rapid "bombing rate" is that students have very little time to think. In fact, research shows that the mean amount of time a teacher waits after asking a question is approximately *one second*! If the students are not able to think quickly enough to come up with a response at this split second pace, the teacher repeats the question, rephrases it, asks a different question, or calls on another student. Moreover, if a student manages to get a response in, the teacher reacts or asks another question within an average time of nine-tenths of a second. It is little wonder that high rates of teacher questioning tend to be associated with low rates of student questions and student declarations. In classrooms where questions are asked at this "bombing rate," students have little time to think, little time to express themselves, and often little desire to express themselves in an atmosphere so charged with a sense of verbal evaluation and testing.

When teachers break out of the "bombing rate" pattern and learn to increase their wait time from one second to three to five seconds after asking a question, many significant changes occur in their classrooms. For example:

1. Students give longer answers.
2. Students volunteer more appropriate answers, and failures to respond are less frequent.
3. Student comments on the analysis and synthesis levels increase. They make more evidence–inference responses and more speculative responses.
4. Students ask more questions.
5. Students exhibit more confidence in their comments, and those students whom teachers rate as relatively slow learners offer more questions and more responses.

Simply by increasing his or her ability to wait longer after asking a question, a teacher can effect some striking changes in the quantity and the quality of student response. It is not as easy as you might think to learn to wait three to five seconds after asking a question. If teachers do not get an immediate response to a question, the natural reaction seems to be one of panic — an assumption that the question is not a good one and that the students do not know the answers. Indeed, teachers who have experimented with trying to increase their wait time find that they become frustrated at about the second or third week of practice. They go through a period of indecision, uncertain as to exactly how long they should wait after asking a question. However, if they receive encouragement during this difficult time, most teachers are able to increase wait time from one second to three to five seconds. Some teachers have found that the following suggestions are helpful to them as they try to increase their wait time.

1. Avoid repeating portions of student response to a question (teacher echo).
2. Avoid the command "think" without giving the student clues to aid his thinking or sufficient time in which to get his thoughts together.
3. Avoid dependency on comments such as "uh-huh" and "okay."
4. Avoid the "yes . . . but" reaction to a student response. This construction signals teacher rejection of the student's idea.

Currently, too many classrooms are characterized by an incredibly rapid rate of interaction as teachers fire one question after another at students without giving them sufficient time to think, to formulate their answers, and to respond. If teachers can master the skill of increasing wait time from one second to three to five seconds, particularly after questions at a higher cognitive level, they will probably find some very positive changes in both the quantity and quality of student response.

## Reinforcement

Reinforcement, or the rewarding of desired student performance, has been a long-recognized teaching skill; however, it is used with surprising infrequency.

Reinforcement techniques fall into two broad categories: verbal and nonverbal. Probably the most common verbal reinforcers are the one-word or brief-phrase responses: "Good," "Nice job," "That's right," "Excellent," and the like. But there are a number of other verbal reinforcers that are not used as extensively, yet can provide students with other powerful rewards. An important type of verbal reinforcement occurs when teachers use student ideas in developing their lessons. Applying, comparing, and building on the contributions of students are important reinforcement techniques, and research shows us that they provide students with a voice in directing their own learning. Moreover, in classes where such reinforcement techniques are applied, students have more positive attitudes and higher achievement than in classrooms where student ideas are not incorporated into the development of the lessons. Such verbal reinforcement can be an important motive for increasing the student's desire to participate.

Nonverbal reinforcement may, in fact, be even more powerful than verbal reinforcement. Nonverbal reinforcement refers to the physical messages sent by teachers through cues such as eye contact, facial expression, and body position. Does the teacher smile, frown, or remain impassive as a student comments in class? Is the teacher looking at or away from the student? Where is the teacher standing? Does the instructor appear relaxed or tense? All these physical messages indicate to the student whether the teacher is interested or bored, involved or passive, pleased or displeased with a student's comment. In various, subtle ways, nonverbal reinforcement can be used to encourage student participation or to inhibit it.

Several interesting studies comparing the relative effect of nonverbal and verbal reinforcement on students have been undertaken. One study actually had teachers send out conflicting reinforcement messages to determine which message students accepted as the more powerful. In one group, the teacher displayed positive nonverbal reinforcement (smiled, maintained eye contact, indicated positive attitude to student answers with facial and body cues) but, at the same time, sent out negative verbal messages. In the second case, the process was reversed, and negative nonverbal reinforcement was coupled with positive verbal reinforcement (frowns, poor eye contact, and the like, coupled with "good," "nice job," etc.).

Although no evidence was accumulated as to whether the teacher was perceived as schizophrenic, the results of the study were nonetheless interesting. In both cases the nonverbal reinforcement was accepted as the primary message by the majority of students. Whether the nonverbal message was positive or negative, most students responded to the nonverbal rather than to the verbal reinforcement. This study provides fascinating support to the notion of "silent language," or of "body language," and it emphasizes the importance of teachers' attending to what they do not say as well as to what they do say as they reinforce student participation.

For many years educators have assumed that reinforcement, verbal and nonverbal, was a positive tool in promoting student learning, and, certainly, this is frequently the case. But reinforcement is not always an effective teaching skill. In some cases reinforcement is ineffectual and, on occasion, it is actually detrimental to learning.[20]

When a teacher relies totally on one or two favorite types of reinforcement and uses these reinforcers repeatedly, the eventual result may be that the reinforcement becomes ineffectual. The teacher, for example, who continually says "Good" after each student response is not reinforcing, but simply verbalizing a comment that has lost its power to reward. Overusing a word or phrase is a pattern that many teachers, both new and experienced, fall into. Continual repetition of a word like "Good" seems only to ease teacher anxiety and to provide the teacher with a second or two to conceptualize his or her next comment or question.

In other cases reinforcement can actually detract from educational objectives and student learning. Reinforcement given too quickly and too frequently may interfere with or block the complete development of student ideas and interactions. When students are engaged in problem-solving activities, continual reinforcement can be an interruption to their thought processes and may actually terminate the problem solving altogether. Reinforcement can also interfere with pupil-to-pupil interactions. Teachers who react to each student comment refocus the discussion on themselves, inhibiting the possibility of student-to-student interactions.

Another misuse of reinforcement is exemplified by those teachers who are unable to differentiate the student's comment from the student's ego and, as a result, praise virtually every student response, regardless of its appropriateness. To these teachers, fearful of alienating or discouraging students, every student comment is automatically rewarded, and critical thinking and accuracy are sacrificed for the sake of goodwill. It is possible, however, for teachers to reward student participation ("Thanks for that answer") and still indicate that the student response is not appropriate. ("Remember now, we are focusing on

American civilization before the introduction of the railroad. Can someone tackle the question again, keeping this in mind?") In other words, it is possible to separate a student's ego from the answer. Rewarding all answers indiscriminately is an example of a poor use of reinforcement, but rewarding the student's participation is possible even when the answer itself may be incorrect.

Finally, it should be pointed out that different individuals respond to different kinds of reinforcement. Teachers should learn to recognize that while some students find intensive eye contact rewarding, others find it uncomfortable; that some students respond favorably to a teacher referring to their contributions by name, but others find it embarrassing. Although it is unrealistic to expect that a teacher will be able to learn the various rewards to which each individual student responds, it is possible for teachers to try, in general, to be sensitive to the effects of different rewards on students.

Researchers who have studied teacher praise conclude that it must have the following characteristics to be effective. (1) Praise must be contingent on the student's answer; (2) praise should indicate the specific student performance to be reinforced; (3) praise should be honest and sincere.[21]

In summary, praise is a traditional but infrequently used skill. Although reinforcement is a positive prod for learning and can increase student participation, it is sometimes misused and can result in decreasing student participation and learning. Praise should be contingent on student behavior, specific, and honest. It should be planned with care, so that such rewards encourage, rather than inhibit, the quantity and quality of student response.

## Probing Questions

Reinforcement and increased wait time are two means whereby teachers can increase student participation in classroom discussion. A third technique designed to increase the quantity, and particularly the quality, of student participation is the probing question.

Probing questions follow student responses and attempt to stimulate students to think through their answers more thoroughly. They cause students to develop the quality of their answers and to expand on their initial responses. Probing questions require students to provide more support, to be clearer or more accurate, and to offer greater specificity or originality.

Probing questions may be used to prompt student thinking on any level of the *Taxonomy*, but they are probably most effective at the analysis, synthesis, and evaluation levels. Here are some examples of probing questions as they might appear in a classroom discussion.

*Teacher:* How is a President elected?
*Student:* By the people.
*Teacher:* How? Be more specific. (probe)
*Student:* They vote.
*Teacher:* Explain how the votes determine who is President. (probe)
*Student:* I think that an electoral college — state representatives — actually do the voting. The people's votes decide which representatives will be chosen. The representatives actually choose the President.
*Teacher:* How are the people certain that these representatives, these electors, wouldn't vote for someone else? (probe)
*Student:* They give their word. They promise to vote for a certain candidate.

*Teacher:* Was there ever a case when an elector did not keep this promise? (probe)

*Student:* Yes. I remember that one elector in the 1960 election decided not to vote for Kennedy even though most of the people in his state voted for Kennedy. I think he voted for Senator Byrd, who wasn't even running.

In this brief dialogue the teacher asks a series of probing questions at various levels of the *Taxonomy.* The teacher does not accept the student's initial response, "By the people," but probes for more specificity as to how the electoral system works and eventually moves the student to a higher cognitive response. Without probing the student's initial answer, the teacher would have been left with a superficial answer, and the student would not have had the opportunity to consider his response more carefully. Probing questions increase the level of student thinking as well as the quality of student response.

Here is another sample classroom dialogue, with some more examples of probing questions.

*Teacher:* How can we convince auto manufacturers to build smaller cars, cars that burn less gasoline?

*Student:* Pass a law.

*Teacher:* Can you be more specific? (probe)

*Student:* Sure. Put a limit on the size of cars.

*Teacher:* Why do you think that would work? (probe)

*Student:* Well, smaller cars burn less gas. If you just ask them to make smaller cars, they wouldn't do it. So pass a law requiring it.

*Teacher:* Wouldn't car manufacturers rebel at being forced to make smaller cars? (probe)

*Student:* I guess. But they would do it.

*Teacher:* What effect might such a law have on businessmen in other industries? How would they perceive such a law? (probe)

## Equity in Interaction

If you ask teachers if they treat male and female students differently, most would be surprised — maybe even offended. "Of course not," they might respond, "I treat all my students the same." If you probed a little more, teachers might acknowledge that they discipline boys more often and more harshly than they do girls. And, in fact, research shows that boys receive from three to ten times as many reprimands as do their female counterparts.[22] However, researchers who have observed classroom interaction closely have discovered another difference in the way teachers tend to talk with girls and boys in classrooms. Analyze the following discussion that took place in a sixth grade accelerated English class. See if you can detect any differences in the way the teacher talks to male and female students.

*Teacher:* Class, the poem I have put up on the board is called "Stopping by Woods on a Snowy Evening." It's one of the poems that you had for your assignment last night. Can you remember who wrote the poem? Marsha?

*Marsha:* Robert Frost.

*Teacher:* Yes, he's a poet from New England who writes a lot about nature. What is the setting for this particular poem, Alice?

*Alice:* There's someone in a sleigh, and he's watching the woods get covered with snow. I think he says that there aren't any farm houses nearby, so it must be far away from people.

*Teacher:* That's right. Describe in more detail what this scene is like. How does the man feel about it? Put it in your own words. Arthur?

*Arthur:* It's night. The man is all alone. There're no people and no noise — except for the sounds of the horse. The woods are turning all white in the dark, and it's beautiful. The man feels very peaceful. It's almost as if he wants to walk right into the woods and stay there. But at the end of the poem he says he can't because he's promised things to people and he has responsibilities.

*Teacher:* Arthur, you've captured the mood exactly. Arthur says that the man feels so drawn to the scene before him that he almost wants to walk into the woods and stay there. Why do you think he feels this way? Jim?

*Jim:* It seems as though there are two reasons. He says that the woods are "lovely, dark and deep." They're so beautiful and peaceful, they're pulling him to become part of them. It also sounds as if he's got some hassles on his mind because he's got these promises he's made to people. Maybe he'd just like to stay in the woods and forget about these problems.

*Teacher:* That's an excellent analysis, Jim. In the last line of the poem the man says that he has miles to go before he sleeps. I want you to think carefully about this line. Is there another meaning sleep could have besides just resting for the night? Tony?

*Tony:* It's probably way-out, but when a man talks about "miles to go before I sleep," could he mean before he dies? It's as though he's saying that he has a lot to do during his life before he can rest at peace in the woods forever.

*Teacher:* Tony, that's not way-out at all. You've done a wonderful job interpreting this poem. It's one of those poems that can be read on more than one level. And, on a deeper level, it may be a poem about death and how this man feels about it.[23]

  If you read this vignette carefully, you might have noticed that the teacher directs more questions to boys than to girls. Also, boys receive more of the questions that call for higher-order thinking and more creative responses. Several studies indicate that boys, particularly high-achieving boys, are likely to receive most of the teacher's active attention.[24] They receive more praise on the quality of their academic work,[25] and they are asked more complex and abstract questions.[26] Other research has shown that teachers in mathematics classrooms give significantly more wait time to boys than to girls. The researchers conclude that "this difference could possibly have a negative effect on girls' achievement in mathematics."[27]

  When teachers realize that they are distributing their attention and their questions in an unfair manner, they can change their teaching behavior. It is important to check yourself for equity in interaction and questioning so that you actively involve all your students in classroom discussions. The four techniques discussed in this section — wait time, reinforcement, probing questions, and equity in interaction — provide teachers with classroom approaches designed to make the student a more active participant in the learning process. When you feel that you understand these skills, go directly to the Mastery Test. In order to pass the Mastery Test, you need to demonstrate a knowledge and comprehension level understanding of the major points contained in the preceding four sections.

# Mastery Test

## OBJECTIVE 3

To describe additional teaching strategies for increasing the quantity and quality of student response.

Discuss how wait time, reinforcement, probing questions, and equity in interaction can increase the quantity and/or quality of student response in the classroom. You should include the following in your discussion:

(a) A description of typical teacher reactions to student comments.
(b) A description of the "bombing rate" and the amount of "wait time" characteristic of most classrooms today.
(c) A description of four positive effects that increased "wait time" has on student participation.
(d) A description of how reinforcement can promote, as well as how it may, if used ineffectively, inhibit student response.
(e) A description of how probing questions can increase the quality of student response.
(f) A description of how patterns of inequity may characterize the interaction and questioning process.

## ANSWER KEY

### Mastery Test, Objective 3

(a) Teachers most frequently react to student responses with acceptance comments such as "Uh-huh" or "O.K." Acceptance is used so frequently that it may lead to a flat classroom environment. The second most used reaction is remediation — comments and probing questions that will help students reach the best possible response. Teacher praise and criticism are reactions that teachers do not use frequently.

(b) *Bombing rate:* Teachers ask questions at an extremely rapid rate, on the average of two or three per minute. It is not unusual to find as many as seven to ten questions asked during a single minute of classroom instruction.
*Wait time:* The mean amount of time a teacher waits after asking a question is only one second.

(c) Increased "wait time" has these positive effects on student participation (you may have chosen any four):

 1. Students give longer answers.
 2. They volunteer more appropriate answers.
 3. Failures to respond are less frequent.
 4. Student comments on the analysis and synthesis levels increase.
 5. Students ask more questions.
 6. Slower students offer more questions and responses.

 7. Students exhibit more confidence in their comments.

(d) Reinforcement could promote student participation by rewarding students for their comments, thus encouraging further participation. This reward may be verbal or nonverbal in nature.
 Reinforcement can hinder student participation when (1) teacher comments interfere with student thinking, (2) teacher eye contact is so strong that it detracts from student-to-student interaction, (3) a particular verbal reinforcer is overused and loses its power, (4) reinforcement is given too frequently or too quickly, without a thorough analysis of the quality of student response.

(e) Probing questions increase the quantity and quality of student participation by requiring the student to go beyond the initial answer and extend his or her thinking.

(f) Boys receive not only more teacher reprimands but also more teacher attention in general. They are praised more often and are asked more higher-order questions. It is important that teachers recognize this potential inequity so that they will involve all students as active participants in the learning process.

NOTES

1. Charles DeGarmo, *Interest and Education* (New York: Macmillan Co., 1902), p. 179.

2. John Dewey, *How We Think*, rev. ed. (Boston: D. C. Heath, 1933), p. 266.

3. Joseph Green, "Editor's Note," *Clearing House* 40 (1966): 397.

4. Thomas Merton, *The Seven Storey Mountain* (Garden City, N.Y.: Doubleday Co., 1948), p. 139.

5. Romiett Stevens, "The Question as a Measure of Classroom Practice," *Teachers College Contributions to Education*, no. 48 (New York: Teachers College Press, Columbia University, 1912).

6. O. L. Davis and Drew Tinsley, "Cognitive Objectives Revealed by Classroom Questions Asked by Social Studies Teachers and Their Pupils," *Peabody Journal of Education* 44 (July 1967): 21–26. Also see O. L. Davis and Francis P. Hunkins, "Textbook Questions: What Thinking Processes Do They Foster?," *Peabody Journal of Education* 43 (March 1966): 285–292. Also see P. E. Blosser, "Review of Research: Teacher Questioning Behavior in Science Classrooms," *ERIC Clearinghouse for Science, Mathematics, and Environmental Education*, ED 18418 (Columbus, Ohio: December 1979); D. Trachtenberg, "Student Tasks in Text Material; What Cognitive Skills Do They Tap?" *Peabody Journal of Education* 52 (1974): 54–57.

7. Stevens, *op. cit.* See also E. Dale and L. Raths, "Discussion in the Secondary School," *Educational Research Bulletin* 24 (1945): 1–6; Davis and Hunkins, *op. cit.;* W. D. Floyd, "An Analysis of the Oral Questioning Activity in Selected Colorado Primary Classrooms" (Ph.D. diss., Colorado State College, 1960); and Roger T. Cunningham, "A Descriptive Study Determining the Effects of a Method of Instruction Designed to Improve the Question-Phrasing Practices of Prospective Elementary Teachers" (Ph.D. diss., Indiana University, 1968), p. 156.

8. Mary Budd Rowe, "Wait-Time and Rewards as Instructional Variables: Their Influence on Language, Logic and Fate Control" (Paper presented at the National Association for Research in Science Teaching, Chicago, April 1972).

9. Hilda Taba, Samuel Levine, and Freeman Elzey, *Thinking Elementary School Children*, Cooperative Research Project No. 1574, San Francisco State College, San Francisco, California, April 1964, p. 177; see also Francis P. Hunkins, *Questioning Strategies and Techniques* (Boston: Allyn and Bacon, 1972). See also D. L. Redfield and E. W. Rousseau, "A Meta-Analysis of Experimental Research on Teacher Questioning Behavior," *Review of Educational Research* 51 (1981): 237–245. See also William Wilen, *Questioning Skills for Teachers* (Washington, D.C.: National Education Association, 1982). See also Paul Otto and Robert Schuck, "The Effect of a Teacher Questioning Strategy Training Program on Teaching Behavior, Student Achievement, and Retention," *Journal of Research in Science Teaching* 20 (1983): 521–528.

10. Rowe, *op. cit.*

11. G. L. Fahey, "The Questioning Activity of Children," *Journal of Genetic Psychology* 60 (1942): 337–357. See also V. M. Houston, "Improving the Quality of Classroom Questions and Questioning." *Educational Administration and Supervision* 24 (1938): 17–28; and W. D. Floyd, *op. cit.*

12. Virginia Rogers, "Varying the Cognitive Levels of Classroom Questions in Elementary Social Studies: An Analysis of the Use of Questions by Student Teachers" (Ph.D. diss., University of Texas at Austin, 1968). See also Hilda Taba, *Teaching Strategies and Cognitive Functioning in Elementary School Children*, Cooperative Research Project No. 2404 (Washington, D.C.: U.S. Office of Education, 1966).

13. Meredith D. Gall, Barbara Dunning, and Rita Weatherby, *Minicourse 9: Higher Cognitive Questioning, Teacher's Handbook,* Far West Laboratory for Educational Research and Development (Beverly Hills: Macmillan Education Services, 1971).

14. Benjamin Bloom, ed., *Taxonomy of Educational Objectives,* Handbook I: Cognitive Domain (New York: David McKay, 1956).

15. J. Brophy and C. Evertson, *Learning from Teaching: A Developmental Perspective* (Boston: Allyn & Bacon, 1976).

16. S. R. Mills, C. T. Rice, D. C. Berliner, and E. W. Rousseau, "The Correspondence Between Teacher Questions and Student Answers in Classroom Discourse," *Journal of Experimental Education* 48 (1980): 194–209.

17. John Goodlad, *A Place Called School* (New York: McGraw-Hill, 1984), p. 124.

18. David Sadker and Myra Sadker, *Promoting Effectiveness in Classroom Instruction, Final Report,* Contract No. 400-80-0033 (Washington, D.C.: Department of Education, 1984).

19. The findings in this section are based on work by Mary Budd Rowe, *op. cit.* See also J. Swift and C. Gooding, "Interaction of Wait Time Feedback and Questioning Instruction on Middle School Science Teaching," *Journal of Research on Science Teaching* 20 (1983): 721–730.

20. Jere Brophy, "Teacher Praise: A Functional Analysis, Occasional Paper No. 2" (East Lansing: Michigan State University, The Institute for Research on Teaching, 1979).

21. Jere Brophy, *op. cit.*

22. Jere Brophy and Thomas Good, *Teacher-Student Relationships: Causes and Consequences* (New York: Holt, Rinehart and Winston, 1974).

23. Myra Sadker and David Sadker, *Sex Equity Handbook for Schools* (New York: Longman, 1982).

24. Brophy and Good, *op. cit.*

25. Carol Dweck, William Davidson, Sharon Nelson, and Bradley Enna, "Sex Differences in Learned Helplessness: II. The Contingencies of Evaluative Feedback in the Classroom and III. An Experimental Analysis," *Developmental Psychology* 14, no. 3 (1978): 268–276.

26. Sadker and Sadker, *Promoting Effectiveness in Classroom Instruction, Final Report,* Contract No. 400-80-0033 (Washington, D.C.: Department of Education, 1984).

27. Delores Gore and Daniel Roumagoux, "Wait-Time as a Variable in Sex Related Differences During Fourth-Grade Mathematics Instruction," *Journal of Educational Research* 76 (1983): 273–275.

ADDITIONAL READINGS   Berliner, David. "The Half-Full Glass: A Review of Research on Teaching." In *Using What We Know About Teaching.* Edited by Philip Hosford. Alexandria, Virginia: Association for Supervision and Curriculum Development, 1984.

Bloom, Benjamin, ed. *Taxonomy of Educational Objectives, Handbook I: Cognitive Domain.* New York: David McKay, 1956.

Cunningham, Roger T. "Developing Question-Asking Skills." In *Developing Teacher Competencies,* edited by James Wiegand. Englewood Cliffs, New Jersey: Prentice-Hall, 1971.

Gall, Meredith; Barbara Dunning; and Rita Weatherby. *Minicourse 9: Higher Cognitive Questioning, Teacher's Handbook.* Far West Laboratory for Educational Research and Development. Beverly Hills: Macmillan Educational Services, 1971.

Gillin, Caroline; Marcella Kysilka; Virginia Rogers; and Lewis Smith. *Questionineze: Individual or Group Game Involvement for Developing Questioning Skills*. Columbus, Ohio: Charles E. Merrill, 1972.

Hyman, Ronald T. *Strategic Questioning*. Englewood Cliffs, New Jersey: Prentice-Hall, 1979.

Sanders, Norris. *Classroom Questions: What Kinds*. New York: Harper and Row, 1966.

Wilen, William. *Questioning Skills for Teachers*. Washington, D.C.: National Education Association, 1982.

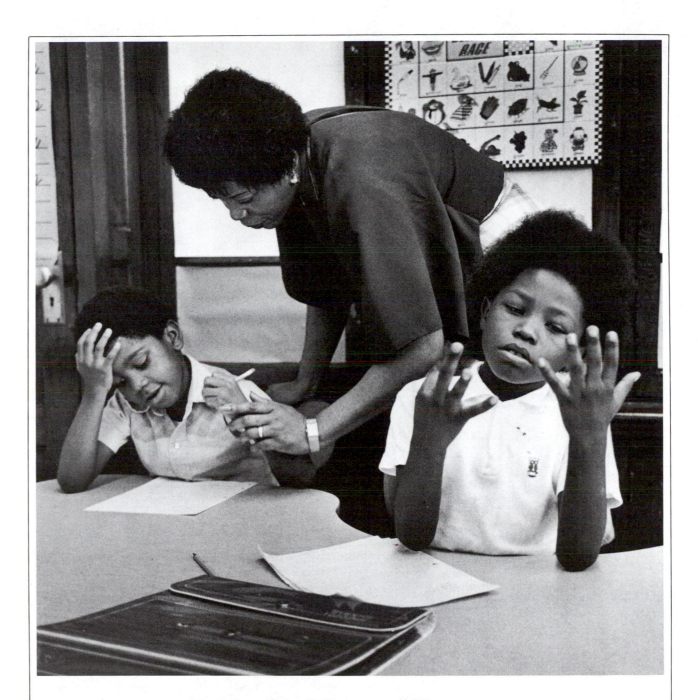

Peter H. Martorella

# 6. Teaching

## Concepts

# Objectives

**1** (a) To identify five different ways in which the term "concept" is used in educational literature; (b) to identify the basic characteristics of concepts; and (c) to distinguish between essential and nonessential characteristics of a concept.

**2** (a) To classify concepts according to types, using four classification systems; and (b) to identify developmental differences that occur among students in concept learning.

**3** (a) To distinguish between the private and public dimensions of concept learning; and (b) to identify and briefly describe the three stages of preparation for the teaching of concepts.

**4** (a) To identify five dimensions of concept learning that can be measured and to arrange them according to their level of complexity; and (b) to identify and briefly describe three procedures for measuring the private dimensions of students' concepts.

---

It began like any other day. Ginny Peters awoke at approximately 7 o'clock, stretched, and rolled out of bed. She put on her clothes, neatly folded on the chair where she had placed them the night before, rolled her pajamas into a ball, and stuffed them under her pillow. Unaware of what was happening downstairs, she brushed her hair the usual 100 times and then washed her face and hands and brushed her teeth.

As she descended the stairs, she greeted her dog Missy and bounded into the kitchen. "Mornin', mom, dad," she said with her usual good cheer. The worried looks on her parents' faces called her up short, and signaled to her that something was amiss. "Sh-h, we're trying to hear the latest report," her mother said gently.

The radio on the kitchen table continued blaring out a news bulletin in excited tones. "Last night while most of Dublin City slept, an unprecedented robbery took place. Striking swiftly and quietly, the thieves moved with unusual efficiency. Informed sources report that law enforcement officials are completely baffled by the case. No clues have been uncovered nor have any eye witnesses come forth. A night watchman working in the 1700 block of Highland Avenue, however, reported that a speeding blue car was observed at approximately 3:00 A.M. No one in Dublin City recalls such a theft occurring where . . . ." Ginny's patience gave out, "What's going on? What happened?" she interrupted.

Her father switched off the radio. Glancing nervously at his wife, he said in solemn tones, "I guess we better tell her, Martha. She's sure to find out about it from someone else, if we don't." Martha began with slow and measured phrases, "Ginny, I don't want you to be upset by what I am about to tell you. Things may be difficult at first, but you — we all — will learn to adjust to it. After a while, our lives will go on just as before."

"Mother, please tell me *what* has happened. I can't stand the suspense," Ginny implored.

Her father leaned across the table and picked up the conversation. Ginny thought she saw a tear in his eye. "Ginny, someone has stolen *happiness*. From now on, no one will ever be able to know about, feel, or share happiness." Just then Ginny awoke with a start. "Wow," she shuddered, "that was a terrible dream."

Fortunately for all of us, as well as our hypothetical Ginny, we still have the concept of happiness among us. The above melodrama was contrived to draw attention to the importance of concepts. The loss of even one of our most precious concepts would be a significant personal, as well as a social, loss.

## The Importance of Concepts

We build our world on concepts. They come in all types, and some are much more significant than others. Throughout any day, hundreds, perhaps thousands of them, will be pressed into service. Ginny's concepts of "tooth brushing," "politeness," "news," "radio," and "sadness" — to name just a few — were employed in her brief dream. Countless other concepts were at work also, just as they are for each of us every conscious moment of our lives. As we learn and experience new things, we both draw upon and increase our conceptual banks. We constantly put old concepts to use and, in the process, frequently extend them and acquire new, related ones.

Where does it all end? The chain of concept acquisition, usage, enlargement, and revision is continuous for as long as we are able to think. For some of us, the conceptual juices flow faster or slower depending upon such factors as our current and past experiences and the formal instruction we receive.

Everyone learns concepts, whether they like to or not. Most of us enjoy learning them — at least, some of the time. Concepts enrich, as well as extend and order, our psychological worlds. Many concepts, such as *chair*, are acquired because they have functional value; they are useful for something we need or want to do. Others, such as *cowboy*, are learned just because they are fun or because they make our lives more interesting and pleasant. Still others, such as *square root, balance of trade, verb*, and the like, are learned on a "good faith" basis. They are not immediately functional nor are they much fun, so we must simply take it on faith that some day they will be useful or entertaining. Much of our concept learning in schools is on such a good faith basis. When a teacher appears to tax or violate our good faith, we may balk at learning. We begin to suspect that we are "being had."

In addition to their ability to entertain us and to help satisfy our immediate needs, concepts serve us in three additional ways.

1. They simplify our learning tasks.
2. They expedite communication.
3. They help us distinguish between reality and imagery.

Our intellectual world is comprised of millions of bits and pieces of knowledge. If each of these items required a separate category in our knowledge network, information retrieval would be extremely unwieldy. Concepts allow us to organize and store similar pieces of information efficiently. Once formed, they eliminate our need to treat each new piece of knowledge as a separate category. In a sense, concepts are *hooks* on which we can hang new experiences. When we confront a sufficiently novel situation for which we have no hooks, we either force the information onto an incompatible hook or else we create a new one. In short, concepts organize our knowledge structure and keep it from becoming unwieldy and dysfunctional.

Perhaps the most useful aspect of concepts lies in their ability to speed up and simplify communication among people. Because you and I share similar concepts, we can easily communicate without any need on my part to explain in great detail every idea, event, or object. Each new concept builds upon preceding ones; their cumulative pattern and sequencing make extended descriptions of each one unnecessary. When communication between two people breaks down, it is often because one member has not learned concepts that are basic to the conversation. Frequently, this problem occurs in textbooks when the author incorrectly assumes knowledge of certain concepts on the part of the readers. On the other hand, communication proceeds very efficiently between individuals who are at a similar stage of conceptual learning. We frequently refer to such people as "being on the same wavelength." However, for communication to proceed at all, mutual knowledge of some concepts is essential.

One of the more subtle functions of concepts is their ability to help us distinguish between illusion and reality. One who has acquired the concept of cow has no trouble distinguishing between a picture or a three-dimensional model of a cow and a real Holstein. Similarly, knowledge of other concepts allows one, without much conscious analysis, to recognize that various pictures and models are only representations. Confusion between real examples of concepts and their secondhand representation can occasionally be detected in children, as with a little girl who believed that chickens were an inch and a half high.

What is the nature of concepts? How are they different from one another? How are they learned? The remainder of this chapter revolves about these three fundamental questions.

# Your Turn

## WHAT DO YOU KNOW ABOUT CONCEPTS?

Let's see what you already know about concepts. Mark a "T" for true and an "F" for false statements.

_____ 1. This page is filled with concepts.

_____ 2. Down deep, all concepts are alike.

_____ 3. Every subject matter area is built around concepts.

_____ 4. It is the subject matter area from which a concept is drawn that makes it easy or difficult to learn.

_____ 5. Another name for a concept is "generalization."

_____ 6. No matter what your age, concept learning occurs in the same way.

_____ 7. Learning a concept occurs in the same way that everything else does.

_____ 8. The more information we have about a concept, the easier it is to learn.

_____ 9. You teach for concept learning in the same way that you teach for other objectives.

_____ 10. Unless you can tell what a concept is in your own words, you have not really learned it.

Compare your answers to these questions with the Answer Key that follows.

## ANSWER KEY
Your Turn: What Do You Know About Concepts?

| | | | |
|---|---|---|---|
| 1. T | | 6. F | |
| 2. F | | 7. F | |
| 3. T | | 8. F | |
| 4. F | | 9. F | |
| 5. F | | 10. F | |

# Objective 1

(a) To identify five different ways in which the term "concept" is used in educational literature; (b) to identify the basic characteristics of concepts; and (c) to distinguish between essential and nonessential characteristics of a concept.

## LEARNING ACTIVITY 1

**THE NATURE OF CONCEPTS**

People's concepts of a concept vary considerably. Some use the term concept synonymously with *idea:* "That's my concept of how a house should be designed." Others use the term to mean a *theme* or *topic:* "These are the concepts we will study in history: 'the Great Depression,' 'the New Deal,' . . . ." A third way to use "concept" is to express a *general, all-encompassing statement:* "All men are mortal." And a fourth way is to refer to the most fundamental *elements* or *structures of disciplines,* such as in the sciences and social sciences: "The concept of culture underlies all of anthropology."

In psychology and specifically in areas where different types of learning outcomes are being considered, concepts have a distinct fifth meaning with which the remainder of this chapter will be concerned. Concepts in this last sense refer to the *categories* into which we group our knowledge and experiences. Once formed, these categories act as intellectual magnets that attract and order related thoughts and experiences. The categories we create generally have single or multiword *labels* or *names* that serve to identify them, such as *tree* or *balance of trade.* As we experience objects or events, we sort them into the various categories we have created; once sorted, we begin relating them to other items in the same category. This relating process may be very brief and simple, or it may evolve into an extended analysis of multiconcept interrelationships.

### Concepts Defined

Thus, we may simultaneously speak of concepts as being (1) *categories* into which our experiences are organized and (2) *the larger network of intellectual relationships brought about through categorization.* We do not merely sort out and label the objects and events we encounter; we actively reflect upon them to greater or lesser degrees. As we are faced with new or old phenomena, we must relate them, sometimes very quickly, to what we already know in order to make much sense of them. Thus, our concepts not only organize our experience but also affect *how* we attend to or reflect upon that experience. Suppose that each day we pass a hole in the ground partially filled with dirt and water. We may label it a "hazardous mud hole," thereby ensuring that we carefully avoid it. On the other hand, a passing biologist, using a different set of conceptual glasses, might experience the hole as a scientific gold mine filled with interesting organisms. His or her conceptual glasses, developed through specialized training, produce a different set of categories that, in turn, lead to different reflections concerning the same object.

Conceptual categories and related reflections may be limited or extensive, simplistic or complex, depending on one's interests and experiences. Occasionally, concepts may lack labels or precise referents. When this is so, communication with others may be difficult. We say things such as "I can't exactly describe it; you sort of have to *feel* it." "I don't know what you call it, but all of these paintings have it." "They don't have any names. I just call them 'squiggles' because they are sort of squiggly."

Objects or events are sorted into concept categories through a check of their basic characteristics or *criterial attributes*. If an item of information meets the criteria for a concept category we hold, we attach the concept name to the item and begin to relate it to other information we have. A check of criterial attributes alone, however, does not produce efficient categorization. The criterial attributes must be present in a particular sequence, relationship, or pattern to qualify for category placement. This specific ordering of attributes is known as the concept definition or *rule*.

Let's examine why the rule, as well as the identification of the criterial attributes, is necessary for accurate categorization. Suppose we fly over a small area and observe the following environmental characteristics: *land, water,* and a *surrounding* body. Into what conceptual category do we place our observation? Without the *rule* or way in which each of the three observed criterial attributes are related, we cannot be sure whether the correct answer is *island* or *lake*. The rule tells us that "land surrounded by water" is an island, whereas "water surrounded by land" is a *lake*.

Essentially then, concepts consist of (1) names such as "island," (2) criterial attributes such as "body of land," and (3) rules such as "body of land surrounded by water." Cases or illustrations of a concept are referred to as *examples; nonexamples* of a concept are any cases or illustrations that lack one or more of the criterial attributes of the concept or else have a different rule. Each concept is a nonexample for

"I guess it goes in the rectangle box, Charlie."

**FIGURE 6.1**

every other one; for instance, island is a nonexample of the concept of isthmus. The closer the "resemblance" of the concepts (i.e., their sets of related criterial attributes), the greater the difficulty in discriminating among them. In Figure 6.1 there is some potential confusion since the three nonexamples of the concept "rectangle" are very similar to the concept "rectangle."

As with examples and nonexamples, criterial attributes also have a negative counterpart — *noncriterial attributes*. These are features that frequently are present in concept illustrations, though they are *not* an essential part of the concept. They are analogous to accessories on a car. Almost always, some accessories come with an automobile though they are unnecessary for the vehicle to function. Noncriterial attributes are present under many forms as seen in the following table. They may appear as *length* in examples of the concept "sentence"; as *color* when dealing with the concept "chair"; as *size* in examples of "triangle" or "island"; and so on.

| Concept | Noncriterial Attribute |
| --- | --- |
| sentence | length |
| chair | color |
| triangle | size |
| island | size |

The list of possibilities for noncriterial attributes is endless.

### Stereotypes and Generalizations

When we attend too closely to noncriterial attributes and begin to treat them as criterial ones, we often create *stereotypes* and *over-generalizations*. For example, on the basis of three dates with three different Italian men, a girl might conclude that all Italian men are great lovers. A child being introduced to geometric shapes notes that in all examples of the concept *triangle* there are two equal sides and that the third side is always parallel to the plane of the floor. He or she overgeneralizes these conditions as essential for all triangles. A high school boy observes that every poem he has ever heard or read has rhymed. He mistakenly concludes that verse must rhyme to be classified as poetry. Children in a family grow up in a neighborhood where most of the blacks they encounter are physically aggressive, poor, and boisterous. From these limited and isolated cases, they begin to form their concepts of all blacks.

Much of the instruction we give and receive inadvertently confuses noncriterial and criterial attributes. To correct this error and sharpen our discrimination capabilities, we must periodically be called up short and be made to analyze carefully the similarities and differences in diverse cases of concept examples and nonexamples.

Almost never, except perhaps with certain abstract concepts, are examples completely free of any noncriterial distractors. Inevitably, there are some details in nearly all illustrations that may serve to mislead us concerning the concept's essential properties. For one whose grasp of a concept is shaky, noncriterial properties may be a source of great perplexity. On the other hand, for one who has a clear understanding of the concept, noncriterial features often provide enrichment. They enhance our already formed concept and enlarge our range of examples. Having already learned to sort out cases on the basis of defining characteristics, we can appreciate and even seek out new, subtle variations on old themes.

# Mastery Test

## OBJECTIVE 1

(a) To identify five different ways in which the term "concept" is used in educational literature; (b) to identify the basic characteristics of concepts; and (c) to distinguish between essential and nonessential characteristics of a concept.

1. In brief, what are five different ways in which the term "concept" is used in educational literature?

_____

_____

_____

_____

_____

2. List below the basic characteristics of concepts.

_____

_____

3. Take a moment to examine the list of concepts in the left-hand column. What are some of the more common noncriterial attributes that might be present in examples of these concepts? (Record your answers in the right-hand column.)

| Concepts | *Typical Noncriterial Attributes* |
|---|---|
| mammal | |
| tree | |
| river | |
| winter | |
| prime number | |
| mountain | |
| state | |
| death | |
| cloud | |
| comb | |

Now compare your answers with those that follow in the Answer Key.

## ANSWER KEY

### Mastery Test, Objective 1

1. (a) to mean the same thing as an "idea"; (b) to mean a "theme" or "topic"; (c) as a general, all-encompassing, or broad statement; (d) to mean the basic structure or elements of a discipline; (e) as categories into which we group our knowledge and experience.
2. Names, criterial attributes, rules.

3. There are a number of possible noncriterial attributes that you might have listed. Consider the following ones for comparisons:
mammal — color; tree — size; river — length; winter — temperature; prime number — size; mountain — location; state — size; death — age; cloud — shape; comb — color.

# Objective 2

(a) To classify concepts according to types, using four classification systems; and (b) to identify developmental differences that occur among students in concept learning.

## LEARNING ACTIVITY 2

**TYPES OF CONCEPTS**

What makes a concept easy or hard to learn? Let's try an experiment to find out. Detach (along the dotted lines) the various cards shown at the back of the book in Appendix B; sort them into two piles. Place those you consider *easy* to learn into the first pile and those you consider *hard* into the second. Arrange these two piles into nine new piles, ranging from easiest to hardest. You may sort as many cards as you wish into each pile, but each pile must have *at least one* card in it. When you finish your sorting, take some time to compare your results and the rationale you used with someone else.

What were the similarities and differences in the two sets of piles and in the two rationales? When your discussion is completed, record the names of the concepts from the nine piles in the appropriate boxes on the continuum in Figure 6.2.

Below the listing, note the criteria you used in judging the concept's level of difficulty. After reading the remainder of the section you may wish to refer back to your conclusions.

## Classifying Concepts

There are many different bases by which to classify concepts as easier or harder to learn. A frequently cited criterion of difficulty is the extent to which concepts are perceived to be *concrete* or *abstract*. For purposes of simplification, let us use the rough definition that concreteness refers to what we can perceive directly through one of the five senses: taste, smell, touch, sound, sight. In contrast, abstractness refers to what we acquire only indirectly through the senses or cannot perceive directly through the senses. There are some problems with these distinctions in practice, but they will suffice to illustrate one type of classification system. Clearly, in this system, chair, tree, glass, and similar objects are concrete concepts and presumably easier to learn. Similarly, beauty, freedom, justice, empathy, and similar terms are abstract and presumably harder to learn. In between are a wide range of concepts that defy simple classification in this system.

Another way to view concepts is to examine whether they are most frequently learned in *formal* or *informal* contexts. Many of the concepts we acquire come through informal channels of experience (car, house, television, fire), while others come through systematic channels of instruction such as schools, job-training programs, or parents (legislature, hydrogen, preposition, square). Not all abstract concepts are acquired formally, however. Beauty and truth, for example, result from a complex blend of formal and informal instruction. It would be difficult to assess which type of instruction is generally dominant for such concepts.

A third perspective on concept types divides them into three classes: *conjunctive*, *disjunctive*, and *relational*. According to this frame of reference, a *conjunctive* concept is less difficult to learn because it has only a *single* set of qualities or characteristics that one has to learn. A little girl might say to herself, "If it has this and that and those things, it must be a whatchamacallit." *Chair* is a conjunctive concept, as the dictionary definition testifies: "A piece of furniture consisting of a seat, legs and back, and often arms, designed for one person." There *are* many kinds or examples of chairs, but the *easy* part of learning the concept is that the basic set of defining characteristics always are essentially the same.

A *disjunctive* concept is slightly more complicated. In order to learn this type of concept, one must learn two or more sets of alternative conditions under which the concept appears. *Citizen* is such a concept. The dictionary states that a citizen is "a native *or* naturalized member of a state or nation who owes allegiance to its government and who is entitled to its protection." Either being born in a country or fulfilling some test of citizenship can lead to the status of *citizen*. In short, disjunctive concepts can have more than one set of criterial attributes.

The most complex type of concept to learn is a *relational* one. Waste, resource, pollution, a little, a lot, parallel, and symmetry are all relational concepts. Their meaning stems from a comparison or a

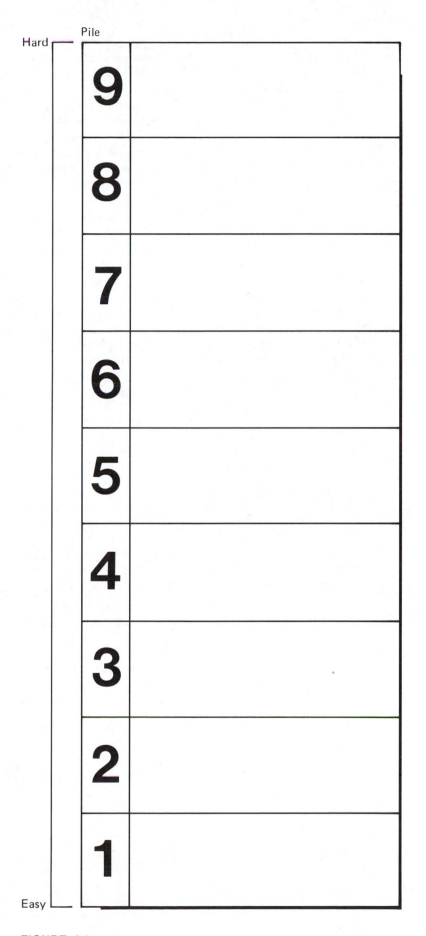

**FIGURE 6.2**

relationship between objects or events. A line segment or an object cannot be assessed "parallel" unless something specific about its relationship to another line or object is known. Similarly, one cannot tell if something is "a lot" unless it is compared to something else — another item, an average or norm of some kind, or the whole of which it is a part.

So it is with all relational concepts; they describe *relationships* between items. A line segment that is parallel on some occasions can be perpendicular on other occasions. Only its particular relationship to *another* line segment makes it perpendicular or parallel. Five apples are a lot of apples for a small child's snack; but they are only a little for a troop of boy scouts. Learners of relational concepts must focus on the characteristics of the items being compared and also on the basis being used for comparison. In observing a line segment, for example, a student also must note another line segment, as well as the relationship between the two.

Figure 6.3 summarizes the characteristics and the relationships among conjunctive, disjunctive, and relational concepts. Determining whether a concept is one of the three preceding types allows a teacher to anticipate learning difficulties and to prepare corresponding instruction. One investigator discovered, for example, that preschoolers have a tendency to treat relational concepts as if they were conjunctive ones.

When the four-year-old first learns the concept dark, he regards it as descriptive of an absolute class of color — black and related dark hues. The phrase "dark yellow" makes no sense to him, for dark signifies dark colors, not relative darkness.[1]

Older students who have misconceptions of *resource* and *waste* reflect similar problems when they fail to understand that oil, water, wood, and the like may be examples of resources and waste simultaneously.

A fourth system for classifying concepts has a developmental basis. It concentrates on the dominant medium through which our concepts are represented as we develop chronologically. According to Jerome

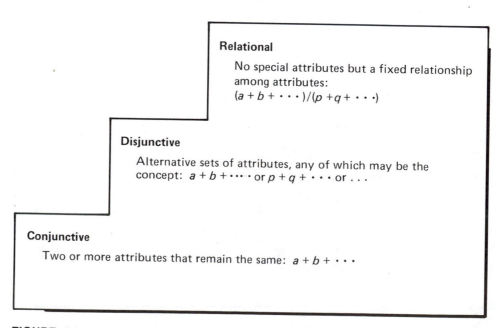

**Relational**

No special attributes but a fixed relationship among attributes:
$(a + b + \cdots)/(p + q + \cdots)$

**Disjunctive**

Alternative sets of attributes, any of which may be the concept: $a + b + \cdots$ or $p + q + \cdots$ or ...

**Conjunctive**

Two or more attributes that remain the same: $a + b + \cdots$

**FIGURE 6.3** Levels of concept difficulty.

Bruner, three representational media for acquiring concepts exist: enactive — "knowing something through doing it"; iconic — "through a picture or image of it"; and symbolic — "through symbols such as language."[2] Thus one might learn the concept of swimming through doing it (enactive); through viewing a filmstrip on swimming techniques (iconic); or through reading a book on the topic (symbolic). Bruner also notes of these three representational forms: "Their appearance in the life of the child is in that order, each depending upon the previous one for its development, yet all of them remaining more or less intact throughout life — barring such early accidents as blindness or deafness or cortical injury."[3] Enactive representation is dominant during infancy and early childhood; iconic representation becomes the norm through preadolescence; thereafter, symbolic representation dominates.

From a teacher's perspective, this system of classifying concepts has two basic applications. Concepts may be analyzed with respect to which one of the three representational forms — enactive, iconic, or symbolic — seems most appropriate for teaching that concept. Another application is to match the developmental level of the children with the mode of representation. A rule-of-thumb approximation for such planning might be

| | |
|---|---|
| Up to 7 years: | Enactive forms |
| Up to 11 years: | Enactive moving to iconic forms |
| 11 years and beyond: | Iconic moving to symbolic forms |

As noted earlier, the process of examining and categorizing concepts may take many forms. The four perspectives, summarized in Figure 6.4, suggest only some of the possibilities. From an instructional viewpoint, the important issue is that we, as teachers, try to: (1) determine which concepts are most likely to present learning difficulties, (2) identify what the potential problems are likely to be, and (3) use such data to build systematic assistance into learning activities. All concepts are not alike with respect to how they are learned and, to the extent that our instruction reflects this fact, it will be more or less effective.

### CLASSIFICATION SYSTEM FOR CONCEPTS

| Basis for Classification | Types of Concepts |
|---|---|
| Degrees of concreteness | 1. concrete (chair, lake) <br> 2. abstract (lonely, hot) |
| Context in which learned | 1. formal (school, training program) <br> 2. informal (socializing, casual observation) |
| Nature of criterial attributes | 1. conjunctive (chair) <br> 2. disjunctive (citizen) <br> 3. relational (dark) |
| Form or manner in which learned | 1. enactive (play tennis) <br> 2. iconic (watch tennis match on TV) <br> 3. symbolic (read book on tennis) |

**FIGURE 6.4**  Concept types.

# Your Turn

## SUBJECT MATTER CONCEPTS

You may wish to try a simple activity to help you identify the sorts of concepts students typically are asked to learn in subject matter areas. For the focus of your investigation, pick a grade level range in which to explore a particular subject matter.

1. A subject matter area (mathematics, social studies, etc.) for grades 1 through 6.
2. A subject matter area for grades 7 through 12.
3. A subject matter area for grades 4 through 9.

Within that subject matter area and for each of those six grade levels identify a popular related textbook. Examine each of the six texts and locate twenty concepts that seem to occur with some frequency. List your concepts on the Concept Tabulation Form that follows. Examine the list and note five conclusions at the bottom of the form that you have drawn based on your data.

## CONCEPT TABULATION FORM

| Textbooks | Concepts |
|---|---|
| A.  Grade: | 1. |
|      Title: | 2. |
|      Publisher: | 3. |
|      Copyright Date: | 4. |
| | 5. |
| B.  Grade: | 6. |
|      Title: | 7. |
|      Publisher: | 8. |
|      Copyright Date: | 9. |
| C.  Grade: | 10. |
|      Title: | 11. |
|      Publisher: | 12. |
|      Copyright Date: | 13. |
| | 14. |
| D.  Grade: | 15. |
|      Title: | 16. |
|      Publisher: | 17. |
|      Copyright Date: | 18. |
| E.  Grade: | 19. |
|      Title: | 20. |
|      Publisher: | |
|      Copyright Date: | |

F.  Grade:

   Title:

   Publisher:

   Copyright Date:

Conclusions
about the
types of
concepts:

1.

2.

3.

4.

5.

Share your results with others who are working in similar areas. If possible, arrange to examine alternative textbooks so that collectively you will have sampled a wide range of texts. Compare similarities and differences in your lists, as well as your individual conclusions. Conclude your discussion by noting what overall conclusions seem warranted based on the collective set of tabulations.

## Mastery Test

**OBJECTIVE 2**     (a) To classify concepts according to types, using four classification systems; and (b) to identify developmental differences that occur among students in concept learning.

1.  Give a brief definition of the following types of concepts, each of which was used in one of the concept classification systems.

   (a) concrete  _____

   _____

   (b) abstract  _____

   _____

   (c) formal  _____

   _____

   (d) informal  _____

   _____

   (e) conjunctive  _____

   _____

(f) disjunctive    _____

_____

(g) relational    _____

_____

(h) enactive    _____

_____

(i) iconic    _____

_____

(j) symbolic    _____

_____

_____

_____

_____

_____

_____

2. Which of the concept types you have just defined are most closely related to developmental differences among children?

_____

_____

_____

_____

_____

_____

_____

_____

_____

_____

## ANSWER KEY

### Mastery Test, Objective 2

1. Answers should be similar to the following definitions:
   (a) *Concrete.* Those concepts we can perceive directly through one of the five senses.
   (b) *Abstract.* Those which cannot be directly perceived through one of the senses.
   (c) *Formal.* Concepts acquired through systematic channels of instruction.
   (d) *Informal.* Concepts acquired through undirected and unorganized means.
   (e) *Conjunctive.* Concepts defined by a single set of qualities or characteristics.
   (f) *Disjunctive.* Concepts defined by two or more alternative sets of qualities or characteristics.
   (g) *Relational.* Concepts defined by the relationships among objects or events.
   (h) *Enactive.* Concepts acquired through doing or acting.
   (i) *Iconic.* Concepts acquired through imagery or pictures.
   (j) *Symbolic.* Concepts acquired through verbal or symbolic forms (such as reading or speaking).
2. Enactive, iconic, and symbolic; concrete and abstract.

# Objective 3

(a) To distinguish between the private and public dimensions of concept learning; and (b) to identify and briefly describe the three stages of preparation for the teaching of concepts.

## LEARNING ACTIVITY 3

**LEARNING AND TEACHING CONCEPTS**

No matter what the subject area or the particular concept, each of us has a unique personal history that influences how we use concepts. My concepts of *primate, rhombus,* or *whiskers* are slightly different from anyone else's, the unique product of specific percepts being processed through my total conceptual network. Compared to the biologist, mathematician, and dermatologist, I may appear to be a conceptual dunce if the conversation deals solely with primates, rhombi, or whiskers. Still we can communicate at a very basic level since we share a minimal level of concept learning.

### Personal and Public Dimensions of Concepts

We may label the unique, personalized side of concepts their *personal dimension.* This idiosyncratic aspect is not really teachable, although traces may sometimes be acquired through formal instruction. For concepts to function as shared experiences, they must also possess a *public dimension* that each of us holds in common. These are the shared attributes or properties that serve as the basis of communication and which must be understood by anyone claiming to have learned the concept. When we move beyond that basic public level of understanding, we generally need to explain in some detail our *personal* associations with the concept. Two individuals who find they "have a lot in common" often mean they have discovered their personal associations with concepts are surprisingly similar.

Try an experiment to discover your own personal associations with a concept that you share with most other people in our culture. Refer to the object shown in Figure 6.5. Give it a name and write that name in the circle at the center of the diagram in Figure 6.6 Next jot down your immediate associations following the first set of arrows in the spaces marked 1. Now consider what the words in these spaces remind you of and record these new associations in the spaces marked 2. Repeat the process for the spaces marked 3.

**FIGURE 6.5**

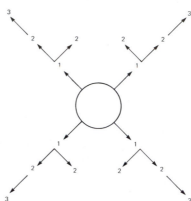

**FIGURE 6.6**  An illustration of a conceptual network.

Take no more than two minutes to complete the diagram. Compare your results with those of others. First examine the names used to categorize the object, then the associations found in the spaces marked 1, 2, and 3. In what ways were all of the associations similar? In what ways did they differ? At what points, if any, did some of the concepts' criterial attributes get listed? At what points were noncriterial attributes listed? What did you learn about your own personal concept from Figure 6.6?

Whatever the character of the personal network each of us generates, it would seem that the *criterial* attributes are the common or *public* aspects of concepts that provide the basis of communication. While formal instruction, such as that occurring in classrooms, always makes some contribution to the personal dimensions of concept learning, its primary focus initially should be on the *public* dimensions. Such basic, culturally shared elements of concepts generally can be derived from dictionaries, encyclopedias, scholarly works, tradition, authoritative experience, or the mass media. While the vast majority of concepts are learned informally, with highly personal and public elements intertwined, many are so specialized that they can only be acquired through formal instruction. Also, a person's lifestyle may be so limited or different from the lifestyles of others that he or she requires assistance in learning the public elements of concepts.

### What's It Like To Learn a Concept?

Everyone learns hundreds of new concepts without ever giving much thought to the matter. Trial-and-error, question-and-answer, and chance observations bring us a wealth of concepts that we are not even aware we are learning. As time passes and we mature, many of these concepts are reinforced, refined, and amplified. This process continues naturally throughout our lives.

Let us try to capture the sensation of someone who is trying to learn a new concept. What strategies are employed? What feelings do we have? What successes and failures do we encounter and what led to them?

## Your Turn

## COMPARE FOUR CONCEPT EXAMPLES

Shown below are some materials taken from the elementary science study unit of *Teacher's Guide for Attribute Games and Problems*.[4] We can treat each of the four sets of figures as a concept to be learned. Examine the first two rows of each set, looking for the criterial attributes (defining properties) of that concept, then select the examples of that concept from the third row. Below each of the four sets, write as specifically and clearly as possible what you consider to be the definition or criterial attributes of the concepts. Compare your conclusions with others who have examined the four sets. If your choices and definitions differ, consider whose results seem most accurate and why. Then turn to the Answer Key that follows.

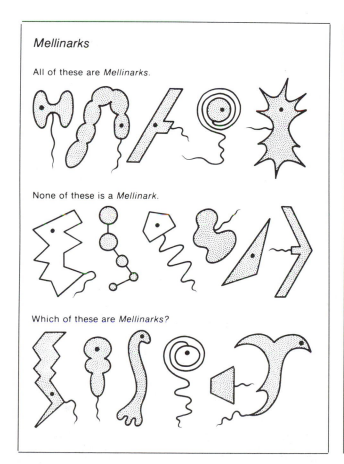

**FIGURE 6.7**

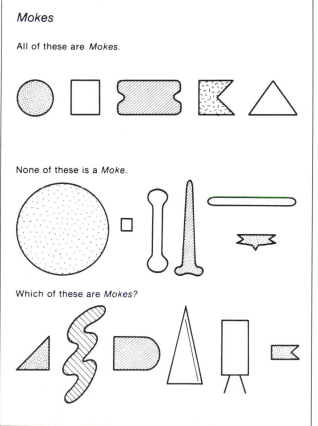

**FIGURE 6.8**

Figures 6.7, 6.8, 6.9, and 6.10 were originally published in *Teacher's Guide for Attribute Games and Problems* (New York: McGraw-Hill, 1968), pp. 75 and 77. They are reprinted here by permission of the Elementary Science Study of Education Development Center, Inc., Newton, MA.

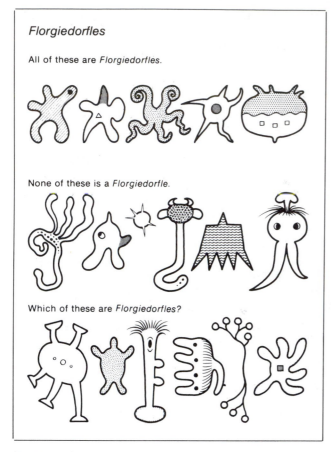

**FIGURE 6.9**

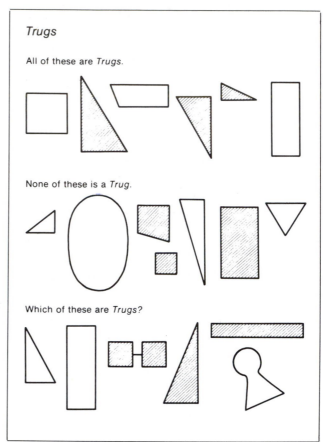

**FIGURE 6.10**

Consider the following questions:

1. In what ways are the four sets alike?
2. What makes some of the concepts easier to learn than others? (In other words, what is the meaning of the term "easier" in these cases?)
3. If you or anyone else was unable to identify or define one or more of the concepts correctly, what were the problems you encountered?
4. In what ways is the learning of these artificial concepts similar to the learning of other reality-based new concepts?
5. Were any of you able to *identify* concept examples correctly but not *define* them accurately? If so, what are the implications of this fact for school learning?
6. What were the feelings you experienced in the various stages of trying to learn the concepts?

## ANSWER KEY
### Your Turn: Compare Four Concept Examples

These four examples should have sensitized you to what it's like to confront a concept for the first time. In order to qualify as a Mellinark, examples must have spots, a black dot, and a tail. Moke examples have only one defining attribute, the fact that they are of the same height. The criterial attributes of Florgiedorfles are their height and number of arms, while Trugs may be *either* shaded triangles *or* unshaded quadrilaterals.

The phenomenon of confusing noncriterial attributes with criterial properties, while deliberately introduced into this demonstration, occurs naturally in the learning of academic concepts. On these occasions, unless a teacher is willing to reexamine his or her instruction rather than fault the learner's capabilities, little progress toward the learning of concepts will occur. An instructor must *resist* the easy defensive position, "Most of the class got the correct answer when I explained the concept. If you didn't, then I guess you are just not trying hard enough!"

Let's reflect a moment on some of the instructional assistance given you relative to the preceding concepts, Mellinarks, Mokes, Florgiedorfles, and Trugs. Most of the conditions provided for your instruction are not available in a typical concept learning situation.

> *Condition 1.* Very little irrelevant material was included in your instruction — material that might have diverted your attention from the essential characteristics of the concept.
>
> *Condition 2.* All the cases you needed, examples and nonexamples, were put before you *simultaneously*. This allowed you to recheck conclusions and to compare cases easily.
>
> *Condition 3.* The characteristics of the concepts were relatively simple ones. Mellinarks were *conjunctive* concepts, the least difficult type to learn (see Figure 6.3), while the fourth concept, Trugs, was *disjunctive* and the second and third, Mokes and Florgiedorfles, were *relational*.
>
> *Condition 4.* All our concepts had concise graphic referents that required little or no verbal ability to understand.

Those readers who experienced difficulty with the pronunciation of concept names or who could not now correctly spell some of them should be able to empathize with students' linguistic burden. Similarly, some readers may have discovered it is possible to identify *instances* of a concept correctly without being able to explain accurately or define the concept in one's own words. Students frequently exhibit this phenomenon, and it often leads to a misinterpretation of their learning level. Persons who can consistently discriminate examples of a concept from nonexamples may be said to have "learned" that concept, whether or not they can articulate a definition of it.

## What's It Like To Teach a Concept?

To initiate the teaching process, you need to ask yourself several sets of questions. The first set pertains to whether the concept is appropriate to *teach*, and the second relates to prerequisite instructional planning.

## Concept Appropriateness Inventory

1. Is the concept considered to be significant? That is, do educators and subject matter specialists seem to suggest that the concept is an important one for students to acquire?

2. Is the concept one that should be taught formally? That is, should a student receive systematic instruction in the concept or is it more appropriately acquired through informal means?

3. Is there sufficient agreement on the criterial attributes and the concept rule to have a basis for designing instruction? That is, can clear and specific guidelines concerning the essential characteristics of the concept be inferred from readings and reference sources?

Assuming the answers are "yes" to these three questions, you are ready to move on to the next set that actually starts the instructional planning.

## Prerequisite Planning Inventory

1. What name is most commonly applied to the concept? (*Example:* lake)

2. What is the concept's rule or definition (i.e., the arrangement of its criterial attributes)? (*Example:* body of water surrounded by land)

3. What are the essential characteristics or *criterial attributes* of the concept, based upon your readings and reference sources? (*Example:* land, water, surrounding)

4. What are some *noncriterial attributes* typically associated with the concept? (*Example:* size, location, depth)

5. What are some interesting and learner-relevant *examples* or cases of the concept which you can use in its explanation? (*Example:* local lakes, mountain lakes, desert lakes)

6. What are some contrasting *nonexamples* of the concept that will help clarify and illustrate the concept? (*Examples:* ocean, stream)

7. What are some *cues, questions,* or *directions* that you can employ to call attention to criterial attributes and noncriterial attributes in the concept examples? (*Example:* "Look at all the points where the water meets the land.")

8. What is the most efficient, interesting, and thought-provoking *medium* (or media) by which to present examples and nonexamples? (*Example:* slides, air photos)

9. What level of *concept mastery* do you expect of students and how will you measure it? (*Example:* Be able to define "lake" and state the similarities and differences this body of water has with other major bodies of water through a project.)

As noted earlier, there are many types of concepts, and the process of learning them differs from that used for other kinds of knowledge such as generalizations. Among concept types there are also differences that require alternative methods of instruction. Detailed discussions of these variations exist elsewhere. In this chapter we shall limit ourselves to a single basic model for organizing concept learning instruction. It emphasizes essential phases of instruction underlying the approach to all types of concepts.

Outlined below is a system for analyzing concepts in some detail that was developed at the University of Wisconsin Research and Development Center in Cognitive Learning. It uncovers some of the data on concepts that a teacher would need to know in order to organize an instructional activity. The example, using the concept "mammal," is adapted from a publication by the Center.[5]

### Example of Concept Data

*Subject area:*   Biological science

*Concept name:*   Mammal

*Criterial attributes:*   Mammals
1. Feed their young on mother's milk.
2. Have hair.
3. Are warm-blooded.

*Noncriterial attributes:*   Color, habitat, pattern in coat, eating habits

*Concept rule:*   A mammal is a warm-blooded animal that has hair and feeds its young on the mother's milk.

*Some concept examples:*   Cow, dog, cat, pig, goat, rabbit, camel

*Some concept nonexamples:*   Chicken, toad, bird, fish, duck, alligator, snake

*Relationship with another concept:*   Mammals use lungs for breathing.

Select a concept from your lists on page 200 or one that interests you and seems suitable for an analysis. Then locate information to complete the Concept Analysis Form that follows. Where a simple word or two will not suffice to indicate examples and nonexamples, briefly outline the nature of the appropriate illustrations.

## CONCEPT ANALYSIS FORM

*Subject area:* _____

*Concept name:* _____

*Criterial attributes:* _____

_____

_____

_____

*Noncriterial attributes:* _____

_____

_____

_____

*Concept rule:* _____

_____

*Some concept examples:* _____

_____

_____

_____

_____

*Some concept nonexamples:* _____

_____

_____

_____

_____

*Relationship with another concept:* _____

_____

_____

_____

## Basic Model for Concept Instruction

1. Complete the Concept Appropriateness Inventory and the Prerequisite Planning Inventory.
2. Develop an introduction to the instructional sequence. The introduction should orient the learner to the task and arouse his or her curiosity. It might be a short story, anecdote, relating of experiences, or brief sequence of questions that focus attention on the topic.
3. Present the series of varied examples and nonexamples of the concept that you have developed in some logical order. (There are no hard and fast rules on "how many." Consider a minimum of seven examples as a rule of thumb.)
4. If possible, present all the examples and nonexamples simultaneously or in close succession, so that the learner can compare all of the cases.
5. Interject the cues, directions, and questions throughout the materials as necessary to draw attention to criterial and noncriterial attributes and to similarities and differences in examples and nonexamples. Correspondingly, encourage learner questions. In written material, cues may be arrows, marginal notes, underlining, and the like.
6. Assess concept mastery at a minimal level, namely, whether students can correctly discriminate among *new* examples and nonexamples.
7. Assess concept mastery at more advanced levels, as consistent with the developmental capabilities of the students and with your own objectives.

The psychologist Robert Gagné offers a brief example of how such a basic model may be employed and, in addition, how *two* related concepts may be taught together — the examples for one serving as the nonexamples for the other.

1. Show the child a glass containing water and a glass containing a rock. Say "This is a solid" and "This is a liquid."
2. Using a different container, show the child some powdered substance in a pile in a container and some milk in another container. Say "This is a solid; this is a liquid."
3. Provide still a third example of solid and liquid, using different materials and containers.
4. Show the child a number of examples of liquids and solids which he has not seen before. Ask him to distinguish the liquids and the solids. (In this example, I assume the child has previously learned to repeat the words "liquid" and "solid" readily when he hears them; they are familiar in sound.)[6]

## Organizing Instructional Materials for Concept Learning

The organization of instructional materials for concept learning may take many forms. Several years ago, an engaging 16-mm film entitled *Model Man*[7] developed the concept of *model,* defined as a disjunctive concept. Blending examples and nonexamples in a humorous story, the film communicated clearly the criterial attributes of the concept in less than 20 minutes. Slides and pictures, though a more static medium, can be used in the same way, and the focus of learning can be controlled more easily.

Suppose we wish to teach the concept of *island* to a class of third graders. We have completed the Concept Appropriateness Inventory and have concluded that the concept is considered by social studies educators to be an important one for children to learn, that it should be taught formally, and that its essential characteristics can be spelled out. The Prerequisite Planning Inventory then is completed. The concept rule is "a body of land surrounded by water," and the criterial attributes are "land," "water," and "surrounding" (all-aroundness). After a brief introduction and a short question-and-answer session, the students are shown a series of slides as characterized below, accompanied by related questions and commentary.

| | | |
|---|---|---|
| Slide 1: | Example | Shot of large uninhabited island with vegetation. |
| Slide 2: | Example | Shot of small uninhabited island with no vegetation. Arrows on slide are pointing to the surrounding water. |
| Slide 3: | Nonexample | Shot of peninsula. |
| Slide 4: | Example | Shot of large island with buildings, etc. |
| Slide 5: | Example | Shot of small island with inhabitants. |
| Slide 6: | Nonexample | Shot of bay with inhabitants adjacent. |
| Slide 7: | Example | Shot of uninhabited island with unusual shape. |
| Slide 8: | Nonexample | Shot of an isthmus. |
| Slide 9: | Example | Shot of an island with a lake within. |

Slide 10: Nonexample    Shot of a lake with arrows pointing to the land all around.

Slide 11: Example    Shot of an uninhabited island with mountains.

Slide 12: Example    Shot of an inhabited island with mountains.

Slide 13: Example    Shot of an island with an unusual shape.

After the slide presentation, a series of simple charts with hand-drawn and/or pasted pictures may be used to measure learning in conjunction with the following basic set of questions.

Chart 1:    Which of these pictures is a picture of an island?

Chart 2:    Which of these pictures is not a picture of an island?

Chart 3:    Which of these pictures shows something that all islands have? (illustrates one attribute)

Chart 4:    Which of these pictures shows something that all islands have? (illustrates another attribute)

Let us now consider an older group of students about to learn the concept of *nonverbal communication*. We might follow a similar format, using pictures and/or role-played episodes as examples and nonexamples. Both scenes from printed advertisements, as well as commercially made photographs and pictures, could be used.

Three-dimensional models also can be employed effectively as examples and nonexamples, particularly in the areas of science and mathematics, for demonstrating concepts like molecules and sets. Three-dimensional models have the additional advantage of providing "hands on" experience with the concept. Simple hand-prepared charts and posters are another medium that lends itself to all subject matter areas. In mathematics, for example, the concept of *mode* can be cleanly and quickly illustrated through a series of charts or through a single one, as shown here.

---

*Examples of Mode*

---

5, 6, 7, _8, 8,_ 9, 10

9, 10, _12,_ 13, 10, _12,_ 8, _12, 12,_ 6

_97,_ 94, 32, _97,_ 75, 63, 29, 85, _97_

1, 13, _22, 22,_ 12, 14, 27, 83, 15, _22_

_72, 72, 72, 72, 72, 72_

_65,_ 64, _65,_ 63, 71, 62, 63, _65_

_1,_ 0, 9, 6, 5, 7, 7, 8, _1,_ 3, _1, 1_

---

An alternate format for the instruction would be to use the chalkboard or the overhead projector. A simple mastery test could consist of a series of new number examples and nonexamples for correct identification, or else a sequence of open-ended questions such as: "What do all the examples have in common?" "How would you define a *mode* in your own words?"

Materials for concept learning also may be designed as self-instructional units. A basic self-instructional sequence or *minitext* designed to teach the concept of *organization* is shown on the next few pages.[8]

**ORGANIZATION**

In this booklet, you are going to learn some things about an organization. Please be sure to read *all* the material on *all* the pages.

This booklet is short and will not take very long to complete.

After you have finished reading the material, you will be asked some questions about what you have just learned.

PLEASE DO *NOT* WRITE IN THE BOOKLET.

PLEASE TURN TO THE NEXT PAGE.

### ORGANIZATION

Tia is a member of the Girl Scouts. James is a member of the Boy Scouts. The Girl Scouts and Boy Scouts *are* organizations. Girl Scouts and Boy Scouts agree to follow certain rules. They enjoy playing games and going on trips together.

All of the boys in one third grade class started a Pirate Club. It *was* an organization. The boys were interested in the same things — pirate stories and ships. So, when they made up a set of rules for the club, one rule was that they would meet once a month to hear pirate stories.

The people in the stands at a baseball game are *not* an organization. They are all interested in baseball, but they did *not* join a group and did not agree to rules in order to see the baseball game. All the fans in the stands at the game do not form an organization. But each of the baseball teams the fans are watching *is* an organization. All nine team members wish to play baseball, and they must obey the rules. Unless they agree to the rules of the team, they are not allowed to belong to it. During the year the team members practice and play together.

Susan and her parents belong to the temple near their house. Thomas and his parents belong to the church two miles from their house. Both the temple and the church *are* organizations. Their members come together to learn about God. Their members all agree to follow certain customs of the temple and the church. They all agree to believe certain things.

Mr. Morton owns a small bread company. He is the only member of the company. He bakes the bread himself and delivers it himself. His company is *not* an organization. Mr. Morton is very interested in his company, and he has set up rules to follow for himself. But since the company has only one member, it is *not* an organization.

All the neighbors in a block have a problem they want to solve. There is too much trash in the neighborhood. They form a Neighborhood Council. It *is* an organization. The members of the Neighborhood Council agree to report all cases of trash in the streets. They also agree to spend two hours a week picking up trash. Once every two weeks, the members call each other to report on the trash pickup.

The Senate of the United States *is* an organization. Senators must follow certain rules to become members of the Senate. There may only be 100 Senators. One of their main interests is to make laws for the country. In order to help pass a law, the Senators must come together in the Senate and vote.

Ten people are shipwrecked on an island. They are all interested in saving their lives. However, they do *not* belong to an organization. No one is able to make a set of rules that all ten can agree to.

Do you think you know now what an *organization* is?

If the answer is *yes,* return this booklet to the person who gave it to you.

If the answer is *no,* read over the material in the booklet again. Then, return the booklet.

When you are ready, you will be asked some questions about what you have just read.

Following completion of the minitext, students take a mastery test. The sample measure shown here also includes a simple evaluation of the minitext itself.

1. Which of these is an organization?
   (a) children playing in the street
   (b) the President of the United States
   (c) people at a concert
   (d) the Boy Scouts

2. Which of these is *not* an organization?
   (a) the football team in your neighborhood
   (b) the children on swings at the playground
   (c) the City Council
   (d) Girl Scouts

3. The Hot Rod Club is
   (a) a meeting
   (b) a council
   (c) an organization
   (d) a government

4. Which is true about *all* organizations?
   (a) They have rules and common interests.
   (b) They must have at least 10 members.
   (c) The members must pay dues.
   (d) The oldest member is always the leader.

5. Which is true about *all* organizations?
   (a) There must be at least two members.
   (b) Only adults may belong.
   (c) Members must meet every week.
   (d) They are always interested in governmental matters.

6. Which is *not always* true about an organization?
   (a) The members of an organization are all the same age.
   (b) There is more than one member.
   (c) All the members have the same problem or interests.
   (d) All the members agree to certain rules.

7. An organization is:
   (a) A gathering of people in the same place.
   (b) A group of people who vote for the same man.
   (c) A group of people who are used to doing many things in the same way every time that they get together.
   (d) A group of people with accepted rules who do things together because they have the same interests or problems.

8. An organization is a kind of
   (a) government
   (b) person
   (c) group
   (d) meeting

9. Look at the pictures below. Which face best describes how *you feel* about organizations. Write the letter of the face on your answer sheet.

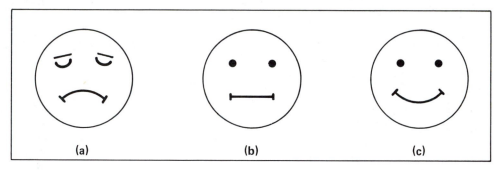

(a)                    (b)                    (c)

**FIGURE 6.11**

10. Which of the answers below tells best how *you feel* about the booklet on organization?
    (a) I feel very happy about it.
    (b) I feel sort of happy about it.
    (c) It was okay.
    (d) I did not like it.
    (e) I really did not like it at all.

11. Would you tell a friend that he or she ought to read this booklet if he or she asked you about it?
    (a) Yes, all of it.
    (b) Yes, parts of it.
    (c) No.
    (d) I am not sure.

*Note:* If you are done, please return these questions and your answer sheet to the person who gave them to you.

Several dimensions of concept mastery are measured in this test, as well as some characteristics of the instructional materials.

*Item 1* measures whether, given the name of a concept, the student can select an example of the concept.

*Item 2* measures whether, given the name of a concept, the student can select a nonexample of the concept.

*Item 3* measures whether, given an example of a concept, the student can identify its name.

*Items 4 and 5* measure whether, given the name of the concept, the student can select the names of relevant attributes of the concept.

*Item 6* measures whether, given the name of the concept, the student can select the names of irrelevant attributes of the concept.

*Item 7* measures whether, given the name of the concept, the student can select the correct definition of the concept.

*Item 8* measures whether, given the name of a concept, the student can select a broader concept to which it is closely related.

*Items 9, 10, and 11* measure the student's affective reaction to the instruction he or she has just received.

Audio recordings also are a useful medium for concept instruction, particularly for the areas of language arts, foreign language, and music. Playing contrasting examples and nonexamples of concepts such as *polyphony* and *counterpoint*, for example, offers learners concrete and structured experiences with the concept. Similarly, certain concepts from other subject matter areas, such as *soliloquy, feedback,* and *idiomatic expression*, are effectively presented through audio formats.

Case studies are a general vehicle for concept instruction. They may be drawn from commercially prepared materials, constructed by a teacher, or adapted from a variety of sources, including commercial materials. Such materials contain carefully structured vignettes with as much noncriterial material as possible removed and with focusing instructions and questions included. Where case studies are used in conjunction with teacher directions, the questions and focusing may occur in the context of general discussion. Case studies are suitable for all areas of the curriculum, especially social studies, science, language arts, music, and health education.

A concept learning activity that can take many forms and which can be used at all grade levels and for a variety of subject matter areas involves students in the construction of *concept folders*. Older students can use 8½ × 11 folders, and young children boxes, to store data on particular concepts. A concept is identified, and after its attributes and rule have been identified and clarified and some examples provided, students are asked to collect data — pictures and/or cases, etc. — over a period of time that are examples of the concept. When the projects are completed, the various folders may be exchanged and shared. Where required, students may be asked to explain the meaning and content of their collections. Several different concepts may be assigned simultaneously.

# Mastery Test

## OBJECTIVE 3

(a) To distinguish between the private and public dimensions of concept learning; and (b) to identify and briefly describe the three stages of preparation for the teaching of concepts.

1. What is meant by the "public" and "private" dimensions of concepts?

_____

_____

_____

_____

_____

2. Identify and briefly describe the three stages of preparation for the teaching of concepts.

_____

_____

_____

_____

_____

## ANSWER KEY

### Mastery Test, Objective 3

1. The "private" dimensions of concepts are all of the personal, noncriterial associations, correct or incorrect, that a given individual identifies with the concept name. The "public" dimensions of concepts are the essential or criterial properties that are agreed upon and shared by those who can correctly identify examples and nonexamples of the concept.

2. Basically, the three-stage process should proceed as follows: Initially, the teacher determines whether the concept is an appropriate one to *teach* (Concept Appropriateness Inventory). If the concept is appropriate for teaching, then the concept is analyzed and some instructional planning considerations are outlined (Prerequisite Planning Inventory). Finally, a detailed set of procedures for teaching the concept are developed (Basic Model for Concept Instruction).

# Objective 4

(a) To identify five dimensions of concept learning that can be measured and to arrange them according to their level of complexity; and (b) to identify and briefly describe three procedures for measuring the private dimensions of students' concepts.

## LEARNING ACTIVITY 4

**MEASURING CONCEPT LEARNING**

Several approaches to measuring concept learning already have been suggested through the illustrations in the preceding section. A basic measure of whether a concept has been learned involves the ability to discriminate new examples of the concept from nonexamples correctly. Unless a student can perform satisfactorily on this fundamental test, learning may not be inferred. Ability to verbalize the concept rule is another *more complex* dimension of concept learning. Young children particularly have great difficulty with this task, even though they perform satisfactorily on discrimination tasks.

Essentially, measurement of concept learning may be viewed as dealing with the following increasingly more complex dimensions:

1. Identification of criterial attributes and nonattributes
2. Discrimination of examples from nonexamples
3. Identification of the concept rule
4. Ability to relate the concept to other concepts
5. Use of the concept in a novel way

Depending upon the significance of the concept and a teacher's objectives, mastery may be assessed over one or all of these dimensions. For many simple instructional activities, identification of criterial attributes can be presumed and a discrimination test will suffice. Other situations will call for measurement of all five dimensions.

Often a teacher wishes to tap the *personal dimensions* of concept learning, either prior to or following related instruction. Such assessment can proceed informally through open-ended discussions, through simple paper-and-pencil questionnaires, or through inventories. Figure 6.5 is one such approach. Two alternative diagnostic activities are outlined here. The first is borrowed from the studies of Michael Wallach and Nathan Kogan on thinking in young children; the second is based upon research into thinking strategies conducted by Hilda Taba.

The Wallach and Kogan activity, although developed for young children, is applicable to all grade levels and subject areas. We will call it the *Like-Things Game.* Concepts from any curricular area may be substituted for the ones used in the example here. Instructions similar to those provided here are used with the students. The instructions may be modified as necessary for different age levels or concepts.

"In this game I am going to name two objects, and I will want you to think of all the ways that these two objects are alike. I might name any two objects — like door and chair. But whatever I say, it will be your job to think of all the ways that the two objects are alike. For example, tell me all the ways that an apple and an orange are alike." (The child then responds.) "That's very good. You've already said a lot of the things I was thinking of. I guess you could also say that they are both round, and they are both sweet, they both have seeds, they both are fruits, they both have skins, they both grow on trees — things like that. Yours were fine, too."[9]

Sets of similar objects, events, or people along the lines of the following might be used with some basic instructions.

1. Tell me all the ways in which squares and quadrilaterals are alike.
2. Tell me all the ways in which sharps and flats are alike.
3. Tell me all the ways in which a lithograph and a print are alike.
4. Tell me all the ways in which a river and a stream are alike.
5. Tell me all the ways in which rockets and planes are alike.
6. Tell me all the ways in which love and hate are alike.
7. Tell me all the ways in which density and cubic feet are alike.
8. Tell me all the ways in which wind and water currents are alike.
9. Tell me all the ways in which churches and banks are alike.
10. Tell me all the ways in which architects and engineers are alike.

Assume you are dealing with a high school government class. You might wish to use the gamelike activity to compare the students' concepts of

electoral college and legislature
primary and election
city and state
norm and law
executive privilege and judicial review

The list of concepts can be as long or as short as desired.

## The Taba Strategy

Several years ago, Hilda Taba developed, and later her associates refined, a systematic strategy that allows a teacher to diagnose student concept states easily. Her strategy consists of three key steps to be carried out in exactly the sequence indicated, with as much time spent at each point as is required. The three basic steps are as follows:

1. Enumerate and list students' responses to an opening question.
2. Have the students group the responses.
3. Have the students label the groups.

Within each of these three key activities, there is a structured role that the teacher must play. The Northwest Regional Educational Laboratory has developed some appropriate questions and statements for a teacher to use in carrying out this role. The following sequence is drawn and adapted from their analysis of the teacher's role.[10]

1. *Enumeration and Listing*

   *Opening question.*   Raise an open-ended question that calls for remembered information concerning the concept to be analyzed and expanded.

"What comes to mind when you hear the word *heredity*?"
"What do you know about triangles?"
"What do you think of when you hear the word *poetry*?"

*Refocusing statement.*   When the responses indicate that students have begun to stray from the topic, call attention to the opening question.

"Let me repeat the original question."

*Clarifying question.*   Frequently students use a term that is unclear or that has many meanings. Ask for clarification.

"What sort of modern paintings?"
"Can you give me an example of a 'way out' person?"
"Can you help me out? I'm not sure I understand what you mean by getting snookered."

*Summarizing question.*   Frequently a student will respond to your opening question with a paragraph or two. Request that he or she abstract the main idea.

"How could we put that on the board?"
"How could we write that in one sentence?"
"Can you help me out? How could we state that to get it in this little space on the board?"

*Mapping-the-field question.*   Try to get as much information as possible.

"Are there any areas that we have missed?"
"Can you think of any other things?"

2. *Grouping the Responses*

*Grouping questions.*   The initial question in the grouping process requests students to group their responses in any fashion they wish.

"Let's look over our list. Can you find any items that could be grouped together?"
"Are there any items on the board that could be grouped together?"

*Grouping rationale question.*   A key element in the grouping process is focusing attention on the rationale used to categorize items. When students do not provide it automatically, request a reason.

"Why did you put _____, _____, and _____ together?"

3. *Labeling the Groups*

*Labeling question.*   The basic question for the labeling process asks the students to analyze a group of items and state a name or label for the grouping.

"Let's look at the first group. What title could we give to this list?"

Unlike the preceding model, Taba's schema should be followed in *exactly* the order specified. It is also crucial that the teacher accept *all* student responses without judging them as correct or incorrect. While, to be sure, students are likely to offer factually incorrect statements or offer apparently illogical groupings and labels, the teacher's role in this model is *not* to challenge or correct, but to accept and list all responses. Keep in mind that the objective is to analyze and expand conceptual associations. In this vein, when students disagree on classmates' groupings, *they have to be reminded that each individual's conceptual organization is unique, and that the rules of discussion in this case require the freedom of self-expression.*

At this point, refer back to the earlier discussion indicated and reread the procedures before attempting the following activity. You will need to have the Taba procedures clearly in mind to complete this activity successfully.

Complete the following Response Form by yourself. You are about to discover how well you have internalized one dimension of the Taba procedures for concept diagnosis — handling student responses — by engaging in a role-playing activity with a series of hypothetical students.

# RESPONSE FORM

You have the role of the teacher, and you have just asked a group of high school students the question "What comes to mind when you hear the word *drama*?" Some of the students have answered as indicated below. You are poised by the chalkboard, chalk in hand, ready to record responses. After each of their answers, in the space provided, note how you would handle their statements or exactly how you would respond to them. Remember to stay in your role and to answer just as if you were actually talking to each student. Be as specific in your answers as you actually would be when you ask for clarification, etc.

1. *Paula:* "I think of lots of action and fine acting.

   *Your response:* _____

   _____

   _____

2. *Perry:* "It reminds me of when I was a kid and my grandfather took me to see a Shakespeare play. I didn't know what was coming off. There were all these people in funny costumes, and I couldn't understand most of what they were saying."

   *Your response:* _____

   _____

   _____

3. *Tito:* "It reminds me of life, how things really are."

   *Your response:* _____

   _____

4. *Wally:* "When you have a drama, you always have a big cast of characters."

   *Your response:* _____

   _____

   _____

5. *Pam:* "That's not true, Wally. I remember reading about a drama that only had two characters."

   *Your response:* _____

   _____

   _____

6. *Mary:* "Dramas always seem to deal with basic emotions that all people have."

   *Your response:* _____

   _____

   _____

7. *Dorothy:* "I guess for me what comes to mind is Saturday nights and my family."

   *Your response:* _____

   _____

   _____

8. *Jack:* "But drama as I think of it is a bunch of clever lines and speeches."

   *Your response:* _____

   _____

   _____

9. *Taffy:* "It makes me think of how much I like musical plays!"

   *Your response:* _____

   _____

   _____

After you have completed your role playing, check with others who have also completed the exercise to see how they responded to the students. Analyze all the sets of responses against the Taba procedures specified. How closely did your treatments of the responses follow the suggested format?

Finally, consider the following analyses in evaluating your own.

1. *Paula:* Her response can simply be acknowledged and recorded as some variation of "Lots of action and fine acting." A minor

alternative response would be to ask, "Would you like me to list 'lots of action' and 'fine acting' as separate items?"

2. *Perry:* He is just a little verbose. You need to ask him to summarize. Any way to accomplish this without rejecting his original comment is satisfactory. For example, "How could I summarize that to get it in this little space?"

3. *Tito:* You might just accept this response as is. Or, to be sure that everyone understands the point, you might ask, "Could you give us an example of what you mean?"

4. *Wally:* Record "Always have a big cast of characters," *even though the association is incorrect.* You are *diagnosing* the level of knowledge the students have, whatever it may be. In order to get an honest assessment, you must establish the discussion ground rule by explaining that "We just want to find out what people think of when they hear the word *drama.* Later on we can examine whether things are right or wrong."

5. *Pam:* Tell her to remember the discussion ground rules, and verbalize the ground rule just cited.

6. *Mary:* Just record "Always seem to deal with basic emotions that all people have."

7. *Dorothy:* Clarification is in order. Ask, "Can you help us out? What is meant by your reference to 'Saturday nights and my family'?"

8. *Jack:* Just record "A bunch of clever lines and speeches."

9. *Taffy:* Just record "How much I like musical plays." Taffy's negative or indirect association is clear and to the point.

Your final listing on the board would appear in some fashion similar to the following:

1. Lots of action and fine acting.
2. (Perry's summary statement.)
3. Life, how things really are (possibly followed by an example, if you requested one).
4. Always have a big cast of characters.
5. (Pam's response after being reminded of the ground rule.)
6. Always seem to deal with basic emotions that all people have.
7. Saturday nights and my family (followed by a clarification of the meaning of the terms).
8. A bunch of clever lines and speeches.
9. How much I like musical plays.

Once you have internalized some of the basic responding procedures related to the first phase of the Taba strategy, you should be prepared to try all *three* steps with a live audience. If you wish to test your competency, organize a group of seven to ten students for a microteaching lesson. (Fewer than seven students will restrict considerably the amount of interaction, though the activity is still possible.) Select any concept you feel is both appropriate and potentially interesting for the group. Take three minutes or so to introduce the situation, and then begin the strategy.

# Mastery Test

**OBJECTIVE 4**     (a) To identify five dimensions of concept learning that can be measured and to arrange them according to their level of complexity; and (b) to identify and briefly describe three procedures for measuring the private dimensions of students' concepts.

1. List five different dimensions of concept learning that may be measured and arrange them in order of decreasing complexity by starting with the most complex process and working down to the least complex process.

_____

_____

_____

_____

_____

2. Identify and briefly describe three procedures for assessing the "private" dimensions of students' concepts.

_____

_____

_____

_____

_____

_____

Compare your answers with those found in the Answer Key that follows.

## ANSWER KEY

Mastery Test, Objective 4

1. The correct arrangement of the items in order of decreasing complexity is

   Use of the concept in a novel way

   Ability to relate the concept to other concepts

   Identification of the concept rule

   Discrimination of examples from nonexamples

   Identification of criterial attributes and nonattributes

2. One approach is the *Like-Things Game.* It calls for students to describe how sets of objects, events, or people are similar by answering a series of open-ended questions. A second approach is a three-step strategy devised by Hilda Taba to assess what associations a group of students attach to a particular concept. The steps involve enumerating and listing associations, grouping them, and finally labeling them. Still a third approach involves each student completing a simple conceptual network diagram similar to Figure 6.6.

# Final Mastery Test

At the outset, you were asked to assess what you knew about concepts through a basic true–false test. Reexamine your responses in that first test to determine how much information you have mastered in this chapter.

To test your mastery of various objectives established for the chapter, see how many of the following questions you can answer.

1. What are at least four different ways in which the term "concept" is used in educational literature?

   _____

   _____

   _____

   _____

2. What basic information is required to teach a concept?

   _____

   _____

3. How do criterial and noncriterial attributes differ?

   _____

   _____

   _____

4. Identify at least two basic reasons why concepts are important.

   _____

   _____

   _____

5. Identify at least three different systems for classifying concepts and explain their meaning.

   _____

   _____

   _____

6. Which concept classification system takes into account developmental differences? In what way?

   _____

   _____

   _____

   _____

7. How do the "private" and "public" dimensions of concepts differ?

_____

_____

_____

_____

_____

_____

_____

8. Summarize the seven steps in the Basic Instructional Model.

_____

_____

_____

_____

_____

_____

_____

_____

_____

9. What are three different levels of concept learning that may be measured?

_____

_____

_____

_____

_____

_____

_____

_____

_____

_____

# ANSWER KEY

## Final Mastery Test

Your answers should be along the following lines:

1. As ideas; as themes or topics; as a general, all-encompassing statement; as elements or structures of a discipline; or as categories into which we organize and relate our knowledge and experiences.
2. Name, criterial attributes, noncriterial attributes, rule, examples, and nonexamples.
3. Criterial attributes are the essential, defining characteristics of concepts. Noncriterial attributes are those which frequently are present in concept examples but are not essential.
4. Concepts simplify our environment; they simplify our learning task; they make communication easier; they help us distinguish between reality and imagery; they enrich our lives.
5. Concrete and abstract; conjunctive, disjunctive, and relational; formal and informal; enactive, iconic, and symbolic. (Check pages 203–205 for the meanings.)
6. Enactive, iconic, and symbolic. (See page 205 for the meanings.)
7. Private dimensions are the personal associations that each of us has with concepts; public dimensions are the basic or criterial characteristics of concepts that people share in common.
8. (a) Complete the Concept Appropriateness Inventory and the Prerequisite Planning Inventory.
   (b) Develop an introduction to the instruction sequence. The introduction should orient the learner to the task and arouse his or her curiosity.
   (c) Present the series of varied examples and nonexamples of the concept that you have developed in some logical order. (There are no hard and fast rules on "how many." Consider a minimum of seven examples as a rule of thumb.)
   (d) If possible, present all the examples and nonexamples simultaneously or in close succession, so that the learner can compare all the cases.
   (e) Interject the cues, directions, and questions throughout the materials as necessary in order to draw attention to criterial and noncriterial attributes and to similarities and differences in examples and nonexamples. Correspondingly, encourage learner questions. In written material, cues may be arrows, marginal notes, underlining, and the like.
   (f) Assess concept mastery at a minimal level, namely, whether students can correctly discriminate among *new* examples and nonexamples.
   (g) Assess concept mastery at more advanced levels, as consistent with the developmental capabilities of the students and with your objectives.
9. Identification of criterial attributes and nonattributes; discrimination of examples from nonexamples; identification of the concept rule; ability to relate the concept to other concepts; use of the concept in a novel way.

NOTES

1. Jerome Kagan, "Preschool Enrichment and Learning," *Interchange* II (1971): 17.

2. Jerome S. Bruner, *Beyond the Information Given: Studies in the Psychology of Knowing* (New York: W. W. Norton, 1973), p. 316.

3. *Ibid.*, pp. 327–328.

4. *Teacher's Guide for Attribute Games and Problems* (New York: McGraw-Hill, 1968), pp. 74–77.

5. Adapted from A. M. Voelker and J. S. Sorenson, *An Analysis of Selected Classificatory Science Concepts in Preparation for Writing Tests of Concept Attainment*, Working Paper No. 57 (Madison, Wis.: Research and Development Center for Cognitive Learning, University of Wisconsin, 1971).

6. Robert M. Gagné, "The Learning of Concepts," in M. David Merrill, ed., *Instructional Design: Readings* (Englewood Cliffs, New Jersey: Prentice-Hall, 1971), p. 299.

7. Produced by *Project Econ 12* at San Jose State University, California.

8. Peter H. Martorella, "Instructional Products for Concept Learning," Temple University, Philadelphia, Pennsylvania, 1973.

9. Michael Wallach and Nathan Kogan, *Modes of Thinking in Young Children* (New York: Holt, Rinehart & Winston, 1965), p. 32.

10. John A. McCollum and Rose Marie Davis, *Trainer's Manual: Development of Higher Level Thinking Abilities*, rev. ed. (Portland, Oregon: Northwest Regional Educational Laboratory, 1969), pp. 160–161.

ADDITIONAL READINGS

Bank, Adrienne, et al. *A Practical Guide to Program Planning: A Teaching Models Approach.* New York: Teacher's College Press, 1981.

Brown, Roger. *Words and Things.* New York: Free Press, 1968.

Bruner, Jerome S., et al. *A Study of Thinking.* New York: John Wiley & Sons, 1956.

Carroll, John B. "Words, Meanings and Concepts." *Harvard Educational Review* XXIV (Spring 1964): 178–202.

Eisner, Elliot W. *Cognition and Curriculum: A Basis for Deciding What to Teach,* Chapter 2. New York: Longman, 1982.

Gagné, Robert M. *The Conditions of Learning.* 4th ed. New York: Holt, Rinehart & Winston, 1985.

Glaser, Robert. "Concept Learning and Concept Teaching," in I. E. Sigel and F. H. Hooper, eds. *Learning Research and School Subjects.* New York: Holt, Rinehart & Winston, 1963.

Klausmeier, Herbert J., and Frank H. Hooper. "Conceptual Development and Instruction," in F. N. Kerlinger and J. B. Carroll, eds. *Review of Research in Education, 2.* Itasca, Illinois: F. T. Peacock, 1974.

Martorella, Peter H. *Concept Learning: Designs for Instruction.* New York: International Textbook, 1972.

Ribivich, Jerilyn K. "A Methodology for Teaching Concepts," *The Reading Teacher* (December 1979): 285–289.

Taba, Hilda. *Teaching Strategies and Cognitive Functioning in Elementary School Children.* Cooperative Research Project no. 2404. Washington, D.C.: U.S. Office of Education, 1966.

Tennyson, Robert, and O. Park. "The Teaching of Concepts: A Review of Instructional Design Literature," *Review of Educational Research* 50 (1980): 53–70.

Vygotsky, L. S. *Thought and Language.* Ed. and trans. by Eugenia Hanfmann and Gertrude Vakar. Cambridge, Massachusetts: M.I.T. Press, 1962.

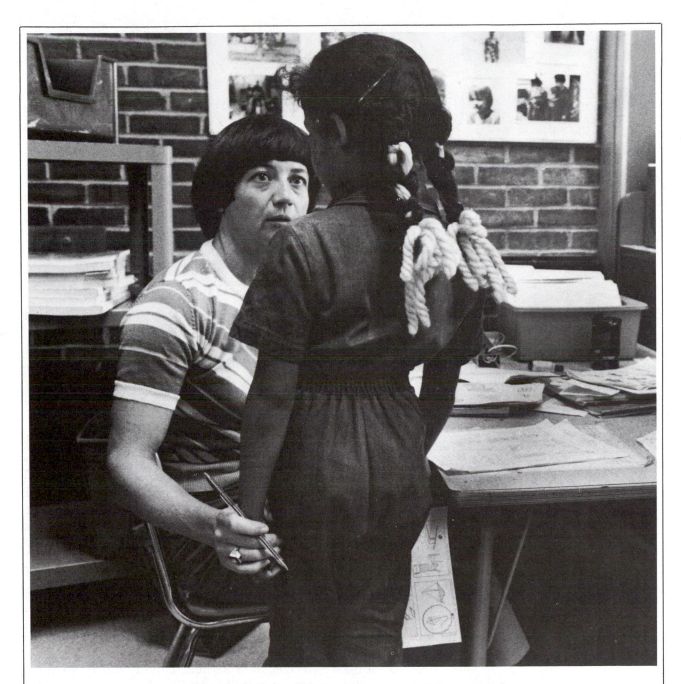

Sandra Sokolove Garrett,
Myra Sadker, and David Sadker

# 7. Interpersonal Communication Skills

# Objectives

**1** To describe the characteristics of attending behavior.

**2** To differentiate between the intellectual and the emotional content of messages (active listening).

**3** To differentiate among the three types of reflecting — word messages, behaviors, inferences.

**4** To differentiate among inventory questions that (1) stimulate communication, (2) clarify information, (3) identify discrepancies, and (4) seek alternatives or solutions.

In times of rapid change, when there are few beliefs to hold on to, there is one maxim that has withstood the test of time: "Know thyself." Socrates' message to his disciples thousands of years ago still has a great deal of relevance for today's teachers and their students. Yet "knowing oneself" is rarely a topic discussed in the classroom. Further, developing teaching strategies to facilitate such inquiry is rarely included in the curriculum of most teacher-training programs.

In this chapter you will have the opportunity to master a series of behaviors that will facilitate positive interpersonal communication between you and your students — communication that leads to self-inquiry and greater self-knowledge. The following introduction establishes the foundation for the role of such inquiry as a critical part of the learning process.

The quest for self-knowledge, as a critical dimension of healthy growth and development, finds its roots in the literature of humanistic psychology. This branch of psychology portrays a dynamic and positive picture of the nature of human beings. Among its basic tenets is a belief that people are free and unique creatures, who, when given a choice, will intuitively choose effective paths of action. Humanistic psychologists describe human beings as self-directed, capable of setting goals, making choices, and initiating action. They also view people as capable of judging the consequences and effectiveness of their own actions. Humanistic psychologists also believe that, in order to function in the most effective manner and to maximize individual potential, people must first become aware of their internal thoughts and feelings regarding both themselves (self-perceptions) and the world at large. By consciously describing these thoughts (cognition) and feelings (affect), people may gain an awareness of how such states influence their behavior. The interrelationships among thoughts, feelings, and behaviors thus form a blueprint for living. Yet, how the individual pieces are shaped within this blueprint need not remain static. All human beings, according to humanistic psychologists, are responsible for and in control of their own actions.

Weinstein and Fantini (1970)[1] propose that often the thoughts and feelings people have about themselves focus around three broad areas of concern which they have termed: identity, connectedness, and power. For example, they state that most persons have deep concerns (thoughts and feelings) about themselves and their sense of *identity*. They ask such questions as, "Who am I? Where am I going? What do I want out of life?" Most people are also concerned about their relationships with others. They may ask: "How do I fit or *connect* with other people? Do people like me? Do they want to be with me?" Still further, all people need to define their own limits, to develop a sense of *power* that will enable them to take some measure of control over their lives.

Although a variety of psychologists have defined other areas of concern [McClelland (1961), achievement, affiliation, power; Schutz (1967), inclusion, control, and affection; Glasser (1965), relatedness, respect; Horney (1942), sense of competence and approval], most of them can be included in the Weinstein and Fantini model. Regardless of the labels presented, humanistic psychologists stress that healthy development depends on people's conscious ability to define behavior. They further state that a critical part of the learning process is the ability to judge whether or not one's thoughts and feelings are productive or unproductive and then to make whatever modifications or adjustments seem necessary. The ultimate goal of this search for self-knowledge is greater self-control and more productive living.

Alschuler and his colleagues (1975) present the following working definition of self-knowledge: "A verbal description of one's characteristics or habitual internal and external responses (thoughts, feelings, and actions) to a set of similar stimuli and the consequences of those specified responses."[2] Further, they state that self-knowledge "increases one's options for going beyond unsatisfying habitual responses."[3] In other words, once human beings gain an increased awareness of how they respond to various situations and what the consequences of these responses are, they can then proceed to choose more satisfying options — options that can lead to more directed, purposeful, and productive lives.

The process of gaining self-knowledge is a continuous and complicated one that is dependent on people's interactions with one another. "How we interact, relate and transact with others, and the reciprocal impact of this phenomenon form the single most important aspect of our existence. Only through interaction with others can we become aware of our own identity."[4]

Within the context of public education, teachers are an integral part of this interactive process. They are the ones who can create a classroom environment that will stimulate and reinforce personal inquiry and help students gain insight into their own identities. Research (Purkey, 1970; Combs, 1965) has shown that students' attitudes (feelings) about themselves are often influenced by how they imagine their teachers perceive them. When teachers project a positive regard for their students, students in return often begin to see themselves and their abilities in more positive ways. Still further, students' attitudes and values are often greatly influenced by their perceptions of their teachers' behaviors (Sokolove, 1975). Students consciously and unconsciously imitate their teachers' styles of behavior and often accept the attitudes and values projected by their teachers as their own.

Therefore, if teachers are to create an environment that is conducive to personal growth, they must first explore their own feelings, attitudes, and values about themselves and their students. Next they must consider the effects these emotions and values have on their actions and, finally, they must deliberately model interpersonal communications that facilitate teacher–student interaction.

Interpersonal communication skills may be defined as a series of specific verbal and nonverbal behaviors that stimulate personal inquiry between two or more persons — inquiry that leads to greater self-knowledge. By employing these behavioral skills, a teacher can help students express and clarify their thoughts and feelings and understand how these internal states affect their behavior. The modeling of such behaviors by the teacher helps initiate this interactive process and provides guidance to students as they too learn to employ these skills.

Before providing a brief overview of these skills, let's look at the dynamics of effective interpersonal communications. As previously mentioned, the personal growth process is interactive in nature. That is, the assistance of other trusted persons is needed before interpersonal sharing can begin. Speakers must be willing to receive both verbal and nonverbal feedback from listeners, and listeners must feel secure enough to provide such feedback.

The following diagram, called the "Johari Window," will help to clarify how self-knowledge is gained through the process of interpersonal communication.

JOHARI WINDOW*

|  | (A) Known to Self | (B) Not known to Self |
|---|---|---|
| (C) Known to others | Area I (A,C) *Public Self* (common knowledge) | Area III (B,C) *Blind Area* |
| (D) Not known to others | Area II (A,D) *Private Self* (secrets, private thoughts) | Area IV (B,D) *Unconscious Self* (undeveloped potential) |

* From *Of Human Interaction* by Joseph Luft, by permission of Mayfield Publishing Co., copyright © 1969 by the National Press. See also *Group Processes*.

There is specific information that is known both to yourself and to others (Area I, Public Self). It may be information received from visual cues such as "You are wearing a red dress today," or it may be information that you are willing to disclose to others, such as a fear of snakes or a vote you cast for a particular candidate in the last election. The content may be thoughts (cognitive) or emotions (affective) and/or behaviors.

At the same time, you may have personal concerns such as "I need money," "I am afraid of speaking in front of others," or "I'm confused" that you may not wish to share with others. This represents the Private Self sector (Area II).

Still other information may be known to others but unknown to you: your face gets red when you are angry, you cut off speakers in the middle of their sentences, or your body is fidgeting when you speak. This information is known as the Blind Area (Area III).

Finally, there exists an area of information that is unknown both to yourself and to others: the Unconscious Self (Area IV). The goal of the personal growth process is to continue gaining more information about yourself (self-knowledge) and, ultimately, to open up areas of unknown potential (Area IV). Consider the following dynamics: As you develop a helping relationship with others and begin *disclosing* information about yourself, Area I (the Public Self) gradually becomes larger, and Area II (the Private Self) becomes smaller. Remember, this is a reciprocal process. Your disclosures prompt *feedback* from others concerning their perceptions of you. Consequently, Area I becomes still larger, while Area III (the Blind Area) becomes smaller. Through the combined interaction of disclosure and feedback, you can also begin opening up Area IV (the Unconscious Self), an area of unexplored thoughts, feelings, and behavior.

This disclosure and feedback process does not denote "telling everything to everybody." Rather, it involves the sharing of information that is relevant to a helping relationship. For example, you may have feelings of shyness or incompetence that can affect your ability to perform well in social situations. By sharing those feelings and receiving feedback from an empathetic listener, you can gain an awareness of how another person sees you and the effects of your actions on that person. You and your friend have not only shared valuable information and clarified possible misperceptions, but the entire process, if honest and sincere, may have built a more satisfying relationship. The process of verbalizing internal thoughts and feelings also helps you to "hear" yourself and to determine if the messages you are sending really reflect what you are feeling inside, that is, if you are sending congruent messages.

Interpersonal communication skills include such behaviors as *attending behavior*, *active listening*, *reflection*, *inventory questioning*, and *encouraging alternative behaviors*. These skills, when practiced effectively, will encourage students: (1) to express their thoughts and feelings; (2) to analyze and clarify their thoughts, feelings, and behaviors; (3) to note potential discrepancies between their actual response patterns and their desired response patterns; and (4) to choose, from among alternatives, new behaviors more in keeping with their desired behavior pattern.

These interpersonal communication skills are hierarchical in nature, with each successive skill including elements of the preceding ones. Together they comprise a taxonomy, with the skills on the lower levels requiring mastery before the skills on the higher levels can be attained.

By gaining proficiency in each of the skills of this taxonomy, a teacher can aid students in the process of gaining greater self-knowledge. Such knowledge will help sensitize students to any discrepancies that might exist between their actual and desired behaviors and, thereby, set the stage for eliminating these discrepancies. Ineffective behavior need not remain static; it can be changed. Once teachers and students become aware of their actions, and realize that not only do they have other choices, but they can also make such changes occur, they are in control.

The following table gives a further explanation of the interpersonal communication skills taxonomy.

### TAXONOMY OF INTERPERSONAL COMMUNICATION SKILLS*

| *Student Process* | *Teaching Skill* | |
| --- | --- | --- |
| *Cluster III* | | |
| Encouraging alternative behaviors | practicing alternative behaviors | |
| *Cluster II* | | |
| Clarifying students' expressions of feelings | reflection | inventory questioning |
| *Cluster I* | | |
| Eliciting students' expressions of feelings | attending behavior | active listening |

\* Adapted from Sadker and Sadker, *Interpersonal Skills of Teaching* (University of Wisconsin-Parkside, 1972).

**Cluster I. Eliciting Students' Expressions of Feelings.**   The two skills or behaviors which initiate teacher–student interpersonal communication and provide the foundation of this taxonomy are (a) attending behavior and (b) active listening behaviors. They may be perceived as climate setting behaviors that stimulate personal disclosure on the part of both teachers and students. Students will not risk sharing their feelings and attitudes if they feel threatened or manipulated. Consequently, an environment that is conducive to sharing is supportive rather than antagonistic, questioning rather than judgmental, flexible and somewhat permissive rather than highly structured and controlled. Students need to feel that their personal disclosures are being listened to seriously and will not lead to ridicule and rejection.

(a) *Attending.*   Through various nonverbal and verbal cues such as eye contact, facial and body gestures, and brief verbal acknowledgments, teachers can demonstrate that they are listening with care and empathy to what is being said. Consequently, they can encourage students to share their thoughts and feelings and know that they are being heard.

(b) *Active listening.*   One of the key steps in active listening is being able to differentiate between intellectual content and emotional content. All messages contain both types of content, and teachers must be able to detect and differentiate them if they are to help their students gain awareness of their own internal thoughts and feelings and ensuing behaviors. Active listening helps the listener make inferences privately about these two types of content by attending to the speaker's verbal and nonverbal cues.

**Cluster II. Clarifying Students' Expressions of Feelings.**   Once students feel comfortable enough to disclose information about themselves, teachers can then help them clarify that information. To do this teachers must be skilled at (a) reflecting and (b) inventory questioning.

(a) *Reflecting.*   The skill of reflecting, in essence, involves holding a mirror up to the student. Teachers can give students direct feedback about the way their verbal and nonverbal messages are being received. They may choose to reflect verbal communication, nonverbal communication, or even to make some inferences regarding the feelings that underlie these verbal and nonverbal messages. Carl Rogers says: "The student, seeing his own attitudes, confusions, ambivalences, feelings and perceptions accurately expressed by another, but stripped of the complication of emotion with which he himself invests them, paves the way for acceptance into the self of all those elements which are now clearly perceived."[5]

(b) *Inventory questions.** By asking inventory questions teachers can help students describe their thoughts, feelings, and manifested actions. Questions like these help students identify specific patterns of behavior or ways in which they characteristically respond to specific events. From that point, students can begin to assess the effectiveness of their behavior patterns. If this assessment shows a discrepancy between their actual and desired behavior, they may begin to consider other behaviors that are more congruent with their personal goals.

**Cluster III. Encouraging Alternative Behaviors.**   The final level of the taxonomy involves the exploration of alternative behaviors. This process includes (a) generating alternative behaviors, (b) practicing them and sensing how they feel, (c) receiving feedback from others regarding their effectiveness, (d) predicting their short-term and long-term consequences, and (e) choosing which pattern of behavior seems most congruent with personal needs.

Only the first two clusters of skills, eliciting and clarifying, will be presented in this chapter. Once you have mastered the skills of attending, active listening, reflecting, and inventory questioning, the transition to the third cluster — Encouraging Alternative Behaviors — will be a natural one.

Several notes of caution are in order before you begin mastering the Taxonomy of Interpersonal Communication Skills. First, the word "skill" in this context is misleading; it often connotes a series of techniques or actions such as technical skills in typing, computers, and the like. There is a great danger in the erroneous assumption that interpersonal communication is composed of a series of skills divorced from attitudes and feelings. It is not enough for teachers to model these skills. Behind teachers' actions there must be a sincere concern for the personal growth of their students; a genuine respect for the inherent good found in each human being; and a real commitment to the growth and actualization of student potential.

In addition, interpersonal communication often takes place in a private situation. Whatever information is shared between you and your students, especially that relating to attitudes, values and feelings, must not be discussed publicly without prior consent of the students involved. It takes a long time to establish a sense of trust; it can be destroyed in an instant if private information is discussed publicly, even in an innocent fashion.

Many of the attending cues discussed in the following section must be adapted to the nature of the individual student. For example, for some students physical touch may be a very uncomfortable form of exchange. This type of contact may have multiple connotations for

---

* Adapted from the Trumpet Model of Weinstein and Fantini. In *Towards Humanistic Education: A Curriculum of Affect* (New York: Praeger, 1970).

different cultures and ethnic groups. Although in general, touch evokes a sense of emotional closeness, some students may find it threatening. The same message also relates to the use of eye contact and physical space during communications.

Finally, behaviors used to stimulate interpersonal communications can be very powerful. When used inappropriately, they can be both manipulative and destructive; however, when used effectively, the taxonomy of interpersonal communications skills may stimulate within the student the greatest level of knowledge — self-knowledge. In addition, "when the teacher has the ability to understand the student's reactions from the inside, has a sensitive understanding of the way the process of education and learning seems to the student, then the likelihood of significant learning is increased."

# Objective 1

To describe the characteristics of attending behavior.

## LEARNING ACTIVITY 1

One of the factors that makes interpersonal communications so complicated is that both participants, the speaker and the listener, are sending and receiving messages simultaneously. For example, when you are involved in a conversation with another person, what cues are you looking at, reacting to, or being affected by? What nonverbal messages are being conveyed through the speaker's body language? What verbal message is the speaker conveying through his/her words? What environmental stimuli distract your attention? In order to create an environment that is conducive to disclosure and inquiry, you must first identify and then seek to control any stimuli that influence the interpersonal communication process. Among the more important stimuli are those labeled "attending behaviors."

We are all aware of what *nonattending* behavior looks like and the frustration that occurs when the listener is occupied with personal thoughts, environmental stimuli or suddenly interjects, "I know exactly what you mean. Let me tell what happened to me . . . ." Such nonattending behaviors detract measurably from effective interpersonal communication. Conversely, attending behaviors are those that put the speaker at ease. The speaker is not interrupted; rather, he or she receives brief verbal or nonverbal acknowledgments during the conversation.

Since communication is both verbal and nonverbal, people's actions often speak louder than their words. In fact, through his research Mehrabian (1966)[6] determined that over 90 percent of the messages teachers send to their students are nonverbal. Teachers can often say more with the wink of an eye than they can with several sentences. Listed below are several suggestions for developing your own attending behavior. They have been divided into both verbal and nonverbal components.

### Nonverbal Cues

**1. Eye Contact.**   Focus your eyes directly on the speaker but be sensitive to the effect such direct eye-to-eye contact may have. Many people feel uncomfortable with direct eye contact and tend to shy away from it. Readjust your focus accordingly.

**2. Facial Expressions.**   Your expressions (or lack of them) provide feedback to the speaker, thereby prompting him or her to say more, to slow down, to clarify. More important, let your face tell the speaker that you empathize with him or her. Smiles, frowns, expressions of surprise or disappointment don't cost very much. In fact, they are priceless, so share them! A word of caution though: too much expression, particularly negative expression, can be very distracting. Be aware of your own facial expressions and the effect that they have on the speaker, and adjust your reactions accordingly. Simultaneously, attend to the facial expressions of the speaker. What nonverbal messages are being conveyed?

**3. Body Posture.**   You can help the speaker relax by relaxing your own body. Body gestures also communicate meaning. Think how you feel when a listener points a finger at you or stands straight with arms folded across the chest. What nonverbal message does that body position communicate to you? Does it stimulate you to say more? Probably not. In fact, Mehrabian (1969)[7] noted that an arms akimbo position most often occurs in conversation with a disliked person. In contrast, when the listener leans toward or touches the speaker, a high level of interest and involvement is communicated. Attend to the body language of the speaker — it also is sending messages.

**4. Physical Space.**   Edward T. Hall (1966)[8] states that the distance people create between themselves has an inherent communication value. He describes an 18-inch distance between speakers as "intimate space," the 18-inch to 4-foot distance as "personal space," the 4-foot to 12-foot distance as "social distance," and beyond 12 feet as "public distance." Each of these distances communicates distinct nonverbal messages — from those of intimacy or emotional closeness where physical touching is possible to the space where physical touch is impossible and fine verbal and nonverbal details are imperceptible. Find a comfortable space between you and your students, one that communicates the message, "I want to make closer contact with you." If you are standing far away, walk across the room toward the student. Don't place physical as well as psychological obstacles in your path.

### Verbal Cues

**1. Silence.**   When used appropriately, silence can, indeed "be golden." It can give both parties a chance to stop and reflect on what has been said. It may also encourage the speaker to say more if he or she doesn't have to anticipate an instant response. Too often listeners feel compelled to make an immediate response and, consequently, they begin searching for a reply before the speaker has concluded. Wait a few seconds to be sure that the speaker has completed his/her thoughts.

**2. Brief Verbal Acknowledgments.**   On the other hand, nothing is more deadly than a "void silence," so you will do well to occasionally interject brief verbal acknowledgments, such as: "I see"; "Wow"; "Oh"; "That's too bad." The goal is to express interest and concern without interrupting or interjecting personal comments. Keep the reactions brief and quickly refocus on the speaker.

**3. Subsummaries.** When appropriate, summarize the essence of what the speaker has said in a sentence or two. By feeding back to the speaker the gist of his or her message, you validate the communication, and this often inspires further conversation.

---

*Summary of effective attending behavior*

Nonverbal cues
1. Eye contact.
2. Facial expressions that reflect empathy.
3. Relaxed body posture and body gestures.
4. Close spatial proximity.

Verbal Cues
1. Effective use of silence.
2. Minimal verbal acknowledgments.
3. Brief subsummaries.

---

# Mastery Test

## OBJECTIVE 1    To describe the characteristics of attending behavior.

Below are three classroom vignettes that contain both effective and ineffective examples of attending behavior. Read each vignette and answer the accompanying questions. You must answer all questions correctly in order to pass this Mastery Test.

### VIGNETTE 1

Mr. Donaldson has had a long day, a typical Monday when everything seems disorganized. As he sits at his desk, preparing the chemistry quiz, Matthew walks in.

> *Matthew:* "Hi, Mr. Donaldson. Do you have a few minutes to talk?"
> *Mr. Donaldson:* (looks up briefly, then back down at his work and continues writing).
> *Matthew:* (rather sheepishly) "I don't understand the equation that you presented today. Can you go over it again?"
> *Mr. Donaldson:* (continues writing) "Go find the equation in the lab manual and read it while I finish this."

Mr. Donaldson finally looks up and sees Matthew huddled in a chair and with a forlorn expression on his face. Remaining seated behind his desk and with an impassive expression, Mr. Donaldson asks: "Well, did you find it yet?"

*Question 1:* List at least two examples of nonattending behavior exhibited by Mr. Donaldson.

_____

_____

*Question 2:* List two nonverbal cues exhibited by Matthew.

_____

_____

## VIGNETTE 2

Mr. Donaldson repeats his question: "Well, did you find it? The formula is on page 66."

> *Matthew:* (looking rather frustrated) "I must be dense or something. I read the description three times but it doesn't make any sense to me. Could you . . ."
>
> *Mr. Donaldson:* (facing the board, interrupts Matthew) "How do you calculate the square root?"

_____

*Question 3:* List at least three attending behaviors (verbal and nonverbal) that Mr. Donaldson could have exhibited to increase the likelihood of effective communication.

_____

_____

_____

## VIGNETTE 3

When Matthew doesn't respond, Mr. Donaldson turns around, and walks over to Matthew: "These formulas can be very confusing in the beginning. Come over to the board with me and we will write them out step by step."

Mr. Donaldson waits a few seconds, looks at Matthew, puts his hand on Matthew's shoulder and smiles: "O.K.?"

*Matthew:* "O.K."

_____

*Question 4:* List at least four attending behaviors that Mr. Donaldson exhibited that facilitated more effective communications.

_____

_____

_____

_____

## ANSWER KEY

### Mastery Test, Objective 1

1. (a) lack of eye contact;
   (b) failure to use physical space in a manner conducive for communication;
   (c) failure to use facial expression that stimulates interpersonal communication.

2. (a) body posture (huddled);
   (b) facial expression (forlorn).

3. (a) used physical space more effectively by inviting Matthew to sit closer to the board and the teacher;
   (b) established eye contact with Matthew;
   (c) didn't interrupt Matthew while he was talking;
   (d) attended to Matthew's nonverbal behavior (look of frustration).

4. (a) established eye contact;
   (b) smiled (facial expression);
   (c) put his hand on Matthew's shoulder;
   (d) established close physical proximity;
   (e) used silence appropriately;
   (f) used subsummary to capture the essence of Matthew's verbal and nonverbal messages.

---

**ON YOUR OWN: FROM THEORY TO PRACTICE**

You have now mastered the first objective in the interpersonal communication skills hierarchy: describing the characteristics of attending behavior. Effective instruction, though, goes beyond the mere "knowing" or "describing" of skills. Effectiveness is measured by performance — actually demonstrating the skills in the classroom with your students. The following exercise, entitled "Practicing Attending Behavior," has been designed as an enrichment activity for you. Similar activities follow the mastery tests in each section of this chapter. You will notice that there are no objectives for these enrichment activities, nor are there any mastery tests to complete. Rather, these activities enable you to practice the interpersonal communication skills "ON YOUR OWN."

## LEARNING ACTIVITY 1.1

### Practicing Attending Behavior

Now that you have had the opportunity to review the basic components of effective attending behavior, you are ready to "try on" the behavior and assess your own effectiveness. You may choose to practice this behavior in your classroom, at home, or anywhere that seems comfortable to you. Described below are several suggestions for setting up a practice experience. (A word of caution, however, may be helpful: Remember that you are acquiring a series of mini-behaviors, one step at a time. Ultimately, these mini-behaviors will be synthesized into a fluid pattern of action — looking, listening, and responding. As you begin practicing the skills, accept the fact that "trying on" a single skill, such as attending, may feel awkward and even unnatural.)

**1. Live Classroom Interaction.** If you are presently teaching or student teaching, you may choose to practice attending behavior directly with your students. You may also choose to practice such a skill with your peers in the teachers' room, at the next staff meeting, or with a visiting parent.

**2. Microteaching Interaction.**   If you have access to videotape equipment, teach a ten-to-fifteen-minute lesson to your peers or to a small group of students. Have this practice session videotaped, and replay it as soon as possible. The content that you choose to transmit in this situation is secondary. Your primary concern is to make a deliberate demonstration of the basic characteristics of attending behavior.

**3. Informal Conversation.**   The ultimate goal in learning to demonstrate interpersonal communication skills is to be able to use them naturally and spontaneously. They form a critical component of your entire style of communicating. Therefore, it need not be necessary to restrict yourself to a classroom situation. The next time you are involved in any one-to-one conversation or in a small group conversation, make a deliberate attempt to attend to the speaker. With continuous practice you will begin to internalize these skills and use them spontaneously. The demonstration of such behaviors will increase the effectiveness of your own communication. This can be quite reinforcing and self-satisfying in itself. Don't be surprised if other people also begin to notice the positive effects of such behavior.

You now have a basic understanding of what behaviors you are to demonstrate, as well as a number of situations in which you can practice them. Now, turn to the criteria that you can use in assessing your own effectiveness.

## Checklists

Included in this learning activity is the first of a series of checklists that will help you assess your ability to demonstrate the skills described in this chapter. Checklists have been developed for each of the four skills presented. Each checklist describes only the characteristics of the specific skill under discussion and therefore helps you focus on one skill at a time. However, keep the hierarchical nature of the skills in mind. A truly effective demonstration requires incorporation of all the skills.

There are two specific types of checklists presented: (1) an Observer's Checklist and (2) a Self-Assessment Checklist. Described below is a series of steps that may be helpful in using these checklists.

**Step 1.**   Read each of the behavior characteristics described on the Observer's Checklist. Then, within any of the situations described above, classroom teaching, microteaching, peer teaching, or informal conversation, observe someone else involved in a conversation. Practice identifying and evaluating tnese behaviors as an observer. How easy or difficult is it for you to spot these behaviors during an ongoing interaction? Try tallying the number of times each specific behavior occurs. As indicated on the checklist, jot down specific examples of the behaviors. Seeing the behaviors in other people may help you in your own practice.

**Step 2.**   Now try demonstrating the skill yourself. If you choose to practice these skills within the context of a classroom, seek the assistance of a peer, a friend, or your supervisor. Have this person observe your interaction over a ten-to-fifteen-minute period. Ask him or her to keep a careful tally of those characteristics described on the Observer's

Checklist. The three categories used to rate the frequency with which you demonstrate these characteristics are: (1) Frequently, (2) Occasionally, and (3) Never. The first two categories are somewhat subjective and will require you to discuss the checklist with the observer. It will be helpful to you if your observer keeps brief notes describing the specific instances in which you displayed the behaviors.

If you are involved in a microteaching situation, you can assess your own performance by using the checklist during the video playback. You may also have a friend assess your demonstration and compare notes. How similar were your respective perceptions of the demonstration?

**Step 3.** After either a live presentation or a videotape laboratory experience, complete the Self-Assessment Checklist. You may then choose to compare your own assessment with that of an impartial observer. How similar are your perceptions?

After completing these three steps, you will have received multiple feedback from a variety of sources — i.e., an observer, perhaps videotape, and your own self-assessment. Strive to develop your eye contact, to relax your body, to let your facial expressions reflect the emotions experienced by the speaker. Be aware of the space that you develop between yourself and the speaker. Stand close enough so that you can reach out and touch one another if it seems appropriate. Try not to interrupt or distract the speaker while he or she is talking. By using subsummaries and/or brief acknowledgments, let the speaker know that you are listening.

## ATTENDING BEHAVIOR CHECKLIST: OBSERVER'S ASSESSMENT

|  | *Frequently* | *Occasionally* | *Never* |
|---|---|---|---|
| 1. The teacher had direct eye contact with the speaker. | _____ | _____ | _____ |
| 2. The teacher seemed distracted by other actions. Examples of distractions: | _____ | _____ | _____ |
| (a) _____ |  |  |  |
| (b) _____ |  |  |  |
| 3. The teacher's facial expressions reflected involvement in the conversation. Examples: | _____ | _____ | _____ |
| (a) _____ |  |  |  |
| (b) _____ |  |  |  |
| 4. The teacher stood close enough to the speaker so that physical contact was possible. | _____ | _____ | _____ |
| 5. The teacher did not interrupt the speaker while he or she was talking. | _____ | _____ | _____ |

6. The teacher used brief acknowledgments and subsummaries that indicated understanding. Examples: _____  _____  _____

(a) _____

(b) _____

---

## ATTENDING BEHAVIOR CHECKLIST: SELF-ASSESSMENT

|  | *Frequently* | *Occasionally* | *Never* |
|---|---|---|---|
| 1. I was aware of the comfort level of the speaker and modified my eye contact accordingly. | _____ | _____ | _____ |
| 2. My body posture was relaxed. I wasn't fidgety. | _____ | _____ | _____ |
| 3. I was conscious of the fact that my face expressed appropriate facial cues in reaction to the speaker's messages. Specific facial expressions that I tried to demonstrate were: | _____ | _____ | _____ |
| 4. I established a physical space that seemed comfortable for both the speaker and me. | _____ | _____ | _____ |
| 5. I felt comfortable with periods of silence. | _____ | _____ | _____ |
| 6. I used brief comments to acknowledge the speaker during the conversation but then quickly refocused attention back on the speaker. Examples of such brief comments were: | _____ | _____ | _____ |
| 7. I used subsummaries to indicate understanding. Examples of such subsummaries were: | _____ | _____ | _____ |
| 8. I observed the facial expressions and body language of the speaker and noticed the following cues. | _____ | _____ | _____ |

# Objective 2

To differentiate between the intellectual and the emotional content of messages (active listening).

## LEARNING ACTIVITY 2

Unlike the reflecting and inventory questioning skills that follow, active listening is difficult to assess through overtly demonstrated behaviors. It is an internal state that can be known only to the listener. Although the listener can demonstrate, nonverbally, most of the characteristics of attending, he or she may still not be listening to the speaker.

As with all of the skills described in this chapter, active listening behavior cannot be developed unless specific motivation is present. What motivates you to be engaged in conversation — necessity or choice? Do you feel obligated to listen or do you have a genuine concern for the speaker? Are you listening to the *person*, his or her thoughts and feelings? Or, are you listening to the words in order to act as a judge, a problem solver, an analyzer, or a critic? Still further, are you entering into the conversation with preconceived expectations of what the speaker is feeling and/or thinking? Do you have any bias or prejudice toward the speaker that may turn you off or distort what you hear?

Charles Kelley (1974)[9] has divided listening into two categories: "deliberate listening" and "empathetic listening." The former describes the ability to "deliberately" hear the intellectual *content* or the information of the message with an intent to analyze it, to recall it at some later point, or to draw conclusions from it. Empathetic listening refers to the listener's ability to participate in the spirit or feeling of the message being expressed. The intent of the empathetic listener is to attend to the speaker's *affective* or emotional needs first. Kelley notes that such empathic listening does not denote that the listener is always uncritical of or always in agreement with the speaker's thoughts, feelings, attitudes, ideas, and values. Rather, the primary concern of the empathetic listener is to be involved fully and accurately with what is being said and felt, both verbally and nonverbally, by the speaker. Once empathetic listeners have heard a message, they can then begin to use their own critical thinking skills — skills that allow them to summarize, describe, infer, and interpret the information.

The skills of deliberate and empathetic listening are not mutually exclusive, for they both aim at a common goal: to understand oral communication accurately. However, such understanding is arrived at through different routes. There is a difference in timing and motivation. The empathetic listener is motivated by his/her need to "hear" the speaker's *feelings*. He/she will analyze the content after the dialogue is complete.

Kelley notes that "deliberate listening" may be a self-contradiction and a misnomer — and that "empathetic listening" may be a redundancy.

To the extent that one is deliberating (mentally criticizing, summarizing, concluding, preparing reports, etc.) he is *not listening*, but formulating his own ideas. Listening by its very nature has to be empathic; a person understands what he has heard, only to the extent that he (she) can share in the meaning, spirit, or feeling of what the communicator has said.[10]

When listeners concentrate on the words being expressed or on their preconceived impressions of the speaker, they are thinking *about* the speaker. By trying to find solutions to problems before the speaker has concluded, they are thinking *for* the speaker. By summarizing or drawing conclusions before the speaker has concluded, they are thinking *ahead* of the speaker. By being empathetic listeners, they are thinking *with* the speakers. They are not anticipating, judging, analyzing — they are just listening.

In order to demonstrate the characteristics of active listening, you must first be an empathetic listener. You must be motivated to listen to the speaker because you have a genuine concern for what he/she is feeling as well as saying. You must temporarily eliminate old impressions and momentarily suspend judgment. Only then can you begin to fully concentrate your energies on looking, listening, and recording the verbal and nonverbal messages of the speaker.

*Active Listening Includes the Following Components:*

1. Blocking out external stimuli.
2. Attending carefully to both the verbal and nonverbal messages of the speaker.
3. Differentiating between the intellectual and emotional content of a message.
4. Making inferences regarding the feelings experienced by the speaker.

Below are the critical steps involved in developing the skill of active listening. The three basic components include: (1) personal inventory, (2) attending skills, and (3) identifying feelings.

**Step 1. Personal Inventory.**   Effective listening requires that you be aware of your own feelings, prejudices, and expectations about the speaker.

You need to inventory your motivation for being involved with him or her. Ask yourself:

1. How do I feel about the speaker and the topic being discussed?
2. Do I really want to hear what that person is saying? What is my role? Am I here to act as critic? As a problem solver?
3. Do I genuinely want to help the speaker if he/she presents a problem?
4. Can I accept the feelings and attitudes of the speaker even if they are different than my own?

Even though the spontaneous nature of most conversations may make such a self-inventory seem difficult, try to discipline yourself to ask one or two of these inventory questions at the onset. If your answers are positive, you can then say: "I have accounted for my personal feelings regarding this speaker, and I can now block them out of my mind and concentrate on the intellectual and the emotional content of the messages being conveyed."

Dealing with people's feelings, attitudes, and values is a sensitive matter. It requires not only highly specialized skills like active listening — but also personal honesty about your motivation and commitment to the communication process.

**Step 2. Attending Skills.**   At this point, your *attending skills* become important. Establish eye contact, relax, and listen. Attend directly to both the *verbal* and *nonverbal* cues of the speaker. What messages are being delivered? What is the tone and pitch of the speaker's voice? Is he/she speaking loudly or softly; rapidly or slowly? What are the hand and body movements saying? This is a "doubly difficult" task. It requires you to look and listen simultaneously.

Those specialists involved in the study of interpersonal communication often differentiate between the actual words used in conversation and the manner in which those words are delivered. They apply the term *verbal* in describing the actual words being spoken and the term *vocal* in describing the volume, note, tone, pitch, and inflection of the words being expressed.[11] Usually, a speaker's emotions have a direct bearing on both the verbal and vocal messages. For example, Joel Davitz[12] concludes that when someone is feeling angry, he or she may communicate through blaring timbre, fast rate, high pitch, and loud delivery. Conversely, when someone is feeling bored, he or she may speak at a slower rate, lower pitch, and with less amplitude. If you wish to attend to the speaker's affect, you will need to listen for these vocal cues.

**Step 3. Identifying the Speaker's Feelings.**   As the conversation proceeds, try and make private inferences about what the speaker is *feeling*. Is he or she sending congruent messages? In other words, are the verbal and nonverbal messages consistent with each other? An incongruent message is easy to spot. It is like looking at a child whose body is rigid, whose hands are clenched, and who says to you with stuttering words, "Everything is t-t-terrific." Try to answer the question, "How does this person feel toward the topic being discussed?" Finding the right "feeling" words to describe the speaker's messages may initially present some difficulty, since emotions have not traditionally been viewed as a topic of open discussion and, consequently, most people suffer from the lack of an appropriate "feeling" vocabulary.

At this point, you have probably received a great deal of information that you would like to pull together and test out for yourself. Try the following review exercise.

**Scene I:**

You are seated at your desk, after school, organizing your materials. It is the end of a very busy day and you are getting ready to leave. Suddenly you look up and see Bruce, one of your fifth grade students, seated at his desk. He's been moody all day and you sense that he has something on his mind. As he approaches you, you begin to inventory your own thoughts and feelings about the potential conversation.

What questions do you ask yourself?

1. _____     3. _____

2. _____     4. _____

Did you ask yourself if you really wanted to stay and listen to Bruce? Did you consider how you felt about him and any previous "after school" conversations that you had had with him? Did you review the different issues that he might want to talk about with you?

If as a result of the inventory, you decide that you really don't want to talk with Bruce (don't have the energy; don't have the time, etc.), what could you say? Perhaps, "Bruce, I'm so tired that I am not sure that I could listen to you in a way that you deserve. Could it wait until tomorrow?" There are times when this may be the wisest response for a caring educator. If you do not have time or are not in a frame of mind that will facilitate effective interpersonal communication, then it is appropriate to set another time. However, remember tomorrow to hold your discussion with Bruce. Also, before putting the discussion off for a day, attend to Bruce carefully to see how pressing his needs and concerns appear to be.

If you have decided to talk with Bruce, are you going to be a: (check one)

_____ 1. deliberate listener

_____ 2. empathic listener

What criteria did you use in determining your role?

If you chose the latter, you have committed yourself to both listening to and observing Bruce's affective or feeling messages, as well as becoming actively involved in the conversation by demonstrating effective attending skills.

## Scene II:

Bruce says: "Do you have a couple of seconds?" Slowly, he begins to talk about the upcoming math test. He drops his eyes to the floor and quietly says, "You know, this stuff is really silly." You may consider Bruce's past performance in math and think to yourself, "Now, he is usually an excellent student. I wonder what he is trying to say."

Based on both Bruce's verbal cues ("this stuff is silly") and his nonverbal cues (head and voice drop), what do you imagine he is feeling? What inferences can you make?

1. _____

2. _____

3. _____

Perhaps he is saying:

"I feel *scared* about the test."

"I'm not prepared."

"I don't understand it."

Or,

"I'm feeling *bored* with this material. It's too easy."

"If I get 100 on the test tomorrow, everyone will make fun of me."

Remember, not every message may have an emotional overtone, so don't exhaust yourself trying to "hear" one. But, if a student does respond with such emotions, attend to them. Interestingly enough, the absence of emotional reaction from a student when circumstances would warrant one (i.e., a fight or some other highly emotional experience) could alert you to listen more actively and intently.

---

*Summary of active listening*

1. Inventory your personal motivation for listening. Put aside preconceived expectations. Suspend judgment.
2. Attend to speaker's (a) verbal cues and vocal cues and (b) nonverbal cues.
3. Begin making private inferences concerning the speaker's feelings. Tune into incongruent messages if any are apparent.

---

# Mastery Test

## OBJECTIVE 2

To differentiate between the intellectual and the emotional content of messages (active listening).

---

Read each statement and try to differentiate between the intellectual (cognitive) content and the emotional (affective) content being transmitted. Sometimes it helps to read the statements aloud. Each time you read one put the accent on a different word. Does it communicate a different emotional message? In the right-hand columns record both the intellectual message and the emotional message. Some of the statements may contain several different emotions. List them all. When you have finished, compare your list with those in the Answer Key. In order to pass this test, you must receive a total score of at least 85. If you disagree with any of the answers listed, ask friends for their reactions. What messages do they receive?

| Statements | Intellectual (Cognitive) (I'm Saying) | Emotional (Affective) (I'm Feeling) |
|---|---|---|
| 1. "I don't need any help. I'm old enough to do it myself." | | |
| 2. "Just go away and leave me alone. I don't want to talk to you or anyone else." | | |
| 3. "I couldn't believe it. Imagine me, getting an A on that paper." | | |
| 4. "I tried to do it three times and I still don't understand it." | | |
| 5. "No matter what I do, I can't seem to please him." | | |

| Statements | Intellectual (Cognitive) (I'm Saying) | Emotional (Affective) (I'm Feeling) |
|---|---|---|
| 6. "I don't feel that I have to answer that. It's none of your business." | | |
| 7. "Every place I turn, you are always there, standing over me." | | |
| 8. "Just trust me." | | |
| 9. "Cool it, I'll do it when I'm good and ready." | | |
| 10. "Just give me a chance, I know I can do it." | | |

# ANSWER KEY

## Mastery Test, Objective 2

Give yourself 3 points for each item which matches those on the key. Give yourself 2 points for those items where your choices only partially match. (There is some similarity between the responses.) Give yourself 0 points if you missed altogether. If you received below 85, reread the preceding Learning Activity. Also share these statements with a friend and compare your perceptions.

| Intellectual (Cognitive) (I'm Saying) | Emotional (Affective) (I'm Feeling) |
|---|---|
| 1. I can do it myself. | I feel — angry frustrated annoyed belittled cocky independent |
| 2. I don't want to talk to anyone. | I feel — angry depressed upset withdrawn isolated |
| 3. I got an A. | I feel — surprised amazed delighted |
| 4. I can't do it. | I feel — frustrated confused tired |

| Intellectual (Cognitive) (I'm Saying) | Emotional (Affective) (I'm Feeling) |
|---|---|
| 5. I can't please him. | I feel — frustrated manipulated controlled pressured |
| 6. I won't answer that. | I feel — confronted angry annoyed irritated obstinate arrogant |
| 7. Stop following me around. | I feel — annoyed put upon cornered |
| 8. Trust me. | I feel — confident secure afraid worried manipulating |
| 9. I'll do it later. | I feel — harried annoyed angry flippant |
| 10. Let me try it. | I feel — eager confident desperate |

**ON YOUR OWN: FROM THEORY TO PRACTICE**

You have now mastered the second objective in the interpersonal communication skills hierarchy: differentiating between the intellectual and the emotional content of messages. As described in Learning Activity 1.1 effective teaching goes beyond the mere "knowing" of differences between word messages and feeling messages. It demands actually using the skill and incorporating it into your own interpersonal communication. So, try practicing this behavior ON YOUR OWN.

## LEARNING ACTIVITY 2.1

### Practicing Active Listening

All the situations described in Learning Activity 1.1 — classroom teaching, microteaching, and informal conversations — are also appropriate for practicing your active listening skills. Within any of these contexts, engage yourself in a conversation with another person. If you have the opportunity to initiate the conversation, you may wish to select a topic that has some emotional overtones. For example, if you are reading an interesting story, you may ask your student, "How did you feel about the ending of the story?" Or, at a party you may ask, "What were your reactions to last night's debate?" Then look, listen, and make private inferences about the speaker's affective messages.

Although active listening skills are important in all forms of communication, they are especially critical when there are emotional overtones in the speaker's messages. When you demonstrate the skills of active listening, you are performing several tasks simultaneously. You are looking at the nonverbal cues of the speaker, you are listening to the verbal cues, and you are also making private inferences about the emotions the speaker may be experiencing. However, all these actions are happening privately. Other than the overt demonstration of attending behavior, the effectiveness of your listening ability is often known only to yourself. So the only checklist used in assessing your ability to listen actively is a self-inventory.

## ACTIVE LISTENING CHECKLIST: SELF-ASSESSMENT

1. I quickly inventoried my personal feelings, attitudes, and expectations toward the speaker and did or did not feel that they would block effective communication. Two specific questions I asked myself were:

   (a) _____

   (b) _____

2. I focused my attention directly on the speaker while he or she was talking. Two specific ways I showed the speaker that I was listening were:

   (a) _____

   (b) _____

3. Two nonverbal cues that gave me information about the speaker's feeling were:

   (a) _____

   (b) _____

   Inferences I made regarding these cues were:

   (a) _____

   (b) _____

4. I listened to the speaker's word messages as well as the tone, pitch, and rate of speech, and I was able to differentiate between the content and the affect messages.

   (a) The content message was:

   _____

   _____

   (b) The affect message might be:

   _____

   _____

# Objective 3

To differentiate among the three types of reflecting — word messages, behaviors, inferences.

## LEARNING ACTIVITY 3

Take a few moments to review objectives 1 and 2. Hopefully, these eliciting behaviors will help provide an environment that is conducive to sharing and self-disclosure. By first attending to your students' nonverbal and verbal cues and then differentiating between the intellectual and the emotional content of their messages, you say to them: "I see you, and I am listening carefully to what you are saying and doing."

Suppose a student expresses an emotional reaction that you wish to respond to. What do you do? What do you say? Consider the following situation and then write down your responses to the students' comments.

*Attending to Students*

You notice that a student is seated at her desk, with her math book opened. She has been staring into space for several minutes and can't seem to concentrate on her work. She is playing with the pages of the book. You go over to her desk and she suddenly says:

*Actively Listening to Students*

"Math is dumb. I don't want to do any of this stuff."

Depending on your past information regarding this student, you may decode the message as:

*Content:* Math is hard, dumb, boring, etc.

*Affect:* 1. "I'm *frustrated*. I need help."
(or)   2. "I'm feeling *tired*, and I don't want to work."
(or)   3. "I'm dumb. I can't do it."
(or)   4. "I'm feeling bored. This stuff is too easy."

How would you respond to this student?

1. _____

2. _____

3. _____

Obviously there are numerous approaches a teacher could take in responding to this student. One appropriate way would be to use the skill of *reflecting*. You could reflect at any one of three levels: (1) You might choose to pick up on the student's *words* and try to capture and reflect back the gist of the verbal message; (2) You could respond to the student's nonverbal or body cues by describing his or her actions; or (3) You could make an inference regarding the emotions being transmitted and share this inference with the student.

The effective use of reflecting behavior by the teacher can communicate to the student: "I have listened carefully to what you have said, and I would like to share my observations with you." Following are sentence stems that often begin reflections on each of these three levels.

| | |
|---|---|
| "I heard you say . . . | (reflecting the student's words, the verbal content of the message) |
| "I saw you do . . . | (reflecting the student's actions, the nonverbal behavior) |
| "I imagine you're feeling . . . | (reflecting the student's feelings that may underlie the verbal and nonverbal behavior) |

The teacher's response, in effect, serves as a mirror for the student's words, feelings, and behaviors, thus providing direct feedback regarding the success of the student's communication. Additionally, effective reflecting behavior often facilitates self-exploration, since it provides speakers with an opportunity to ponder their listeners' feedback before reorganizing and clarifying their messages. Reflection can also provide an opportunity for teachers and students to clarify any misinterpretations that may block the process of communication.

The skill of reflecting is comprised of successive behaviors ranging from simply paraphrasing the speaker's words to describing the speaker's body cues or behaviors to reflecting the speaker's affective or feeling messages in order to make inferences or interpretations.

## Reflecting Word Messages (paraphrasing)

To reflect word messages, a teacher repeats or paraphrases the essence of the thought (words) just communicated. No attempt is made to reflect the feelings being conveyed or the nonverbal cues or behaviors being displayed. Sometimes hearing an exact repetition or paraphrase of what was just said can be a clarifying experience for both the speaker and the listener.

Look again at the dialogue at the beginning of Learning Activity 3. To reflect the student's word message, the teacher could respond to the student by saying: "So you think that the math is dumb," or, "You don't want to do your math today." Even though such a response may sound trite and mechanical, practice using it for a while — it will not only help to develop your own listening skills, but it will also serve as a means for clarifying the speaker's messages. A teacher may choose to use this type of response before deciding whether to continue the interaction by reflecting the emotional messages that appear to underlie the verbal content. Reflecting word messages thus serves several purposes: (1) It initiates dialogue between the teacher and students; (2) It provides some "lead time" for the teacher to decide whether to continue the discussion; (3) It may motivate the student to provide additional information regarding his or her thoughts and feelings.

Such a response is reflecting rather than confrontative; it does not force the student to respond. Simply letting a student know that you are listening may be all that is needed to stimulate further dialogue.

## Reflecting Nonverbal Messages (behavior description)

The second component of reflecting requires you to describe the physical behaviors of the speaker. When reflecting nonverbal messages, only use the visible behavioral evidence. Following are some of the ways you might begin a response to reflect a student's nonverbal messages.

I noticed that when you did . . . ,     your face . . . .
When you did . . . ,     your body . . . .
    your hands . . . .

Referring again to the interaction at the beginning of Learning Activity 3, if the teacher had chosen to reflect the student's nonverbal message, he or she might have said: "I see you sitting here, staring into space, and playing with your math book. What's up?" Usually the behavior description is followed by a question that will open up some dialogue. You observe, give some feedback by describing the behavior, and then check it out by asking a question.

By describing specific, observed behaviors, you provide insight to the speaker about how he or she is "coming across" or being perceived. Such responses are descriptive and nonevaluative. They do *not* include accusations or inferences about the other person's motives, attitudes, or personality traits. Telling a child that he or she is rude is offering an accusation rather than a description of specific behavior. Often young children have a difficult time differentiating between themselves and their actions. Are they, as human beings, rude people, or are their *actions* inappropriate to the situation? Remember, describe specific *actions* only.

### Reflecting in Order to Make Inferences or Interpretations

This third level of reflecting incorporates the skills described in the two preceding behaviors. However, it goes beyond both the paraphrasing of words and the reflection of nonverbal cues. It represents an attempt on the part of the teacher to summarize what he or she saw and heard and to "check out" those observations by sharing some inferences regarding the speaker's feelings. Did the listener's perceptions match the original intentions of the speaker; was the speaker really "in touch" with his or her own messages? In the earlier interaction concerning the student who seemed to have problems with his math, the teacher might have responded at this level as follows: "I see you sitting there, playing with the math book (reflecting behavior), saying that math is dumb (reflecting the word messages). Are you feeling frustrated by the problems?" (interpretation of the student's feelings).

Effective reflecting behavior is not a semantic game or a way of putting the other person's ideas in new terms. Rather, it comes from a genuine desire to understand exactly what the student is expressing and feeling both verbally and nonverbally. You are never expected to play the role of a mind reader. You do not have to try to guess what the speaker is thinking or feeling. After summarizing what you saw (behavior description) and what you heard (reflection of content), you share your inference about whatever thoughts or feelings you associate with such a response. In short, "check out" your interpretations with a question. How accurate were your inferences? Did they match the speaker's intentions?

Introductions which can be helpful in checking out your interpretations are:

"It seems to me that what you were saying was . . . ."

"Could it be that . . . ?"

"Were you trying to say . . . ?"

These introductions differ from those used in reflecting word messages in that you go beyond restating the gist of the words by adding an inference of your own. For example, a student says to you: "He makes me sick." You respond by saying: "Are you trying to say that he made you angry when he stole third base?" In this example, you added your own interpretation.

You may also choose to use lead-in sentences that incorporate behavior description and/or paraphrasing.

"I saw you do . . . and I imagine that you are thinking . . . ."

"I noticed that you did . . . and I imagine that you were thinking . . . ."

"I noticed that you did . . . and I imagine that you were feeling . . . ."

"I heard you say . . . . Were you thinking . . . feeling . . . ?"

For additional clarification you could also ask questions at the end of each statement of inference. For example:

"Does that sound accurate to you?"

"Does that seem right to you?"

"Did I perceive (hear, see) that correctly?"

Both the *timing* and the *number* of reflected statements are critical elements in practicing this skill. It can be just as ineffective to reflect too much as too little. It becomes annoying to the speaker to have his or her verbal or nonverbal communications reflected and interpreted constantly. It can often cause students to doubt that you really are seeking clarification. They may suspect that you are trying to manipulate them by putting your own thoughts and values in their mouths. Communication then becomes unbalanced and strained.

Frequent reflecting seems especially appropriate under two conditions: (1) when mistakes could be very costly and, consequently, accuracy becomes vital; and (2) when strong feelings in either the sender or the receiver increase the probability of misunderstanding. In such cases, reflecting becomes crucial as a way of ensuring that the message comes through undistorted. The next time you are having a disagreement with someone, try reflecting what has been said until he or she corroborates your understanding. Note what effect this has on the other person's feelings and also your own.

When used effectively, reflecting enhances the development of a nonthreatening environment in which learners can feel free to express themselves. Reflections should never be judgmental, advisory, challenging, or ridiculing in nature. Rather, they should be *questioning* and exploratory.

---

*Summary of effective reflecting behavior*

1. Become aware of any preconceived thoughts or feelings you may have regarding the speaker and/or the topic being discussed. Will they hinder communication? If so, how?
2. Attend carefully to both the verbal and nonverbal messages of the speaker. *Observe.*
3. Make a mental note of the exact words being spoken and the specific behaviors being demonstrated. *Look, listen, and record.*
4. Differentiate between the verbal messages and the emotional messages being delivered. What is the speaker saying? What feelings are associated with the words? *Look, listen, record, and infer.*
5. Respond to the student by:
   (a) Paraphrasing the words. *Reflect words.*
   (b) Describing the specific observed behaviors of the speaker. *Describe.*
   (c) Share your inferences concerning the student's thoughts and feelings that may underlie verbal and nonverbal behavior. *Interpret.*
6. Be aware of the tone of voice you use. Avoid sarcasm, judgment, reprimand.
7. Ask for clarification to assess the accuracy of your perceptions. *Clarify.*

---

# Mastery Test

## OBJECTIVE 3

To differentiate among the three types of reflecting — word messages, behaviors, inferences.

---

Code each of the following responses to determine which of the three types of reflecting behavior is being exhibited. Use the following abbreviations: WM = reflecting word messages, B = reflecting behavior, I = interpretive reflections. To pass this test successfully, you must accurately code at least 9 of the 10 responses.

_____ 1. *Student*    (twisting in seat, biting pencil): "I don't like creative writing. I'm no good at writing."

   *Teacher:*    "You don't care for the writing assignments, and you don't feel you have much talent as a writer. What do you find the most difficult about writing?"

_____ 2. *Student*    (smiling broadly and displaying a medal): "Look at the medal I just won. I took first prize in the swimming competition."

   *Teacher:*    "It looks to me as though you're really proud and happy to have done so well."

_____ 3. *Student*    (frowning and slumped in chair): "I don't want to go to the school dance. I hate standing in a line hoping some dumb boy will ask me to dance."

   *Teacher:*    "It sounds like you feel awkward or maybe left out and as if you're standing alone while your friends are dancing. Is that true?"

_____ 4. *Student* (with his hands in his pockets and shrugging his shoulders): "You know my father. He is really big on sports. He played football, so I have to play football."

    *Teacher:* "It sounds as if you feel resentful. Is that true?"

_____ 5. *Student:* "That was a stupid thing for him to do. I told him he'd probably get caught."

    *Teacher:* "So you warned him."

_____ 6. *Student:* "I can do that as well as any boy can. Why can't I try it?"

    *Teacher:* "Are you saying that you feel like you're being discriminated against?"

_____ 7. *Student* (running across the room, almost knocking over the fish tanks)

    *Teacher:* "When you run across the room like that, you could easily knock over the tanks."

_____ 8. *Student* (seated under a tree, reading a book, while the rest of the class is playing kickball)

    *Teacher:* "Are you sitting here because you would rather read or because you didn't get picked for the team?"

_____ 9. *Student* (seated under a tree, reading a book, while the rest of the class is playing kickball)

    *Teacher:* "I see you sitting here reading instead of playing with the class. What's happening?"

_____ 10. *Student* (seated under a tree, reading a book, while the rest of the class is playing kickball): "I'd rather read than play kickball. I have to finish this book by fourth period."

    *Teacher:* "Oh, you didn't finish your assignment?"

---

## ANSWER KEY

Mastery Test, Objective 3

1. WM   2. I   3. I   4. I   5. WM   6. I   7. B   8. I   9. B   10. WM

**ON YOUR OWN: FROM THEORY TO PRACTICE**

You have now completed the third objective, differentiating among the three types of reflecting behaviors. It is difficult to make the transition from "knowing" the three types of reflecting and actually "demonstrating" these behaviors in your own interpersonal communication. To help you make this transition, we have included an additional enrichment activity, "Constructing Responses." Because of the complexity of this skill, we encourage you to try your hand at writing the three types of reflecting responses before you actually practice this new behavior. When you feel confident that you can construct the messages, move from theory to practice — ON YOUR OWN.

## LEARNING ACTIVITY 3.1

### Constructing Responses

*Directions:* Working alone or with a partner, read each of the brief vignettes and dialogues that follow. Then write a statement incorporating the reflecting response indicated in the parentheses. When you have completed the activity, compare your responses with the sample answers that follow.

### VIGNETTE 1

Teri, at the age of eight, still has difficulty in sharing her materials with other children. She often begins fighting with them when they "borrow" her materials, even when she is not working with them. Cheri innocently picks up one of her games, which is lying on the table. Teri immediately runs up to her and grabs it away.

(a) The teacher walks over to the table and says to Teri:

_____

(reflecting behavior)

(b) Teri is screaming: "It's my game and she can't play with it. Tell her to give it back to me."

The teacher says: _____

(reflecting word message)

(c) Teri, red in the face, seems very angry. She says: "It's mine and she didn't ask if she could borrow it."

The teacher says: _____

(interpretive reflection)

(d) *Teri:* "She'll probably just break it anyways."

*Teacher:* _____

(interpretive reflection)

(e) Cheri, getting very flustered and her eyes filling with tears, says: "I didn't know it was yours. Stop pulling at my arm."

*Teacher:* _____

(reflecting behavior)

(f) Cheri pulls the game away from Teri and puts it back on the table. She looks at the teacher and says: "Can I play with it?"

*Teacher:* _____

(open response)

### VIGNETTE 2

For the big History Fair, the class has decided to recreate the landing on the moon by the first astronaut. The students are to decide among themselves who will play the astronaut. The selection process has turned into a big popularity contest between two students, Mike and Frank. They both seem to be "battling" with each other.

(a) Frank gets red in the face and quite defensive. He says, "I even look like the guy. I should be it."

*Teacher:* _____

(reflecting behavior)

(b) *Frank* (still demanding): "So what's the big deal? Just let me play the bit."

*Teacher:* _____

(reflecting word message)

(c) Mike, equally agitated, shouts: "Just wait one big minute — let me say something."

*Teacher:* _____

(interpretive reflection)

(d) *Mike:* "You bet I'm angry. What happened to the big democratic thing we were supposed to have here?"

*Teacher:* _____

(reflecting word messages)

(e) *Frank:* "Why don't we both read the part and let the kids decide?"

*Teacher:* _____

(interpretive reflection)

(f) *Mike:* "That will probably turn out to be one big game . . . a popularity contest."

*Teacher:* _____

(reflecting word message)

## VIGNETTE 3

Half of the class is gathered together for a class meeting. There have been several incidents of stealing in the lockers lately, and the teacher thinks that it is necessary to discuss it openly.

(a) *Judy:* "What difference does it make who's taking all the stuff. Let's just put guards out in the hall and keep a lookout for the thief."

*Teacher:* _____

(reflecting word messages)

(b) *Kenny:* "That doesn't make sense to me. Let's just set a reward system. Give money to anyone who knows anything about it."

*Teacher:* _____

(reflecting word messages)

(c) *Dorie* (seated quietly in her chair, suddenly blurts out): "That's *crazy*."

*Teacher:* _____

(interpretive reflection)

(d) Donald opens his eyes wide and nods his head.

*Teacher:* _____

(reflecting behavior)

(e) *Donald:* "Boy, we are *assuming* a lot. How do we know that there is just one thief?"

*Teacher:* _____

(reflecting word messages)

(f) *Melissa:* "Wait a minute. Why don't we just give the thief a chance to return everything before we start a big hunt team."

*Teacher:* _____

(interpretive reflection)

# Potential Responses

## Constructing Responses

Take a look at the responses listed below. Obviously, unless you are clairvoyant, you will not have written the identical statements. The critical issue is to determine if your statements follow the basic guidelines of effective reflecting behavior. Ask yourself if you have successfully captured the "intent" of the speaker.

### Vignette 1

(a) "I saw you pull that box away from Cheri. What's happening?"
(reflecting behavior)
(b) "It's yours and no one else can play with it."
(reflecting word message)
(c) "Your face is getting red . . . I imagine that you are angry because Cheri didn't ask you if she could borrow it. Is that true?"
(interpretive reflection)
(d) "Are you worried that if someone borrows your game they will break it?"
(interpretive reflection)
(e) "I can see that you are about to cry. Calm down."
(reflecting behavior)
(f) open response

### Vignette 2

(a) "Your face is getting red."
(reflecting behavior)
(b) "So you think it's not such a big issue and that you should play the role."
(reflecting word messages)

(c) "You look angry. Do you feel like you haven't had a chance to speak?"
(interpretive reflection)
(d) "You don't think that the selection process is fair? democratic?"
(reflecting word messages)
(e) "You think the kids will be fair judges. Is it because you think that they will vote for you?"
(interpretive reflection)
(f) "You think the kids will vote for the most popular? Do you have any other suggestions?"
(reflecting word messages)

### Vignette 3

(a) "You think a guard system is a way to deal with the problem."
(reflecting word messages)
(b) "So you are suggesting a reward system."
(reflecting word messages)
(c) "You obviously disagree with those two ideas. Is it because they seem unfair to you?"
(interpretive reflection)
(d) "I see you nodding your head. Is it because you think they are unfair?"
(reflecting behavior)
(e) "You think we are assuming a lot . . . that maybe there is more than one thief."
(reflecting word messages)
(f) "When you used the term 'hunt team,' I imagine you thought that there was something inhuman or scary about the process of finding the thief. Is that true?"
(interpretive reflection)

# LEARNING ACTIVITY 3.2

## Practicing Reflecting Behavior

Now that you have refined your skill in constructing responses, you are ready to actually "try on" the three types of reflecting behaviors. As the skill becomes more complicated, so does the checklist. Take a few moments to analyze the checklists before using them to assess your own performance. Note that both the effective and the ineffective characteristics of this skill are listed. Both types of characteristics are included in order to focus on some of the common errors that may occur as you begin practicing this new behavior.

When setting the scene to practice this skill with your friends or students, keep the situation simple. Limit the number of people and distracting variables. Start with reflecting word messages. You may also choose to tell the people you are working with that you are practicing new skills and would like some feedback from them. How did they react when they heard their statements being reflected? How accurately did you reflect their messages?

## REFLECTING BEHAVIOR CHECKLIST: OBSERVER'S ASSESSMENT

| | Frequently | Occasionally | Never |
|---|---|---|---|
| 1. The teacher accurately summarized the gist of the speaker's message. | _____ | _____ | _____ |
| 2. The teacher responded by describing the specific behaviors of the speaker. | _____ | _____ | _____ |
| 3. The teacher responded by describing specific behaviors of the speaker and also summarizing the content of the conversation. ("I saw you do . . . and I heard you say . . . .") | _____ | _____ | _____ |
| 4. The teacher responded by sharing personal perceptions (inferences) of the speaker's thoughts and feelings. ("I imagine you are feeling . . . .") | _____ | _____ | _____ |
| 5. The teacher's inferences appeared to be inaccurate. | _____ | _____ | _____ |
| 6. At the end of the reflections (verbal, nonverbal, and/or inferential), the teacher asked a question for clarification. ("What's happening?" "Is that true?") | _____ | _____ | _____ |
| 7. The teacher responded with a judgment instead of a reflection. ("That's wrong." "You're rude.") | _____ | _____ | _____ |
| 8. The teacher's tone seemed to communicate a sense of acceptance. | _____ | _____ | _____ |
| 9. The teacher paraphrased the student's messages so often during the conversation that it was distracting. | _____ | _____ | _____ |

## REFLECTING BEHAVIOR CHECKLIST: SELF-ASSESSMENT

I. *Initiating the Interaction*

1. I initiated the interaction by describing the student's nonverbal behavior.

   Specifically, I said: _____

2. The student initiated the interaction by asking a question or making a statement. I summarized the student's verbal message.

   Specifically, I said: _____

3. I added personal inferences and/or interpretations to my observations.

   Specifically, I said: _____

4. I "checked out" my perceptions of the student's verbal and/or nonverbal messages by asking a direct question for clarification.

   The specific question I asked was: _____

II. *Use of Reflecting*

5. I made inferences to myself regarding the content and the nonverbal messages of the speaker.

   (a) The content message was:

   _____

   (b) The nonverbal cues were:

   _____

   (c) The specific inferences I made regarding these messages were:

   _____

   _____

6. My responses were/were not well timed, and I did/did not interrupt the speaker. The specific cues that told me it was an appropriate time to speak were:

   _____

   _____

7. When I misinterpreted the message, I asked for clarification.

   (a) The misinterpretation was:

   _____

   (b) The way I asked for clarification was:

   _____

   (c) The clarified message was:

   _____

   _____

8. The most comfortable type of reflecting for me was:                                   (check one)

    (a) Reflecting verbal messages                                                     _____

    (b) Reflecting nonverbal messages                                                  _____

    (c) Reflecting with an attempt to make inferences or interpretations               _____

# Objective 4

To differentiate among inventory questions that (1) stimulate communication; (2) clarify information; (3) identify discrepancies; and (4) seek alternatives or solutions.

## LEARNING ACTIVITY 4

Let's take a few moments and review the development of the interpersonal communication skills taxonomy thus far. The skills involved in the first cluster, entitled *Eliciting Students' Expressions of Feelings*, are mood behaviors that stimulate teacher and student interaction and enhance the potential for effective interpersonal communication. When you model attending and active listening behaviors, you are communicating to your students that you have put aside other business and are ready to listen and interact with them.

By effectively attending to your students, you have communicated that you can see them, hear them, and even touch them. Your body posture reflects a comfort level that puts others at ease. By observing *their* facial expressions and body postures and by listening to the pitch and tone of their voices, as well as to their actual words, you are listening actively and differentiating between feeling and word messages. The Cluster II skills, *Clarifying Students' Expressions of Feelings*, teach you how to respond to students in very specific ways. By paraphrasing your students' verbal messages, you allow them to hear their own words, and in doing so, you help clarify any misinterpretations. By describing their behaviors, you help them become more aware of the physical reactions that accompany their verbal dialogue. By adding interpretation to these descriptions, you share your perceptions of why they may be speaking or acting in a certain manner. Such interpretations can provide additional insights regarding the connection between their thoughts, feelings, and behaviors.

At any of these three levels of reflecting, your students are given the opportunity to accept or reject your reactions and perceptions. Mutual feedback will enable both of you to gain valuable information regarding one another. Such interpersonal interactions will help students become more aware of their own thoughts, feelings, and resulting behaviors. At this point they may begin to see the effects of their actions on other persons.

Inventory questions may now be appropriate. Such questions will enable your students to further clarify specific aspects of their behavior. Too often, people simply take their style of behavior for granted and give little thought as to whether it serves them productively or unproductively. Inventorying one's behavior pattern is a necessary condition for growth, one that is prerequisite to the search for alternative response patterns.

### Inventory Questions

Questioning behavior has been an integral part of the interpersonal communications hierarchy from the onset. As you were attending to your students' verbal and nonverbal messages, you may have been asking yourself questions such as: "What is he/she thinking?" "I wonder what lies behind that calm exterior?" As you initiated the reflective listening stage, you had to inventory your own motivation for listening and you asked yourself a series of self-confronting questions: "Do I really want to be involved in this conversation?" "What past experiences have I had with the speaker that could positively or negatively affect my ability to listen?" Questioning skills were also inherent in the reflective listening stage, when you followed each type of message — words, behaviors, and inferences — with a question for clarification: "Is that what you said?" "Did I describe your feelings accurately?" "Do you agree with my perception of the situation?"

Questioning, therefore, is a multifaceted form of communication. In their most positive form, questions can (1) invite communication; (2) express lack of understanding; (3) clarify misperceptions or inaccurate information; (4) focus attention on specific thoughts, feelings, actions, events; and (5) show concern and involvement. When used inappropriately, they can be threatening, interrupt the thought process, carry an accusatory or judgmental message, and generate defensiveness and hostility with the student.

Inventory questions are a unique subset of questions that stimulate introspection. When used effectively, they enable individuals to get inside themselves and to (1) stimulate communication related to thoughts, feelings, and behaviors; (2) clarify communications related to these personal states; (3) identify any discrepancies between their intended words and actions and how the messages are actually received by others; and (4) seek out potential alternatives and/or solutions. When students respond to inventory questions, they assume a very active role in interpersonal communications.

Inventory questions may be viewed as a process of shared problem solving; a way of identifying and bringing to the surface pieces of the behavioral puzzle. The ultimate goal is to move the student to a greater understanding of his/her behavior; to assess the effects of this behavior, and to determine if change is necessary.

Weinstein (1975)[13] states that the product of self-knowledge is to create more "response-ability," or more choices in the way people behave. Once people understand how their thoughts and feelings affect their behavior, they can begin predicting, analyzing, and modifying that behavior. In short, the better people understand the causes and consequences of their behavior, the greater their ability to control their actions. Maturity is reflective of continuous assessment, alteration, and reassessment of one's behaviors.

Described below are four types of inventory questions. These questions serve to (1) stimulate communication; (2) clarify information; (3) identify discrepancies; and (4) seek alternatives or solutions.

**Level 1. Stimulate Communication.** Inventory questions that stimulate communication are open invitations to talk. They give the student the opportunity to explore and discuss thoughts and feelings. They say to the student: "I am interested in you and concerned about what happens to you." Examples of inventory questions that stimulate communication are:

- "Can you tell me what happened?"
- "Can we talk about what's on your mind?"
- "How are you feeling about this?"

Remember that the purpose of these questions is to engage the student in the self-inquiry process and to help him/her discuss specific actions or events and related feelings.

Consider the following vignette:

Kevin, a student in your homeroom, has been sent to you by the playground monitor because he was involved in a fight. Which of the following inventory questions stimulates communication that can lead to further inquiry?

- "Kevin, whom were you fighting with this time?"
- "Kevin, can you tell me a little about what happened out on the playground?"
- "Kevin, why were you fighting?"

If you selected the first response, you may block all further communication. "Whom were you fighting with *this time*?" is accusatory and confrontative.

If you selected the third response, it is unlikely that you will help Kevin disclose thoughts and feelings. Answering the question "why" often requires the student to analyze or intellectualize about his/her behavior. Furthermore, such questions can divert attention from real, immediate feelings and may cause the student to become defensive. Remember that inventory questions encourage individuals to reflect on "their behavior and their inner experiences with a minimum of obstructive self-judging, defensiveness, or ambitious striving for results."[14]

If you selected the second response, you have increased the likelihood that Kevin will share thoughts and feelings with you. You have effectively stimulated communication.

**Level 2. Clarify Information.** Inventory questions at this level seek to expand and/or clarify thoughts, feelings, and actions and enable students to begin recognizing patterns of behavior. Specifically, the goal of these questions is to (1) obtain more information, both factual and emotional; (2) relate specific examples, thus moving from vague generalizations to more concrete information; (3) clarify ambiguous terms or statements; and (4) focus on specific thoughts, feelings, and action as well as on patterns of behavior. Following are examples of inventory questions that clarify information:

- "Can you give me more information about what happened?"
- "Why don't you tell me more about what you were feeling?"
- "What did you mean when you said — ?" "Can you give me a specific example of when you felt that way?" "Can you say more about that?" "Has this ever happened before?"

- "Is this typical of the way you act/react?" "How do you usually react/act when this happens?" "What usually triggers this reaction?"

Let's continue with the preceding vignette and watch how the teacher uses clarifying questions to obtain more information and to help Kevin focus on specific feelings.

> *Kevin:* Jack and I were fighting.
> *Teacher:* Can you tell me specifically what happened?
> *Kevin:* He called me a cheater and told me I played dirty ball.
> *Teacher:* Can you say more?
> *Kevin:* We were shooting baskets and I pushed him accidentally.
> *Teacher:* And what were you thinking?
> *Kevin:* It was an accident. I was all excited . . . and I just wanted to hit the basket.
> *Teacher:* What did you say?
> *Kevin:* Nothing. . . . I guess I just kicked him.
> *Teacher:* You said that you were all excited, what else were you feeling?
> *Kevin:* I just wanted to hit the basket this time. . . . I wanted to win. . . . I guess I got angry.
> *Teacher:* Do you usually kick or fight when you get angry?

By effectively using inventory questions that clarify information, the teacher was able to receive a more accurate and comprehensive description of events that occurred. The teacher asked just one question at a time, did not ask questions that focused on "why" Kevin acted as he did, and was not accusatory or judgmental.

**Level 3. Identify Discrepancies.**   This level of inventory questions looks at the consequences and outcomes of specific behaviors or behavior patterns. It helps students determine if the outcomes of their actions are what they want or expect them to be and to identify any discrepancies that may exist. Inventory questions that identify discrepancies include these specific examples.

- "What was the outcome of your actions?"
- "Did things work out the way you wanted them to?"
- "What price did you pay for responding that way?"
- "How did it serve you to act this way?"

Now let's continue with the next stage of the vignette. Here are sample questions that could help Kevin identify the results of his behavior.

- "What does kicking and fighting get you in the end?"
- "You wanted to win, but what was the result of the fight?"
- "You were angry, so you kicked Jack. How did that serve you?"

Notice that inventory questions identifying discrepancies are open-ended. These questions can be more confrontative than the others in this series. However, there are times when this may be appropriate.

**Level 4. Seek Alternatives or Solutions.**   This level of inventory question brings students to the next logical step. Once they realize that their behavior does not result in desirable consequences, students are ready to explore alternatives and consider new solutions.

This type of inventory question serves as a transition to the next cluster of skills in the taxonomy of interpersonal communications skills — Encouraging Alternative Behavior. Specific questions that can be used at this level include:

- "If you don't like the outcomes of your actions, in what other ways can you behave?"
- "If you had it to do all over again, how would you react?"
- "How could you change your behavior to achieve more positive outcomes?"
- "What else could you do to achieve your goal, that has more positive consequences?"

In terms of our ongoing vignette, the teacher can explore with Kevin other strategies he could try when he gets excited and angry. These inventory questions can help Kevin become aware of choices and options.

# Your Turn

## DIFFERENTIATING AMONG THE FOUR TYPES OF INVENTORY QUESTIONS: (1) STIMULATING COMMUNICATION; (2) CLARIFYING INFORMATION; (3) IDENTIFYING DISCREPANCIES; (4) SEEKING ALTERNATIVES OR SOLUTIONS.

Before you read further, test your skill by completing the following review exercise. Read the vignette and, in the spaces provided, code the type of inventory question. Use *SC* for stimulating communication; *CI* for clarifying information; *ID* for identifying discrepancies, and *PA* for seeking out potential alternatives or solutions. When you complete the review, check your responses with those provided.

As Mrs. Peterson walks down the hall, she overhears Mindy and Lisa arguing:

> *Mindy:* Why did you tell me yesterday that you would go?
> *Lisa:* I forgot that I already promised Sue that I would go with her.
> *Mindy:* Thanks a lot, FRIEND.

Lisa walks into the resource room and slumps into her chair.

_____ 1. *Mrs. Peterson:* Lisa, you look so sad. Is anything wrong?
    *Lisa:* Nothing.
_____ 2. *Mrs. Peterson:* Does it have anything to do with your conversation with Mindy?
    *Lisa:* Yeah, Mindy is mad at me because I can't go to the show with her today.
_____ 3. *Mrs. Peterson:* Can you tell me what happened?
    *Lisa:* It's all so stupid. . . . I promised her I'd go to the show with her . . . . I forgot that I had already made plans to go with Sue.

_____ 4. *Mrs. Peterson:* How did Mindy react?

        *Lisa:* Bad, I guess. I don't want Mindy to be mad.

_____ 5. *Mrs. Peterson:* What's your reaction to the situation?

        *Lisa:* That I shouldn't have made two sets of plans again.

_____ 6. *Mrs. Peterson:* Has this happened before?

        *Lisa:* Yeh.

_____ 7. *Mrs. Peterson:* Can you give me another example when you acted this way?

        *Lisa:* Last week I did the same thing with Kathy.

_____ 8. *Mrs. Peterson:* So you make two different plans with two different friends. What usually happens? What does it get you in the end?

        *Lisa:* I guess one friend ends up getting mad at me. Why don't I think sometimes, instead of just absentmindedly saying yes?

_____ 9. *Mrs. Peterson:* If you had it to do over again, what other ways could you act?

---

## ANSWER KEY

### Your Turn

1. SC, 2. CI, 3. CI, 4. CI, 5. CI, 6. ID, 7. CI, 8. ID, 9. PA

---

This dialogue was brief. One or two questions from each of the four types of inventory questions were enough. Remember, the teacher's questions merely guide the personal inquiry process. It is not our place to probe or analyze.

The inventory process is a continuous and somewhat complicated process. It requires patient, supportive, and sensitive teachers who have mastered a series of specific, focused questions that they can use spontaneously. The entire interactive process necessitates a sensitivity in attending to students' nonverbal cues, sensing when to stop — stop questioning, stop probing. Teachers must protect their students from getting hurt, mocked, or ostracized by others.

---

*Summary of effective inventory questions*

*Level 1: Stimulate communication.* Questions at this level offer an open invitation to talk. They make students aware of your interest and concern.

*Level 2: Clarify information.* Questions at this level seek to (1) obtain more information; (2) relate specific examples; (3) clarify ambiguous terms or statements; (4) focus on specific thoughts, feelings, and actions.

*Level 3: Identify discrepancies.* Questions at this level focus on the consequences and outcomes of specific behaviors; they aid in the identification of discrepancies that may exist between desired versus actual outcomes of one's behavior.

*Level 4: Seek alternatives or solutions.* Questions at this level help students explore and identify more productive behaviors that are likely to achieve desired outcomes.

# Mastery Test

**OBJECTIVE 4**    To differentiate among four types of inventory questions that (1) stimulate communication; (2) clarify information; (3) identify discrepancies; and (4) seek potential alternatives or solutions.

Read the following dialogue and code the underlined sentences according to the four different levels of inventory questions: *SC* = stimulating communication; *CI* = clarifying information; *ID* = identifying discrepancies; *PA* = seeking potential alternatives or solutions. To complete this test successfully, you must accurately code all eight inventory questions.

Mr. Cotter explained the rules of the game and then asked the students to divide themselves into four equally numbered teams. As they were selecting their teams, Mr. Cotter noticed Julia slipping quietly out the back door. She didn't return until all the teams were selected and the game was under way. Mr. Cotter motioned to Julia to meet him in the hall. Once outside he said:

_____ 1. *Mr. C:* "I noticed that you left the room as soon as the kids started to select their teams, and you didn't come back until the game started. What made you leave? Do you want to talk about it?"

       *Julia:* "I didn't want to stay."

_____ 2. Mr. C.: "Can you tell me more about that?"

       *Julia:* "I didn't think anyone would pick me for the team. I never get picked for any team — like yesterday when we had to play kickball, I probably would have been the last one picked . . . just because I'm new here nobody picks me."

_____ 3. *Mr. C.:* "How did you act then?"

       *Julia:* "I told Mr. Gold that I had to go to the lavoratory."

       *Mr. C.:* "So when the class is dividing themselves into teams, you usually leave before you get picked."

       *Julia:* "I guess so."

_____ 4. *Mr. C.:* Tell me Julia, what does running away get you? How does it serve you?"

       *Julia:* "Well, if I can't stick around, then I don't have to be the last one picked."

_____ 5. *Mr. C.:* "What are some other consequences?"

       *Julia:* "I guess I just end up sitting and watching the others play."

_____ 6. *Mr. C.:* "How do you feel when you watch the others play?"

       *Julia:* "Well . . . I guess I feel left out."

_____ 7. *Mr. C.:* "So you leave before you can get picked and then feel left out when you have to sit back and watch. Did your behavior get you what you wanted?"

       *Julia:* "No."

_____ 8. *Mr. C.:* "What other ways could you act so that you don't feel left out?"

## ANSWER KEY

Mastery Test, Objective 4

1. SC, 2. CI, 3. CI, 4. ID, 5. ID, 6. CI, 7. ID, 8. PA

## LEARNING ACTIVITY 4.1

### Practicing Inventory Questions

You are now ready to practice the fourth and final interpersonal communication skill presented in this chapter. Review the checklist, become comfortable with the items, and establish the settings for practicing inventory questions, making sure that the situation is not too complex. Only a few people need be involved in the dialogues. Use only one or two questions from each of the inventory categories.

The final words of caution are worth repeating: Keep your practice settings simple, keep the number of people involved in the dialogue to a minimum, and use just one or two questions from each of the inventory categories.

### INVENTORY QUESTIONING BEHAVIOR CHECKLIST: OBSERVER'S ASSESSMENT

|  | Frequently | Occasionally | Never |
|---|---|---|---|
| 1. The teacher asked questions that stimulated communication related to the student's thoughts, feelings, and/or behaviors. | _____ | _____ | _____ |
| 2. The teacher avoided questions that required the student to justify his or her thoughts and feelings. | _____ | _____ | _____ |
| 3. The teacher asked questions that enabled the student to clarify his or her thoughts and feelings. | _____ | _____ | _____ |
| 4. The teacher asked questions that helped the student to recognize patterns of behavior. | _____ | _____ | _____ |
| 5. The teacher asked questions that helped the student to see the consequences of his or her behavior. | _____ | _____ | _____ |
| 6. The teacher asked questions that enabled the student to identify discrepancies between actual and desired outcomes of his or her actions. | _____ | _____ | _____ |
| 7. The teacher asked the student questions that helped him or her to seek alternative behaviors. | _____ | _____ | _____ |

### INVENTORY QUESTIONING BEHAVIOR CHECKLIST: SELF-ASSESSMENT

1. I asked questions to stimulate communication with the student related to thoughts, feelings, and behaviors.

   Specifically, I asked: _____

2. I avoided asking questions that would require the student to justify his or her thoughts, feelings, and/or behaviors. Instead, I asked:

_____

3. In order to obtain more information and enable the student to clarify his or her thoughts, I asked:

_____

4. In order to help the student recognize specific behavior patterns, I asked:

_____

5. In order to help the student identify the consequences and/or outcome of his or her behavior, I asked:

_____

6. In order to help the student recognize discrepancies between the actual versus desired outcomes of his or her behavior, I asked:

_____

7. In order to help the student seek alternative behaviors, I asked:

_____

_____

**SUMMARY**

You have now mastered the first two clusters of skills in the interpersonal communications taxonomy and have set into motion a meaningful pattern of communication and interaction between you and your students. The third cluster of skills — Encouraging Alternative Behaviors — will bring the process to the next logical point in the cycle. We encourage you to explore the skills inherent at this level of the hierarchy by referring to the original Weinstein and Fantini model alluded to on p. 227.

Stop for a moment and consider the hierarchical nature of the skills that you have practiced in this chapter. You have learned to observe both yourself and your students and have become aware of, and sensitive to, verbal and nonverbal behavior. Hopefully, your students have also become sensitized to these cues, both in themselves and in others. You have learned to listen to both the intellectual and emotional content of your own messages and those sent by your students. Hopefully, they too have developed this skill. You have also learned to reflect, or describe to your students, the messages that they are sending through their words and actions. As a result, your students are gaining insight into their own thoughts and feelings and ensuing behaviors. They are learning how their behaviors are perceived by others. You have also learned to ask inventory questions; these will help both you and your students to identify discrepancies between actual and desired behavior and to explore potential alternatives and solutions.

Through practice and genuine respect for yourself and your students, you will move effectively to the next stage, Encouraging Alternative Behavior. In essence, you will be saying to your students: "If you don't like the consequences of your behavior, you have the power to change."

NOTES

1. Gerald A. Weinstein and Mario F. Fantini, *Toward Humanistic Education: A Curriculum of Affect* (New York: Praeger, 1970).

2. Alfred Alschuler, Judith Evans, Gerald Weinstein, and Roy Tamashiro, "Search for Self-Knowledge," *Me Forum* (Spring 1975). University of Massachusetts Press.

3. *Ibid.*

4. J. E. Weigand, ed., *Developing Teacher Competencies* (Englewood Cliffs, New Jersey: Prentice-Hall, 1971), p. 247.

5. Carl Rodgers, *On Becoming a Person* (Boston: Houghton Mifflin, 1961).

6. A. Mehrabian and M. Wiener, "Non-immediacy between communication and object of communication in a verbal message," *Journal of Consulting Psychology* 30 (1966).

7. A. Mehrabian, "Significance of Posture and Position in the Communication of Attitude and Status Relationships," *Psychological Bulletin* 71 (1969): 359–372.

8. Edward T. Hall, *The Hidden Dimensions* (Garden City, New York: Doubleday, 1966), p. 108.

9. Charles Kelley, *Journal of Humanistic Psychology* 14 (1974).

10. *Ibid.*

11. Gerald Miller, *Speech Communication: A Behavioral Approach* (Indianapolis: Bobbs-Merrill, 1966), p. 73.

12. Joel Davitz, ed., *The Communication of Emotional Meaning* (New York: McGraw-Hill, 1964), p. 195.

13. Gerald Weinstein, "Introduction" in *Discovering Your Teaching Self: Humanistic Approaches to Effective Teaching* by Richard Curwin and Barbara Fuhrmann (Englewood Cliffs, New Jersey: Prentice-Hall, 1975), p. xix.

14. Daniel Malamud and Solomon Machover, *Toward Self-Understanding: Group Techniques in Self-Confrontation* (Springfield, Illinois: Charles C Thomas, 1970).

ADDITIONAL READINGS

Barbara, Dominick A. *The Art of Listening*. Springfield, Illinois: Charles C Thomas, 1966.

Brammer, Lawrence M. *The Helping Relationship Process and Skills*. Englewood Cliffs, New Jersey: Prentice-Hall, 1973.

Combs, Arthur. *The Professional Education of Teachers*. Boston: Allyn and Bacon, 1965.

Carkuff, Robert, and Richard Pierce. *The Art of Helping III*. Amherst, Massachusetts: Human Resource Press, 1977.

Davitz, Joel R. et al. *The Communication of Emotional Meaning*. New York: McGraw-Hill, 1964.

Ekman, Paul, and Wallace V. Friesen. *Unmasking the Faces*. Englewood Cliffs, New Jersey: Prentice-Hall, 1975.

Gazda, George. *Human Relations Development*. Boston: Allyn and Bacon, 1973.

Glasser, William. *Reality Therapy. A New Approach to Psychiatry*. New York: Harper and Row, 1965.

Glasser, William. *Schools Without Failure*. New York: Harper and Row, 1969.

Hall, Edward T. *The Silent Language*. New York: Fawcett, 1959.

Hennings, Dorothy Grant. *Mastering Classroom Communication: What Interaction Analysis Tells the Teacher*. Santa Monica, California: Goodyear, 1975.

Horney, Karen. *Self-Analysis*. New York: W. W. Norton, 1942.

Kagan, Norman. *Interpersonal Process Recall: A Method of Influencing Human Interaction*. East Lansing: Michigan State University Press, 1975.

Katz, Robert L. *Empathy: Its Nature and Uses*. Glencoe, Illinois: Free Press, 1963.

Long, Lynette. *Listening/Responding Human Relations Training for Teachers*. Monterey, California: Brooks/Cole Publishing Company, 1978.

Long, Lynette; Louis Paradise; and Thomas Long. *Questioning Skills for the Helping Process*. Monterey, California. Brooks/Cole Publishing Company, 1981.

Luft, Joseph. *Group Process: An Introduction to Group Dynamics*, 2nd ed. Palo Alto, California: National Press Books, 1970.

Maslow, Abraham H. *The Farther Reaches of Human Nature*. New York: Viking Press, 1971.

Maslow, Abraham H. *Toward A Psychology of Being*. New York: Van Nostrand Reinhold Co., 1968.

Matson, Floyd, and Ashley Montagu. *The Human Dialogue, Perspectives on Communication*. New York: Free Press, 1967.

McClelland, David. *The Achieving Society*. Princeton: D. Van Nostrand, 1961.

Montagu, Ashley. *The Humanization of Man*. Cleveland, Ohio: World Publishing Co., 1962.

Moustakas, Clark E., ed. *The Self: Explorations in Personal Growth*. New York: Harper and Row, 1956.

Purkey, William. *Self Concept and School Achievement*. Englewood Cliffs, New Jersey: Prentice-Hall, 1970.

Rogers, Carl. *Client-Centered Therapy*. Boston: Houghton Mifflin, 1951.

Rogers, Carl. *Humanistic Psychology*. Columbus, Ohio: Charles E. Merrill, 1971.

Schutz, William. *Firo: A Three-Dimensional Theory of Interpersonal Behavior*. New York: Rinehart and Winston, 1958.

Schutz, William. *Joy: Expanding Human Awareness*. New York: Grove Press, 1967.

Sokolove, Sandra. *A Competency-Based Approach to Humanizing Education*. Ed.D. dissertation. University of Massachusetts, 1975.

Stanford, Gene, and Albert E. Roark. *Human Interaction in Education*. Boston: Allyn and Bacon, 1974.

Wilford A. Weber

# 8. Classroom Management

# Objectives

**1** To define the term "classroom management," to differentiate the instructional and managerial dimensions of teaching, and to make a case for the importance of effective classroom management.

**2** To describe the four stages of the analytic-pluralistic classroom management process.

**3** To specify classroom conditions deemed desirable because they promote student on-task behavior and facilitate effective and efficient instruction.

**4** To analyze existing classroom conditions and to identify managerial problems, potential managerial problems, and desirable conditions.

**5** To describe the nature and dynamics of the authoritarian, intimidation, permissive, cookbook, instructional, behavior-modification, socioemotional-climate, and group-process approaches to classroom management.

**6** To identify managerial strategies believed to be effective.

**7** To analyze a given classroom situation and to describe and justify the managerial strategy or strategies most likely to be effective in facilitating and maintaining those classroom conditions deemed desirable.

**8** To design a data-gathering instrument and a set of data-collection procedures that might be used to evaluate managerial effectiveness.

No other aspect of teaching is so often cited as a major concern by prospective, beginning, and experienced teachers as classroom management. No other aspect of teaching is more frequently discussed in the professional literature — or the faculty lounge. The reason is quite simple. Classroom management is a complex set of behaviors the teacher uses to establish and maintain classroom conditions that will enable students to achieve their instructional objectives efficiently — that will enable them to learn. Thus, effective classroom management is the major prerequisite to effective instruction. Classroom management may be considered the most fundamental — and the most difficult — task the teacher performs.

The teacher's competence in classroom management is largely a function of his or her understanding of the dynamics of effective classroom management. Therefore, the purpose of this chapter is to enable you to cope more effectively with classroom management problems by helping you to understand the management dimension of teaching more fully. More specifically, because no one "best" approach to classroom management has been found, eight different approaches are examined: the authoritarian, intimidation, permissive, cookbook, instructional, behavior-modification, socioemotional-climate, and group-process approaches. Your own teaching should be more effective if you understand the managerial process and the full range of managerial strategies that characterize each of those eight approaches and are able to select and apply those specific managerial strategies most likely to be effective in a given situation.

# Objective 1

To define the term "classroom management," to differentiate the instructional and managerial dimensions of teaching, and to make a case for the importance of effective classroom management.

## LEARNING ACTIVITY 1

### Definitions

Although it is something of an oversimplification, a search of the literature on teaching reveals nine rather different definitions of the term "classroom management." The nine differ because each represents a particular philosophical position and operational approach regarding classroom management.

The authoritarian approach, for example, views classroom management as the process of *controlling student behavior*. In this position, the role of the teacher is to establish and to maintain order in the classroom. Primary emphasis is on preserving order and maintaining control through the use of discipline. Indeed, advocates of this position often regard discipline and classroom management as synonymous terms.

A second position — one that is somewhat related to the authoritarian approach — is the intimidation approach. This approach also views classroom management as the process of controlling student behavior. However, unlike the authoritarian approach, the intimidation approach seems to be predicated on the assumption that student conduct is best controlled through the use of intimidating teacher behaviors — sarcasm, ridicule, coercion, threats, force, and disapproval, for example. The role of the teacher is to *compel the student to behave* as the teacher wishes out of a fear to do otherwise.

A third point of view — one directly contrary to the intimidation approach — is the permissive approach. To advocates of this approach, the role of the teacher is to *maximize student freedom* — to help students feel free to do what they want whenever and wherever they want. To do otherwise, it is claimed, is to inhibit their natural development.

Unlike the other positions discussed here, a fourth viewpoint —the cookbook, or "bag-of-tricks," approach — is not derived from a single, well-conceptualized theoretical or psychological base. Instead, it consists of an ill-fitting combination of old wives' tales, folklore, and common sense presented as a set of prescriptions the teacher is to follow religiously. The cookbook approach is most often represented by rather simplistic lists of "dos" and "don'ts" describing what the teacher should and should not do in reaction to various problem situations. This approach is called the cookbook approach because these lists resemble step-by-step recipes; the role of the teacher is to "*follow the recipes.*"

The instructional approach — a fifth viewpoint regarding classroom management — is based on the premise that carefully planned and executed instruction will prevent most student behavior problems and will solve those it does not prevent. This approach advocates the use of instructional teacher behaviors to prevent or to stop inappropriate student behaviors. The role of the teacher is to *plan and implement "good" lessons* — lessons that are appropriate to the needs and interests of students, lessons that motivate students.

The principles of behavior modification provide the basis for a sixth position. This position views classroom management as the process of *modifying student behavior*. The role of the teacher is to foster desirable student behavior and to eliminate undesirable behavior. In short, the teacher helps the student learn appropriate behavior by applying principles derived from theories of reinforcement.

A seventh position views classroom management as the process of *creating a positive socioemotional climate* in the classroom. The assumption of this position is that learning is maximized in a positive classroom climate, which, in turn, stems from good interpersonal relationships — both teacher-student and student-student relationships. It is also assumed that the teacher is the key to those relationships. Therefore, the teacher's role is to *develop a positive socioemotional classroom climate* through the establishment of healthy interpersonal relationships.

An eighth viewpoint conceives the classroom to be a social system in which group processes are of major importance. The basic assumption is that instruction takes place within a group context. Therefore, the nature and behavior of the classroom group are viewed as having a significant effect on learning, even though learning is seen as an individual process. The role of the teacher is to *foster the development and operation of an effective classroom group*.

The eight positions presented above represent eight different classroom management approaches. Each approach has its advocates and its practitioners. However, no one of these eight managerial approaches has been proved best. Therefore, you are discouraged from adopting any one of these eight positions and from relying on only one managerial approach. Rather, you are encouraged to consider accepting a pluralistic definition of the term "classroom management." Such a definition broadens the range of approaches from which to select managerial strategies having the potential to create and to sustain conditions that facilitate effective and efficient instruction. It is argued here that only the teacher who adopts a pluralistic operational definition — who draws from each of the eight approaches — is able to select from a full range that managerial strategy which is most likely to be effective given an accurate analysis of a particular situation. A pluralistic approach does not tie the teacher to only one set of managerial strategies as he or she attempts to establish and to maintain those conditions in which students can learn. The teacher is free to consider all strategies that appear viable. The advantage of this position seems clear.

A definition sufficiently broad to reflect a pluralistic approach might state: Classroom management is that set of activities by which the teacher establishes and maintains those classroom conditions which facilitate effective and efficient instruction.

## Instruction and Management

Teaching consists of two major sets of activities: instruction and management. Instructional activities are intended to facilitate the student's achievement of specific educational objectives directly. Diagnosing learner needs, planning lessons, presenting information, asking questions, and evaluating learner progress are examples of instructional activities. Managerial activities are intended to create and maintain conditions in which instruction can take place effectively and efficiently. Rewarding promptness, developing teacher–student rapport, and establishing productive group norms are examples of managerial activities. Admittedly, it is often difficult to decide whether a particular teaching behavior is instructional or managerial, because the two are usually intertwined. It is important, however, to try to make this distinction when faced with classroom problems.

Inasmuch as teaching consists of instructional and managerial activities, it follows that the teacher faces both types of problems. The effective teacher must be able to distinguish between instructional problems that require instructional solutions and managerial problems that require managerial solutions. Too often, teachers attempt to solve managerial problems with instructional solutions. (The reverse is also true but occurs with somewhat less frequency.) For example, making the lesson more interesting — a commonly suggested instructional remedy — is not likely to solve the problem of children who are withdrawn because they have not been accepted by their classmates. Nonacceptance and withdrawal are management problems and require a managerial solution.

## Importance

If instruction is that set of activities intended to facilitate the student's achievement of educational objectives directly and if management is that set intended to create conditions in which instruction can take place, it follows that effective management is a critical prerequisite to effective instruction. Thus, simple logic supports the notion that effective classroom management is an important aspect of the teaching–learning process.

In addition to the logical argument that can be made for the importance of effective classroom management, an increasingly strong case can be made on the basis of results from teacher effectiveness research. A growing body of research suggests that there is a positive relationship between certain teacher classroom management behaviors and desirable learner outcomes, including student on-task behavior, student achievement, and student attitudes. For example, the literature indicates that: (1) using "gentle desists" — an authoritarian managerial strategy — is effective in decreasing student misconduct; (2) applying "positive reinforcement" — a behavior-modification managerial strategy — is effective in promoting appropriate student behavior; (3) communicating "unconditional positive regard" — a socioemotional-climate managerial strategy — is effective in fostering positive teacher-student interpersonal relationships; and (4) employing "classroom meetings" — a group-process managerial strategy — is effective in promoting productive classroom group norms. The Additional Readings section of this chapter lists a number of sources that make a case for the effectiveness of these and other managerial strategies.

# Mastery Test

**OBJECTIVE 1**    To define the term "classroom management," to differentiate the instructional and managerial dimensions of teaching, and to make a case for the importance of effective classroom management.

Answer each of the following questions in the spaces provided. When finished, check your responses with the Answer Key that follows.

1. You have read several definitions of the term "classroom management." Each is somewhat different from the others because of the philosophical position it represents. Write a brief operational definition of the term "classroom management" that you feel would be useful to you as you think about the concept.

_____

_____

_____

2. Contrast the managerial and the instructional dimensions of teaching through: (a) a comparison of their respective purposes; (b) a description of their chief characteristics; and (c) the presentation of several examples of each.

_____

_____

_____

_____

_____

_____

_____

3. As noted earlier, there are two major viewpoints which stress the importance of effective classroom management. The first of these was described as being based on logic; the second was described as being based on research. Try to restate each argument in your own words. You might find this a more interesting exercise if you role-play a bit in responding. In the first case, you might write as if you were an experienced teacher attempting to explain "the facts of life" to a teacher-education student. And in the second case, you might write as if you were an educational researcher summarizing research findings in a scholarly paper.

*Logical Viewpoint*

_____

_____

_____

_____

_____

*Research Viewpoint*

# ANSWER KEY
## Mastery Test, Objective 1

The following are suggested responses that might have been given to the questions asked above. Because the questions tend to be rather open-ended, your answers may not be identical, but they should be similar. In those cases where they are not, compare the two sets of responses and try to account for any large discrepancies. If it appears that you may have misunderstood some aspect of the information presented so far, you may want to reread certain parts of Learning Activity 1 or the appropriate resource materials listed in the Additional Readings.

1. An operational definition of the term "classroom management," it is argued here, should be a pluralistic definition — one that is broad enough to embrace a variety of viewpoints. The following definition is suggested: Classroom management is that set of activities by which the teacher establishes and maintains those classroom conditions that facilitate effective and efficient instruction. Your definition may not be identical to this one, but it should incorporate these two notions: (1) Classroom management is a set of teaching behaviors or activities performed by the teacher; that is, classroom management is something the teacher does; and (2) Classroom management — to be effective — is pluralistic; that is, the teacher employs strategies from a variety of approaches rather than relying on a single approach.

2. The distinction between managerial and instructional teaching behaviors is very often not an easy one to make because they tend to be intertwined. However, in simple terms, the purpose of instructional activities is to facilitate student achievement relevant to specific educational objectives, while the purpose of managerial activities is to establish and maintain conditions in which instruction can take place effectively and efficiently. Instructional activities are characterized by teacher behavior intended to facilitate achievement of specific student outcomes directly. Managerial activities are characterized by teacher behavior that creates and maintains conditions in which instructional activities can take place. Diagnosing learner needs, planning lessons, presenting information, asking questions, and evaluating learner progress are examples of instructional activities given in Learning Activity 1. Rewarding promptness, developing teacher-student rapport, and establishing productive group norms are examples of managerial activities presented in Learning Activity 1. (You might have given many other examples.)

3. Logic suggests that effective classroom management is an important aspect of the teaching-learning process because effective management is prerequisite to effective instruction. If the goal of instruction — and of schooling — is to foster student achievement, this goal cannot be realized in the absence of effective classroom management. Thus, effective classroom management is of crucial importance.

   A growing body of teacher effectiveness research suggests that there is a positive relationship between certain teacher classroom management behaviors and desirable learner outcomes. While this research has not shown one particular classroom management approach to be superior, it has shown that certain managerial strategies are effective. Thus, it can be claimed that the appropriate use of those strategies is important in fostering desirable student outcomes.

# Objective 2

To describe the four stages of the analytic-pluralistic classroom management process.

## LEARNING ACTIVITY 2

The previous section argued for a definition of the term "classroom management" that views classroom management as a process — a set of activities — by which the teacher establishes and maintains those conditions that facilitate effective and efficient instruction. The purpose of this section is to expand on that position by providing a description of classroom management as a four-stage, analytic-pluralistic process in which the teacher: (1) specifies desirable classroom conditions; (2) analyzes existing classroom conditions; (3) selects and utilizes managerial strategies; and (4) assesses managerial effectiveness.

### Specifying Desirable Classroom Conditions

The classroom management process is purposeful; that is, the teacher uses various managerial strategies in order to achieve a well-defined, clearly identified purpose — the establishment and maintenance of those particular classroom conditions the teacher feels will facilitate effective and efficient instruction with his or her students. Consequently, the first step in an effective classroom management process is the specification of those conditions the teacher deems desirable — the specification of "ideal" conditions. The teacher should develop a clear, thoughtful conceptualization of those conditions he or she believes will enable him or her to instruct effectively. In so doing, the teacher should recognize that the conditions identified as desirable will to a large extent reflect his or her personal philosophy rather than any set of universally accepted and empirically validated truths. Additionally, the teacher should recognize the need to continually assess the utility of his or her conceptualization and to modify it as circumstances dictate.

The teacher who takes care to specify the classroom conditions he or she believes are desirable has two major advantages over the teacher who does not: (1) The teacher will be far less likely to view classroom management as a process in which he or she simply reacts to problems as they occur; and (2) The teacher will have a set of objectives toward which his or her efforts are directed and by which his or her accomplishments are evaluated. It is argued here that the teacher who has a clear understanding of his or her managerial objectives is far more likely to be effective than the teacher who does not. Learning Activity 3 will provide you with an opportunity to identify conditions you feel would facilitate instruction in your classroom.

### Analyzing Existing Classroom Conditions

Having specified those classroom conditions he or she feels are desirable, the teacher is in a position to analyze existing classroom conditions — to compare the "real" with the "ideal." Such an analysis allows the teacher to identify: (1) discrepancies between existing conditions and desired conditions and decide which require immediate attention, which require eventual attention, and which require monitoring; (2) potential problems — discrepancies that are likely to arise if the teacher fails to take preventive measures; and (3) those existing conditions the teacher wishes to maintain, encourage, and sustain because they are desirable. Thus, the second stage of the process is based on the assumption that the effective teacher is one who is skilled at analyzing classroom interaction and particularly sensitive to what is happening in his or her classroom. That is, the teacher has an accurate understanding of what his or her students are doing — and not doing — and what they are likely to do. He or she is fully aware of "what's going on." Learning Activity 4 will give you an opportunity to increase your ability to analyze classroom conditions.

## Selecting and Utilizing Managerial Strategies

When the teacher's analysis of existing conditions suggests the need for intervention, the teacher should carefully select and apply the managerial strategy or strategies having the greatest potential to be effective in achieving his or her goal — be it to solve a problem, prevent a problem, or maintain a desirable condition. This suggests that the effective teacher is one who understands the full range of managerial strategies implied by each of a variety of approaches to classroom management and is able to select and apply the strategy or strategies most appropriate to a particular situation given his or her analysis of that situation.

This selection process may be thought of as a "computer search" in which the teacher considers the strategies "stored" in his or her "computer bank" and selects that strategy or those strategies holding the greatest promise in promoting the conditions deemed desirable. Learning Activities 5, 6, and 7 will provide you with an opportunity to examine managerial strategies you may wish to put in to your "computer" and to practice selecting managerial strategies most likely to be effective in various situations.

## Assessing Managerial Effectiveness

In the fourth stage of the managerial process, the teacher assesses his or her managerial effectiveness. That is, from time to time the teacher should evaluate the extent to which his or her efforts are establishing and maintaining desirable conditions — the extent to which he or she is narrowing the gap between the "real" and the "ideal." This evaluation process focuses on two sets of behaviors: teacher behaviors and student behaviors. In the first case, the teacher evaluates the extent to which he or she is using those managerial behaviors he or she intends to be using. The teacher assesses whether the managerial strategies he or she is using are most likely to bring about those conditions deemed desirable. In the second case, the more important of the two, the teacher evaluates the extent to which his or her students are behaving in desirable ways. Here the major emphasis is on the extent to which students are behaving appropriately — the extent to which they are doing what they are supposed to be doing. Teacher and student behavioral data may be collected from three sources: the teacher, the student, and an independent observer. Learning Activity 8 will give you an opportunity to increase your ability to evaluate your managerial effectiveness.

# Mastery Test

## OBJECTIVE 2 To describe the four stages of the analytic-pluralistic classroom management process.

In the spaces below, briefly describe each of the four stages of the analytic-pluralistic classroom management process. When you have done so, compare your responses to those in the Answer Key that follows.

Stage One _____

_____

_____

_____

Stage Two _____

_____

_____

_____

Stage Three _____

_____

_____

_____

Stage Four _____

_____

_____

_____

_____

## ANSWER KEY

### Mastery Test, Objective 2

The four stages of the analytic-pluralistic classroom management process are: (1) specifying desirable classroom conditions; (2) analyzing existing classroom conditions; (3) selecting and utilizing managerial strategies; and (4) assessing managerial effectiveness. If you have any reason to believe that your descriptions of these four stages are inadequate, you may want to refer to the appropriate section or sections of Learning Activity 2. Although it is important that you feel reasonably comfortable with your understanding of these four stages, subsequent learning activities are designed to provide the opportunity for more complete understanding.

# Objective 3

To specify classroom conditions deemed desirable because they promote student on-task behavior and facilitate effective and efficient instruction.

## LEARNING ACTIVITY 3

As noted in the previous section, the first step in the analytic-pluralistic classroom management process is for the teacher to specify his or her managerial objectives as conditions deemed desirable — those conditions that promote student on-task behavior and facilitate effective and efficient instruction. It is argued here that effective classroom management is a purposive, goal-directed process. Thus, the effective teacher is one who has clearly and thoughtfully identified those conditions he or she feels will encourage students to do what they are supposed to do — to be on-task rather than off-task, to behave appropriately rather than inappropriately. Although there is some research that offers guidance as to conditions that may be related to student achievement, the unfortunate reality is that too little is known in this regard. Thus, the conditions identified by a teacher are necessarily largely a reflection of his or her personal philosophy. The purpose of Learning Activity 3 is to provide you with an opportunity to examine your own thinking in this regard. That is, you are asked to identify those classroom conditions you feel are desirable because you think that they are likely to foster student on-task behavior and to promote instructional effectiveness. In short, you are asked to specify your managerial objectives. As you will see, the bias here is that they are best specified as student behaviors and attitudes the teacher wishes to promote.

# Mastery Test

### OBJECTIVE 3

To specify classroom conditions deemed desirable because they promote student on-task behavior and facilitate effective and efficient instruction.

Unlike most of the other mastery tests in this chapter, this test has no right or wrong answers. You are asked to examine each of the statements below and to indicate which of them you feel describes a classroom condition you believe would facilitate effective and efficient instruction in your classroom. Place a check mark in the space in front of each statement you think represents an "ideal" condition. Additionally, five spaces are provided for you to describe any other conditions you favor. The Answer Key following the statements provides a brief discussion you may wish to consider.

_____ Students exhibit on-task behavior.

_____ Students understand the teacher's expectations and act accordingly.

_____ Students exhibit productive work and study behaviors.

_____ Students understand and adhere to school and classroom rules.

_____ Students evidence feelings of self-worth.

_____ Students feel free to express themselves to the teacher and to one another.

_____ Students follow clearly established routines.

_____ Students show respect for persons and property.

_____ Students communicate openly and honestly.

_____ Students manifest positive interpersonal relationships.

_____ Students feel accountable for their own behavior.

_____ Students exhibit group cohesiveness.

_____ Students understand and accept the consequences of their actions.

_____ Students feel that they are treated fairly.

_____ Students exhibit cooperativeness and a sharing attitude.

_____ Students display productive group norms.

_____ Students quickly return to task after interruptions.

_____ Students follow directions.

_____ Students are prepared for the task at hand.

_____ Students function at a noise level appropriate to the activity.

_____ Students participate actively in learning tasks.

_____ Students display positive feelings about classroom processes.

_____ Students manifest the ability to adjust to changing situations.

_____ Students exhibit self-discipline and self-control.

_____ Students feel comfortable and safe.

_____ Students display initiative and creativity.

_____ Students serve as resources to one another.

_____ Students move from one task to another in an orderly manner.

_____ Students accept and respect authority.

_____ Students support and encourage one another.

_____ Students are responsible for individual supplies and materials.

_____ Students pay attention to the teacher and to one another.

_____ Students like being members of the classroom group.

_____ Students feel that the teacher understands them.

_____ Students believe that they have opportunities to be successful.

_____

_____

_____

_____

_____

## ANSWER KEY
Mastery Test, Objective 3

As noted earlier, the statements you checked — the statements that described conditions you would like to establish and maintain in your classroom — reflect your personal views. Whether you checked all of the statements or only a few is not the issue. The important thing is for you to keep those conditions that you identified in mind as you work through the remainder of this chapter. Those conditions you identified — those you checked and any additional ones you might have described — constitute your "managerial objectives." These conditions should serve as a guide as you undertake Learning Activities 4 through 8. These activities call for you to analyze problem situations, select managerial strategies you believe would be effective given your analyses, and design procedures to evaluate your managerial effectiveness. Your analyses of given situations should take into account the conditions you deem desirable; the managerial strategies you select should promote — not hinder — the achievement of the conditions you deem desirable; and the assessment procedures you design should enable you to determine the extent to which the conditions you deem desirable have been achieved. In short, all subsequent steps in the managerial process are influenced by the outcomes of the first step — the specification of classroom conditions you believe promote student on-task behavior and facilitate effective and efficient instruction. The managerial behaviors of the competent teacher are purposive. Consequently, you should strive to manage the classroom so as to achieve and to sustain those conditions you deem desirable. Your efforts should be directed toward the achievement of *your* managerial objectives.

# Objective 4

To analyze existing classroom conditions and to identify managerial problems, potential managerial problems, and desirable conditions.

## LEARNING ACTIVITY 4

In the second stage of the analytic-pluralistic classroom management process, the teacher analyzes existing classroom conditions. Having identified the classroom conditions he or she feels are desirable, the teacher attempts to determine the extent to which those conditions are present. It is argued here that the effective teacher is one who is able to accurately and thoroughly analyze classroom conditions on an ongoing basis — one who at all times knows what is going on in his or her classroom.

Sometimes an analysis of existing conditions appears to be relatively simple and straightforward. Two students fighting over the ownership of a pencil, a student cheating on an examination, a kindergarten student throwing a temper tantrum because he cannot be first in line, and a tenth grade student throwing a paper wad at a friend across the room may appear to be problems that are easily analyzed. That is not the case, however. Each is a complex situation that requires careful analysis. The purpose of this section is to provide you with some guidelines you may find useful as you attempt to analyze classroom conditions. In addition, this section provides you with a series of exercises to give you practice with regard to this important skill.

### Instructional and Managerial Problems

Clearly, the first step in solving classroom management problems is to identify accurately those problems that are instructional problems and those that are managerial problems. (Here, the term "managerial problem" is used broadly. A managerial problem is any instance in which there is a discrepancy between desirable and existing conditions — any instance in which a managerial objective is not being achieved. Additionally, as shown later in this section, managerial problems also include: (1) potential problems — instances in which discrepancies between desirable and existing conditions are likely to arise if the teacher fails to take preventive measures; and (2) desirable conditions — instances in which there is no discrepancy between desirable and existing conditions. When the teacher has identified a managerial problem, he or she should next identify the managerial objective or objectives not being achieved — the managerial objective or objectives he or she will attempt to achieve in order to solve the managerial problem identified. This process requires that the teacher be able to distinguish between instructional and managerial problems. The section that follows provides some guided practice in making those kinds of distinctions. Three typical classroom problems are described; some are instructional problems and some are managerial problems. Read each description carefully and decide whether you believe the problem to be instructional or managerial. Indicate your decision by placing a check in the appropriate space. Additionally, whenever you identify a managerial problem, briefly note at least one managerial objective that is not being achieved. (You may wish to refer to the list of managerial objectives on pages 281 and 282 for assistance.) For example, if there was an instance in which a student destroyed another student's art project, the managerial objective at issue would be: Students show respect for persons and property. Because instructional and managerial problems are so often intertwined, in making your decision be sure to go to the cause of the problem, not its symptoms. However, be careful not to read too much into the description. A discussion of each problem is presented immediately after the spaces provided for your responses.

# Your Turn

## IDENTIFYING INSTRUCTIONAL AND MANAGERIAL PROBLEMS

1. Johnny is a sixth grade boy of low-average ability. His academic record is very poor; in reading, for example, he is two years below grade level and nearly a year below any of his peers. His teacher, Mrs. Miller, describes him as "the worst kid in the class," for he seems to be misbehaving continuously. Johnny refuses to do his own assignments and frequently disrupts others in the class while they are doing their assignments. Mrs. Miller feels that he could do the same work the other children do if he would simply apply himself.

Instructional Problem _____          Managerial Problem _____

Managerial Objective _____

_____

_____

_____

*Discussion.* Although on the surface this may appear to be a managerial problem, the underlying problem here is instructional. Because Johnny is unable to be successful in his academic work, he is frustrated. His frustration manifests itself in the form of misbehavior. Expecting Johnny to be able to do the same kind and quality of work as his classmates is probably an unrealistic expectation. The teacher will need to provide instruction which is appropriate to Johnny's level of ability and achievement if he is to be successful. It is likely that success would eliminate Johnny's need to misbehave.

2. Although it is now eight weeks since she transferred to her new school, Barbara is still the "new kid in class." She transferred in midyear when her family moved to the city but has not yet become an accepted member of her fourth grade class. She appears to be shy and withdrawn. Barbara's teacher, Mr. Johnson, has made numerous attempts to "bring her out of her shell." He has formed small groups to work on social studies projects and has placed Barbara with a group of three particularly friendly girls.

Instructional Problem _____          Managerial Problem _____

Managerial Objective _____

_____

_____

_____

*Discussion.* This is a managerial problem. If Barbara is to become a fully participating, active member of the classroom group, her teacher will have to help her perceive the group as attractive and its members as accepting. Certain kinds of instructional activities — such as small group work — may facilitate this process, but the problem is essentially managerial, not instructional. The managerial objectives here might include: (1) Students manifest positive interpersonal relationships; (2) Students exhibit group cohesiveness; and (3) Students like being members of the classroom group.

3. Ms. Roth enters her fourth grade classroom to find Billie and Steve scuffling on the floor. Their classmates have gathered in a circle around them; they quickly notice Ms. Roth and take their seats. "Stop it this minute!" she calls to the fighting boys. They jump up, surprised that she is there.

Instructional Problem _____          Managerial Problem _____

Managerial Objective _____

_____

_____

_____

*Discussion.* This is clearly a managerial problem. Indeed, it is one of those few problems which is exclusively managerial. In addition, it is an interesting case because there are really two problems — one which is very apparent and one which is not. The obvious problem is that two members of the class are fighting. The second problem — one often overlooked — is that the classroom group sanctioned their behavior. Group norms had not developed to the point where the class would stop the fighting because it was violating their rules of how to behave in the classroom. The teacher will need to deal with both the conflict between the boys and the lack of productive norms within the classroom group. A number of managerial objectives might be listed here; these include: (1) Students manifest positive interpersonal relationships; (2) Students understand and adhere to school and classroom rules; and (3) Students display productive group norms.

Note: *Because it is a managerial objective that applies to most problem situations, "Students exhibit on-task behavior" is an appropriate managerial objective for each of the two managerial problems.*

## Individual and Group Managerial Problems

There are two major categories of classroom management problems: individual problems and group problems. This is a somewhat risky classification because individual problems and group problems — as with instructional problems and managerial problems — are often intertwined. However, the classification is a useful one for the teacher who recognizes and appreciates their interrelationship.

Although there are numerous descriptions of both individual and group classroom management problems, we will limit ourselves to two sources, the work of Dreikurs and Cassel[1] for individual problem categories and the work of Johnson and Bany[2] for group problems. These two sources are among the soundest available and, in addition, they are among the most easily understood and readily applied because of their relative simplicity.

## Individual Problems

Dreikurs and Cassel's categorization of individual classroom management problems derives from their assumption that human behavior is *purposive and goal-seeking*. Each individual has a fundamental need to belong and to feel worthwhile. When the individual is frustrated in developing a feeling of belonging and a sense of self-worth through socially acceptable means, he or she behaves inappropriately, that is, misbehaves. The authors identify four types of misbehavior: (1) attention-getting behaviors, (2) power-seeking behaviors, (3) revenge-seeking behaviors, and (4) behaviors that are displays of inadequacy. These misbehaviors are given in order of increasing severity. For example, the attention-seeking child who fails to gain attention may become a power-seeker.

The student who is unable to gain status in a socially acceptable manner usually seeks it through either active or passive *attention-getting* behaviors. The active form of destructive attention-getting is found in the show-off, the clown, the mischief maker, the brat, the incessant questioner; the nuisance, in a word. The passive form of destructive attention-getting is found in the lazy or inept student who attempts to get others to pay attention to him or her by requiring constant help.

*Power-seeking* behaviors are similar to but more intense than those of destructive attention-getting. The active power-seeker argues, lies, contradicts, has temper tantrums, refuses to do what he or she is told to do, and is openly disobedient. The passive power-seeker is one whose laziness is so pronounced that he or she usually accomplishes no work at all. Such a student is forgetful, stubborn, and passively disobedient.

The *revenge-seeking* student is so deeply frustrated and confused that he or she seeks success through hurting others. Vicious, openly defiant behavior is common, and physical attacks (scratching, biting, kicking) against fellow students, authority figures, and animals are not uncommon. He or she is a sore loser and poor sport. Usually the revenge-seeking child is active rather than passive. The active revenge-seeking child is described as vicious and revengeful. The passive revenge-seeking child is described as sullen and defiant.

The student who displays *inadequacy* is one who has become so deeply discouraged in attempting to achieve a feeling of belonging that he or she has given up any hope of succeeding and expects only continued failure. Feelings of hopelessness and helplessness accompany the withdrawal or dropout behavior of such a student, who equates participation with further failure. Such displays of inadequacy always take a passive form.

In addition to describing these four types of individual classroom management problems, Dreikurs and Cassel suggest a rather simple technique by which the teacher can identify the nature of the problem. They suggest that (1) if the teacher feels *annoyed* by the child's behavior, it is probable that the child's goal is attention-getting; (2) if the teacher feels *defeated or threatened,* the child's goal is probably power-seeking; (3) if the teacher feels *deeply hurt,* the child's goal is likely revenge-seeking; and (4) if the teacher feels *helpless,* the child's goal is likely a display of inadequacy. Dreikurs and Cassel assert that the teacher must correctly identify and understand the goals of the student's misbehavior to be effective in dealing with it.

## Group Problems

Johnson and Bany, advocates of the group-process approach, identify seven group classroom management problems: (1) lack of unity; (2) nonadherence to behavioral standards and work procedures; (3) negative reactions to individual members; (4) class approval of misbehavior; (5) being prone to distraction, work stoppage, and imitative behavior; (6) low morale and hostile, resistant, or aggressive reactions; and (7) inability to adjust to environmental change.

A *lack of unity* is characterized by conflicts between individuals and subgroups. Examples include conflicts between students of one sex or race and students of the other sex or race. The classroom climate in such situations is marked by conflict, hostility, and tension. Students are dissatisfied with the group and find it unattractive. Students fail to support one another.

When the classroom group exhibits inappropriate behavior in situations where there are clearly established norms, it is categorized as *nonadherence* to behavioral standards. Examples include noisy, disorderly behavior at times when students are expected to be quiet and well behaved. Loud talking and disruptive behavior while students are supposed to be engaged in quiet work at their seats is a typical example. Pushing and shoving in the cafeteria line is another.

*Negative reactions to individual members* of the class are characterized by expressions of hostility toward persons who are not accepted by the group, who deviate from the group's norms, or who hinder the group's efforts. Typical of this type of problem are instances in which the classroom group picks on the student they consider different. The group's efforts are directed toward getting the individual to conform.

*Class approval of misbehavior* occurs when the group encourages and supports an individual who is behaving in a socially unacceptable way. The most common example is classroom support for the "class clown." If such misbehavior is advocated by the class, it is both a group and an individual problem. The group problem, however, is the more serious of the two.

A problem exists when the group is easily *distracted or prone to work stoppage.* The group overreacts to minor distractions and allows minor problems to interfere with productivity. The instance in which the class refuses to work because they perceive the teacher as having been unfair is a typical example. Such situations are marked by uncertainty and anxiety.

When the class engages in covert or overt *acts of protest and resistance*, causing work slowdowns or stoppage, it is a most difficult group problem. The expressions of resistance are generally very subtle. Repeated requests for clarity regarding assignments, lost pencils, forgotten homework, and petty grievances are typical. However, overt, hostile, aggressive behavior is relatively uncommon.

Classroom groups who react inappropriately when there is a new rule, an emergency situation, a change in group membership, a schedule interruption, or a substitute teacher are exhibiting an *inability to adjust to environmental change*. Generally, such groups are reacting to stress; they perceive the change as a threat to group unity. The most common example is the normally well-behaved class that behaves very badly with a substitute teacher.

Six typical managerial problems are described below; some are individual problems, some are group problems, and some are both individual and group problems. Read each description carefully and decide whether you believe the problem to be an individual problem, a group problem, or both. Indicate your judgment by placing a check mark in the appropriate space or spaces. Then identify the particular type of individual or group problem according to the lists below. Finally, identify at least one managerial objective appropriate to each situation. A list of recommended responses follows the description.

# Your Turn

## IDENTIFYING INDIVIDUAL AND GROUP MANAGERIAL PROBLEMS

The following section presents six brief descriptions of classroom management problems. Your task is to identify the general type of problem (individual or group), identify the particular kind of individual or group problem according to the lists below, and identify at least one managerial objective that is not being achieved to the extent desirable. As earlier, you may find the list of managerial objectives on pages 281 and 283 to be helpful.

*Individual Problem (Dreikurs and Cassel)*

1. Attention-getting
2. Power-seeking
3. Revenge-seeking
4. Display of inadequacy

*Group Problem (Johnson and Bany)*

1. Lack of unity
2. Nonadherence to behavioral standards and work procedures
3. Negative reactions to individual members
4. Class approval of misbehavior
5. Being prone to distraction, work stoppage, and imitative behavior
6. Low morale and hostile, resistant, or aggressive reactions
7. Inability to adjust to environmental change

1. Michael has displayed the ability to disrupt Ms. Hamilton's mathematics lessons. He constantly interrupts her with criticisms. He argues about assignments he is given. He refuses to do what he is told to do even if reprimanded. Ms. Hamilton is afraid he may have the upper hand.

   Individual Problem _____                    Group Problem _____

   Type of Problem _____

   Managerial Objective _____

2. Mr. Clarkson's eighth grade algebra class is usually very well behaved and hard working. However, Ms. Felder, their substitute teacher, finds that they refuse to work and are quite sullen and defiant, even though she is following Mr. Clarkson's lesson plans to the letter.

   Individual Problem _____                    Group Problem _____

   Type of Problem _____

   Managerial Objective _____

3. Mrs. Appleton finds Barry to be a very annoying child. He is always into one or another form of mischief. His misbehavior is relatively minor but, nonetheless, rather obnoxious.

   Individual Problem _____                    Group Problem _____

   Type of Problem _____

   Managerial Objective _____

4. In his twenty-five years of teaching Mr. Ramiriz had never experienced a class which was so defiant as his eleventh grade auto body repair class. The students were constantly complaining about something. Indeed, it appeared to Mr. Ramiriz that they were too busy complaining to get any work done.

   Individual Problem _____                    Group Problem _____

   Type of Problem _____

   Managerial Objective _____

5. Miss Franklin felt that Susan was the most disruptive child in her fifth grade class. She was argumentative and defiant. This in itself concerned Miss Franklin, but of even greater concern was the way in which the other children encouraged this misbehavior. Susan knew that she was acting with the full approval of her peers.

   Individual Problem _____                    Group Problem _____

   Type of Problem _____

   Managerial Objective _____

6. Manny spends most of his time in Mr. Bishop's class daydreaming and looking out of the window. He plays with his pencil and doodles. He takes no part in the discussions and is oblivious to the teacher. Mr. Bishop is at a loss at trying to get Manny to take an active part in class sessions.

   Individual Problem _____                    Group Problem _____

   Type of Problem _____

   Managerial Objective _____

# ANSWER KEY

## Your Turn: Identifying Individual and Group Managerial Problems

The following is a list of the responses recommended for the preceding exercise. Compare your responses to them. You should not be satisfied with your performance unless you have correctly identified at least 5 out of 6 as individual or group problems. You should get at least 4 correct responses with regard to the specific type of problem. While the managerial objectives you have identified may not be identical to those listed here, you should attempt to justify the validity of both sets and reconcile any significant differences.

1. Individual problem; power-seeking; students understand the teacher's expectations and act accordingly, exhibit productive work and study habits, show respect for persons and property, and follow directions.
2. Group problem; inability to adjust to environmental change; students manifest the ability to adjust to changing situations.
3. Individual problem; attention-getting; students exhibit productive work and study habits and exhibit self-discipline and self-control.
4. Group problem; low morale and hostile, resistant, or aggressive reactions; students display productive group norms and follow directions.
5. Group problem; class approval of misbehavior; students display productive group norms; and individual problem; power-seeking; students understand the teacher's expectations and act accordingly and manifest positive interpersonal relationships.
6. Individual problem; display of inadequacy; students participate actively in learning tasks.

Two additional comments: First, as noted earlier, it would have been appropriate for each of the six problems to have listed "Students exhibit on-task behavior" as a managerial objective as this covers almost all problem situations. Second, in problem 5, the group problem described is viewed as having greater importance than the individual problem. You should recognize, however, that there are conflicting views in this regard. Some argue that resolution of the group problem will solve the individual problem. Others argue that resolution of the individual problem will solve the group problem. Still others argue that they are two separate and distinctly different problems, both of which require attention. You will need to reach your own conclusions about this issue.

## Problems Requiring Attention and Problems Requiring Monitoring

Thus far, our discussion about the analysis of existing classroom conditions has focused on the ability of the teacher to distinguish between: (1) instructional and managerial problems; (2) individual managerial problems and group managerial problems; and (3) various types of individual and group managerial problems. As difficult as it sometimes is to make these sorts of distinctions, they are crucial. For example, it can be argued that instructional problems require instructional solutions and that managerial problems require managerial solutions. It can also be argued that individual problems require managerial strategies that focus on the individual, whereas group problems require managerial strategies that focus on the classroom group. To do otherwise invites failure. Now we shall turn to an aspect of the analysis process that is not quite as straightforward — the identification of managerial problems requiring immediate attention, managerial problems requiring eventual attention, and managerial problems requiring monitoring.

In the main, managerial problems requiring immediate attention present a serious physical or psychological danger or potential danger to the student or students involved. These situations demand that the teacher act — and act quickly. There are other situations in which the teacher feels the need to act quickly so that a relatively minor problem does not become more serious. A fight involving two students represents an example of the first type of problem — there is the danger of serious physical harm, so the teacher acts immediately to deal with the problem so as to minimize the consequences. An instance in which one student is teasing another student who the teacher knows is likely to react violently if provoked is an example of the second type of problem — a situation in which the teacher moves quickly so as to prevent a minor problem from becoming more serious. Here the teacher would take immediate action in order to forestall the possibility of a violent reaction from the teased student. Unfortunately, there are no firm guidelines a teacher can use to determine whether certain situations require immediate attention. Although there is the need to not let things "get out of hand," there is also the need to not overreact to minor problems which will go away by themselves. The ability to make good judgments in this regard comes with experience — and a commitment to constant alertness. The effective teacher can "spot" a situation requiring immediate attention. As a rule of thumb, it is usually better to act immediately than to not do so. Sins of omission are likely to lead to more serious consequences than are sins of commission.

Although the purpose of this section is to discuss the analysis process, it is perhaps an appropriate place to comment further on situations that require immediate action on the part of the teacher. Because such situations give the teacher little time to consider the nature of the strategy he or she will use in dealing with the problem and because such situations often evoke a strong emotional response on the teacher's part, they are the types of situations the teacher is most likely to handle badly. Two suggestions are made in this regard. First, the teacher should develop a repertoire of "prepackaged" strategies he or she can "pull off the shelf" when confronted with such situations. The teacher should try to anticipate the kinds of serious problems he or she is likely to confront in the course of the school year and to map out a strategy he or she would use if that sort of problem were to occur. For example, the teacher might anticipate his or her students being involved in a fight. The teacher should have given this possibility a great deal of consideration and should have planned a sequence of actions to take if a fight were to break out in his or her classroom. The teacher should rehearse the specific steps he or she would take. Were a fight to start in his or her classroom, the teacher would be prepared to put his or her plan into action. Just as airline pilots use simulation exercises to become "programmed" to deal with various types of emergency situations, so too must the teacher be similarly prepared.

Second, when confronted with a situation he or she feels must be dealt with swiftly, the teacher should do whatever can be done to safely "buy time." That is, the teacher should do as little as is absolutely necessary at once and should reserve further actions for later — after the immediate danger has passed and emotions have had an opportunity to calm down. For example, a teacher who has managed to "break up" two fighting students might buy time by sending them to opposite corners of the room, with instructions that each write a description of what happened. That would give the teacher time to collect his or her thoughts, to plan the next steps to be taken, and to let teacher and student emotions subside. Not all problems give the teacher an opportunity to buy time, but the teacher who is able to do so when appropriate is far less likely to do or say something he or she later regrets.

Not all managerial problems require that the teacher act immediately. Indeed, most give the teacher time to consider various courses of action. Those problems that require attention — but not immediate attention — give the teacher an opportunity for careful analysis. The teacher is able to go beyond symptoms and to consider causes. He or she is able to more accurately diagnose the problem and to more thoughtfully select a strategy or a set of strategies which will address that problem.

For example, the teacher who discovers that a member of his or her class is not accepted by the other members of the classroom group is faced with a managerial problem to solve. The teacher would like to help that student become an accepted member of the classroom group and would like to help that group accept the student as a member of the group. Over several days, the teacher might carefully observe the dynamics that seem to hinder acceptance of the student by his or her peers. Having identified those factors and having identified a set of managerial strategies he or she believes will foster acceptance, the teacher implements those strategies having the best potential to solve the problem. The implementation of those strategies extends over two months, during which the teacher monitors the effect of his or her interventions and makes such modifications as are indicated. Eventually, some ten weeks after becoming aware of the problem, the teacher determines that his or her efforts have been successful — the student has been accepted as a valued, contributing member of the classroom group. In this example, the teacher's analysis revealed a problem needing attention; however, the nature of the problem — and its impact on the instructional process — allowed the teacher to take a considerable amount of time to diagnose and address the problem.

We have seen that an analysis of existing classroom conditions can reveal problems that require immediate attention and problems that require eventual attention; it also can reveal problems — discrepancies between existing and desirable conditions — that do not warrant direct, overt teacher intervention. Any overt action on the part of the teacher would be an unwise investment of teacher and/or student time. Most typically, no teacher intervention is needed in minor types of student misbehavior which do not appear to be disturbing the instructional process and seem unlikely to become more serious. The student who taps his or her pencil during quiet seat-work activities may be an example of such a problem. The teacher determines that this minor misbehavior does not disturb the teacher or the students and therefore elects to take no overt action to change the student's behavior. Rather, the teacher opts to simply "keep an eye on the situation" — to monitor the student's behavior. Such monitoring allows the teacher to determine whether the student's behavior has become disruptive. Should the teacher find that the behavior has become disruptive, he or she would have to intervene in an attempt to change the student's behavior. Clearly, the decision to take action or to not take action is a "judgment call." The teacher who is particularly sensitive to the dynamics of the classroom is more likely to make the right "call." The effective teacher is one who knows when an intervention is likely to be a good investment and when it is likely to be a poor investment.

Similarly, the effective classroom manager knows when to move quickly to deal with a problem and when to move more slowly.

## Potential Problems

The analysis process that allows the teacher to identify problems also allows him or her to identify potential problems. It is argued here that the effective teacher is one who is skillful at anticipating potential problems — discrepancies between the desirable and existing conditions which are likely to arise if the teacher fails to take preventive measures. Certainly, the effective manager is one who is able to react to problems. However, he or she is also able to anticipate potential problems and, when necessary, to intervene so as to "nip them in the bud."

A teacher should prepare students for the day when he or she is absent and is replaced by a substitute teacher, for example. Taking steps to prepare the class for that eventuality is not particularly burdensome and can yield important benefits — for the substitute teacher, the students, and the teacher. It is a good investment of teacher and student time and energy. The teacher who returns after a three-day absence and finds that the instructional process has barely "skipped a beat" and learns from the substitute teacher that his or her students behaved "beautifully" understands the wisdom of preparing the class to function in his or her absence and appreciates the benefits to be gained from having things arranged so that a substitute teacher can take over with a minimum of disruption. The substitute teacher who finds no lesson plans, no seating chart, and no established routine cannot be expected to be effective. The competent teacher anticipates potential problems and strives to prevent them.

## Desirable Conditions

Thus far, we have discussed how the second stage of the analytic-pluralistic managerial process can be used to identify problems and potential problems. These aspects of the analysis process are given greatest attention in the literature. However, a largely ignored use of the analysis process is to identify existing conditions that are desirable—instances in which there is no discrepancy between what exists and what is desired. For example, in a classroom of thirty-two students, the teacher is most likely to attend to two students who are misbehaving and being disruptive and to ignore the fact that thirty students are being very well behaved. It is the viewpoint here that the misbehavior of the two students must be reduced *and* that the behavior of those thirty students must be maintained, encouraged, and supported. Too often classroom management is viewed as a change process in which the primary managerial role of the teacher is to change the behavior of students who misbehave. It is very useful to remember that effective classroom management is also a maintenance process; it involves efforts to establish *and to maintain* those conditions that facilitate effective and efficient instruction. The effective teacher is proactive, reactive, *and* supportive.

Appropriate behavior must be rewarded if it is to be maintained. Students who exhibit appropriate behavior must feel that their efforts are appreciated. They very often do not. Thus, the teacher must be aware of existing conditions that are desirable—those students who are behaving acceptably. Unless the teacher strives to identify appropriate student behaviors, he or she will be unlikely to become aware of anything but inappropriate student behaviors. Surely, such a teacher will not reward appropriate behavior when it occurs—and that behavior will be less likely to be exhibited in the future. As some advocates of the behavior-modification approach say, the teacher must "catch 'em bein' good." The tendency too often is to "catch 'em being bad."

### Summary

This learning activity has stressed the importance of processes related to the analysis of existing classroom conditions. You have been asked to distinguish between: instructional and managerial problems, individual and group managerial problems, and various types of individual and group managerial problems. You have been encouraged to view the analysis process as one in which the teacher identifies: problems requiring immediate attention; problems requiring eventual attention; problems requiring monitoring; potential problems to be prevented; and desirable conditions to be maintained. The Mastery Test that follows provides you with an opportunity to practice the skills involved in the analysis process; the Answer Key provides one point of view.

# Mastery Test

## OBJECTIVE 4
To analyze existing classroom conditions and to identify managerial problems, potential managerial problems, and desirable conditions.

This test contains very brief descriptions of five typical classroom problems; some are instructional problems and some are managerial problems. Read each description carefully and indicate, by placing checkmarks in the appropriate spaces, how you perceive the problem. In addition, identify at least one managerial objective that is not being achieved in the problems you identify as managerial problems. Compare your responses to those in the Answer Key that follows.

1. The civics class is divided into six small groups. Each is to select an important event from the early 1900s and report on the people and places involved. Everything seems to be moving smoothly, when a very loud voice comes from a group in the back of the room: "But I don't want to write on that guy. He's dumb! Just because we elected you the chairperson doesn't give you the right to tell us what to do — to tell us which of the people we're to report on!"

_____ Instructional Problem                   _____ Managerial Problem

_____ Individual Problem                      _____ Group Problem

_____ Problem Needing Attention               _____ Immediate Attention Required

_____ Potential Problem Needing Attention     _____ Eventual Attention Required

_____ Desirable Condition Needing Attention   _____ Monitoring Required

Managerial Objective _____

2. It seemed that for the umpteenth time Sarah had turned in a paper that looked as if it had been trampled by a herd of buffalo. Anyone would have thought it was messy. Although Sarah is capable of neat work — she does neat work in some of her other classes — she does not do so in Mr. Reed's room.

_____ Instructional Problem          _____ Managerial Problem

_____ Individual Problem             _____ Group Problem

_____ Problem Needing Attention      _____ Immediate Attention Required

_____ Potential Problem Needing Attention   _____ Eventual Attention Required

_____ Desirable Condition Needing Attention   _____ Monitoring Required

Managerial Objective _____

3. Ms. Jackson began her reading lesson in her third grade as usual. And, as usual, Susan was up to her "old tricks." Everything was one big joke to her, and Susan had a snide comment for everything anyone said or did. Ms. Jackson tried to ignore her misbehavior, but it continued and, indeed, seemed to increase.

_____ Instructional Problem          _____ Managerial Problem

_____ Individual Problem             _____ Group Problem

_____ Problem Needing Attention      _____ Immediate Attention Required

_____ Potential Problem Needing Attention   _____ Eventual Attention Required

_____ Desirable Condition Needing Attention   _____ Monitoring Required

Managerial Objective _____

4. Ms. Freiberg's tenth grade geometry class seemed to be very disinterested in the subject. She had tried to make the class sessions interesting by using a variety of materials and activities, but conditions did not seem to improve. The more she tried, the more apathetic they appeared to be.

_____ Instructional Problem          _____ Managerial Problem

_____ Individual Problem             _____ Group Problem

_____ Problem Needing Attention      _____ Immediate Attention Required

_____ Potential Problem Needing Attention   _____ Eventual Attention Required

_____ Desirable Condition Needing Attention   _____ Monitoring Required

Managerial Objective _____

5. By mid-October, Mr. Michael felt that his social studies class was less productive than it should have been. He had let the students establish and enforce certain rules and regulations, hoping that students would become responsible for their own conduct. He felt the situation was now getting out of hand because the rules were not being followed or enforced.

_____ Instructional Problem          _____ Managerial Problem

_____ Individual Problem             _____ Group Problem

_____ Problem Needing Attention      _____ Immediate Attention Required

_____ Potential Problem Needing Attention   _____ Eventual Attention Required

_____ Desirable Condition Needing Attention   _____ Monitoring Required

Managerial Objective _____

## ANSWER KEY

### Mastery Test, Objective 4

1. Managerial problem; group problem; problem needing attention; immediate attention required; students exhibit cooperativeness and a sharing attitude, exhibit productive work and study behaviors, exhibit group cohesiveness, and display productive group norms are some of the managerial objectives one might focus on here; (the fact that five groups are working well could be described as a desirable condition needing attention and immediate attention required).

2. Managerial problem; individual problem; problem needing attention; eventual attention required; students exhibit productive work and study behaviors and understand the teacher's expectations and act accordingly are two managerial objectives one might include here; (this is another problem the teacher will want to work on pretty quickly, but not immediately; the teacher has time to diagnose the situation and to select strategies having the potential to be effective).

3. Managerial problem; individual problem; problem needing attention; eventual attention required; students exhibit productive work and study behaviors, show respect for persons and property, manifest positive interpersonal relationships, and understand the teacher's expectations are a few of the managerial objectives one might have included; (this is another problem that provides the teacher with an opportunity to move carefully).

4. Instructional problem; (the inability of the teacher to motivate the students is most likely an instructional problem; unless she finds learning activities that will be of interest, there is the danger that the students may begin to misbehave). (If you felt this was a managerial problem, students participate actively in learning tasks would be the major managerial objective in this situation.)

5. Managerial problem; group problem; problem needing attention; eventual attention required; students understand and adhere to school and classroom rules and exhibit self-discipline and self-control are the major managerial objectives one might identify here; (the teacher should attempt to understand the situation better while considering various managerial options; he or she should not wait too long before implementing the strategies he or she favors).

# Objective 5

To describe the nature and dynamics of the authoritarian, intimidation, permissive, cookbook, instructional, behavior-modification, socioemotional-climate, and group-process approaches to classroom management.

Earlier, the third stage of the analytic-pluralistic managerial process was described as a "computer search" in which the teacher selects and applies the managerial strategy or strategies that appear to have the greatest potential to be effective in a particular situation given his or her analysis of that situation. It was noted that this stage requires that the teacher understand the full range of managerial strategies implied by each of a variety of approaches to classroom management. The purpose of this section of the chapter is to increase your understanding of the authoritarian, intimidation, permissive, cookbook, instructional, behavior-modification, socioemotional-climate, and group-process approaches. It is not unreasonable to expect that a teacher might utilize strategies from a number of these approaches during a typical school day. However, primary attention will be given to the behavior-modification, socioemotional-climate, and group-process approaches, inasmuch as both the literature and research seem to point to their effectiveness. Somewhat less attention is given to the other five approaches. Limitations of space preclude an in-depth examination of any of the approaches. Consequently, you are encouraged to read broadly in the books listed for Objective 5 in the Additional Readings section of this chapter.

## LEARNING ACTIVITY 5.1

### The Authoritarian Classroom Management Approach

As described earlier, the authoritarian approach to classroom management views the managerial process as one in which student behavior is controlled by the teacher. The approach places the teacher in the role of establishing and maintaining order in the classroom through the use of controlling strategies; the major goal of the teacher is to control student behavior. The teacher assumes responsibility for controlling the conduct of the student because the teacher "knows best." The teacher is "in charge." This is most often done by creating and enforcing classroom rules and regulations.

However, one should not view authoritarian strategies as intimidating. The teacher who draws from the authoritarian approach does not force compliance, does not demean the student, and does not use harsh forms of punishment. The authoritarian teacher acts in the best interests of the student. This position is perhaps best explained by Canter and Canter, advocates of an approach they have called "assertive discipline."[3]

Canter and Canter argue that the teacher has the right to: establish clear expectations, limits, and consequences; insist on acceptable behavior from his or her students; and follow through with an appropriate consequence when necessary. Canter and Canter take great pains to emphasize that assertive discipline is a humane approach. They argue that all students need limits and that teachers have the right to set and enforce such limits.

Although it is an oversimplification, it is suggested here that the authoritarian approach offers five strategies that the teacher might wish to include in his or her repertoire of managerial strategies: (1) establishing and enforcing rules; (2) issuing commands, directives, and orders; (3) utilizing mild desists; (4) utilizing proximity control; and (5) utilizing isolation and exclusion.

**Establishing and Enforcing Rules.** The process of *establishing rules* is one in which the teacher sets limits by telling the student what is expected of him or her and why. Thus, it is a process that clearly and specifically defines the teacher's expectations concerning classroom behavior. Rules are statements — usually written — that describe and make public appropriate and inappropriate student behaviors. Rules are formalized guidelines that describe acceptable and unacceptable student behaviors; their purpose is to guide and limit student conduct. It is argued that well-defined rules are necessary if students are going to work within known boundaries. Rules that specify what is and is not acceptable are necessary if students are to know where they stand; students have a right to know "the rules of the game." In addition, they have a right to know the consequences of "breaking the rules." Advocates of the authoritarian approach insist that the teacher should establish and enforce rules that are realistic, reasonable, well defined, limited in number, and clearly understood and that he or she should do so beginning with the first day of the school year. They stress that no group can work together successfully without established standards of behavior — rules that are public and enforced.

Many recommendations have been made regarding the establishment of classroom rules. Space limitations allow only two major issues to be highlighted here. The first issue has to do with the extent to which students are involved in "making the rules." The second issue, somewhat related to the first, has to do with the number of rules that should be established. There are various positions concerning student involvement in rule establishment. The polar positions are: (1) Students should have a central role in making rules, inasmuch as they are more likely to follow rules they have had a hand in developing; the role of the teacher is to guide the students' efforts to develop good rules; and (2) The teacher should make the rules, inasmuch as the teacher — not the students — has the responsibility to determine which student behaviors are acceptable and which are not; the role of the students is to follow the rules, not to make them.

A position somewhere between these extremes seems to be most attractive. That is, the teacher should first specify a limited number of nonnegotiable rules and then work with students to add such additional rules as deemed necessary. This viewpoint also incorporates what appears to be the most appealing position with regard to the "number of rules" issue: Teachers should work to keep the number of rules to a minimum. The argument is that fewer rules, consistently enforced, are more likely to be effective than are many rules, because a great number of classroom rules make enforcement impossible. When rules go unenforced, the teacher's ability to manage the classroom is greatly diminished. Thus, the teacher should establish a reasonable number of enforceable rules.

**Issuing Commands, Directives, and Orders.**   The use of *commands, directives, and orders* is the third authoritarian managerial strategy discussed here. A command is a statement the teacher uses to tell the student that he or she is supposed to do something the teacher wants him or her to do. Clearly, there are times when it is necessary and appropriate for the teacher to tell the student that he or she is supposed to do something the teacher wants him or her to do. The kindly kindergarten teacher who asks her students to move to the story center is issuing a command; the friendly French teacher who asks his students to open their texts to page 47 is issuing a command; and the businesslike calculus teacher who asks one of her students to distribute the midterm examinations is issuing a command. Even in the most democratically run classrooms, teachers issue commands. Advocates of this authoritarian strategy argue that the use of clearly stated, easily understood commands, directives, and orders is a perfectly acceptable way for the teacher to control student behavior so long as the teacher does not use force to compel the student to obey. They recommend that commands should describe what the student is expected to do in very specific terms. One is hard pressed to disagree with this viewpoint.

**Utilizing Mild Desists.**   A wide variety of recommendations have been made with regard to the enforcement of classroom rules. Most typically, these recommendations have ranged from mild forms of punishment to very harsh forms of punishment. Many who might be categorized as supporting the authoritarian viewpoint recognize that severe types of punishment have been shown to be largely ineffective in the classroom setting. However, they do point to the effectiveness of a mild form of punishment — *"mild desist behaviors."* The terms "mild desist," "gentle desist," "soft reprimand," and "corrective" are used as labels for that managerial strategy in which the teacher reproves the student for behaving in an unacceptable way — for violating a rule. That is, the teacher — in a kindly manner intended to promote more acceptable behavior and not in a hostile manner intended to condemn the unacceptable behavior — informs the student that he or she is behaving inappropriately, should stop behaving inappropriately, and should return to behaving appropriately. The literature suggests that the use of mild desists is an effective strategy for helping the student who is exhibiting minor forms of misconduct — who is off-task — to get back on-task with a minimum of "muss and fuss." Those who support the use of this strategy are quick to remind others that mild desist behaviors are intended to be helpful, not hostile. They are verbal or nonverbal teacher behaviors intended to inform, not to indict.

**Utilizing Proximity Control.**   A teacher may be described as utilizing *proximity control* when he or she moves closer to a student whom the teacher sees misbehaving or whom the teacher believes is on the verge of misbehaving. This sort of action is based on the assumption that the physical presence of the teacher will be sufficient to cause the student to refrain from misbehaving. Proximity control is intended to defuse a disruptive or potentially disruptive situation; it is not intended to be punitive or intimidating. Its primary function is to let the student know — by the teacher's presence — that the teacher is aware of the student's behavior. Much like the mild desist, its intent is to inform, not to indict.

**Utilizing Isolation and Exclusion.**   *Isolation, exclusion,* inschool suspension, inschool detention, suspension and other forms of exile are strategies which teachers and school administrators are encouraged to consider as a response to serious student misbehavior. Authors representing a wide range of philosophies support the use of various types of exile. All attest to the effectiveness of these strategies, and most view them as nonpunitive. On the other hand, Wallen and Wallen describe isolation as the "ultimate punishment," the most severe allowable form of punishment.[4] The growing use of isolation suggests that various forms of exile — particularly inschool suspension — are viewed as effective in dealing with more serious forms of student misbehavior.

Given the arguments presented here, teachers who would build a repertoire of classroom management strategies would do well to consider the inclusion of at least five authoritarian managerial strategies: the establishment and enforcement of classroom rules; the use of commands, directives, and orders; the use of mild desists; the use of proximity control; and the use of isolation and exclusion.

## LEARNING ACTIVITY 5.2

### The Intimidation Classroom Management Approach

Earlier, the intimidation classroom management approach was described as an approach that — like the authoritarian approach — views classroom management as the process of controlling student behavior.

However, unlike the authoritarian approach, which stresses the use of humane teacher behavior, the intimidation approach emphasizes the use of intimidating teacher behaviors — harsh forms of punishment such as sarcasm, ridicule, coercion, threats, force, and disapproval, for example. The role of the teacher is viewed as one in which the teacher forces students to behave according to the teacher's dictates. The student behaves in a manner acceptable to the teacher out of a fear to do otherwise.

Although intimidation strategies are widely used, few authors who have written in the area of classroom management acknowledge that they believe that the intimidation approach is viable. On the contrary, it is often criticized in the literature. Its most articulate critics may be Johnson and Bany, who point to the ineffectiveness of "punitive and threatening practices" and "dominative and pressuring practices," strategies at the core of the intimidation approach.[5] They assert — and it is agreed here — that objective evaluation of intimidation managerial strategies leads to the conclusion that they are, for the most part, ineffective. Their use usually results in only temporary solutions followed by even greater problems, the most serious of which is student hostility and the destruction of teacher–student interpersonal relationships. At the very best, intimidation strategies deal only with a problem's symptoms, not with the problem itself.

The literature suggests that teachers who wish to build a repertoire of effective classroom management strategies will find "slim pickings" in the intimidation approach. The one intimidation strategy that might be viewed as useful in certain situations is the *harsh desist*. A harsh desist or reprimand is a loud, verbal command issued in a situation in which the intent of the teacher is to immediately stop a very serious student misbehavior. For example, the teacher who comes upon two students fighting in the hallway may yell "Stop!" in the hope that the students — hearing the voice of a teacher — would be afraid to continue to misbehave and to break the rules in the presence of a teacher who could bring serious sanctions to bear. Obviously, this type of intimidating behavior would be best used only to *stop* the fight — to stop the misconduct at once. When the fighting has stopped, the continued use of intimidating teacher behaviors would not be as productive as other strategies. The viewpoint here is that the teacher who relies heavily on intimidation managerial strategies — who attempts to control student behavior through the use of intimidating teacher behaviors — is likely to be very ineffective.

## LEARNING ACTIVITY 5.3

### The Permissive Classroom Management Approach

As noted earlier in this chapter, the permissive classroom management approach stresses the need to *maximize student freedom*. The major theme is that the teacher should allow students to do what they want whenever and wherever they want. The role of the teacher is to promote the freedom of students and thereby to foster their natural development. In essence, the teacher is expected to interfere as little as possible. The teacher is to encourage students to express themselves freely so that they might reach their fullest potential. Frankly, the permissive approach has few advocates. It represents a point of view which most consider impossible to put into operation in the public school context. It fails to recognize that the school and the classroom are social systems and as such make certain demands on those who are major actors in those systems. Students — and teachers — are expected to exhibit socially acceptable behavior, for to do otherwise is to risk violating the rights of others.

On the other hand, many who contend that the permissive approach in its "pure" form is not productive in school and classroom environments suggest that the teacher should give students an opportunity to "do their own thing" when it makes sense to do so. Students, they argue, must have the opportunity to be "psychologically free," to take "safe risks," to negotiate those aspects of the school experience that are negotiable, and to develop self-directedness, self-discipline, and self-responsibility. If the teacher does not encourage a measure of freedom when it is appropriate to do so, those things are not likely to happen. Clearly, the teacher must find ways to provide the student with as much freedom as he or she can handle in a responsible manner. Those who would consider drawing on managerial strategies that are representative of the permissive approach would do well to consider the validity of such arguments.

## LEARNING ACTIVITY 5.4

### The Cookbook Classroom Management Approach

The fourth approach discussed here is the cookbook, or "bag-of-tricks," approach. As mentioned earlier, this approach to classroom management — an ill-fitting combination of old wives' tales, folklore, and common sense — takes the form of recommendations touted as remedies for all "managerial ills." Descriptions of the cookbook approach usually consist of lists of things a teacher should do — or should not do — when confronted with various types of classroom management problems. These lists of "dos" and "don'ts" are commonly found in articles with titles like "Thirty Ways to Improve Student Behavior." Because these lists often have the appearance of being quick and easy recipes, this approach is known as the cookbook approach. The following are typical of the kinds of statements one might find on such a list:

Always reprimand a pupil in private.

Never raise your voice when admonishing a student.

Always be firm and fair when dealing with students.

Never play favorites when rewarding students.

Always be sure that a student is guilty before punishing him or her.

Always be sure that all students know all your rules and regulations.

Always be consistent in enforcing your rules.

Because the cookbook approach is not derived from a well-conceptualized base, it lacks consistency. Even though many suggestions put forward by advocates of the cookbook approach make a great deal of sense, there is no set of principles that permits the teacher to generalize to other problems. Additionally, the cookbook approach tends to cause a teacher to be *reactive* in dealing with classroom management. In other words, the teacher who uses a cookbook approach usually is reacting to specific problems and using short-range solutions. It is more effective to be *proactive*, to anticipate problems, and to use long-range solutions. The cookbook approach does not foster this type of managerial behavior, which attempts to deal with (1) possible problems before they actually surface in the classroom and (2) causes rather than with symptoms.

Another difficulty caused by acceptance of the cookbook approach is that when the specific prescription fails to achieve its intended goal, the teacher cannot posit alternatives, because the cookbook approach deals in absolutes. If "such and such" happens, the teacher does "so and so." On the other hand, advocates of a pluralistic approach assert that if "such-and-such" happens, the teacher can do "this" or "this." And if one of those fails to work, it is simply a matter of reanalyzing the situation and selecting from a variety of other attractive alternatives. Teachers who operate from a cookbook framework disadvantage themselves and are unlikely to be effective classroom managers.

A final word of caution: The cookbook approach should not be confused with either an eclectic approach or a pluralistic approach. The cookbook approach consists of ill-fitting bits and pieces of advice concerning the managerial behaviors the teacher is to use in particular situations. An eclectic approach is one in which the best aspects of a variety of managerial approaches are combined to create a well-conceptualized, philosophically, theoretically, and/or psychologically sound whole from which the teacher selects that particular managerial behavior appropriate to a situation. As noted previously, a pluralistic approach is one in which the teacher selects from a wide variety of managerial approaches that managerial strategy or combination of strategies having the greatest potential given an analysis of the situation. It is argued here that the wise teacher places value on those managerial approaches and strategies that are conceptually sound. He or she does not blindly follow a recipe.

## LEARNING ACTIVITY 5.5

### The Instructional Classroom Management Approach

The instructional approach to classroom management is based on the contention that carefully designed and implemented instruction will prevent most managerial problems and solve those it does not prevent. This approach argues that effective management is the result of quality instructional planning. Thus, the role of the teacher is to carefully plan "good lessons" — learning tasks that are tailored to the needs and abilities of each student, provide each student with a reasonable opportunity to be successful, gain and hold the interest of each student, and motivate each student. The "war cry" of those who advocate the instructional managerial approach is: "Make your lessons interesting."

Advocates of the instructional approach to classroom management tend to view instructional teacher behaviors as having the potential to achieve two central managerial goals: (1) preventing managerial problems; and (2) solving managerial problems. It is argued here that well-planned and well-executed instructional activities make a major contribution to the first of these goals — the prevention of managerial problems — and little contribution to the second goal — the solving of managerial problems. There is considerable evidence to indicate that well-designed, well-implemented instructional activities are a primary factor in preventing managerial problems. In addition, there is overwhelming support for the contention that poorly designed, poorly implemented instructional activities are a major contributor to managerial problems. However, there is little evidence to support the notion that instructional activities are effective in solving managerial problems once they have occurred. At best, it seems that instructional managerial behaviors are useful in dealing with only very minor sorts of student misbehavior.

An examination of the arguments made by advocates of the instructional approach suggests that the teacher should consider the following instructional managerial strategies: (1) providing interesting, relevant, and appropriate curriculum and instruction; (2) employing effective movement management; (3) establishing classroom routines; (4) giving clear directions; (5) utilizing interest boosting; (6) providing hurdle help; (7) planning for environmental changes; (8) planning and modifying the classroom environment; and (9) restructuring the situation.

**Providing Interesting, Relevant, and Appropriate Curriculum and Instruction.**   Davis states that "a well-planned curriculum implemented by a well-prepared teacher who presents a study topic so that it holds the interest of the students has traditionally been considered a deterrent to disruptive classroom behavior."[6] Kounin has reported research findings that are particularly relevant in this regard.[7] He found that the key to effective classroom management is the teacher's ability to prepare and conduct lessons that prevent inattention, boredom, and misbehavior. He found that successful teachers: teach well-prepared lessons that proceed smoothly and at a good pace with a minimum of confusion or loss of focus; waste little time moving students from one activity to another; and provide seatwork activities geared to the abilities and interests of students. Successful teachers, he found, are prepared and therefore able to exhibit what he called "smoothness" and "momentum." Such teachers employ effective movement management.

**Employing Effective Movement Management.**   *Effective movement management* is evidenced by a teacher who is able to move students smoothly from one activity to the next (smoothness) and to maintain momentum within an activity (momentum). The ability to regulate the flow and pace of classroom activities is viewed by many as crucial to preventing student off-task behavior.

Kounin also found that unsuccessful teachers are inadequately prepared and therefore unable to exhibit smoothness and momentum; they exhibit "jerkiness" and "slowdowns." They do not move students smoothly from one activity to the next; nor do they maintain momentum within an activity. Instead, they display behaviors Kounin saw as contributing to jerkiness (thrusts, dangles, truncations, and flip-flops) and slowdowns (overdwelling and fragmentation). A thrust is an instance in which the teacher suddenly bursts into an activity with a statement or direction for which the group is not ready. A dangle is an instance in which the teacher leaves one activity dangling in midair to start another activity and then returns to the first activity. A truncation is an instance in which the teacher simply leaves one activity dangling in midair and starts another activity. A flip-flop is an instance in which the teacher terminates one activity, starts a second, and then returns to the first. Overdwelling is an instance in which the teacher spends too much time giving explanations and/or directions. Fragmentation is an instance in which the teacher breaks down an activity into several unnecessary steps when it could have been appropriately handled as a whole.

Kounin's contention is that these teacher behaviors hinder smoothness and momentum and contribute to jerkiness and slowdowns that result in student inattention, boredom, and misbehavior. It is his position that unsuccessful teachers display ineffective behaviors primarily because they have not given adequate attention to planning and preparing the instructional activities they would have their students undertake. Since space does not permit a thorough description of Kounin's work, you are encouraged to refer to his 1970 book if you feel that his findings are of particular interest; that book has become something of a classic in the classroom management literature.

**Establishing Classroom Routines.** The process of *establishing classroom routines* is one in which the teacher — beginning with his or her first encounter with the classroom group — helps students understand what it is they are to do with regard to typical daily activities. Clear explanations of the teacher's expectations regarding classroom routines are viewed as a critical first step in effectively managing the classroom and developing a productive classroom group. It is a process that minimizes the potential for problems.

**Giving Clear Directions.** A number of authors emphasize the importance of giving clear, concise *directions*. Long and Frye argue that clear, simple instructions are fundamental to promoting desired behaviors.[8] Others argue that directions should be clear, precise, concise, to the point, and carefully sequenced. The effective classroom manager gives clearly understood directions. The teacher who says to his or her students "Please open your books to the problems you worked for homework" is much more likely to create problems than is the teacher who says "Please open your math books to page 47 so we can take a look at the six problems you did for last evening's homework." Obviously, students are far more likely to do what the teacher would like them to do if the teacher is very clear in communicating what students are to do. Giving good directions contributes to managerial effectiveness in that it helps avoid problems that can result from poor directions.

**Utilizing Interest Boosting.** *Interest boosting* is a process in which the teacher makes a special effort to show genuine interest in a student's work when the student first begins to show signs of boredom or restlessness. The teacher might go over to the student, look at his or her work, compliment his or her effort, and make suggestions for further improvements. In this way the teacher helps the student stay on task and prevents misbehavior.

**Providing Hurdle Help.**   *Hurdle help* is assistance given by the teacher to help the student cope with a frustrating problem just when the student really needs it in order not to explode or give up. The intent is to provide assistance before a situation gets out of hand. Hurdle help is a particularly useful way to prevent disruptive behavior.

**Planning for Environmental Changes.**   The classroom management literature suggests that, in order to minimize managerial problems, the teacher should anticipate certain environmental changes and prepare the classroom group to deal with them. For example, students should be prepared for the possibility of the teacher's absence — and a substitute teacher. Advance planning helps students know how to behave before potentially disruptive situations arise. Thus, managerial problems are prevented.

**Planning and Modifying the Classroom Environment.**   A number of authors have pointed to the importance of a classroom environment that is cheerful and orderly, that is organized so as to maximize productivity and minimize misbehavior, and that is well designed with regard to the physical placement of students. These authors stress the need to plan and to modify the classroom environment in order to prevent or eliminate certain types of unacceptable behaviors.

**Restructuring the Situation.**   *Situation restructuring* is a managerial strategy in which the teacher, through the use of a simple cue — a sentence or two at most — initiates a new activity or causes an old activity to be performed in a different manner. Changing the nature of the activity, changing the focus of attention, or finding new ways of doing the same old things appear to be effective in preventing managerial problems — particularly those that result from boredom.

In summary, the teacher would do well to remember the following with regard to instructional managerial strategies: (1) Well-planned and well-conducted instructional activities are a key factor in preventing managerial problems but not in solving them; (2) The teacher should design instructional activities that take into account the abilities and interests of each student; (3) The teacher should move students smoothly from one activity to the next and should maintain momentum within an activity; (4) The teacher should establish classroom routines and give clear directions; (5) The teacher should use interest boosting and hurdle help; and (6) The teacher should plan the classroom environment, plan for environmental changes, and restructure the situation when necessary. The use of these instructional managerial strategies will prevent many managerial problems.

<u>LEARNING ACTIVITY 5.6</u>

## The Behavior-Modification Classroom Management Approach

As discussed earlier, the behavior-modification approach is based on principles from behavioral psychology. The major principle underlying this approach is that behavior is learned. This applies both to appropriate and to inappropriate behavior. Advocates of the behavior-modification approach contend that a student misbehaves for one of two reasons: (1) The student has learned to behave inappropriately; or (2) The student has not learned to behave appropriately.

The behavior-modification approach is built on two major assumptions: (1) There are four basic processes that account for learning; and (2) Learning is influenced largely, if not entirely, by events in the environment. Thus, the major task of the teacher is to master and apply the four basic principles of learning that behaviorists have identified as influencing human behavior. They are: positive reinforcement, punishment, extinction, and negative reinforcement.

**Utilizing Positive Reinforcement, Punishment, Extinction, and Negative Reinforcement.** Terrence Piper[9] provides an easily understood explanation of the four basic processes. He suggests that when a student behaves, his or her behavior is followed by a consequence. Furthermore, he argues that there are only four basic categories of consequences: (1) when a reward is introduced; (2) when a punishment is introduced; (3) when a reward is removed; or (4) when a punishment is removed. The introduction of a reward is called *positive reinforcement,* and the introduction of a punishment is simply called *punishment.* The removal of a reward is called either *extinction* or *time out,* depending upon the situation. The removal of a punishment is called *negative reinforcement.*

Behaviorists assume that the frequency of a particular behavior is contingent (depends) upon the nature of the consequence that follows the behavior. Positive reinforcement, the introduction of a reward after a behavior, causes the reinforced behavior to increase in frequency. Rewarded behavior is thus strengthened and is repeated in the future.

### Example

Brad prepares a neatly written paper, which he submits to the teacher (student behavior). The teacher praises Brad's work and comments that neatly written papers are more easily read than those which are sloppy (positive reinforcement). In subsequent papers, Brad takes great care to write neatly (the frequency of the reinforced behavior is increased).

Punishment is the introduction of an undesirable or aversive stimulus (punishment) after a behavior and causes the punished behavior to decrease in frequency. Punished behavior tends to be discontinued.

### Example

Jim prepares a rather sloppily written paper, which he submits to the teacher (student behavior). The teacher rebukes Jim for failing to be neat, informs him that sloppily written papers are difficult to read, and tells him to rewrite and resubmit the paper (punishment).

In subsequent papers, Jim writes less sloppily (the frequency of the punished behavior is decreased).

Extinction is the withholding of an anticipated reward (the withholding of positive reinforcement) in an instance where that behavior was previously rewarded. Extinction results in the decreased frequency of the previously rewarded behavior.

### Example

Susie, whose neat work has always been praised by the teacher, prepares a neatly written paper, which she submits to the teacher (student behavior previously reinforced by the teacher). The teacher accepts and subsequently returns the paper without comment (withholding of positive reinforcement). Susie becomes less neat in subsequent papers (the frequency of the previously reinforced behavior decreases).

Time out is the removal of the student from the reward; it reduces the frequency of reinforcement and causes the behavior to become less frequent.

### Example

The students in Ms. Clark's English class have come to expect that she will give them an opportunity to play a word game if their work is satisfactory. This is an activity they all enjoy. Ms. Clark notes that all their papers were neatly done except Jim's paper. She tells Jim that he will not be allowed to participate in the class game and must, instead, sit apart from the group (removal of the student from the reward). Subsequently, Jim writes less sloppily (the frequency of the behavior decreases).

Negative reinforcement is the removal of an undesirable or aversive stimulus (punishment) after a behavior, and it causes the frequency of the behavior to be increased. The removal of the punishment serves to strengthen the behavior and increase its tendency to be repeated.

### Example

Jim is the one student in the class who consistently presents the teacher with sloppy papers. Despite the teacher's constant nagging of Jim, his work becomes no neater. For no apparent reason, Jim submits a rather neat paper. Ms. Clark accepts it without comment — and without the usual nagging (the removal of punishment). Subsequently, Jim's work becomes neater (the frequency of the behavior is increased).

In summary, then, the teacher can encourage appropriate student behavior by using: positive reinforcement — the introduction of a reward; and negative reinforcement — the removal of a punishment. The teacher can discourage inappropriate student behavior by using: punishment — the introduction of an undesirable stimulus; extinction — the withholding of an anticipated reward; and time out — the removal of the student from the reward. It must be remembered that these consequences exert influence on student behavior in accordance with established behavioral principles. If the teacher rewards misbehavior, it is likely to be continued; if the teacher punishes appropriate behavior, it is likely to be discontinued.

According to Buckley and Walker,[10] timing and frequency of reinforcement and punishment are among the most important principles in behavior modification. Student behavior that the teacher wishes to encourage should be reinforced immediately after it occurs; student behavior that the teacher wishes to discourage should be punished immediately after it occurs. Behavior that is not reinforced at once tends to be weakened; behavior that is not punished at once tends to be strengthened. Thus, the teacher's timing of rewards and punishment is important. "The sooner the better" should be the watchword of those teachers who would maximize their management effectiveness.

Of equal importance is the frequency with which a behavior is reinforced. Continuous reinforcement, reinforcement which follows each instance of the behavior, results in learning that behavior more rapidly. Thus, if a teacher wishes to strengthen a particular student behavior, he or she should reward it each time it occurs. While continuous reinforcement is particularly effective in the early stages of acquiring a specific behavior, once the behavior has been established, it is more effective to reinforce intermittently.

There are two approaches to intermittent reinforcement: an interval schedule and a ratio schedule. An *interval schedule* is one in which the teacher reinforces the student after a specified period of time. For example, a teacher using an interval schedule might reinforce a student every hour. A *ratio schedule* is one in which the teacher reinforces the student after the behavior has occurred a certain number of times. For example, a teacher using a ratio schedule might reinforce the student after every fourth occurrence of the behavior. For the most part, an interval schedule is best for maintaining a consistent behavior over time, while a ratio schedule is best for producing more frequent occurrence of a behavior.

Positive reinforcement has been defined as the introduction of a reward; extinction and time out have been defined as the removal of a reward. Punishment has been defined as the introduction of a punishment; negative reinforcement has been defined as the removal of a punishment. In other words, behavioral consequences have been discussed as either the introduction or the removal of rewards or the introduction or removal of punishment. Therefore, let's take a closer look at the notions of reward and punishment.

By definition, a reward or reinforcer is any stimulus which increases the frequency of the behavior that preceded it; and, by definition, a punishment (or aversive stimulus) is anything which decreases the frequency of the behavior that preceded it.

Different authors classify reinforcers differently. The behavior-modification literature is replete with labels. There is general agreement, however, that reinforcers may be classified in two major categories: (1) *primary reinforcers*, which are not learned and which are necessary to sustain life (food, water, and warmth are examples); and (2) *conditioned reinforcers*, which are learned (praise, affection, and money are examples).

Conditioned reinforcers are of several distinct types, including *social reinforcers* — rewarding behavior by other individuals within a social context (praise or applause); *token reinforcers* — intrinsically nonrewarding objects, which may be exchanged at a later time for tangible reinforcers (money or a system of check marks that can be traded in for free time or school supplies); and *activity reinforcers* — rewarding activities offered the student (outdoor play, free reading time, or being allowed to choose the next song).

Space limitations preclude a complete description of how various types of unconditioned and conditioned reinforcers can be used by the teacher to manage student behavior effectively. Many of the resources listed in the Additional Readings do that quite well. However, it is important to emphasize one point here: a reward is defined in terms of its ability to increase the frequency of the rewarded behavior. Thus, reward (and punishment) can be understood only in terms of an individual student. One student's reward may be another student's punishment. A response that the teacher intended to be rewarding may be punishing, and a response intended to be punishing may be rewarding. The latter is very often the case. A very common example occurs when a student misbehaves in order to get attention. The teacher's subsequent scolding actually rewards rather than punishes the attention-hungry student and, consequently, the student continues to misbehave in order to get the attention he or she seeks.

The above example suggests that the teacher must take great care in selecting a reinforcer that is appropriate to a particular student. While this is true, the selection process need not be difficult. Because reinforcers are idiosyncratic to the individual student, the student is in the best position to designate them. Thus, the best reinforcer is one selected by the student. Givener and Graubard[11] suggest three methods by which to identify individually oriented reinforcers: (1) obtain clues concerning potential reinforcers by observing what the student likes to do; (2) obtain additional clues by observing what follows specific student behaviors; that is, try to determine what teacher and peer behaviors seem to reinforce his or her behavior; and (3) obtain additional clues by simply asking students what they would like to do with free time, what they would like to have, and what they would like to work for.

Teachers who feel that it is important to reward appropriate student behavior do so in many ways. These range from "pats on the back" to "happy notes" informing a student's parents that the student has improved his or her conduct. Most teachers recognize that praise and encouragement are very powerful social reinforcers. Additionally, behavior modification offers the teacher a number of managerial strategies that involve the use of reinforcement. Although much has been written about each of these strategies and their effectiveness, space allows only a very brief description here.

**Utilizing Modeling.**   *Modeling* is a process in which the student, by observing another person behaving, acquires new behaviors without himself being exposed to the consequences of the behavior. Modeling, as a managerial strategy, may be viewed as a process in which the teacher demonstrates by his or her own actions the values and behaviors he or she wants students to acquire and display.

**Utilizing Shaping.**   *Shaping* is a procedure in which the teacher requires the student to perform a series of behaviors that approximate the desired behavior and, each time the student performs the required approximation or one a bit closer to the desired behavior, the teacher reinforces the student until the student is consistently able to perform the desired behavior. Thus, shaping is a behavior modification strategy used to encourage the development of new behaviors.

**Utilizing Token Economy Systems.**    A *token economy system* usually consists of three elements intended to change the behaviors of groups of students: (1) a set of carefully written instructions that describe the student behaviors the teacher will reinforce; (2) a well-developed system for awarding tokens to students who exhibit the behaviors that have been specified as appropriate; and (3) a set of procedures that allows students to exchange tokens they have earned for "prizes" or opportunities to engage in special activities. The implementation and operation of a token economy requires a great investment of time and energy on the part of the teacher. Consequently, its most typical — and efficient — use is in situations in which a large percentage of the students in a class are misbehaving and the teacher seeks to very rapidly change the behavior of those students. A well-managed token economy can be a very effective means for modifying the behavior of groups of students.

**Utilizing Contingency Contracting.**    A *contingency contract* or behavioral contract, an agreement negotiated between the teacher and a misbehaving student, specifies the behaviors the student has agreed to exhibit and indicates what the consequences — the pay off — will be if the student exhibits those behaviors. A contract is a written agreement between the teacher and a student detailing what the student is expected to do and what reward he or she will be given for doing those things. As in all contracts, both parties obligate themselves. The student is committed to behave in certain ways deemed appropriate, and the teacher is committed to reward the student when he or she does so. Contracting tends to be a somewhat time-consuming process. Therefore, it is usually reserved for those instances in which a student is exhibiting serious misbehaviors on a rather routine basis. Contracting can be a very effective tool in such instances.

**Utilizing Group Contingencies.**    The use of *group contingencies* consists of using a procedure in which the consequences — reinforcement or punishment — that each student receives depend not only on his or her own behavior but also on the behavior of the members of his or her group. Usually, it involves an instance in which the rewards for each individual member of the class are dependent on the behavior of one or more or all of the other students in the class.

**Reinforcing Incompatible Alternatives.**    *Reinforcing an incompatible alternative* involves a situation in which the teacher rewards a behavior that cannot coexist with the disruptive behavior the teacher wishes to eliminate.

**Utilizing Behavioral Counseling.**    *Behavioral counseling* is a process involving a private conference between the teacher and the student — a conference intended to help the misbehaving student see that his or her behavior is inappropriate and plan for change. It is argued that such conferences help the student to understand the relationship

Spence 2

between his or her actions and the resulting consequences and to consider alternative actions likely to result in desired consequences.

**Utilizing Self-Monitoring.** *Self-monitoring* — self-management, self-recording — is a strategy in which the student records some aspect of his or her behavior in order to modify that behavior. Self-monitoring systematically increases the student's awareness of a behavior he or she wishes to decrease or eliminate. Self-monitoring promotes self-awareness through self-observation.

**Utilizing Cues, Prompts, and Signals.** A *cue* is a verbal or nonverbal prompt or signal — a reminder — given by the teacher when he or she feels the student needs to be reminded either to behave in a certain way or to refrain from behaving in a certain way. Thus, a cue can be used to encourage or discourage a given behavior. Unlike a reinforcer, a cue precedes a response; it "triggers" a behavior.

Having briefly discussed the use of rewards, let us now turn to the thorniest of dilemmas faced by advocates of the behavior-modification approach — the use of punishment to eliminate inappropriate behavior. This is a subject of great controversy, controversy which is far from resolution. While it appears that every author has a somewhat different opinion, three major viewpoints seem most prominent: (1) the appropriate use of punishment is highly effective in eliminating student misbehavior; (2) the judicious use of punishment in limited types of situations can have desirable immediate, short-term effects on student misbehavior, but the risk of negative side effects requires its use to be carefully monitored; and (3) the use of punishment should be avoided completely, because student misbehavior can be dealt with just as effectively with other techniques that do not have the potential negative side effects of punishment.

Few authors present a viewpoint other than their own. However, Sulzer and Mayer[12] do help the reader examine the advantages and disadvantages of using punishment. They identify the following advantages: (1) Punishment does stop the punished student behavior immediately, and it reduces the occurrence of that behavior for a long period of time; (2) Punishment is informative to students because it helps students to discriminate rapidly between acceptable and unacceptable behaviors; and (3) Punishment is instructive to other students because it may reduce the probability that other class members will imitate the punished behaviors.

Disadvantages include: (1) Punishment may be misinterpreted. Sometimes a specific, punished behavior is generalized to other behaviors; for example, the student who is punished for talking out of turn may stop responding even when appropriate to do so; (2) Punishment may cause the punished student to withdraw altogether; (3) Punishment may cause the punished student to become aggressive; (4) Punishment may produce negative peer reactions; for example, students may exhibit undesirable behaviors (ridicule or sympathy) toward the punished student; and (5) Punishment may cause the punished student to become negative about himself or herself or about the situation; for example, punishment may diminish feelings of self-worth or produce a negative attitude toward school.

In weighing the advantages and disadvantages of using punishment, Sulzer and Mayer conclude that alternative procedures for reducing student behaviors should always be considered. Furthermore, they contend that once a punishment procedure is selected, it should be employed with the utmost caution and its effects should be carefully monitored. They also suggest that the teacher anticipate and be prepared to handle any negative consequences that might arise. Finally, they recommend that teachers find desirable behaviors to reinforce at the same time they are withholding reinforcement or punishing undesirable behavior.

Other behaviorists also point to research that suggests that punishment is largely ineffective in the classroom setting and argue against its use. As noted earlier, advocates of the authoritarian approach view mild forms of punishment (mild desists) as effective, whereas advocates of the intimidation approach view harsher forms of punishment as effective. Advocates of the socioemotional-climate approach argue for the effectiveness of another form of punishment — the application of logical consequences. Many behaviorists argue that the effective teacher is one who is able to modify inappropriate student behavior through the use of strategies other than punishment. As noted earlier, they advocate the use of extinction and time out. Several other strategies are also advocated; these include: overcorrection, response cost, negative practice, satiation, and fading.

**Utilizing Overcorrection.**    *Overcorrection* is a mild form of punishment in which the teacher requires a disruptive student to restore the environment to a better condition than existed before his or her disruptiveness. The student is required to go beyond simple restitution and to make things better than they were before he or she misbehaved.

**Utilizing Response Cost.**    *Response cost* is a procedure in which a specified reward is removed following an inappropriate behavior. The teacher arranges the rules of the classroom so that a particular cost — a fine — is levied for certain misbehaviors. Inappropriate behavior costs the student an already earned reward.

**Utilizing Negative Practice.**    *Negative practice* is a process in which the student who exhibits an undesirable behavior is required by the teacher to repeatedly perform that behavior until it becomes punishing — to repeat that behavior to the point at which the behavior itself becomes aversive. Those who advocate the use of negative practice encourage teachers to use this procedure only to eliminate undesirable behaviors that can be repeated without causing additional harm or disruption.

**Utilizing Satiation.**    *Satiation* — saturation — is the process of presenting a reinforcing stimulus at such a high rate that it is no longer desirable and becomes aversive. An "oversupply" of a particular reinforcer is presented so that the effectiveness of the reinforcer is diminished. In the typical situation, a teacher might insist that a misbehaving student continue to perform that misbehavior until he or she tires of doing it.

**Utilizing Fading.**    *Fading* is a process in which the teacher gradually eliminates the cues and prompts for a given kind of behavior. Supporting stimuli — cues and prompts — originally provided are gradually omitted until the student can perform the desired behavior without assistance.

Clearly, this section on the behavior modification approach cannot begin to describe in detail the many managerial strategies that constitute this approach. Should you feel the need for more information on this subject, it is suggested that books by Axelrod[13] and Clarizio[14] provide particularly good descriptions of behavior modification strategies.

Given the discussion in this section, the following seems to be an accurate summary of the lessons to be gained from the behavior-modification approach: (1) Rewarding appropriate student behavior and withholding the rewarding of inappropriate behavior are very effective in achieving better classroom behavior; (2) Punishing inappropriate student behavior may eliminate that behavior, but may have serious negative side effects; and (3) Rewarding appropriate behavior is probably the key to effective classroom management.

# Your Turn

## IDENTIFYING STATEMENTS REPRESENTING THE BEHAVIOR-MODIFICATION APPROACH

The following exercise was designed to give you an opportunity to assess your understanding of the information in this section. Please check each statement which represents the behavior-modification approach to classroom management. Compare your responses to those in the Answer Key that follows.

_____ 1. The teacher should use positive reinforcement to encourage the continuance of appropriate student behavior.

_____ 2. The teacher should recognize that the failure to reward a behavior tends to weaken that behavior.

_____ 3. The teacher should avoid punishing appropriate student behavior.

_____ 4. The teacher should understand that punishment and negative reinforcement are synonymous terms.

_____ 5. During the early stages of the student's acquisition of a desirable behavior, the teacher should reinforce that behavior immediately after it occurs.

_____ 6. The teacher should know that a ratio schedule of reinforcement is one in which the teacher reinforces the student's behavior after a certain number of occurrences of that behavior.

_____ 7. The teacher should ignore appropriate student behavior and promptly punish inappropriate student behavior.

_____ 8. The teacher should recognize that extinction is the withholding of an anticipated reward after a behavior occurs.

_____ 9. The teacher should understand that the use of negative reinforcement tends to increase the frequency of the behavior which caused the removal of the aversive stimulus.

_____ 10. The teacher should be aware that those things he or she perceives as rewards may not be perceived as rewards by students.

_____ 11. The teacher should avoid reinforcing student misbehavior.

_____ 12. The teacher should use the same rewards for all students so as to be perceived as fair.

_____ 13. The teacher should recognize that intermittent reinforcement is useful for strengthening desirable behaviors the student has learned.

_____ 14. The teacher should operate on the assumption that all student behavior is learned.

_____ 15. The teacher should recognize that the use of token reinforcers is inappropriate because it is nothing more than bribery.

_____ 16. The teacher should always consider alternatives to using punishment to eliminate unacceptable student behavior.

_____ 17. The teacher should understand that there are many types of reinforcers that may be effectively and appropriately used in the classroom.

_____ 18. The teacher should recognize that different students have different — often conflicting — perceptions regarding those things they view as rewarding.

_____ 19. The teacher should use an interval schedule of reinforcement when attempting to maintain a consistent behavior over an extended period of time.

_____ 20. The teacher should never fail to reward appropriate student behavior.

_____ 21. The teacher should recognize that the effectiveness of a token system is enhanced because it allows students to select their own rewards.

_____ 22. The teacher should understand that all behaviors have consequences, including behaviors which are ignored.

_____ 23. The teacher should know that continuous reinforcement is reinforcement which follows each occurrence of a particular behavior.

_____ 24. The teacher should reward only exceptional student behavior because typical behavior does not deserve special attention.

_____ 25. The teacher should recognize that the sole use of teacher attention as a reinforcer tends to increase student dependency.

_____ 26. The teacher should recognize that the timing and frequency of reinforcement influence its effectiveness.

_____ 27. The teacher should view ignoring student behavior as having the potential of being perceived as withholding reward or withholding punishment.

_____ 28. The teacher should reward acceptable student behavior and avoid rewarding inappropriate student behavior.

_____ 29. The teacher should recognize that ignoring student misbehavior is the same as approving of that behavior.

_____ 30. The teacher should understand that rewards are unique to the individual student.

_____ 31. The teacher should recognize that even the careful and judicious use of punishment may bring about serious negative side effects.

_____ 32. The teacher should always carefully monitor the effects of using punishment.

_____ 33. The teacher should view a well-managed token system as a means of promoting appropriate student behavior.

_____ 34. The teacher should anticipate and be prepared to deal with the possible negative effects of using punishment.

_____ 35. The teacher should observe and/or question students to obtain clues concerning potential rewards.

**ANSWER KEY**

Your Turn:  Identifying Statements Representing the Behavior-Modification Approach

The listing below presents the numbers of those statements suggested here as representative of the behavior-modification approach. You can feel that you have a good grasp of the information in this section if at least 30 of your responses are in agreement with those listed. Should you feel uncomfortable with the results, reread the materials in this learning activity and/or study those applicable resources listed for objective 5 in the Additional Readings. Statements that reflect the behavior-modification approach are: 1, 2, 3, 5, 6, 8, 9, 10, 11, 13, 14, 16, 17, 18, 19, 21, 22, 23, 25, 26, 27, 28, 30, 31, 32, 33, 34, and 35.

## LEARNING ACTIVITY 5.7

### The Socioemotional-Climate Classroom Management Approach

The socioemotional-climate approach to classroom management has its roots in counseling and clinical psychology and, consequently, places great importance on interpersonal relationships. It builds on the assumption that effective classroom management — and effective instruction — is largely a function of positive teacher-student relationships. Advocates of the socioemotional-climate approach emphasize that the teacher is the major determiner of interpersonal relationships and classroom climate. Consequently, the central managerial task of the teacher is to build positive interpersonal relationships and to promote a positive socioemotional climate.

Many of the ideas that characterize the socioemotional-climate approach may be traced to the work of Carl Rogers.[15] His major premise is that the facilitation of significant learning is largely a function of certain attitudinal qualities that exist in the interpersonal relationship between the teacher (the facilitator) and the student (the learner). Rogers has identified several attitudes that he believes are essential if the teacher is to have maximum effect in facilitating learning: realness, genuineness, and congruence; acceptance, prizing, caring, and trust; and empathic understanding.

**Communicating Realness.**  *Realness* is viewed by Rogers as the most important attitude the teacher can display in facilitating learning. Realness is an expression of the teacher being himself or herself. That is, the teacher is aware of his or her feelings, accepts and acts on them, and is able to communicate them when appropriate. The teacher's behavior is congruent with his or her feelings. In other words, the teacher is genuine. Rogers suggests that realness allows the teacher to be perceived by students as a real person, a person with whom they can relate. Thus, the establishment of positive interpersonal relationships and of a positive socioemotional climate is enhanced by the teacher's ability to display realness. Sincere expressions of enthusiasm or boredom are typical examples of realness.

**Communicating Acceptance.**  *Acceptance* is the second attitude which Rogers views as important to teachers who would be successful in facilitating learning. Acceptance indicates that the teacher views the student as a person of worth. It is nonpossessive caring for the learner. It is an expression of basic trust — a belief that the student is trustworthy. Accepting behaviors are those which make the student feel trusted and respected, those which enhance his or her self-worth. Through acceptance, the teacher displays confidence and trust in the ability and potential of the student. Consequently, the teacher who cares, prizes, and trusts the student has a far greater chance of creating a socioemotional climate which promotes learning than does the teacher who fails to do so.

**Communicating Empathic Understanding.** *Empathic understanding* is an expression of the teacher's ability to understand the student from the student's point of view. It is a sensitive awareness of the student's feelings and is nonevaluative and nonjudgmental. Expressions of empathy are all too rare in the classroom. When they occur, the student feels that the teacher understands what he or she is thinking and feeling. Rogers argues that clearly communicated, sensitively accurate, empathic understanding greatly increases the probability that positive interpersonal relationships, a positive socioemotional climate, and significant learning will occur.

In summary, then, Rogers suggests that there are certain conditions which facilitate learning and most prominent among these is the attitudinal quality of the interpersonal relationship between the teacher and the student. He has identified three attitudes which are crucial to the rapport-building process: realness, acceptance, and empathy.

Ginott[16] has presented views which are similar to those of Rogers. His writings also stress the importance of congruence, acceptance, and empathy and give numerous examples of how these attitudes may be manifested by the teacher. In addition, Ginott has emphasized the importance of *effective communication* in promoting good teacher-student relationships. How the teacher communicates is viewed as being of decisive importance.

**Utilizing Effective Communication.**    Ginott has written that the cardinal principle of communication is that the teacher talk to the situation, not to the personality and character of the student. When confronted with undesirable student behavior, the teacher is advised to: describe what he or she sees; describe what he or she feels; and describe what needs to be done. The teacher accepts the student but not the student's behavior; the teacher "separates the sin from the sinner." This notion has been called unconditional positive regard. (As you can see, it is identical to Rogers's notion of acceptance.) The teacher views the student as a person of worth regardless of how the student behaves. In addition, Ginott has provided a long list of recommendations describing ways in which the teacher might communicate effectively. Although a lengthy explanation of each is not possible here, a summary of these recommendations follows:

1. Address the student's situation. Do not judge his or her character and personality, because this can be demeaning.
2. Describe the situation, express feelings about the situation, and clarify expectations concerning the situation.
3. Express authentic and genuine feelings that promote student understanding.

4. Diminish hostility by inviting cooperation and providing students with opportunities to experience independence.

5. Decrease defiance by avoiding commands and demands which provoke defensive responses.

6. Recognize, accept, and respect the student's ideas and feelings in ways which increase his or her feelings of self-worth.

7. Avoid diagnosis and prognosis, which result in labeling the student, because this may be disabling.

8. Describe processes and do not judge products or persons. Provide guidance, not criticism.

9. Avoid questions and comments that are likely to incite resentment and invite resistance.

10. Avoid the use of sarcasm, because this may diminish the student's self-esteem.

11. Resist the temptation to provide the student with hastily offered solutions; take the time to give the student the guidance needed to solve his or her own problem. Encourage autonomy.

12. Attempt to be brief; avoid preaching and nagging, which is not motivating.

13. Monitor and be aware of the impact one's words are having on students.

14. Use appreciative praise, because it is productive; avoid judgmental praise, because it is destructive.

15. Listen to students and encourage them to express their ideas and feelings.

The list above cannot do justice to Ginott's views. The reader who desires a fuller explanation of these recommendations and who wishes to examine examples which support Ginott's suggestions is encouraged to refer to his last book, *Teacher and Child.*

Many of those who share Ginott's views regarding effective communication stress the importance of active listening and humor. *Active listening* is a process in which the teacher listens carefully to the student and then feeds back the message in an attempt to show that he or she understands what the student was attempting to say. Advocates of this strategy argue that active listening creates a situation in which the student is more likely to feel understood and valued; some view it as a way to operationalize the concept of acceptance. *Humor* is a strategy that can be used to ease tension in an anxiety-producing situation or to make a student aware of a lapse in behavior. Humor should be genial, kindly, and gentle and should not be sarcastic or ridiculing, as this endangers teacher-student relationships and student feelings of self-worth.

A third viewpoint that might be classified as a socioemotional approach is that of Glasser.[17] Although an advocate of teacher realness, acceptance, and empathy, Glasser does not give these primary emphasis. Rather, he stresses the importance of teacher involvement and the use of managerial strategy called *reality therapy.*

**Utilizing Reality Therapy.** Glasser asserts that the single basic need that people have is the need for identity — feelings of distinctiveness and worthiness. He argues that in order to achieve a "success" identity in the school context, one must develop social responsibility and feelings of self-worth. Social responsibility and self-worth are the result of the student developing a good relationship with others — both peers and adults. Thus, it is involvement that is crucial to the development of a success identity. Glasser argues that student misbehavior is the result of the student's failure to develop a success identity. He proposes an eight-step, one-to-one counseling process the teacher might use to help the student change his or her behavior; this process has been called *reality therapy* and is in many ways similar to behavior contracting, a behavior-modification strategy discussed in the previous learning activity. Glasser suggests that the teacher should:

1. Become personally involved with the student; accept the student but not the student's misbehavior; indicate a willingness to help the student in the solution of his or her behavior problem.

2. Elicit a description of the student's present behavior; deal with the problem, do not evaluate or judge the student.

3. Assist the student in making a value judgment about the problem behavior; focus on what the student is doing which is contributing to the problem and to his or her failure.

4. Help the student plan a better course of action; if necessary, suggest alternatives; help the student reach his or her own decision based on his or her evaluation, thereby fostering self-responsibility.

5. Guide the student in making a commitment to the course of action he or she has selected.

6. Reinforce the student as he or she follows the plan and keeps the commitment; be sure to let the student know that you are aware that progress is being made.

7. Accept no excuses if the student fails to follow through with his or her commitment; help the student understand that he or she is responsible for his or her own behavior; alert the student of the need for a better plan; acceptance of an excuse communicates a lack of caring.

8. Allow the student to suffer the natural and realistic consequences of misbehavior, but do not punish the student; help the student try again to develop a better plan and expect him or her to make a commitment to it.

Glasser views the above process — reality therapy — as effective for the teacher who wishes to help the misbehaving student develop more productive behavior. In addition, Glasser proposes a similar process for helping a whole class deal with group behavior problems — the social problem-solving classroom meeting. As a managerial strategy, the classroom meeting is perhaps best thought of as a group-process managerial strategy. Therefore, it is described in Learning Activity 5.8, the next section of this chapter.

A fourth and final viewpoint which might be seen as a socioemotional-climate approach is that of Dreikurs.[18] While it is true that works by Dreikurs and his colleagues contain many ideas that have important implications for effective classroom management, there are two which stand out from the others: (1) an emphasis on the democratic classroom in which the students and the teacher share responsibility for both process and progress; and (2) a recognition of the impact which natural and logical consequences have on the behavior — and misbehavior — of students.

**Developing a Democratic Classroom.**  A dominant theme in this approach is the assumption that student conduct and achievement are facilitated in a *democratic classroom*. The autocratic classroom is one in which the teacher uses force, pressure, competition, punishment, and the threat of punishment to control student behavior. The laissez-faire classroom is one in which the teacher provides little, if any, leadership and is overly permissive. Both the autocratic classroom and the laissez-faire classroom lead to student frustration, hostility, and/or withdrawal; both result in a devastating lack of productivity. True productivity can occur only in a democratic classroom — one in which the teacher shares responsibility with students. It is in a democratic atmosphere that students expect to be treated and are treated as responsible, worthwhile individuals capable of intelligent decision making and problem solving. And it is the democratic classroom that fosters mutual trust between the teacher and the students and among students.

The teacher who attempts to establish a democratic classroom atmosphere must not abdicate his or her responsibilities as a leader. The effective teacher is not an autocrat, but neither is he or she an anarchist. The democratic teacher guides; the autocratic teacher dominates; and the laissez-faire teacher abdicates. The democratic teacher teaches responsibility by sharing responsibility.

The key to a democratic classroom organization is regular and frank group discussions. Here the teacher — acting the role of leader — guides the group in group discussions that focus on problems of concern. Three products of that process have been identified: (1) the teacher and the students have an opportunity to express themselves in a way that is sure to be heard; (2) the teacher and the students have an opportunity to get to know and understand one another better; and (3) the teacher and the student are provided with an opportunity to help one another. He notes that an essential by-product of such group discussions is the opportunity the teacher has to influence those values of his or her students that may differ from those considered more productive.

Although there is an emphasis on the importance of the teacher's developing a democratic socioemotional classroom climate, you will see in the next learning activity that these views on the value of shared leadership and group discussions are very similar to those of the advocates of the group-process approach.

**Employing Logical Consequences.**  The second major emphasis concerns the impact of consequences on student behavior. In the classroom setting, natural consequences are those that are solely the result of the student's own behavior. *Logical consequences* are those which are more or less arranged by the teacher, but are a logical outcome of the student's behavior. The natural consequence of the student's grasping a hot test tube is that he or she will burn his or her hand. The logical consequence of breaking the test tube is that the student will have to pay the cost of replacing it. In order to be considered a logical consequence, however, the student must view the consequence as logical. If it is viewed as punishment, the positive effect is lost. Although most behaviorists do not make a distinction between logical consequences and punishments, most advocates of the socioemotional-climate approach do. Dreikurs and Grey suggest five criteria they view as useful in distinguishing logical consequences from punishment:

1. Logical consequences express the reality of the social order, not of the person; punishment expresses the power of a personal authority; a logical consequence results from a violation of an accepted social rule.

2. Logical consequences are logically related to the misbehavior; punishment rarely is logically related; the student sees the relationship between the misbehavior and its consequences.

3. Logical consequences involve no element of moral judgment; punishment inevitably does; the student's misbehavior is viewed as a mistake, not a sin.

4. Logical consequences are concerned only with what will happen next; punishment is in the past; the focus is on the future.

5. Logical consequences are involved in a friendly manner; punishment involves either open or concealed anger; the teacher should try to disengage himself or herself from the consequence.

In summary, then, logical consequences: express the reality of the social order; are intrinsically related to the misbehavior; involve no element of moral judgment; and are concerned only with what will happen next. On the other hand, punishment: expresses the power of personal authority; is not logically related to the misbehavior; involves moral judgment; and deals with the past. As Glasser does, Dreikurs stresses the importance of the positive effect which the application of logical consequences has on the behavior of students. Both argue it is crucial that teachers help students understand the logical relationship between their behavior and the consequences of that behavior. Both also argue that it is important that the teacher be able to use logical consequences appropriately — and avoid punishment — in helping students change their behaviors to those that are more desirable.

The teacher who would be an effective classroom manager would do well to consider including the following socioemotional climate strategies in his or her behavioral repertoire: communicating realness, acceptance, and empathic understanding; utilizing effective communication, exhibiting unconditional positive regard, exhibiting active listening, and utilizing humor; utilizing reality therapy; developing a democratic classroom; and employing logical consequences. All are strategies that facilitate the establishment and maintenance of positive teacher-student interpersonal relationships and a positive socioemotional climate.

# Your Turn

## IDENTIFYING STATEMENTS REPRESENTING THE SOCIOEMOTIONAL-CLIMATE APPROACH

The following exercise is designed to assist you in determining the extent to which you understand the information presented in this section. Check each statement you feel represents the views of the socioemotional-climate approach to classroom management. Please compare your responses with those in the Answer Key that follows.

_____ 1. A teacher should allow students to suffer the natural and logical consequences of their behavior unless these consequences involve physical danger.

_____ 2. A teacher should recognize that punishment is a powerful tool for dealing with both individual and group problems.

_____ 3. A teacher should accept no excuses from the student who fails to follow the behavior change plan to which he or she has made a commitment.

_____ 4. A teacher should help the student identify and describe the behavior problem rather than evaluate the student.

_____ 5. A teacher should recognize that the acceptance of the student implies approval of his or her behavior.

_____ 6. A teacher should direct attention toward solving behavior problems rather than finding fault or assigning blame.

_____ 7. A teacher should help students identify group problems, assign blame, and fix the appropriate punishment.

_____ 8. A teacher should never express feelings not congruent with those he or she is experiencing.

_____ 9. A teacher should address the student's situation, not the student's character or personality.

_____ 10. A teacher should remain aloof and businesslike in dealing with students.

_____ 11. A teacher should recognize that the laissez-faire classroom is unproductive.

_____ 12. A teacher should recognize that he or she cannot abdicate his or her responsibility if a democratic classroom climate is to be achieved.

_____ 13. A teacher should help the student understand the logical relationship between the misbehavior and the consequence.

_____ 14. A teacher should recognize that students view teacher expressions of emotion as a sign of weakness.

_____ 15. A teacher should encourage and accept the expression of student ideas and feelings.

_____ 16. A teacher should understand that effective management is the result of the teacher assuming an authoritarian posture and maintaining control.

_____ 17. A teacher should promote a nonpunitive climate when working with a student who has misbehaved.

_____ 18. A teacher should recognize that even well-led group discussions are little more than bull sessions of questionable value.

_____ 19. A teacher should understand that effective communication is essential to positive interpersonal relationships.

_____ 20. A teacher should express empathy toward students so that they feel he or she understands them and their feelings.

_____ 21. A teacher should avoid sarcasm, because this tends to demean the student and decrease his or her feelings of self-worth.

_____ 22. A teacher should avoid becoming overly involved with students and their nonschool problems.

_____ 23. A teacher should understand that the nature of the interpersonal relationship between the teacher and the students is a function of the student behaviors.

_____ 24. A teacher should recognize that he or she has the right to expect students to show him or her proper respect.

_____ 25. A teacher should view acceptance as a belief that the student is worthy.

_____ 26. A teacher should know that empathic understanding is an expression of the teacher's ability to understand the student from the student's point of view.

_____ 27. A teacher should recognize that the manner in which the teacher communicates is decisively important.

_____ 28. A teacher should consider a student's behavior as a reflection of his personality and character.

_____ 29. A teacher should understand that certain teacher behaviors increase student hostility and defiance.

_____ 30. A teacher should use behaviors that are likely to promote cooperation and avoid those that are likely to promote competition.

_____ 31. A teacher should always be sure that he or she has correctly diagnosed the student's misbehavior before labeling the problem.

_____ 32. A teacher should be brief and avoid preaching and nagging.

_____ 33. A teacher should not tolerate and should carefully control student expressions of feelings, especially expressions of hostility and defiance.

_____ 34. The teacher should commit himself or herself to helping the student develop self-responsibility and feelings of self-worth.

_____ 35. The teacher should use sarcasm very carefully and only after good interpersonal relationships have been established.

## ANSWER KEY

### Your Turn: Identifying Statements Representing the Socioemotional-Climate Approach

The list below contains the numbers of the statements viewed here as representative of the socioemotional-climate approach to classroom management. Compare your responses to these. You can consider that you have done well if you disagree on no more than five statements. If you feel the need to review this topic, reread this learning activity or study applicable resources listed for objective 5 in the Additional Readings. The representative statements are: 1, 3, 4, 6, 8, 9, 11, 12, 13, 15, 17, 19, 20, 21, 25, 26, 27, 29, 30, 32, and 34.

## LEARNING ACTIVITY 5.8

### The Group-Process Classroom Management Approach

As noted earlier, the group-process approach — also known as the sociopsychological approach — is based on principles from social psychology and group dynamics. The major premise underlying the group-process approach is based on the following assumptions: (1) Schooling takes place within a group context — the classroom group; (2) The central task of the teacher is to establish and maintain an effective, productive classroom group; (3) The classroom group is a social system containing properties common to all social systems. The effective, productive classroom group is characterized by certain conditions that are compatible with those properties; and (4) The classroom management task of the teacher is to establish and maintain such conditions. While there is some disagreement concerning the conditions which characterize the effective, productive classroom group, you will examine the conditions described in three excellent sources: the work of Schmuck and Schmuck, Johnson and Bany, and Kounin.

First let us focus on six properties identified by Schmuck and Schmuck[19] regarding classroom management: expectations, leadership, attraction, norms, communication, and cohesiveness.

*Expectations* are those perceptions that the teacher and the students hold regarding their relationships to one another. They are individual predictions of how self and others will behave. Therefore, expectations about how members of the group will behave greatly influence how the teacher and the students behave in relation to one another. The effective classroom group is one in which expectations are accurate, realistic, and clearly understood. The behavior of the teacher communicates to students what behavior the teacher expects of them, and the students, in turn, tend to conform to those expectations. Thus, if students feel the teacher expects them to misbehave, it is likely that they will misbehave; if students feel the teacher expects them to behave appropriately, it is more likely that they will behave appropriately.

*Leadership* is best thought of as those behaviors that help the group move toward the accomplishment of its objectives. Thus, leadership behaviors consist of actions by group members; included are actions which aid in setting group norms, which move the group toward its goals, which improve the quality of interaction between group members, and which build group cohesiveness. By virtue of their role, teachers have the greatest potential for leadership. However, in an effective classroom group, leadership functions are performed by both the students and the teacher. An effective classroom group is one in which the leadership functions are well distributed and where all group members can feel power and self-worth in accomplishing academic tasks and in working together. When students share classroom leadership with the teacher, they are far more likely to be self-regulating and responsible for their own behavior. Thus, the effective teacher is one who creates a climate in which students perform leadership functions. The teacher improves the quality of group interaction and productivity by training students to perform goal-directed leadership functions and by dispersing leadership throughout the group.

*Attraction* refers to the friendship patterns in the classroom group. Attraction can be described as the level of friendship that exists among members of the classroom group. The level of attraction is dependent upon the degree to which positive interpersonal relationships have been developed. It is clear that a positive relationship exists between level of attraction and student academic performance. Thus, the effective classroom manager is one who fosters positive interpersonal relationships among group members. For example, the teacher attempts to promote the acceptance of rejected students and new members.

*Norms* are shared expectations of how group members should think, feel, and behave. Norms greatly influence interpersonal relationships because they provide guidelines that help members understand what is expected of them and what they should expect from others. Productive group norms are essential to group effectiveness. Therefore, one important task of the teacher is to help the group establish, accept, and maintain productive group norms. Such norms provide a frame of reference which guides the behavior of members. The group, not the teacher, regulates behavior by exerting pressure on members to adhere to the group's norms. It is crucial that the teacher assist the group in the development of productive norms. This is a difficult task. Advocates of the group-process approach argue that productive norms can be developed — and unproductive norms changed — through the concerted, collaborative efforts of the teacher and the students using group discussion methods.

*Communication* — both verbal and nonverbal — is dialogue between group members. It involves the uniquely human capability to understand one another's ideas and feelings. Thus, communication is the vehicle through which the meaningful interaction of members takes place and through which group processes in the classroom occur. Effective communication means the receiver correctly interprets the message that the sender intends to communicate. Therefore, a twofold task of the teacher is to open the channels of communication so that all students express their thoughts and feelings freely and, frequently, to accept student thoughts and feelings. In addition, the teacher should help students develop certain communication skills — paraphrasing, perception checking, and feedback, for example (see Chapter 7, "Interpersonal Communication Skills").

*Cohesiveness* is concerned with the collective feeling that the class members have about the classroom group — the sum of the individual members' feelings about the group. Unlike the notion of attraction, cohesiveness emphasizes the individual's relation to the group as a whole instead of to individuals within the group. Schmuck and Schmuck note that groups are cohesive for a variety of reasons: (1) because the members like one another; (2) because there is high interest in a task; and (3) because the group offers prestige to its members. Thus, a classroom group is cohesive when most of its members, including the teacher, are highly attracted to the group as a whole.

Cohesiveness occurs to the extent to which individual needs are satisfied by group membership. Schmuck and Schmuck assert that cohesiveness is a result of the dynamics of interpersonal expectations, leadership style, attraction patterns, and the flow of communication. The teacher can create cohesive classroom groups by open discussions of expectations, by dispersion of leadership, by the development of several friendship clusters, and by the frequent use of two-way communication. Cohesiveness is essential to group productivity. Cohesive groups possess clearly established group norms — strong norms, not necessarily norms that are productive. Thus, the effective classroom manager is one who creates a cohesive group that possesses goal-directed norms.

To summarize the position taken by Schmuck and Schmuck, then, it can be said that they give major importance to the teacher's ability to create and manage an effectively functioning, goal-directed classroom group. The implications of their position are, as they suggest, the following:

1. The teacher should work with students to clarify the interpersonal expectations held by individuals in the group; recognize the expectations he or she holds for each individual student and for the group; modify his or her expectations on the basis of new information; foster expectations that emphasize student strengths rather than weaknesses; and make a deliberate effort to accept and support each student.

2. The teacher should exert goal-directed influences by exhibiting appropriate leadership behaviors; help students develop leadership skills; and disperse leadership by sharing leadership functions with students and by encouraging and supporting the leadership activities of students.

3. The teacher should display empathy toward students and help them develop an empathic understanding of one another; accept all students and encourage them to accept one another; provide opportunities for students to work collaboratively; and facilitate the development of student friendships and teacher–student rapport.

4. The teacher should help students resolve conflicts between institutional rules, group norms, and/or individual attitudes; use various problem-solving techniques and group discussion methods to help students develop productive, goal-directed norms; and encourage students to be responsible for their own behavior.

5. The teacher should exhibit effective communication skills and help students develop effective communication skills; foster open channels of communication which encourage students to express their ideas and feelings freely and constructively; promote student interaction, which allows students to work with and get to know one another; and provide opportunities for students to discuss openly the group's processes.

6. The teacher should foster cohesiveness by establishing and maintaining a classroom group that is characterized by: clearly understood expectations; shared, goal-directed leadership; high levels of empathy, acceptance, and friendship; and open channels of communication.

Although the views held by Johnson and Bany[20] are, in many ways, similar to those of Schmuck and Schmuck, they represent a contribution which warrants their examination here. Johnson and Bany describe two major types of classroom management activities — facilitation and maintenance. Facilitation refers to those management behaviors that improve conditions within the classroom; maintenance refers to those management behaviors that restore or maintain effective conditions. The teacher who manages the classroom effectively exhibits both facilitation and maintenance management behaviors.

Johnson and Bany have identified four kinds of facilitation behavior: (1) achieving unity and cooperation; (2) establishing standards and coordinating work procedures; (3) using problem solving to improve conditions; and (4) changing established patterns of group behavior. They have identified three kinds of maintenance behavior: (1) maintaining and restoring morale; (2) handling conflict; and (3) minimizing management problems. Although we cannot give a full description of these managerial behaviors — Johnson and Bany used over four hundred pages in doing that — a very brief explanation of each behavior is presented here.

*Achieving classroom group unity and cooperation* (cohesiveness) is a worthy and necessary goal if the teacher is to help the group to be maximally effective. Because cohesiveness is largely dependent on group members liking one another and liking the group, the task of the teacher is to make group membership attractive and satisfying. Johnson and Bany assert that cohesiveness is dependent on the amount and frequency of student interaction and communication, the kind of structure which exists within the group, and the extent to which motives and goals are shared. It follows, then, that the teacher should: encourage student interaction and communication by providing opportunities for students to work with one another and to discuss their ideas and feelings; accept and support all students while creating a structure within which each student develops a strong sense of belonging; and help students develop and recognize shared goals.

*Establishing standards and coordinating work procedures* are among the most important — and the most difficult — of the teacher's responsibilities. Standards of conduct specify appropriate behaviors in given situations; work procedures are those standards that apply to interactive instructional processes. For example, a behavioral standard might involve the behavior prescribed for students as they stand in the cafeteria line or as they pass out of the classroom during a fire drill. A work procedure might refer to the behavior expected of students when they are finished with seatwork assignments or when they wish to ask the teacher a question. Clearly, effective instruction is dependent upon the extent to which the teacher is able to establish appropriate standards and the extent to which the teacher is able to facilitate student adherence to those standards. Johnson and Bany emphasize the importance of group decision methods as a means of establishing behavioral standards and gaining adherence to those standards. Standards which are accepted by the group become group norms. In a cohesive group, there is a great deal of pressure on members to conform to those norms. Thus, the effective classroom group is one in which desirable standards and work procedures are accepted group norms.

*The use of group problem-solving discussions* to improve classroom conditions is a strategy highly recommended by advocates of the group-process approach. The problem-solving process is viewed somewhat differently by different authors but, for the most part, may be thought of as consisting of: (1) identifying the problem; (2) analyzing the problem; (3) evaluating alternative solutions; (4) selecting and implementing a solution; and (5) obtaining feedback and evaluating the solution. The basic premise underlying this strategy is that students, given the opportunity, skills, and guidance necessary, can and will make good, responsible decisions regarding their classroom behavior. This premise suggests that the teacher should provide students with the opportunity to engage in group problem-solving discussions; should foster the development of student problem-solving skills; and should guide students in the problem-solving process.

*Changing established patterns of group behavior* involves the use of planned-change techniques similar to those of group problem solving. However, the difference is that the purpose of the problem-solving process is to find a solution to a problem, while the purpose of the planned-change process is to gain acceptance of an already determined solution. Thus, the planned-change process is one of improving conditions by substituting appropriate goals for inappropriate goals. The notion is that group goals exert a strong influence upon the behavior of group members, and when group goals are in conflict with those of instruction, students behave inappropriately. Therefore, it is necessary for the teacher to help the group replace inappropriate goals and behaviors with more appropriate ones, goals that satisfy group needs and that are consistent with those of the school.

Johnson and Bany argue that group planning is the best process to use for changing inappropriate goals and behaviors to more appropriate ones. Their viewpoint is based on the assumption that such changes are much more likely to be accomplished and accepted if members of the group have participated in the decision to change. This suggests that the role of the teacher is to help students understand the goal to be achieved; to involve students in discussions that result in an examination of various plans for achieving the goals, selecting a plan, and identifying tasks that need to be performed; to implement the plan and perform the necessary tasks; and to assess the plan's effectiveness. During the planned-change process, the teacher encourages group acceptance of externally established goals. Students are engaged in decisions regarding the strategies to be used in achieving those goals.

Simply put, then, the facilitation management behaviors of the teacher consist of: (1) encouraging the development of group cohesiveness; (2) promoting the acceptance of productive standards of conduct; (3) facilitating the resolution of problems through the use of group problem-solving processes; and (4) fostering appropriate group goals, norms, and behaviors. The intent of these facilitative management behaviors is the improvement of those classroom conditions which promote effective instruction. Maintenance management behaviors are intended to restore and maintain those classroom conditions. Descriptions of the three types identified by Johnson and Bany follow.

The ability to *maintain and restore morale* is important because the level of classroom group morale greatly influences group productivity. A group with high morale is far more likely to be productive than a group with low morale. Facilitation behaviors build morale. However, the effective teacher recognizes that many factors can cause morale to fluctuate. Thus, the teacher should understand the factors that influence morale and exhibit those behaviors that preserve high morale. Johnson and Bany note that morale is affected by the level of cohesiveness, the amount of interaction and communication, the extent to which members have shared goals, the extent to which the group's goal-directed efforts are hindered, and environmental conditions that cause anxiety and stress or otherwise affect the group adversely.

Thus, the task of the teacher may be viewed as twofold: (1) The teacher should act to rebuild morale; this includes fostering cohesiveness, encouraging increased interaction and communication, and promoting shared goals. (2) The teacher should act to reduce anxiety and relieve stress; this includes fostering cooperation rather than competition, exhibiting shared leadership, eliminating extremely frustrating and threatening situations, neutralizing disruptive influences, and clarifying stress situations through discussion. Crucial to the teacher's effectiveness is the extent to which the teacher is accepted and trusted by the students. The teacher cannot hope to be successful in restoring morale if students perceive him or her as part of the problem or if his or her behavior creates new problems. The use of punishment is an all too common example of the latter.

Handling conflict in the classroom group is among the most difficult tasks a teacher faces. Hostile, aggressive student behaviors are emotion laden, disruptive, and irritating, especially when directed toward the teacher. But conflict and hostility must be viewed as a normal result of the interactive processes that occur in the classroom. It is not realistic to expect otherwise. Indeed, in the initial phases of a group's development, it is not unusual and can be constructive.

There are many causes of conflict. Primary among them is frustration. When the group is hindered or blocked in achieving its goal, the result is frustration. Feelings of frustration manifest themselves as hostility and aggression — or as withdrawal and apathy. The effective teacher should be able to recognize and deal with such problems quickly.

Johnson and Bany suggest a process for resolving a conflict: (1) set guidelines for discussion; (2) clarify what happened; (3) explore differences in points of view; (4) identify the cause or causes of the conflict; (5) develop agreements regarding the cause or causes of the conflict and regarding resolution of the conflict; (6) specify a plan of action; and (7) make a positive appraisal of group efforts. To prevent conflict, the teacher is encouraged to reduce frustrations as much as possible by making it possible for the group to set and reach reasonable goals.

If they are to minimize problems, teachers must understand their classroom group and must be able to anticipate the influence various environmental factors will have on that group. In minimizing management problems, the effective teacher utilizes two major strategies: (1) to use facilitation and maintenance behaviors to establish and maintain an effectively functioning, goal-directed classroom group; and (2) to diagnose and analyze the health of the classroom group continuously and to act on the basis of that diagnosis. For example, symptoms of disunity call for teacher behaviors intended to promote group cohesiveness. Symptoms of inappropriate norms call for teacher behaviors intended to change those norms to more appropriate ones. In addition, certain types of problems — the new student and the substitute teacher for example — can and should be anticipated. The teacher should help the class prepare for such possibilities.

Effective classroom management, according to Johnson and Bany, involves the ability of the teacher to establish the conditions that enable the classroom group to be productive — and the ability to maintain those conditions. The latter involves the ability to maintain a high level of morale, to resolve conflict, and to minimize management problems. Implicit is the need to build good communication, to establish positive interpersonal relationships, and to satisfy both individual and group needs. The overriding emphasis is on the ability of the teacher to use group methods of management, for these behaviors determine the effectiveness of the group and the success of instruction.

So far in this section we have presented two somewhat different viewpoints regarding the group-process approach to classroom management — the views of Schmuck and Schmuck and the ideas of Johnson and Bany. A brief examination of several additional ideas from the research of Kounin[21] and the work of Glasser[22] completes the viewpoints presented in this section.

As noted in Learning Activity 5.5, Kounin has conducted extensive research on the management dimension of teaching. Earlier, several concepts coming from his research were described as instructional managerial strategies. Here, three additional strategies — strategies relevant to the group-process approach — are described:

1. *Withitness behaviors* are those behaviors by which the teacher communicates to students that he or she knows what is going on, that he or she is very much aware of what students are doing — or not doing. Kounin concluded that withitness is significantly related to managerial success. That is, teachers who demonstrated withitness are more likely to have fewer and less serious student misbehaviors.

2. *Overlapping behaviors* are those behaviors by which the teacher indicates that he or she is attending to more than one issue when there is more than one issue to deal with at a particular time. Kounin suggests that overlapping — when combined with withitness — is related to managerial success. The teacher who is able to pay attention to more than one issue at a time is more likely to be effective than the teacher who is unable to do so.

3. *Group-focus behaviors* are those behaviors teachers use to maintain a focus on the group — rather than on an individual student — during individual recitations. Kounin identified two aspects of group-focus behaviors: *group alerting*, which refers to the extent to which the teacher involves nonreciting students (maintains their attention and "keeps them on their toes"); and *accountability*, which refers to the extent to which the teacher holds students accountable and responsible for their task performances during recitations. Kounin found that group alerting and accountability are related to student behavior. He suggests that teachers who maintain a group focus are more successful in promoting student goal-directed behavior and in preventing student misbehavior than are teachers who do not.

In summarizing his studies, Kounin asserts that his findings suggest there are certain teaching behaviors — withitness, overlapping, and group-focus behaviors — that are related to managerial success. He also notes that these techniques of classroom management apply to the classroom group and not merely to individual students. Thus, Kounin may be described as a staunch advocate of group management — a most interesting dimension of the group-process approach to classroom management.

Many behavior problems are best addressed through the use of the class as a problem-solving group under the guidance of the teacher. If each student can be helped to realize that he or she is a member of a working, problem-solving group and that he or she has both individual and group responsibilities, it is likely that discussions of group problems will lead to the resolution of those problems. Without such help students tend to evade problems, depend on others to solve their problems, or withdraw. The social–problem-solving *classroom meeting* is intended to provide the assistance students need in this regard. It is a viewpoint shared by most advocates of the group-process approach and best described by Glasser. He suggests three guidelines to enhance the potential effectiveness of social–problem-solving classroom meetings:

1. Any group problem may be discussed; a problem may be introduced by a student or the teacher.
2. The discussion should be directed toward solving the problem; the atmosphere should be nonjudgmental and nonpunitive; the solution should not include punishment or fault finding.
3. The meeting should be conducted with the teacher and students seated in a tight circle; meetings should be held often; meetings should not exceed 30 to 45 minutes, depending upon the age of the students.

The reader who wishes to be more fully informed about these views should refer to Glasser's book, *Schools Without Failure.*

In summary, it appears that the teacher who wishes to develop a behavioral repertoire that draws on the group-process approach would consider the advantages of the following strategies: fostering reasonable, clearly understood expectations; sharing leadership; fostering open communication; establishing and maintaining group morale and attraction; fostering group unity, cooperation, and cohesiveness; promoting productive group standards and norms; resolving conflicts through discussion; exhibiting withitness, overlapping, and group-focus behaviors; and employing problem-solving classroom meetings.

This section provides an overview of the group-process approach. Space limitations preclude a more detailed treatment of the subject. It is recommended that the reader who wishes to explore this topic in more detail refer to the work of Schmuck and Schmuck, Johnson and Bany, Kounin, and Glasser. An excellent source of practical suggestions related to classroom group development is a book by Stanford.[23]

# Your Turn

## IDENTIFYING STATEMENTS REPRESENTING THE GROUP-PROCESS APPROACH

The exercise below is intended to provide you with an opportunity to assess your understanding of the information presented in this section. Place a check mark in front of each statement that is representative of the group-process approach to classroom management. Check your responses in the Answer Key that follows.

_____ 1. The teacher should demonstrate the ability to attend to more than one issue at a time.

_____ 2. The teacher should help students establish productive norms.

_____ 3. The teacher should reward the student whose accomplishments are of an exceptional nature.

_____ 4. The teacher should use group problem-solving discussions to solve management problems.

_____ 5. The teacher should create open channels of communication in which students are able to express their ideas and feelings freely.

_____ 6. The teacher should recognize that social–problem-solving classroom meetings are most effective when relatively brief and frequent.

_____ 7. The teacher should foster group cohesiveness by helping students perceive membership as attractive and satisfying.

_____ 8. The teacher should encourage competition that enables all students to compete on a fair basis.

_____ 9. The teacher should help students develop communication, leadership, and group problem-solving skills.

_____ 10. The teacher should make it clear that conflict is unproductive and, therefore, cannot be tolerated.

_____ 11. The teacher should recognize that change is more readily accepted if individuals participate in the decision to change.

_____ 12. The teacher should encourage student interaction and communication.

_____ 13. The teacher should force withdrawn students to participate in group activities.

_____ 14. The teacher should behave in ways that let students know the teacher knows what is going on.

_____ 15. The teacher should recognize that the ability to deal with individual student misbehavior is more important than the ability to deal with group problems.

_____ 16. The teacher should help students clarify their interpersonal expectations.

_____ 17. The teacher should share leadership with students.

_____ 18. The teacher should understand that effective management begins with his or her ability to control each individual within the group.

_____ 19. The teacher should recognize that hostility and conflict are among the normal and natural consequences of human interaction.

_____ 20. The teacher should recognize that the social–problem-solving classroom meeting is a powerful tool for dealing with group problems.

_____ 21. The teacher should help students display empathy and acceptance for one another.

_____ 22. The teacher should focus on the group through group alerting and accountability during recitations.

_____ 23. The teacher should recognize that peer group norms are powerful determinants of member behavior.

_____ 24. The teacher should understand that even in a highly cohesive group, morale fluctuates, requires constant monitoring, and needs restoration from time to time.

_____ 25. The teacher should avoid activities that give students an opportunity to voice opposition to school policies and classroom regulations.

_____ 26. The teacher should understand that the behavior of each individual is greatly influenced by the nature of the classroom group and its properties.

_____ 27. The teacher should recognize that the effective management of problem behavior is based on fully understanding individual behavior and its causes.

_____ 28. The teacher should help students establish behavioral standards that are productive.

_____ 29. The teacher should recognize that group management procedures are not compatible with the individualization of instruction.

_____ 30. The teacher should help students identify management problems without assigning blame.

_____ 31. The teacher should encourage teacher–student interaction and discourage student–student interaction.

_____ 32. The teacher should promote a nonjudgmental, nonevaluative climate when guiding a social–problem-solving classroom meeting.

_____ 33. The teacher should be able to cope with more than one event simultaneously.

_____ 34. The teacher should recognize that the ability to handle individual student problems precludes the need to be concerned about group management techniques.

_____ 35. The teacher should understand that preventing classroom management problems is at least as important as solving problems.

## ANSWER KEY

### Your Turn: Identifying Statements Representing the Group-Process Approach

The following is a listing of those statements that reflect the group-process point of view accurately. You should feel comfortable with your level of understanding if at least 30 of your responses agree with those suggested here. If you disagree on more than five statements, reread the materials in this learning activity and/or study the applicable resources listed for objective 5 in the Additional Readings. The statements that represent the group-process view are: 1, 2, 4, 5, 6, 7, 9, 11, 12, 14, 16, 17, 19, 20, 21, 22, 23, 24, 26, 28, 30, 32, 33, and 35.

# Mastery Test

## OBJECTIVE 5

To describe the nature and dynamics of the authoritarian, intimidation, permissive, cookbook, instructional, behavior-modification, socioemotional-climate, and group-process approaches to classroom management.

Learning Activities 5.1 through 5.8 presented brief descriptions of eight different approaches to classroom management. The following exercise provides you with an opportunity to assess your understanding of the basic principles of each of those approaches. Each of the following fifty statements takes a particular position with regard to the teacher and effective classroom management. Your task is to identify correctly the approach each statement represents. In the space provided in front of each statement, please place the code letters of that approach you feel the statement represents. Please use the following code:

AU — authoritarian approach
BM — behavior-modification approach
CB — cookbook approach
GP — group-process approach

IN — instructional approach
IT — intimidation approach
PM — permissive approach
SE — socioemotional-climate approach

When you have responded to all fifty statements, compare your responses to those presented in the Answer Key that follows.

_____ 1. The teacher should recognize that a central role of the teacher is to maintain order and discipline in the classroom by controlling student behavior.

_____ 2. The teacher should recognize that classroom climate greatly influences learning and that the teacher greatly influences the nature of that climate.

_____ 3. The teacher should reward acceptable student behavior and avoid rewarding unacceptable student behavior.

_____ 4. The teacher should recognize that an individualized curriculum can eliminate most classroom management problems.

_____ 5. The teacher should address the student's situation, not the student's character or personality, when dealing with a problem.

_____ 6. The teacher should not impose limits on students, as this will keep them from reaching their full potential.

_____ 7. The teacher should understand that the use of logical consequences minimizes the potential for the negative side effects that can accompany other forms of punishment.

_____ 8. The teacher should understand that effective management begins with his or her ability to control each student through the use of force as necessary.

_____ 9. The teacher should always be fair and firm in dealing with students, as consistency is very important.

_____ 10. The teacher should help students understand, accept, and follow established rules and regulations.

_____ 11. The teacher should view a well-managed token system as an effective means of promoting appropriate student behavior.

_____ 12. The teacher should be tolerant of all forms of student behavior.

_____ 13. The teacher should allow students to suffer the natural and logical consequences of their behavior unless those consequences involve physical danger.

_____ 14. The teacher should behave in ways that let the students know that the teacher is aware of what is going on.

_____ 15. The teacher should recognize that a central role of the teacher is the establishment and maintenance of positive teacher–student relationships.

_____ 16. The teacher should understand that the use of punishment and the threat of punishment can be very effective management tools when used appropriately.

_____ 17. The teacher should recognize that rewards are unique to the individual student.

_____ 18. The teacher should understand that appropriate classroom activities usually ensure appropriate student behavior, as they decrease the potential for frustration and boredom.

_____ 19. The teacher should recognize that the appropriate use of mild desist behaviors can be both effective and efficient in controlling student behavior.

_____ 20. The teacher should treat students with respect and be committed to helping them develop self-responsibility and feelings of self-worth.

_____ 21. The teacher should never punish a student unless there is adequate evidence to establish guilt beyond a reasonable doubt.

_____ 22. The teacher should help students develop a high level of cohesiveness and productive norms.

_____ 23. The teacher should operate on the assumption that both appropriate and inappropriate student behaviors are learned.

_____ 24. The teacher should understand that disruptive students often misbehave because they have been given inappropriate learning tasks.

_____ 25. The teacher should recognize that the manner in which the teacher communicates with students is decisively important.

_____ 26. The teacher should use sarcasm very carefully and only after good interpersonal relationships have been established.

_____ 27. The teacher should always conduct himself or herself in a businesslike and dignified manner when interacting with students.

_____ 28. The teacher should observe and/or question students to obtain clues concerning potential rewards.

_____ 29. The teacher should understand that the use of classroom meetings and group problem-solving sessions can be a very effective means for solving certain managerial problems.

_____ 30. The teacher should "separate the sin from the sinner" when dealing with a student who has behaved inappropriately.

_____ 31. The teacher should recognize that most classroom management problems can be avoided or solved by good instructional practices.

_____ 32. The teacher should understand that it is important to help students develop communication, leadership, and group problem-solving skills.

_____ 33. The teacher should understand that effective classroom management is nothing more than the application of common sense.

_____ 34. The teacher should recognize that the proper use of sarcasm and ridicule can be effective in controlling student behavior.

_____ 35. The teacher should recognize that a central role of the teacher is to use a variety of instructional strategies to prevent and to solve discipline problems.

_____ 36. The teacher should understand that it is important to establish and to enforce reasonable expectations and rules.

_____ 37. The teacher should be fair but firm from the beginning because it is easier to relax control than it is to impose it once it has been lost.

_____ 38. The teacher should foster group cohesiveness by helping students perceive membership as attractive and satisfying.

_____ 39. The teacher should create good discipline with lessons the children will find interesting and motivating.

_____ 40. The teacher should view teacher realness, acceptance, and empathy as keys to effective classroom management.

_____ 41. The teacher should understand that it is important to establish a physical and psychological environment in which the student is completely free to say and do anything he or she wants to.

_____ 42. The teacher should understand that well-planned lessons are an effective means of achieving order in the classroom.

_____ 43. The teacher should reinforce appropriate student behaviors in ways that recognize that rewards are unique to the individual student.

_____ 44. The teacher should understand that effective management is largely a function of his or her ability to punish student misconduct when it occurs.

_____ 45. The teacher should recognize that the teacher must often assume responsibility for controlling the behavior of the student.

_____ 46. The teacher should recognize that a central role of the teacher is to use tried-and-true techniques to prevent and solve discipline problems.

_____ 47. The teacher should recognize that rewarded behavior is likely to be continued and that unrewarded behavior is likely to be discontinued.

_____ 48. The teacher should plan and use appropriate instructional activities to ensure appropriate student behavior.

_____ 49. The teacher should understand that effective classroom management is the result of the teacher's establishing and maintaining control.

_____ 50. The teacher should understand that effective classroom management is intended to help the classroom group become responsible for solving many of its own problems.

## ANSWER KEY

### Mastery Test, Objective 5

The following answers might have been given for the items above. Some of your responses might not agree with those here. Where there is such disagreement, you may want to analyze your position. As you do so, you should recognize that some managerial strategies may be representative of more than one approach, depending on your interpretation and preference. Thus, it is altogether possible for you to give a "correct" response that disagrees with the "key." What is most important here is that you feel comfortable with your responses even if you happen to disagree with the key. You should feel that you are familiar with the information presented in this section of the chapter.

If you correctly identified at least forty-five of the statements, you can be fairly confident that you understand the basic principles of the eight managerial approaches described in this learning activity. If you did not do as well as you would have liked, you may wish to review the information presented in Learning Activities 5.1 through 5.8 and/or study any of the resources listed under Objective 5 in the Additional Readings section of this chapter. When you are confident that you are familiar with each of the eight approaches, you are ready to move on to the next learning activity.

1. AU  2. SE  3. BM  4. IN  5. SE  6. PM  7. SE  8. IT  9. CB  10. AU  11. BM  12. PM  13. SE  14. GP  15. SE  16. IT  17. BM  18. IN  19. AU  20. SE  21. CB  22. GP  23. BM  24. IN  25. SE  26. IT  27. CB  28. BM  29. GP  30. SE  31. IN  32. GP  33. CB  34. IT  35. IN  36. AU  37. CB  38. GP  39. IN  40. SE  41. PM  42. IN  43. BM  44. IT  45. AU  46. CB  47. BM  48. IN  49. AU  50. GP

# Objective 6

To identify managerial strategies believed to be effective.

## LEARNING ACTIVITY 6

Having completed Learning Activities 5.1 through 5.8 and the Mastery Test for Objective 5, you should be reasonably well informed regarding a wide range of managerial strategies, and you should now be prepared to "load your computer." That is, you should have developed some opinions as to the managerial strategies you would feel comfortable in using and which might have the potential to be effective in your classroom with your students. The purpose of this section is to give you an opportunity to identify those managerial strategies you believe would be particularly effective in establishing and maintaining those "ideal" conditions you specified in Learning Activity 3. This intent is based on the assumption that it will be useful for you to take this opportunity to crystallize your thinking about those managerial strategies you perceive to be especially useful. Because you will be identifying managerial strategies you believe to be effective in helping you achieve your managerial objectives, this test has no right or wrong answers. The best answers represent viewpoints you can justify to your own satisfaction.

# Mastery Test

## OBJECTIVE 6    To identify managerial strategies believed to be effective.

This Mastery Test contains a listing of many of the managerial strategies discussed in the previous section of this chapter. Place a check mark in front of each managerial strategy you believe would be potentially useful in your efforts to manage the classroom effectively. In addition, space has been provided for you to list several additional managerial strategies you believe to be effective. It is the hope here that your responses will represent informed opinion.

_____   1. Establishing and enforcing rules

_____   2. Using mild desists and soft reprimands

_____   3. Issuing commands and directives

_____   4. Using harsh forms of punishment

_____   5. Maximizing student freedom

_____   6. Following "tried-and-true" prescriptions

_____   7. Planning and implementing interesting and appropriate lessons

_____   8. Facilitating smoothness and momentum

_____   9. Giving clear, explicit directions

_____ 10. Using positive reinforcement

_____ 11. Using time out and extinction

_____ 12. Using token economies

_____ 13. Using behavior contracting

_____ 14. Building positive teacher–student interpersonal relationships

_____ 15. Displaying realness, acceptance, and empathic understanding

_____ 16. Exhibiting unconditional positive regard

_____ 17. Using reality therapy

_____ 18. Employing democratic classroom procedures

_____ 19. Applying logical consequences

_____ 20. Fostering reasonable, clearly understood expectations

_____ 21. Developing open channels of communication

_____ 22. Fostering a high level of group cohesiveness

_____ 23. Promoting productive group norms

_____ 24. Resolving conflict and restoring group morale and unity

_____ 25. Employing problem-solving classroom meetings

_____ 26. Exhibiting withitness, overlapping, and group focus

_____ 27. Strategy:

_____ 28. Strategy:

_____ 29. Strategy:

_____ 30. Strategy:

# Objective 7

To analyze a given classroom situation and to describe and justify the managerial strategy or strategies most likely to be effective in facilitating and maintaining those classroom conditions deemed desirable.

## LEARNING ACTIVITY 7.1

The previous learning activities emphasized that the nature of the problem and its context should dictate the strategy that a teacher uses in attempting to solve the problem. In addition, a strong case has been made for the viewpoint that the teacher might appropriately employ any one of a number of strategies in attempting to solve a particular classroom management problem. Indeed, the effective teacher is one who is able to recognize several equally viable alternatives when confronted with the need to employ a managerial strategy. The following exercise is designed to give you an opportunity to practice that skill. As you work through the exercise, keep in mind that your goal is always to establish and maintain those classroom conditions you identified as desirable in Learning Activity 3.

# Your Turn

## RECOGNIZING ALTERNATIVE STRATEGIES

For each case study, please: (1) describe the type of problem, (2) describe two different strategies a teacher might use in solving the problem, and (3) briefly explain and defend the choices you have made.

Because of the wide range of possible responses, this learning activity does not have an answer key. However, after responding to all six case studies, you should analyze your answers. You might consider the extent to which your responses to a particular problem: (1) are really different approaches to the problem; (2) follow logically from the type of problem indicated; (3) deal with the problem's cause and not just the symptoms; (4) would influence a majority of the class in a positive and productive way; (5) would have long-range benefit; and (6) most important, would promote those classroom conditions you deem desirable. If you are pleased with the results of your analysis, you can feel reasonably comfortable with your ability to consider alternative solutions to classroom management problems. If you are not pleased with your responses and feel that additional effort is required, you may find it helpful to review certain of the information contained in Learning Activities 5.1 through 5.8.

1. Although you have no direct evidence that supports the assertion, Eddie has a reputation as a bully. He is rather large for his age and towers over most of his sixth grade classmates. Having attended to a chore that required you to leave your room for a few minutes, you return to find Eddie holding Harry, a much smaller boy, by the shirt. Eddie's clenched right hand is cocked as if he is about to deliver a sharp blow.

Problem _____

_____

_____

_____

Solution 1

*Description* _____

_____

_____

_____

_____

*Justification* _____

_____

_____

_____

_____

Solution 2

*Description* _____

_____

_____

_____

_____

*Justification* _____

_____

_____

_____

_____

2. Having finished lunch, you hurry to the gym to set up the equipment necessary for your one o'clock physical education class. As you enter the gym you find Phil and Allan, both seniors, smoking. Although school regulations forbid smoking and call for an automatic three-day suspension, some of your colleagues fail to enforce the regulation because they feel the punishment is too severe.

Problem _____

_____

_____

_____

Solution 1

*Description* _____

_____

_____

_____

_____

*Justification* _____

_____

_____

_____

_____

Solution 2

*Description* _____

_____

_____

_____

_____

*Justification* _____

_____

_____

_____

3. While your third grade class is working quietly at their seats, Cindy approaches your desk and in a near whisper says: "During recess someone took the pen I got for Christmas out of my desk. I think Ray took it because he's now using one just like it. I don't think he had it before. If I don't get it back, my mom is going to be awful mad."

Problem _____

_____

_____

_____

Solution 1

   *Description* _____

   _____

   _____

   _____

   _____

   *Justification* _____

   _____

   _____

   _____

   _____

Solution 2

   *Description* _____

   _____

   _____

   _____

   _____

   *Justification* _____

   _____

   _____

   _____

   _____

4. Your eighth grade American history class is a delight to teach. They are bright and motivated. Although you have taught them for only three months, they have become your "all-time favorites." As you introduce the day's lesson, you notice immediately that they are angry and sullen. Recognizing that this is such unusual behavior for this group and that it is likely to inhibit your effectiveness that day, you decide to find out the reason for their feelings. Brenda, one of the class leaders, speaks out: "It's that Mr. Underhill. He gave us an exam that was totally unfair. It covered two chapters he hadn't even assigned and now he says he did. None of us did well on the exam; a 62 was the highest score. And he won't let us take a make-up. That's not fair." The rest of the class nods in agreement.

   Problem _____

   _____

_____

_____

Solution 1

*Description* _____

_____

_____

_____

*Justification* _____

_____

_____

_____

Solution 2

*Description* _____

_____

_____

_____

_____

*Justification* _____

_____

_____

_____

5. At recess, you accompany your fifth grade class to the playground. You are watching a group of students skipping rope when you are attracted by noise coming from a group of boys in a cluster. As you approach them, you find eight or ten boys in a tight circle around another boy, Leslie McClendon. The boys in the circle are chanting," "Leslie is a girl's name. Leslie is a girl's name."

Problem _____

_____

_____

_____

Solution 1

*Description* _____

_____

_____

_____

_____

*Justification* _____

_____

_____

_____

_____

Solution 2

*Description* _____

_____

_____

_____

_____

*Justification* _____

_____

_____

_____

_____

6. A month into the school year, you assign small group projects to your tenth grade biology students. You allow students to form their own groups of four or five. Although the class of thirty-four students consists of eighteen boys and sixteen girls and contains twenty white students and fourteen black students, you are surprised and disappointed to see that the groups the students form are composed of white boys, black boys, white girls, or black girls only. Not one of the eight groups is either sexually or racially integrated.

Problem _____

_____

_____

Solution 1

*Description* _____

_____

_____

_____

*Justification* _____

_____

_____

_____

Solution 2

*Description* _____

_____

_____

_____

*Justification* _____

_____

_____

## LEARNING ACTIVITY 7.2

Thus far in this chapter, emphasis has been given to the notion that the effective classroom manager is one who makes good decisions — one who accurately identifies the nature of the problem and who selects the managerial strategy that has the greatest potential for solving the problem. Accurate identification of the problem and selection of an appropriate strategy are crucial factors. Of equal importance is the matter of *timing*. That is, *when* the teacher acts is often as important as *what* the teacher does. Even if the teacher decides not to act, that decision must be made quickly.

In the most simple of terms, there are four such periods with regard to the timing of an intervention. The teacher must: (1) anticipate certain types of problems and act to prevent them from happening; (2) react immediately in instances requiring immediate action; (3) solve problems that do not require immediate action but that must be dealt with promptly; and (4) monitor the effectiveness of attempts to solve identified problems. The following exercise gives you an opportunity to practice the ability to react under the pressure of time —the ability to make good decisions quickly.

## Your Turn

## MAKING QUICK DECISIONS

Eight problems are briefly described on the pages that follow. Your task is to describe what you would do in each case and to justify the course of action you select. However, in this exercise your response should also be timed — so that you experience the pressure of having to make a decision within a limited amount of time. For each case, you will have two minutes within which to describe what you would do if faced with the problem described. The following procedures are recommended for this exercise.

Do *not* read the case studies yourself; have a partner read them to you instead. (You can do the same thing for him or her when you finish the exercise.) It will be most effective to become aware of the problems for the first time when — and only when — you are ready to do this exercise.

Have a partner select six to ten of the problems he or she feels are most relevant to your particular situation. Let him or her begin by reading the first problem and then pausing for exactly two minutes. At the end of that two-minute interval, he or she will read the second problem and make another two-minute pause. Then he or she will read the third problem and so on until all the problems have been read. You should write your solution — and only the solution, *not* the justification — to the first problem during the time in which the problem was read and during the two-minute interval that follows. At the end of the first pause, you should move on to the second problem and so on until you have responded to all of the problems. Then go back and write justifications for each of the problems.

Your justifications ought to describe the reasoning behind your decisions. Additionally, you may find it helpful to describe the assumptions you made about the nature of the problem, and other alternatives you considered, and the condition you would be attempting to establish or reestablish. Having finished writing a justification for each response, carefully and thoroughly examine your responses and your justifications with a peer or group of peers. Or, put your answers aside for a day or two. Then you might review your responses to determine how good you still feel about your answers. Obviously, this exercise has no right or wrong answers. For this reason, none are provided. The best answers are clearly those which make good sense to you as you subject them to an objective analysis that recognizes the assumptions you have made about the problem and the managerial outcomes you would hope to achieve.

1. Jim is one of the brighter students in your third grade class, but he constantly misbehaves. He does nothing really serious, just a continuous series of minor incidents — talking out, laughing loudly, slamming his desk top, throwing wads of paper, and teasing fellow classmates, for example. Although these are not major misbehaviors, they are annoying and disruptive. In addition, the other students think these things are funny. They laugh and treat Jim's behavior as a joke. What do you do?

2. You are not sure of the problem, but the symptoms are obvious. Your seventh period algebra class is not working well. Assignments are generally late. The students are constantly complaining about your assignments, the fairness of tests, and everything in general. During class discussions, no one participates. No one volunteers to answer questions you believe many can answer. Little accidents such as pencils breaking, books falling on the floor, and an overturned waste basket seem frequent. What do you do?

3. Tom has been a member of your Spanish II class for nearly three weeks now, having transferred to Wilson High School after the Christmas break. Although he seems to be a nice young man, it is obvious that he has not been accepted by his classmates. Small group projects designed to involve Tom have not helped. Tom remains outside an otherwise cohesive group. The other students seem to ignore him, and he seems to ignore them. However, you have not seen any signs of hostility on anyone's part. What do you do?

4. Your fourth period social studies class has always been a bit more of a problem than your other tenth grade students. However, after six months, they now work quite well with one bothersome exception. Despite your telling them on numerous occasions that they are to wait until you dismiss them when the bell rings for them to go to fifth period lunch, they invariably get out of their seats and rush to the door, pushing and shoving into the hallway. As luck would have it, today Mr. Blake, the principal, was almost run over by your stampeding students. What do you do?

5. Your eighth grade history students are working quietly in groups of three or four. As you move around the room checking on the progress the groups are making on their projects, you hear constrained giggling from a far corner of the room. You look up in time to see Bill holding a penknife in his hand. Catching sight of you, Bill slips the knife into his desk. As you near Bill's desk, you notice that an obscene word has been carved in large letters on Bill's desk top. The carving is fresh; indeed, there are still wood chips on the desk. What do you do?

6. The flu has kept you out of school for several days. Handling students after they have had a few days with a substitute teacher is generally something of a problem, and you do not really expect the first day back to go too smoothly. That expectation is reinforced by a note left for you by the substitute teacher. It reads: "I had nothing but trouble with all of your classes, but the first period business math is perhaps the worst group I've ever met. There isn't a polite person in that entire class. I don't know how you stand it. They gave me nothing but trouble. They are the most discourteous group I've ever met." The first period bell rings, and members of the business math class take their seats. What do you do?

7. When Linda's mother brought Linda to your kindergarten class on the first day of school, she warned you that Linda was "a very sensitive child." After only two weeks of school you have some idea of the reason she felt the need to warn you. Linda displays a rare gift for temper tantrums. If she can't be first in line — temper tantrum. If she is not allowed to do what she wants to do — temper tantrum. And Linda's temper tantrums are complete with kicking, crying, screaming, and rolling on the floor. You have tried to ignore her outbursts, but now you find that the other children are making fun of Linda. Typical comments include: "There she goes again!" "What a baby she is!" "Grow up, crybaby!" What do you do?

8. Your ninth grade social studies class is the best you have ever had. They are both bright and well behaved. Class discussions are a delight; test scores are always good. On numerous occasions you have praised the class for their accomplishments. However, the recent assignment of Barbara to the class has created a problem. Barbara has had a miserable home life. She is the illegitimate daughter of a woman with a bad reputation in the community. Barbara herself has been in trouble with the law. Indeed, she has just been released from a school for delinquent girls, having "served" six months for shoplifting — a third such conviction. The principal has assigned her to your class because she is bright and because he feels that she will be better behaved with "good students." Barbara has been in your class for only a few days when you begin to receive complaints that "things are missing." Pencils, pens, compacts, combs, lipsticks, and other things have begun to disappear. What do you do?

# Objective 8

To design a data-gathering instrument and a set of data-collection procedures that might be used to evaluate managerial effectiveness.

## LEARNING ACTIVITY 8

In Learning Activity 2, the managerial process was described as a four-stage process in which the teacher: (1) specifies desirable classroom conditions; (2) analyzes existing classroom conditions; (3) selects and utilizes managerial strategies; and (4) assesses managerial effectiveness. The purpose of this learning activity is to provide you with additional information concerning the fourth stage of the managerial process — the evaluation of managerial effectiveness — and to give you an opportunity to practice several skills related to the evaluation of managerial effectiveness.

Earlier the fourth stage of the managerial process was described as one in which the teacher assesses his or her managerial effectiveness. The point was made that from time to time the teacher should evaluate the extent to which his or her efforts are establishing and maintaining those conditions the teacher views as desirable. It was also noted that this evaluation process focuses on two sets of behavioral indicators (teacher behaviors and student behaviors) and three data sources (the teacher, the student, and an independent observer) as shown in the model below.

## BEHAVIORAL INDICATORS

| Data Source | Teacher Behavior | Student Behavior |
|---|---|---|
| Teacher | Question asked of the teacher:<br><br>Are you doing those things likely to be managerially effective — likely to establish and maintain those conditions you deem desirable? | Question asked of the teacher:<br><br>Are your students behaving in ways that suggest that you are managerially effective — to what extent are they exhibiting those student behaviors you deem desirable? |
| Student | Question asked of the student:<br><br>Is your teacher doing those things likely to be managerially effective — likely to establish and maintain those conditions he or she deems desirable? | Question asked of the student:<br><br>Are you behaving in ways that suggest that your teacher is managerially effective — to what extent are you and your fellow students exhibiting those behaviors your teacher deems desirable? |
| Observer | Question asked of the observer:<br><br>Is this teacher doing those things likely to be managerially effective — likely to establish and maintain those conditions he or she deems desirable? | Question asked of the observer:<br><br>Are these students behaving in ways that suggest that their teacher is managerially effective — to what extent are they exhibiting those behaviors this teacher deems desirable? |

As shown in the model, two sets of behaviors serve as indicators of managerial effectiveness: teacher behaviors and student behaviors. In the first case, the teacher evaluates the extent to which he or she is using those managerial behaviors and strategies he or she should be using and intends to use. That is, the teacher assesses whether the managerial strategies he or she is using are most likely to bring about desirable classroom conditions. In the second case, the teacher evaluates the extent to which his or her students are behaving in desirable ways. Here the major emphasis is on the extent to which students are doing what the teacher would like them to be doing given those conditions he or she deems desirable. In short, in assessing managerial effectiveness, the teacher evaluates what he or she is doing and what his or her students are doing in light of his or her managerial objectives.

The model also indicates that there are three sources from which the teacher can collect data regarding teacher and student behaviors: the teacher, the student, and an independent observer. This suggests that there are six "behavior indicator–data source" categories one might use in assessing managerial effectiveness. The purpose here is not to provide a lengthy discussion of the various types of data-collection instrumentation and procedures one might use with regard to each of these categories. However, a description of each of the six categories is presented with brief mention of several procedures which might be used; additionally, you would no doubt find the Additional Readings listed for Objective 8 and Chapter 9 to be helpful in this regard.

### Teacher Behavior as Perceived by the Teacher

One means by which a teacher can assess his or her managerial effectiveness is to analyze and evaluate his or her managerial behaviors. The teacher simply examines the extent to which he or she is behaving in ways he or she feels are likely to be managerially effective. During such an examination, the teacher considers the questions: Am I doing the things I intend to be doing — and should be doing — given what I hope to accomplish managerially with my students? Are my managerial behaviors likely to contribute to the development and maintenance of those conditions I believe facilitate the instructional process? Am I correctly analyzing the situation and using those managerial strategies having the greatest potential to be effective given my managerial objectives?

Clearly, this form of assessment is one of self-analysis. It is a process intended to allow the teacher to gain greater insight into the management of the classroom so that he or she can make such adjustments as seem reasonable. For example, a teacher who is working to foster more positive teacher–student interpersonal relationships by displaying realness, acceptance, and empathy might elect to examine the extent to which he or she is doing so. The teacher might analyze videotape and audiotape recordings of his or her classroom behavior in an attempt to determine whether he or she displayed those behaviors in a satisfactory manner. That is, the teacher — using his or her own criteria — would judge the extent to which he or she was being successful in displaying realness, acceptance, and empathy. It is the *teacher* who decides whether he or she is doing what he or she wants to be doing — and who decides whether he or she needs to behave differently. Thus, one means by which the teacher can assess his or her managerial effectiveness is to analyze his or her own behavior, determine its appropriateness, and make such adjustments as are appropriate.

## Student Behavior as Perceived by the Teacher

A second method by which the teacher can assess his or her managerial effectiveness is to examine the extent to which students are behaving in desirable ways. The central questions here include: Are my students behaving in ways that indicate that I am being managerially effective? Are they doing the kinds of things I would like them to be doing? Does their behavior suggest that I am making satisfactory progress toward the accomplishment of my managerial objectives?

This form of assessment calls for the teacher to look at the behavior of his or her students — to determine the extent to which they are behaving as the teacher would have them behave. For example, a teacher who feels that it is important for students to work cooperatively — that they serve as resources to one another and interact productively and with a minimum of conflict — might focus on the extent to which students are displaying those sorts of behaviors. The teacher might utilize rather complicated processes or very simple processes. He or she might systematically analyze videotape recordings or might simply lean back and reflect on the happenings of the school day. In any event, the intent of the teacher would be to analyze how well his or her students were working together, inasmuch as the teacher saw this as an important indicator of his or her managerial effectiveness. The teacher who felt that his or her students were working cooperatively would act to support such behavior; one who felt that his or her students were not working cooperatively would move to foster such behavior. By examining student behavior, the teacher makes judgments about his or her effectiveness and acts accordingly.

## Teacher Behavior as Perceived by the Student

A third strategy the teacher might use to assess his or her managerial effectiveness involves the utilization of student perceptual data. Using any of a variety of techniques, the teacher collects information about how his or her students view the managerial behaviors of the teacher. The major sorts of questions asked of the students are: Is your teacher doing those things likely to be managerially effective? Is your teacher behaving in ways likely to establish and to maintain those classroom conditions your teacher thinks facilitate instruction? Is your teacher exhibiting those managerial behaviors he or she wants to be exhibiting?

This type of evaluation requires that the teacher collect and analyze student perceptions regarding the teacher's managerial behaviors. Rating scales and questionnaires are two of the many strategies the teacher might employ for these purposes. For example, "report cards on the teacher" are an interesting and popular type of rating scale. A teacher who wished to know how students perceived his or her attempts to exhibit unconditional positive regard — his or her efforts to accept the students as persons of worth while not approving of their misbehavior — might use a report card format to tap student perceptions. The student would be asked to "fill out a report card on the teacher." The report card would contain a series of statements reflecting various managerial strategies the teacher saw as indicators of managerial effectiveness. The student would "grade" the teacher on each of these statements. In the case of unconditional positive regard, the item might read: "My teacher likes me even when I misbehave." The student would give the teacher a grade, using the grading system used on the students' report cards. The teacher receiving an "A" from his or her students on the unconditional positive regard item could be resonably confident of his or her effectiveness in that regard. The teacher receiving a failing grade from his or her students should consider what he or she might do to improve his or her "grades" on the next report card — and increase his or her managerial effectiveness. Clearly, student perceptual data can be useful in helping the teacher to better understand the impact of his or her behavior and to make necessary adjustments. The use of student perceptions regarding the teacher's managerial behaviors is a very powerful means by which to improve that teacher's managerial effectiveness.

## Student Behavior as Perceived by the Student

Student perceptions of the teacher's managerial behaviors are a valuable source of useful information. So too are student perceptions concerning student behaviors. The fourth form of assessment is one in which the teacher collects and analyzes student perceptual data regarding behaviors of the student and his or her classmates. The primary questions addressed include: Am I and my fellow students behaving in ways my teacher deems appropriate? Is my behavior and that of my classmates evidence that my teacher is managerially effective? Am I and the other students in this class doing those things my teacher would like us to be doing?

This kind of assessment involves the collection and analysis of student perceptions regarding the behavior of the student and of the classroom group. A number of strategies are appropriate for this purpose. Questionnaires and rating scales are among the most popular.

For example, a teacher who is concerned about the extent to which his or her classroom group is cohesive and who wishes to gather information regarding the students' perceptions about the group's cohesiveness might develop a rating scale to measure student perceptions. Among the items on the scale would be items intended to measure the students' perceptions of the group's cohesiveness. The student might be asked to respond to an item such as: I like being a member of this class. The student would respond by checking that point on a scale, which might range from "strongly agree" to "strongly disagree." If a large number of students indicated that they liked being members of the class, the teacher could infer a fairly high level of cohesiveness. If a large number of students indicated that they very much disliked being members of the class, the teacher could infer that the group was not very cohesive. In the latter instance, the teacher would take actions intended to build cohesiveness; in the former instance, he or she would attempt to support the existing condition. Student perceptions regarding their classroom behavior can provide very useful information to the teacher who seeks to improve his or her managerial effectiveness.

## Teacher Behavior as Described by an Independent Observer

A fifth means by which a teacher can assess his or her managerial effectiveness is through the analysis of teacher behavior data collected by an independent observer. An observer — usually using an observational schedule or checklist prepared by the teacher — observes the teacher and collects data concerning the teacher's managerial behaviors. These data are used to respond to several central questions: What managerial behaviors and strategies does the teacher utilize? Is this teacher doing those things he or she has indicated he or she intends to be doing given what it is that he or she hopes to accomplish managerially? Are the managerial behaviors being exhibited by the teacher likely to facilitate the establishment and maintenance of those classroom conditions the teacher believes to be necessary for instructional effectiveness?

This sort of evaluation involves the use of teacher behavior data collected by an observer — a fellow teacher, a supervisor, a principal, or a parent, for example. The observer utilizes an observational schedule or an observational checklist designed by the teacher to yield descriptive information concerning the managerial behaviors and strategies exhibited by the teacher during the period observed. For example, a teacher who opted to use this method of evaluation and who was particularly concerned about the extent to which he or she was rewarding appropriate student behavior might design a checklist including an item stating: "Rewards appropriate student behavior." The teacher might ask a fellow teacher to visit his or her classroom on several different occasions and to use the checklist to note, among other things, the frequency with which he or she rewarded appropriate student behavior. The observer would, in effect, count each instance in which the teacher rewarded appropriate student behavior. After the observations had been completed, the teacher would examine the data and determine whether he or she was satisfied with the frequency with which he or she rewarded student behavior. If the teacher were satisfied, he or she would attempt to continue that pattern of behavior he or she had exhibited during the observation. If the teacher were not satisfied, he or she would attempt to increase or decrease his or her use of this strategy. Clearly, an observer can provide descriptive data which the teacher can find useful in making decisions that might improve his or her managerial effectiveness.

### Student Behavior as Described by an Independent Observer

The sixth and last method a teacher might use to evaluate his or her managerial effectiveness also utilizes descriptive data provided by an observer using an observation schedule or checklist. However, in this case, the focus of the observation is student behavior, not teacher behavior. The observer collects data that describe the behaviors exhibited by the teacher's students. These data are analyzed in an effort to respond to questions such as: What sorts of behaviors do these students exhibit in this classroom with this teacher? Are these students behaving in ways this teacher believes to be appropriate? Does the individual and collective behavior of these students indicate that this teacher is managerially effective?

Responses to these sorts of questions require data concerning student behavior. In this case, the data which have been collected by an observer. Typically, the observer uses an observation schedule or checklist designed to yield descriptive information concerning both student behavior and teacher behavior. A teacher who was particularly concerned about the on-task behavior of his or her students might design an observational schedule that would allow an observer to note the percentage of time during the period observed that each student was "on-task" and "off-task," respectively. For example, the observer might "scan the room" at five-minute intervals to determine whether each student was exhibiting on-task and off-task behaviors; this would allow the teacher to make judgments about his or her ability to promote students' on-task behavior. It would also allow the teacher to make informed decisions regarding future attempts to promote student on-task behavior. Additionally, if teacher managerial behavior data have been collected along with student behavior data, the teacher is in a good position to examine the possible relationships between his or her behavior and that of his or her students. It is argued here that observational data — teacher behavior data and student behavior data — are useful indicators of managerial effectiveness and are useful to the teacher who seeks to improve his or her managerial effectiveness.

### Summary

This section has provided a brief examination of the fourth stage of the analytic-pluralistic managerial process. That stage is one in which the teacher evaluates his or her managerial effectiveness. You have been presented with six different methods a teacher might use to assess his or her managerial effectiveness. These methods yield data regarding two sets of behavioral indicators (teacher behaviors and student behaviors) from three data sources (the teacher, the student, and an independent observer). Teacher behavior data provide information that allows the teacher to determine whether he or she is exhibiting those managerial behaviors he or she wants to be exhibiting. Student data provide evidence that allows the teacher to determine whether he or she is making satisfactory progress toward achieving his or her managerial objectives — the establishment and maintenance of conditions facilitating effective and efficient instruction. Thus, it is clear that student behaviors are more valid indicators of managerial effectiveness. However, the teacher behavior data are useful in this regard. It is argued here that the teacher who periodically evaluates his or her managerial effectiveness is far more likely to be effective than the teacher who does not.

The exercise that follows gives you an opportunity to identify some teacher behaviors and student behaviors you might examine in evaluating your managerial effectiveness. As you consider the teacher behaviors listed, you will want to keep two things in mind: (1) the managerial strategies you identified as effective in Learning Activity 6; and (2) the student behaviors you identified as desirable conditions in Learning Activity 3. These should guide your selections.

# Your Turn

## IDENTIFYING TEACHER AND STUDENT BEHAVIORAL INDICATORS

This exercise presents two lists; one contains a listing of teacher behaviors and the other contains a listing of student behaviors. Your task is to identify from each list at least ten behaviors you regard as important indicators of managerial effectiveness. Place a check mark in front of those behaviors you believe to be important. Space has been provided for any others you might like to add.

### Teacher Behaviors

_____ 1. The teacher encourages students to communicate openly.

_____ 2. The teacher talks to the situation rather than to the character or personality of the student when handling a problem.

_____ 3. The teacher expresses his or her true feelings and attitudes to students.

_____ 4. The teacher makes his or her expectations clear and explicit to students.

_____ 5. The teacher reinforces appropriate student behaviors.

_____ 6. The teacher trains students to perform leadership functions and shares leadership with them.

_____ 7. The teacher listens attentively to students.

_____ 8. The teacher accepts students as persons of worth.

_____ 9. The teacher does not behave in a punitive or threatening manner.

_____ 10. The teacher displays an awareness of what is going on in the classroom.

_____ 11. The teacher praises the accomplishments of the group.

_____ 12. The teacher uses expressions indicating that the students constitute a group of which he or she is a member.

_____ 13. The teacher elicits and accepts student expressions of feelings.

_____ 14. The teacher clearly communicates appropriate standards for student behavior.

_____ 15. The teacher clarifies the norms of the group.

_____ 16. The teacher provides students with an opportunity to work cooperatively.

_____ 17. The teacher ignores inappropriate student behavior to the extent possible.

_____ 18. The teacher encourages the establishment of productive group norms.

_____ 19. The teacher does not ridicule or belittle students.

_____ 20. The teacher does not encourage student competition.

_____ 21. The teacher communicates an awareness of how students feel.

_____ 22. The teacher respects the rights of students.

_____ 23. The teacher accepts all student contributions.

_____ 24. The teacher guides students in practicing productive group norms.

_____ 25. The teacher encourages and supports individual and group problem solving.

_____ 26. The teacher provides students with opportunities to succeed.

_____ 27. The teacher removes students from rewarding situations or removes rewards from students in the event of misbehavior under certain circumstances.

_____ 28. The teacher initiates, sustains, and terminates classroom activities with smoothness.

_____ 29. The teacher directs attention toward the group rather than toward the individual during general classroom activities.

_____ 30. The teacher allows students to experience the logical consequences of their behavior when physically safe to do so.

_____ 31. The teacher praises the accomplishment of the student rather than the student himself or herself.

_____ 32. The teacher accepts students and encourages them to be accepting of one another.

_____ 33. The teacher promotes group morale by helping students engage in total-class activities.

_____ 34. The teacher makes use of "time out" to extinguish inappropriate student behavior.

_____ 35. The teacher uses nonverbal communication that supports and is congruent with his or her verbal communication.

_____ 36. The teacher promotes group unity.

_____ 37. The teacher encourages students to use time wisely.

_____ 38. The teacher trains students to behave appropriately in the teacher's absence.

_____ 39. The teacher displays the ability to attend to more than one issue at a time.

_____ 40. The teacher discusses issues with students rather than arguing with them.

_____ 41. The teacher accepts a productive level of noise in the classroom.

_____ 42. The teacher is nonjudgmental in discussing problem situations.

_____ 43. The teacher anticipates certain types of problems and works to prevent them.

_____ 44. The teacher respects student privacy.

_____ 45. The teacher treats students as persons who are capable of dealing with their own problems.

_____ 46. _____

_____

_____

_____ 47. _____

_____

_____ 48. _____

_____ 49. _____

_____ 50. _____

*Student Behaviors*

_____ 1. Students are learning subject matter.

_____ 2. Students are able to settle disagreements by using the democratic process.

_____ 3. Students are receptive to new ideas and changes in routine.

_____ 4. Students work together well in groups.

_____ 5. Students do not feel that the teacher is going to ridicule them.

_____ 6. Students feel free to communicate their ideas and feelings.

_____ 7. Students feel good about themselves both individually and collectively.

_____ 8. Students do not view the teacher as being punitive or threatening.

_____ 9. Students view the teacher as being objective.

_____ 10. Students feel very good about being part of the class.

_____ 11. Students are willing to chance opinion and comments without fear.

_____ 12. Students speak of themselves as group members.

_____ 13. Students feel that the teacher understands their feelings.

_____ 14. Students work on-task.

_____ 15. Students feel as though they know the "real" teacher.

_____ 16. Students perform leadership functions.

_____ 17. Students do not feel guilty about their mistakes.

_____ 18. Students feel rewarded when they behave appropriately.

_____ 19. Students are aware of the standards for appropriate behavior.

_____ 20. Students perceive the teacher as accepting.

_____ 21. Students explore new situations.

_____ 22. Students adhere to established norms.

_____ 23. Students do not form small cliques and subgroups.

_____ 24. Students accept responsibility for their behavior.

_____ 25. Students behave in an increasingly more appropriate manner.

_____ 26. Students are attentive to the teacher, one another, and the task.

_____ 27. Students organize themselves and settle into work procedures easily.

_____ 28. Students feel that the teacher cares about their feelings.

_____ 29. Students do not ridicule one another.

_____ 30. Students share materials unselfishly.

_____ 31. Students use problem-solving techniques to solve problems.

_____ 32. Students perceive the teacher as fair.

_____ 33. Students feel that the teacher has time after class hours to help them with their problems.

_____ 34. Students move smoothly from one activity to another.

_____ 35. Students evaluate their class meetings and give the teacher feedback.

_____ 36. Students display a positive group identity.

_____ 37. Students use time productively.

_____ 38. Students behave appropriately in the teacher's absence.

_____ 39. Students begin, continue, and end work smoothly.

_____ 40. Students resolve their differences without hostility.

_____ 41. Students work at a productive noise level in the classroom.

_____ 42. Students respect the rights of one another and the teacher.

_____ 43. Students feel that they have contributed to their own learning.

_____ 44. Students readily accept new class members.

_____ 45. Students are optimistic about their ability to arrive at successful solutions to problems.

_____ 46. _____

_____

_____ 47. _____

_____

_____ 48. _____

_____

_____ 49. _____

_____

_____ 50. _____

_____

NOTES

1. Rudolf Dreikurs and Pearl Cassel, *Discipline Without Tears* (New York: Hawthorn Books, 1972), pp. 31–41.

2. Lois V. Johnson and Mary A. Bany, *Classroom Management: Theory and Skill Training* (New York: Macmillan Co., 1970), pp. 45–59.

3. Lee Canter and Marlene Canter, *Assertive Discipline* (Los Angeles: Canter and Associates, 1979).

4. Carl J. Wallen and LaDonna L. Wallen. *Effective Classroom Management* (Boston: Allyn and Bacon, 1978), p. 214.

5. Johnson and Bany, *op. cit.*

6. Jean E. Davis, *Coping with Disruptive Behavior* (Washington, D.C.: National Education Association, 1974), p. 21.

7. Jacob S. Kounin, *Discipline and Group Management in Classrooms* (New York: Holt, Rinehart & Winston, 1970).

8. James D. Long and Virginia H. Frye, *Making It Till Friday: A Guide to Successful Classroom Management* (Princeton, New Jersey: Princeton Book Company, 1977), pp. 35–36.

9. Terrence Piper, *Classroom Management and Behavioral Objectives: Applications of Behavioral Modification* (Belmont, California: Lear Siegler/Fearon Publishers, 1974), pp. 10–18.

10. Nancy K. Buckley and Hill M. Walker, *Modifying Classroom Behavior: A Manual of Procedures for Classroom Teachers* (Champaign, Illinois: Research Press Company, 1970), p. 30.

11. Abraham Givener and Paul S. Graubard, *A Handbook of Behavior Modification for the Classroom* (New York: Holt, Rinehart & Winston, 1974), p. 8.

12. Beth Sulzer and G. Roy Mayer, *Behavior Modification Procedures for School Personnel* (Hinsdale, Illinois: Dryden Press, 1972), pp. 174–184.

13. Saul Axelrod, *Behavior Modification for the Classroom Teacher* (New York: McGraw-Hill, 1983).

14. Harvey F. Clarizio, *Toward Positive Classroom Discipline* (New York: John Wiley and Son, 1980).

15. Carl R. Rogers, *Freedom to Learn* (Columbus, Ohio: Charles E. Merrill, 1969).

16. Haim G. Ginott, *Between Parent and Child* (New York: Macmillan Co., 1965); *Between Parent and Teenager* (New York: Macmillan Co., 1969); and *Teacher and Child* (New York: Macmillan Co., 1972).

17. William Glasser, *Schools Without Failure* (New York: Harper and Row, 1969).

18. Rudolf Dreikurs and Loren Grey, *A New Approach to Discipline: Logical Consequences* (New York: Hawthorn Books, 1968); Rudolf Dreikurs and Pearl Cassel, *Discipline Without Tears* (New York: Hawthorn Books, 1972); and Rudolph Dreikurs, Bernice Bronia Grunwald, and Floyd C. Pepper, *Maintaining Sanity in the Classroom: Classroom Management Techniques* (New York: Harper and Row, 1982).

19. Richard A. Schmuck and Patricia A. Schmuck, *Group Processes in the Classroom* (Dubuque, Iowa: William C. Brown, 1979).

20. Johnson and Bany, *op. cit.*

21. Kounin, *op. cit.*

22. Glasser, *op. cit.*

23. Gene Stanford, *Developing Effective Classroom Groups* (New York: A & W Visual Library, 1980).

ADDITIONAL READINGS *Objectives 1, 2, 3, and 4*

Dreikurs, Rudolf, and Pearl Cassel. *Discipline Without Tears*. New York: Hawthorn Books, 1972.

Duke, Daniel L., ed. *Classroom Management. The Seventy-Eighth Yearbook of the National Society for the Study of Education*. Chicago: National Society for the Study of Education, 1979.

Dunkin, Michael J., and Bruce J. Biddle. *The Study of Teaching*. New York: Holt, Rinehart & Winston, 1974.

Johnson, Lois V., and Mary A. Bany. *Classroom Management: Theory and Skill Training*. New York: Macmillan Co., 1970.

*Objectives 5, 6, and 7*

Axelrod, Saul. *Behavior Modification for the Classroom Teacher*. New York: McGraw-Hill, 1983.

Buckley, Nancy K., and Hill M. Walker. *Modifying Classroom Behavior: A Manual of Procedures for Classroom Teachers*. Champaign, Illinois: Research Press Company, 1978.

Canter, Lee, and Marlene Canter. *Assertive Discipline*. Los Angeles: Canter and Associates, 1976.

Charles, C. M. *Building Classroom Discipline*. New York: Longman, 1981.

Clarizio, Harvey F. *Toward Positive Classroom Discipline*. New York: John Wiley and Sons, 1980.

Doyle, Walter. *Classroom Management*. West Lafayette, Indiana: Kappa Delta Pi, 1980.

Dreikurs, Rudolf. *Psychology in the Classroom*. New York: Harper and Row, 1968.

Dreikurs, Rudolf, and Pearl Cassel. *Discipline Without Tears*. New York: Hawthorn Books, 1972.

Dreikurs, Rudolf, and Loren Grey. *A New Approach to Discipline: Logical Consequences*. New York: Hawthorn Books, 1968.

Dreikurs, Rudolf, Bernice Bronia Grunwald, and Floyd C. Pepper. *Maintaining Sanity in the Classroom: Classroom Management Techniques*. New York: Harper & Row, Publishers, 1982.

Duke, Daniel L., ed. *Helping Teachers Manage Classrooms*. Alexandria, Virginia: Association for Supervision and Curriculum Development, 1982.

Duke, Daniel L. *Managing Student Behavior Problems*. New York: Teachers College, Columbia University, 1981.

Duke, Daniel L., and Adrienne M. Meckel. *Teacher's Guide to Classroom Management*. New York: Random House, 1984.

Emmer, Edmund T.; Carolyn M. Evertson; Julie P. Sanford; Barbara S. Clements; and Murray E. Worsham. *Classroom Management for Secondary Teachers*. Englewood Cliffs, New Jersey: Prentice-Hall, 1984.

Evertson, Carolyn M.; Edmund T. Emmer; Barbara S. Clements; Julie P. Sanford; and Murray E. Worsham. *Classroom Management for Elementary Teachers*. Englewood Cliffs, New Jersey: Prentice-Hall, 1984.

Ginott, Haim G. *Teacher and Child: A Book for Parents and Teachers*. New York: Macmillan Company, 1972.

Glasser, William. *Schools Without Failure*. New York: Harper and Row, 1969.

Grey, Loren. *Discipline Without Fear*. New York: Hawthorn Books, 1974.

Howell, Robert G., and Patricia L. Howell. *Discipline in the Classroom: Solving the Teaching Puzzle*. Reston, Virginia: Reston Publishing Company, 1979.

Lehman, Jerry D. *Three Approaches to Classroom Management: Views from a Psychological Perspective*. Washington, D.C.: University Press of America, 1982.

Long, James D., and Virginia H. Frye. *Making It Till Friday: A Guide to Successful Classroom Management.* Princeton, New Jersey: Princeton Book Company, 1977.

Medland, Michael M., and Michael M. Vitale. *Management of Classrooms.* Holt, Rinehart and Winston, 1984.

Rinne, Carl H. *Attention: The Fundamentals of Classroom Control.* Columbus, Ohio: Charles E. Merrill Publishing Company, 1984.

Schmuck, Richard, and Patricia A. Schmuck. *Group Processes in the Classroom.* Dubuque, Iowa: William C. Brown Company, 1979.

Stanford, Gene. *Developing Effective Classroom Groups.* New York: A & W Visual Library, 1980.

Sulzer, Beth, and G. Roy Mayer. *Behavior Modification Procedures for School Personnel.* Hinsdale, Illinois: Dryden Press, 1972.

Tanner, Laurel N. *Classroom Discipline for Effective Teaching and Learning.* New York: Holt, Rinehart & Winston, 1978.

Wallen, Carl J., and LaDonna L. Wallen. *Effective Classroom Management.* Boston: Allyn and Bacon, 1978.

Walker, James E., and Thomas M. Shea, *Behavior Modification: A Practical Approach for Educators.* St. Louis: C.V. Mosby Company, 1984.

Weber, Wilford A., and Linda A. Roff. "A Review of the Teacher Education Literature on Classroom Management," *Classroom Management: Reviews of the Teacher Education and Research Literature.* Princeton, New Jersey: Educational Testing Service, 1983. Pages 7–42.

*Objective 8*

Fox, Robert; Margaret Luszki, and Richard Schmuck. *Diagnosing Classroom Learning Environments.* Chicago: Science Research Associates, 1966.

TenBrink, Terry D. *Evaluation: A Practical Guide for Teachers.* New York: McGraw-Hill Book Company, 1974.

Terry D. TenBrink

# 9. Evaluation

# Objectives

**1** To define evaluation and to describe each of the four stages in the evaluation process.

**2** To select appropriate information-gathering instruments when seeking to make classroom evaluations.

**3** To write good test items for evaluating achievement.

**4** To develop checklists and rating scales for evaluating student products and performances.

**5** To describe how to use information to evaluate—that is, to grade, to judge student progress, to judge changes in student attitudes, and to judge the effectiveness of your own instruction.

Educational evaluation is useful only to the extent that it helps the educator (administrator, teacher, student) make sound educational judgments and decisions. In this chapter you will learn about some of the basic principles of evaluation as applied to classroom problems. This chapter can be very helpful when you are faced with the task of evaluating your students. However, I would encourage you to go beyond this introductory level of understanding. Purchase a good basic text on classroom evaluation techniques. Practice your test-writing skills whenever possible. Learn from your mistakes as you begin to evaluate your own students, and learn to use evaluation as a necessary and important teacher tool. Use evaluation to help you teach better and to help your students learn better.

# Objective 1

To define evaluation and to describe each of the four stages in the evaluation process.

## LEARNING ACTIVITY 1.1

Stated most simply, to evaluate is to place a value upon — to judge. However, forming a judgment is not an independent action. In order to judge, one must have information. The act of judging depends upon this prerequisite act of obtaining information. Furthermore, the act of forming a judgment is itself prerequisite to an action one step further: decision making. So, evaluation, the process of forming judgments, depends upon information gathering and leads to decision making. Picture it this way:

Or, this way:

> Evaluation is the process of obtaining information and using it to form judgments which, in turn, are used in decision making.

The above definition clearly specifies the interrelatedness among the various stages in the evaluation process; and yet, it also clearly indicates the centrality of forming judgments. If you have not formed a judgment, you have not evaluated. This chapter, therefore, will deal primarily with the procedures for forming judgments.

However, it is important for you to understand the *total* evaluation process. So, let's expand this definition some. So far it is obvious that evaluation involves at least three stages: obtaining information, forming judgments, and using those judgments in decision making. By adding a preparation stage and enlarging a bit on the last stage, we come up with the following four stages:

---

*The evaluation process*
*Stage 1:* Preparing for evaluation.
*Stage 2:* Obtaining needed information.
*Stage 3:* Forming judgments.
*Stage 4:* Using judgments in making decisions and preparing evaluation reports.

---

Let's look at a rather typical teaching–learning situation. Notice how this teacher goes through these four stages as she attempts to make her instruction more effective.

*Stage 1.* Preparing for evaluation.

Bonnie, a third grade teacher, has become concerned about Billy. He seems to be having trouble keeping up in reading. Bonnie wonders how long he will be able to function within the reading group he is in. She wonders whether or not she should move him to a slower group. Perhaps there is something she can do to help — some extra work, for example, or some extra attention. She decides she needs more information before she can accurately judge Billy's level of achievement in reading. After determining the kind of information she needs (e.g., information about the kind of errors made when reading orally, information concerning Billy's use of various word attack skills, information about Billy's interests), Bonnie determines when and how to obtain that information.

*Stage 2.* Obtaining needed information.

Over a period of several days Bonnie obtains a great deal of information about Billy. She gives him a standardized reading test, listens to him read orally, carefully records the kind of errors he makes, and observes him throughout the day watching for patterns of behavior that might indicate particular attitudes toward various subject matters.

*Stage 3.* Forming judgments.

After analyzing all the information she has obtained, Bonnie comes to the following conclusions:

1. Billy is not capable of reading material written at a third grade level.
2. Billy reads comfortably only that material written on a second grade level or lower.
3. Billy's primary weakness lies in the area of word attack skills.
4. Billy does not have a comprehension problem. He understands what is read to him.
5. Billy likes the children in his reading group.
6. Billy enjoys the stories in the third grade reader.

*Stage 4.* Using judgments to make decisions and evaluation reports.

On the basis of the above judgments Bonnie decides that she should keep Billy in his present reading group. She further decides to take the following action:

1. Prepare a check list of word attack skills.
2. Systematically teach Billy those skills on a one-to-one basis.
3. Continue to have the stories read to Billy so that he will not fall behind on his comprehension skills.
4. Have Billy check off each word attack skill as he demonstrates competence in using it.

Having made these decisions, Bonnie writes a brief summary of her judgments, noting the actions she anticipates making. She files this in her own files for future reference. She also calls in Billy's parents and shares her findings with them, asking them to cooperate and to give Billy lots of encouragement and praise, supporting him as he struggles to make up the deficiencies she has discovered.

Note the key features of each of the stages illustrated above:

1. *Stage 1. Preparation:* Determine the kind of information needed and decide how and when to obtain it.
2. *Stage 2. Information Gathering:* Obtain a variety of information as accurately as possible.
3. *Stage 3. Forming Judgments:* Judgments are made by comparing the information to selected criteria.
4. *Stage 4. Decision Making and Reporting:* Record significant findings and determine appropriate courses of action.

## LEARNING ACTIVITY 1.2

Talk to a teacher about how he or she decides what to teach, when to teach, and how to teach. Probe for specific answers. Try to identify the various stages in the evaluation process as that teacher explains his or her decision making to you. Could you use the terminology of this chapter to explain what the teacher has done?

# Mastery Test

**OBJECTIVE 1**   To define evaluation and to describe each of the four stages in the evaluation process.

1. Give a brief definition of evaluation.

_____

_____

2. List the four stages in the evaluation process. Describe briefly what goes on in each stage. Use examples from the classroom to clarify your descriptions.

   (a) *Stage 1.* _____

   _____

   _____

   _____

   _____

   _____

   _____

   _____

   (b) *Stage 2.* _____

   _____

   _____

   (c) *Stage 3.* _____

   _____

   _____

   (d) *Stage 4.* _____

   _____

   _____

## ANSWER KEY

### Mastery Test, Objective 1

1. Evaluation is the process of obtaining information and forming judgments to be used in decision making.

2. (a) *Preparing for evaluation.* In this stage you need to determine the judgments and decisions you anticipate making (e.g., when to begin Unit 2, what assignments to give, where to place Johnny). Next you must decide what information you will need in order to make those judgments and decisions (e.g., how quickly the students are moving through Unit 1, what the students' interests are, how well Johnny reads). Finally, you will decide when and how to obtain the information needed (e.g., weekly, through quizzes; first week of class, using an interest inventory; second week of class, using a standardized test of reading and observing students during oral reading).

(b) *Obtaining needed information.* Involves asking students (inquiry), observing students (watching students setting up an experiment), or testing students (giving a multiple-choice test of history facts).

(c) *Forming judgments.* In this stage you compare the information with some referent and make a value judgment. Grades reflecting achievement and predictions about how well a student might be expected to do are both common examples of classroom judgments.

(d) *Using judgments in decisions and preparing evaluation reports.* Deciding what action to take (e.g., move Johnny to a slower reading group) and reporting the evaluation results that led to that decision comprise the major tasks of the final stage of evaluation. Note that the emphasis is on the *use* of judgments.

# Objective 2

To select appropriate information-gathering instruments when seeking to make classroom evaluations.

## LEARNING ACTIVITY 2.1

The first step in preparing to evaluate is determining what you will be evaluating and what kind of information you will need in order to make that evaluation.[1] Once that has been determined, you are ready to choose a tool for obtaining that information. There are basically two steps involved: (1) determine the information-gathering technique you want to use; and (2) select the type of instrument that should be used.

STEP 1

### Choose an Appropriate Technique

There are basically four different techniques classroom teachers use to obtain information about themselves and their students: inquiry, observation, analysis, and testing.

To inquire is to ask. Whenever you wish to know someone's opinions, feelings, interests, likes and dislikes, etc., ask that person. Good teachers are always asking their students how they feel about what is going on. They know the value of information gained through inquiry.

Observations are made by teachers whenever they look, listen, feel, or use any other senses to find out what is going on in the classroom. Observations of student performances, habit patterns, and interpersonal interactions all provide the teacher with helpful information.

Analysis is the process of breaking something down into its component parts. For example, a teacher might analyze a math assignment to discover the kinds of errors students are making. Or, a vocational education teacher might analyze a coffee table made by a woodworking student, evaluating the project according to the design, overall construction, and finish of the table.

Testing is being used whenever there is a common situation to which all students respond (e.g., a test question), a common set of instructions governing the students' responses, a set of rules for scoring the responses, and a description (usually numerical) of each student's performance—a score.

The chart below compares these four techniques. Study the chart and then try to do the exercise that follows.

### A SUMMARY OF THE MAJOR CHARACTERISTICS OF THE FOUR INFORMATION-GATHERING TECHNIQUES*

| | Inquiry | Observation | Analysis | Testing |
|---|---|---|---|---|
| Kind of information obtainable | Opinions<br>Self-perceptions<br>Subjective judgments<br>Affective (especially attitudes)<br>Social perceptions | Performance or the end products of some performance<br>Affective (especially emotional reactions)<br>Social interaction psychomotor skills<br>Typical behavior | Learning outcomes during the learning process (intermediate goals)<br>Cognitive and psychomotor skills<br>Some affective outcomes | Attitude and achievement<br>Terminal goals<br>Cognitive outcomes<br>Maximum performance |
| Objectivity | Least objective<br>Highly subject to bias and error | Subjective but can be objective if care is taken in the construction and use of the instruments | Objective but not stable over time | Most objective and reliable |
| Cost | Inexpensive but can be time-consuming | Inexpensive but very time-consuming | Fairly inexpensive<br>Preparation time is somewhat lengthy but crucial | Most expensive but most information gained per unit of time |

* Terry D. TenBrink, *Evaluation: A Practical Guide for Teachers* (New York: McGraw-Hill, 1974), p. 140. ©1974 by McGraw-Hill Book Co. Used with the permission of the McGraw-Hill Book Company.

# Your Turn

## CHOOSING AN EVALUATION TECHNIQUE

For each of the following questions, decide on the evaluation technique that would probably be most helpful. Use the following key: A, inquiry; B, observation; C, analysis; D, testing.

1. What kind of errors does Sally make when reading aloud?
2. How well can Sammy read?
3. What is George's attitude toward math?
4. Why isn't Ernest completing his workbook during spelling?
5. What is the average reading level of this class?
6. Who does Johnny have as friends?
7. What mistakes are most common in long division problems?
8. How well did the students learn the concepts in Chapter 7?
9. How well does Mary interact with her classmates during recess?
10. What are Kevin's primary handwriting errors?

## ANSWER KEY

Your Turn: Choosing an Evaluation Technique

1. B   2. D or B   3. A   4. B or A   5. D   6. A or B   7. C   8. D   9. B   10. C or A

STEP 2

**Select the Best Instrument to Obtain the Kind of Information You Need**

Once you have selected an appropriate information-gathering technique, you should choose the type of information-gathering instrument to be used. An information-gathering technique is a *procedure* for obtaining information. An information-gathering instrument is a *tool* we use to help us gather information. We will briefly examine four basic types of instruments: tests, checklists, rating scales, and questionnaires.

A test is an instrument that presents a common situation to which all students respond, a common set of instructions, and a common set of rules for scanning the students' responses. Tests are used primarily for determining aptitude and achievement. When we want to know how much a student knows or how well he or she can perform certain skills, a test is an appropriate instrument to use.

Most classroom tests are constructed by the teacher and are referred to as "teacher-made tests" or "classroom tests" to distinguish them from standardized tests. The instructions on standardized tests have been carefully standardized so that everyone taking the test does so under similar conditions. Most standardized tests are developed and sold by test publishers and have been carefully developed, tried out, revised, standardized, and evaluated for reliability and validity.

A checklist is basically a list of criteria (or "things to look for") for evaluating some performance or end product. One uses a checklist by simply checking off those criteria that are met. For example, one could use a checklist to be certain that a student goes through all the routines in an exercise program. Or, a list of criteria for a good speech could be checked as an indication of what a speech student did correctly when making a speech to inform. Whenever it is helpful to know whether an important characteristic is present in a performance (or is found in some end product), a checklist would be an appropriate instrument to use.

If we wish to rate the quality of a performance or end product, a rating scale would be the instrument to use. We might judge a speech, for example, by whether or not gestures were used. But if we want to determine the quality of those gestures (whether they were good, fair, poor, etc.), a rating scale should be used. A rating scale provides a scale of values that describe someone or something being evaluated.

The advantages and disadvantages of each type of instrument are highlighted for you in the following table. Again, study the table carefully and then take "your turn" at trying to select an appropriate instrument.

## ADVANTAGES AND DISADVANTAGES OF EACH
## TYPE OF INFORMATION-GATHERING INSTRUMENT

| Type of Instrument | Advantage | Disadvantage |
|---|---|---|
| *Standardized tests:* used when very accurate information is needed | Usually well developed and reliable. Include norms for comparing the performance of a class or an individual. | Often not measuring exactly what had been taught. Expensive. Limited in what is measured. |
| *Teacher-made tests:* used routinely as a way to obtain achievement information | Usually measure exactly what has been taught. Inexpensive. Can be constructed as need arises. | No norms beyond the class are available. Often unreliable. Require quite a bit of time to construct. |
| *Checklists:* used to focus observations | Helpful in keeping observations focused on key points or critical behaviors. | Measure only presence or absence of a trait or behavior. |
| *Rating scales:* used to judge quality of performance | Allow observational data to be used in making quality judgments as well as quantitative judgments. | Take time and effort to construct. Can be clumsy to use if too complex. |
| *Questionnaires:* used to inquire about feelings, opinions, and interests. | Keep inquiry focused and helps teacher to obtain the same information from each student. | Take time and effort to construct. Difficult to score — no right answers and therefore hard to summarize the data. |

# Your Turn

# SELECTING AN INFORMATION-GATHERING INSTRUMENT

Read each of the following classroom situations. First decide what technique is being used (inquiry, observation, analysis, testing), and then write down which instrument you would use and why. Compare your answers with those of your peers and those found in the answer key.

1. A second grade teacher wants to find out if her pupils now understand how to form the vowels in cursive writing.
2. A high school social studies teacher wants to know how his students feel about the outcome of the latest elections.
3. A fourth grade teacher wants to know how well his class compares to other fourth grade classes in their achievement of the basics: reading, writing, arithmetic.
4. An eighth grade teacher just finished teaching her students to compute the volume of a cube and wants to know how well her students learned this skill.
5. A music teacher wants to rank-order her clarinet players so that she can assign them chairs in the band.
6. A shop teacher wants to make sure that his students all follow the safety precautions when operating a radial arm saw.

## ANSWER KEY

### Your Turn: Selecting an Information-Gathering Instrument

1. Observation is the best choice because in order to find out *how* the pupils form their letters, you must watch them forming them.
2. Feelings are best discovered by inquiry. This teacher should ask his students how they feel.
3. Achievement is best measured through testing.
4. Whenever you want a measure of maximum performance of a cognitive skill, test.
5. Observing their performance and perhaps analyzing what she hears—that's the answer to this music teacher's evaluation problem.
6. Observation is best, preferably without the students knowing that they are being watched.

# Mastery Test

**OBJECTIVE 2**   To select appropriate information-gathering instruments when seeking to make classroom evaluations.

For each of the situations described in the questions below, determine the best technique and/or instrument to be used.

1. A fifth grade teacher wants to ask all her students how they feel about each of the subjects they are studying:
   a. testing—classroom test
   b. observation—questionnaire
   c. inquiry—rating scale
   d. inquiry—questionnaire

2. A high school math teacher wants to know if her class is ready to go on to the next unit. To measure the students' level of achievement, she should use a:
   a. classroom test
   b. standardized test
   c. checklist
   d. rating scale

3. The school superintendent wants an overall picture of the level of achievement for each class in the school system:
   a. checklist
   b. classroom test
   c. standardized test
   d. rating scale

4. A speech teacher is trying to improve her ability to judge impromptu speeches:
   a. analysis
   b. observation
   c. testing
   d. inquiry

5. An English teacher examines each student's theme very carefully so she can get a good idea about each person's particular strengths and weaknesses in writing:
   a. analysis—checklist
   b. analysis—test

   c. inquiry—checklist
   d. inquiry—test

6. To determine academic aptitude for placement in special programs, one should use a:
   a. rating scale
   b. checklist
   c. classroom test
   d. standardized test

---

## ANSWER KEY

**Mastery Test, Objective 2**

1. d  2. a  3. c  4. b  5. a  6. d

# Objective 3

To write good test items for evaluating achievement.

## LEARNING ACTIVITY 3.1

The first step in test construction is to determine what it is you are trying to test and what kind of item would be best suited to testing that type of information. Most classroom tests are used to measure learning outcomes. The best statements of learning outcomes are instructional objectives. As you may recall from the discussion in Chapter 3, instructional objectives define clearly, in observable terms, the achievement we expect of our students. In that chapter the importance of well-chosen verbs in writing instructional objectives was emphasized. The verb should describe precisely the kind of response you expect the student to make to a particular subject matter content. If the verb used in an instructional objective does do that, it is a relatively simple matter to determine the type of test item you should use. For example, suppose that you are trying to find out if your students have mastered the following objectives:

1. To list the names of the first ten presidents of the United States.
2. To describe the major contributions of Washington and Lincoln.
3. To explain the changes that occur when a different political party takes control of Congress.

The first objective obviously calls for a short-answer–type question in which the student is asked to list names. The other two objectives would best be tested with an essay question because the student would have to describe or explain—not the kind of thing they could do on an objective test such as true/false or multiple choice. What kinds of learning outcomes are best measured with objective-test items (true/false, matching, multiple choice)? These types of items are best suited for measuring learning outcomes for which the student must be able to choose among alternatives. For example:

1. To choose the word that best describes the author's feelings.
2. To select the sentence that best represents the democratic position.
3. To identify the emotive language in a paragraph.
4. To determine which of several experiments would most likely provide the information needed by a particular researcher.

Note that each of these objectives could readily be measured with an objective test. However, it is possible to measure some of them with some other type of item. For example, the third objective in the list above (to identify emotive language) could be measured with a variety of test items:

1. *True/false:* The statement underlined in the paragraph above is emotive language.
2. *Multiple choice:* Which of the following sentences (as numbered in the paragraph above) represents emotive language?
   (a) Sentence 2      (c) Sentence 6
   (b) Sentence 3      (d) Sentence 9
3. *Short answer:* Pick out three emotive statements from the paragraph above and write them on your paper.

You can readily see that the first step in selecting the type of item to use is to examine the instructional objectives. However, there is often still room for choice; some objectives can be measured by more than one item type. Consequently, other things must be taken into account. The following table highlights the advantages and disadvantages of the major types of test items. Study this table carefully and then try the exercise "Your Turn."

### ADVANTAGES AND DISADVANTAGES OF DIFFERENT TYPES OF TEST ITEMS

| Type | Advantages | Disadvantages |
|------|-----------|---------------|
| Short Answer | Can test many facts in short time. Fairly easy to score. Excellent format for math. Tests recall. | Difficult to measure complex learning. Often ambiguous. |
| Essay | Can test complex learning. Can evaluate thinking process and creativity. | Difficult to score objectively. Uses a great deal of testing time. Subjective. |
| True/False | Test the most facts in shortest time. Easy to score. Tests recognition. Objective. | Difficult to measure complex learning. Difficult to write reliable items. Subject to guessing. |
| Matching | Excellent for testing associations and recognition of facts. Although terse, can test complex learning (especially concepts). Objective. | Difficult to write good items. Subject to process of elimination. |
| Multiple Choice | Can evaluate learning at all levels of complexity. Can be highly reliable, objective. Tests fairly large knowledge base in short time. Easy to score. | Difficult to write. Somewhat subject to guessing. |

# Your Turn

## SELECTING THE TYPE OF ITEM

For each learning outcome, determine the type of test item you would use and briefly state the reason you would use that type.

1. To explain the value of using strong, active verbs in writing paragraphs.

_____

_____

_____

2. To list the steps to take when processing a film.

_____

_____

_____

3. To select, from among alternatives, the best way to introduce a new topic.

_____

_____

_____

4. To discuss the implications of the new morality.

_____

_____

_____

5. To write down the names of at least five generals from World War II.

_____

_____

_____

6. To choose the most likely cause of a given kind of engine malfunction.

_____

_____

_____

7. To recognize each of the major parts of speech.

_____

_____

_____

# ANSWER KEY
## Your Turn: Selecting the Type of Item

1. *Essay:* In order to "explain," the student needs considerable freedom to respond.
2. *Short answer:* No freedom here, just the steps.
3. *Multiple choice:* Selection from among alternatives is being called for.
4. *Essay:* To discuss requires freedom to respond.
5. *Short answer:* This objective calls for just a list, no explanation.
6. *Multiple choice:* This requires choosing among alternatives or *matching,* with types of malfunctions in one column and the possible causes in another.
7. *Multiple choice:* An example of this type of item might be: "The underlined word represents which of the following parts of speech" or *matching,* with words in one column and parts of speech in the other.

## WRITING TEST ITEMS

### Writing Essay Questions

The secret to good item writing is to be as clear and as concise as possible. Don't try to trick the students. Test each learning outcome (instructional objective) in as straightforward a manner as possible. When reading a test question a student should understand exactly what is being asked. If the student knows the material, he or she should be able to answer the question correctly.

The objectivity that comes from an item written in this way is especially difficult to attain when writing and grading essay questions. However, by following the simple guidelines listed below, you should be able to produce well-written essay questions.

*Guidelines for Writing Essay Questions*

1. Make certain that your question really tests the learning outcome of interest.

2. Each essay item should include:
   (a) a clear statement of the problem
   (b) any restrictions on the answer

3. For each item, construct a model answer. It should include:
   (a) the content of an ideal answer
   (b) any important organizational features
       one might expect in an ideal answer

Once you are certain that an essay is the type of item you wish to use, you need to formulate the question so that every student reading it will have the same understanding about what is expected in the answer. *Note:* Not every student need be able to answer the question. However, every student should know what the question is asking. That criterion for a well-written essay question will be easier to meet if you:

1. Use clear, concise language.
2. Be very precise about any restrictions you want to place on the answer.

Examine the following sets of questions. Note that the questions that are easiest to understand are shorter, contain simpler language, involve simple sentence structures, and do not include extraneous verbage.

*Set A*

Clear: Describe a wedge and list three or four of its uses.

*Not so clear:* Explain what a wedge is and its functions with a few examples.

*Down-right confusing:* Produce a descriptive paragraph concerning the wedge and its functional utility.

*Set B*

*Clear:* Explain why certain chemicals should always be mixed in a certain order.

*Ambiguous:* Exploding chemicals can be dangerous, which should not happen. How do you avoid this?

*Impossible:* Sometimes reactions occur which are potentially volatile when the proper order of mixing certain chemicals is not maintained. Can you explain this?

Using clear, concise language is not enough. A good essay question must also indicate the level of specificity you expect in the answer. It must let the student know whether opinions are acceptable, whether or not arguments must be substantiated, and, if so, whether or not references are needed. It should provide the student with an indication of just how much freedom he or she has in responding.

Take, for example, the following essay item:

Discuss the various properties of water.

The language of this item is certainly clear and concise. But what kind of response would be acceptable? Would "water tastes good and gets you wet when you fall in it" be an acceptable answer? Maybe. Only the author of the question knows. Look at the following alternative ways of writing this item. Each one imposes slightly different restrictions on the student's answers, and each one is better than our original item because of those added restrictions.

Describe what happens to water when it is exposed to extreme temperatures.

List the chemical properties of water.

List the nutritional properties of drinking water.

Why does the taste of water vary so greatly from one location to another?

List and briefly describe five ways that water helps to sustain life.

Note that each of the items above clearly calls for a different kind of response. Note too the variety of ways one can restrict or shape a student's response. Now try your hand at writing essay items by doing the following exercise.

# Your Turn

## WRITING ESSAY ITEMS

Write two essay questions. One should be a very open-ended question. The other should place restrictions upon the response the student is asked to make.

1. An open-ended question with little restrictions:

_____

_____

_____

_____

_____

_____

_____

_____

_____

_____

2. An essay question that somehow restricts or limits the student's response in one or more of the following ways by:
   (a) limiting the amount of time to answer or the number of words that can be used in the answer.
   (b) limiting the topic to certain specified subtopics.
   (c) asking the student to focus on one aspect of the topic.
   (d) restricting the response to only one point of view.

_____

_____

_____

_____

_____

_____

_____

_____

_____

_____

## ANSWER KEY

### Your Turn: Writing Essay Items

1. *An open-ended question:* This question should allow the student a great deal of freedom to respond, but it should be quite clear about what is being asked. You can see from the samples given below that open-ended questions can be difficult to grade because each student may choose to restrict his or her own answer in a different way.

   *Sample Questions*
   (a) Discuss some ways you might use to reduce your anxiety when preparing to make a contemporaneous speech.
   (b) What could you do to reduce the number of germs on medical instruments if you have no sterilization equipment?
   (c) Discuss the pros and cons of the draft registration.
   (d) Convince me that it is important to understand the history of the English language.

2. *A restricted essay question:* Again, make certain that your question has been clearly written. Further, check to see that your question limits the answers in a way that will help the student to be able to respond (i.e., the student will know how to answer *if* he or she knows the information being asked for).

   *Sample Questions*
   (a) List and explain each of the steps we discussed for setting up an experiment.
   (b) In no more than ten lines, describe a typical Eskimo village from the early 1900s.
   (c) Cite five reasons for having a 55-mph speed limit. Defend one of your reasons with supporting evidence.

Well-written essay items will help make it easier for the students to respond *and* easier for the teacher to grade. The biggest problem with essay tests is that they are difficult to grade objectively. However, that problem can be greatly reduced if a model answer is developed and used as a guide when the students' answers are graded. There are two major considerations when writing a model answer:

1. All important content should be included in a model answer.
2. Any important organizational features that would be expected in a good answer should be specified.

# Your Turn

## CONSTRUCTING A MODEL ANSWER

Write two or three essay questions with various degrees of freedom. Then write a model answer for each question.

_____

_____

_____

_____

_____

First, then, a model answer should contain any content you hope to find in the students' answers. When comparing a student's answer to the model answer, you should only have to check through the student's answer to see whether or not it includes the items listed as important content in the model answer. Facts, concepts, principles, and acceptable problem solutions are the kinds of things one should list in a model answer.

Below are two examples of model answers: the first, for an essay question calling primarily for factual material; the second calling for a specific type of answer, but allowing the student some freedom in the particular content to be discussed.

### *Example of a Model Answer for a Factual Essay Question*

*Question:* Describe the steps to take when developing black-and-white film.

*Model answer:* Student answers should include the following information:

*Step 1:* Load film onto developing reel, grasp film by edges, in darkened room (red light only), check to see that film surfaces are not touching each other.

*Step 2:* Place reel in developing tank and cover with light-tight lid.

*Step 3:* Wet down the film, etc.

### *Example of a model answer for an essay question allowing some freedom of content.*

*Question:* Defend *or* refute the following statement:

Civil wars are necessary to the growth of a developing country.

Cite reasons for your argument and use examples from history to help substantiate your claim.

*Model Answer:* All answers, regardless of the position taken, should include:

1. A clear statement of the position
2. At least five logical reasons
3. At least four examples from history that *clearly* substantiate the reasons given.

Note that in the second example the student has great freedom to choose what to discuss, but restrictions are placed instead on the *type* of information to be included in the answer. For some essay questions, the order in which topics are included in the answer may be important. Other questions may call for a carefully developed logic, and the specific content is less important. Just remember this basic rule: A model answer should highlight the features that best reflect the learning outcome being measured by the essay question.

## ANSWER KEY

### Your Turn: Constructing a Model Answer

Check your model answer against the criteria for model answers. Compare your model answers with those of your peers. If you are uncertain about your answers, ask your instructor to check them.

## Writing Multiple-Choice Questions

Multiple-choice questions are perhaps the most frequently used type of test item. To make it easier to talk about these items, labels have been developed for each part of such an item:

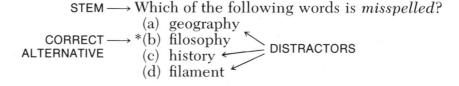

The multiple-choice item is the most versatile of all item types. You can ask questions at virtually all levels of understanding and do so with a high degree of reliability. However, to be both a reliable and a valid measure of a learning outcome, a multiple-choice item should meet the following criteria:

1. Present a single problem or question.
2. Measure a learning outcome that can be tested by selecting a right or best answer from among several alternatives.
3. Include alternatives that are terse—most of the item's information occurring in the stem.
4. Include alternatives that are very similar in wording, writing style, length, etc.
5. Include alternatives that follow logically and grammatically from the stem.
6. Include distractors that are plausible but not correct.

Let's examine a few multiple-choice items to see if they meet the criteria above. Then you will have an opportunity to evaluate items and try writing some of your own.

*Examples of Multiple-Choice Items*

*Poor item:* Alternatives too lengthy, question unclear.
1. Frozen foods
    (a) Can be quick-frozen and then stored at zero degrees and only then for specified periods of time.
    (b) Are tastier than any other kind of processed foods.
    (c) Should always be washed and blanched before being packed for freezing.
    (d) Can be stored at 28° or less if they are properly packaged and sealed.

*Improved:* Question clarified, alternatives shortened.
1. What is most important to a long shelf life for frozen foods?
    (a) Zero degrees temperature
    (b) Air-tight packages
    (c) Blanching food before freezing
    (d) Selection of food for freezing

*Poor item:* Alternatives do not follow grammatically from stem
1. The constituents of air that are essential to plant life are
    (a) oxygen and nitrogen
    (b) carbon monoxide
    (c) nitrogen and iodine
    (d) water

*Improved:* All alternatives are plural, stem shortened.
1. Which of the following pairs are essential to plant life?
    (a) oxygen and nitrogen
    (b) carbon oxide and iodine
    (c) polyethyl and water
    (d) water and carbon monoxide

*Improved:* All alternatives are singular.
1. Which of the following is essential to plant life?
    (a) nitrogen
    (b) carbon monoxide
    (c) polyethylene
    (d) iodine

# Your Turn

## Evaluating and Writing Multiple-Choice Questions

Choose a subject with which you are familiar and write five multiple-choice questions. Try to write at least two of them at a level of learning higher than just the memorization of facts.

_____

_____

_____

_____

_____

_____

## ANSWER KEY

### Your Turn: Evaluating and Writing Multiple-Choice Questions

Check your items against the criteria for good multiple-choice items. In addition, exchange your items with a classmate and evaluate each other's.

### Writing True/False Items

True/false items are often criticized because they are so susceptible to error due to guessing. However, certain kinds of learning outcomes lend themselves naturally to a true/false format. If the items are carefully written so as to make them as reliable as possible, it would seem reasonable to include a few true/false items in a test.

The most important rule to remember when writing true/false items is that each item must be clearly true or clearly false. Look at the following examples:

1. Squares have only three sides and two right angles.
2. Liquids always flow in the direction of gravitational pull.
3. Complete sentences include both a subject and predicate.
4. Cities are built on major traffic routes.
5. Our moon reflects the light of the sun.
6. Extroverts are outgoing and always popular.

Note that items 3 and 5 are clearly true and that only item 1 is clearly false. Item 2 is basically true, but "always" is extremely strong language. Might there be some exceptions? And what about item 4? It is a reasonable generalization, to be sure, but not true in every case. Finally, item 6 is partially true (outgoing, yes, but not always popular). Does the part that is false make the whole statement false?

The problem with item 6 can often be avoided by remembering a second rule: Each true or false statement must present one and only one fact. For example, we could improve item 1 above by making two items from it:

(a) Squares have a total of three sides.
(b) Squares have only two right angles.

A final rule to remember when constructing a true/false item is: Do not try to trick the students. Don't take a perfectly true statement, for example, and insert a "not" or other qualifying word that would make the statement false.

*Good item:* The sun is closer to the earth at the equator.
*Good item:* The sun is farther from the earth at the equator.
*Bad item:* The sun is not closer to the earth at the equator.

Don't lift a statement out of context, hoping that the student will remember reading it and think it true because it is familiar.

Poor:　　　Nouns modify nouns
Improved: Although they do not normally do so, in some situations nouns can modify nouns (e.g., baseball bat)

There are many other ways to trick students. You'll know it when you are doing it. Avoid that temptation. Always ask yourself: "Am I really measuring an important learning outcome in a straightforward manner?"

# Your Turn

## WRITING TRUE/FALSE ITEMS

Try the exercise below. Remember the three rules cited above, and also remember to avoid: (1) using statements lifted directly from the "book," (2) double negatives, and (3) long, complex statements.

A professor has just assigned several children's books to his literature class and wants to spot-check to find out if they remember the stories they have read. Write six to eight true/false items about the story "Little Red Riding Hood."

_____

_____

_____

_____

_____

_____

_____

_____

_____

## ANSWER KEY

### Your Turn: Writing True/False items

Compare your questions to those of your classmates and to the examples below. The content of your questions may be different from the examples, but they should not violate the rules for writing good true/false items.

_____  1. Little Red Riding Hood was on her way to the store when she met the wolf.

_____  2. The wolf was very friendly to Little Red Riding Hood at first.

_____  3. The basket Little Red Riding Hood carried contained food for her grandmother.

_____  4. The wolf followed Little Red Riding Hood to her grandmother's.

_____  5. Little Red Riding Hood immediately recognized the wolf when she found him in her grandmother's bed.

_____  6. The wolf was finally caught and killed.

### Writing Matching Items

Matching items are written as a group of items and provide two lists; the student's task is to match each item from one list with an item from the other list. A well-written set of matching items will illustrate some particular relationship between pairs of items from the two lists. A very common use of the matching exercise, for example, is to test the relationship between a term and its definition. Other kinds of relationships that might be tested with a matching exercise are:

1. Historical events and dates
2. Novels and their authors
3. Tools and their uses
4. Problems and their solutions
5. Elements and their symbols
6. Causes and their effects
7. Drawings and their interpretations

Relationships like these are relatively easy to test with a matching exercise. Simply make two lists and write a clear set of instructions telling the student the kind of relationship you are testing (i.e., the rationale, or basis, for matching). Try your hand at writing a matching exercise as instructed in the next exercise. Make sure that you keep the following points in mind:

Points to Remember When Writing a Matching Exercise

1. An obvious, natural relationship must exist between the items in the two lists.
2. The basis for matching must be made clear to the student.
3. One of the lists should be approximately 50% longer than the other list (makes it difficult to obtain correct match by the process of elimination).
4. The shorter list should not contain more than seven or eight items.

# Your Turn

## WRITING A MATCHING EXERCISE

Write a matching exercise to measure elementary science facts (e.g., properties of water, uses of elementary tools, weather conditions and their signs). Your shorter list should include five items to be matched with items from a seven-item list. Make certain that you have written clear instructions to the pupils.

_____     _____

_____     _____

_____     _____

_____     _____

_____     _____

_____     _____

_____

### ANSWER KEY

Your Turn: Writing Matching Items

Check your work according to the criteria for matching exercises. Ask a friend to read your instructions to see if they are clear.

## LEARNING ACTIVITY 3.2

As an optional learning exercise, you may find it helpful to examine a variety of test items, judging them in light of the criteria set down in the last few pages.

Ask your instructor to help you locate both standardized and teacher-made tests for you to examine. For each item, ask yourself what makes the item a good one or what makes it a poor one. Also ask: "What is the writer of this item really trying to measure?"

This activity can be done individually or in small groups, but any findings should be shared with others in a general class discussion.

# Mastery Test

## Objective 3   To write good test items for evaluating achievement.

Write a set of objectives for a unit of instruction. (Choose the subject matter and grade level.) Next, develop a test designed to find out whether students have mastered the objectives.

*Objectives:* _____

_____

_____

_____

_____

_____

_____

_____

*Test Items:* Put on a separate page. (You may wish to put your items on index cards to file for future use.)

## Answer Key

Mastery Test, Objective 3

Evaluate your test against these criteria:

1. The test clearly measures the objectives.
2. The items are clear and concise (unambiguous).
3. The type of items used represent the most direct way to measure the objectives.

4. The readability of the items is appropriate for the grade level you selected.
5. Any necessary instructions to the students are clearly stated.

## Objective 4

To develop checklists and rating scales for evaluating student products and performances.

There are many times when tests will not give you the information you need. You want to rate a student's musical performance. You are judging a speech contest. You are trying to grade an art project. You are on a committee evaluating textbooks for possible adoption. These and similar situations represent the kind of evaluation problem best solved through the use of checklists or rating scales.

### Developing Checklists

Checklists provide a systematic way of checking whether or not important characteristics are present in someone's performance (or in a product that someone had produced). Note the key consideration: Are some characteristics of this performance or product so important that it is valuable simply to know whether or not they are present? When the answer to that question is yes, a checklist is what you are looking for.

Below is a list of the kinds of performances and products that might be evaluated through the use of checklists.

| *Performances* | *Products* |
|---|---|
| Playing a musical instrument | Drawings and paintings |
| Singing | Sculptures |
| Speaking | Maps |

Participating in a discussion
Leading a discussion
Conducting an experiment
Working through a math problem
Conducting a library search
Painting in oils
Sculpturing

Wood products
Handicrafts
Outlines

When developing a checklist for evaluating a performance, your focus will be on behaviors; in developing one for use with products, it will be on observable features or characteristics. Note this difference by comparing the two checklists below. The first has been designed to evaluate a student while he is doing an oil painting (performance). The second has been designed to evaluate an oil painting after a student has completed it (product). How are these lists similar? How are they different?

*Example: Evaluating a Student's Oil Painting*

| *Performance* | *Product* |
| --- | --- |
| \_\_\_\_ General layout sketched out first | \_\_\_\_ Overall layout pleasing |
| \_\_\_\_ Background wash painted over the large areas | \_\_\_\_ Colors crisp and clean |
| \_\_\_\_ Colors mixed on canvas | \_\_\_\_ Composition appropriate to subject matter |
| \_\_\_\_ Paints "worked" very little to keep them crisp | \_\_\_\_ Sufficient details but not overdone |
| \_\_\_\_ Brushes and painting knives selected carefully to produce the desired textures | |

The process of developing a checklist is relatively simple: First, list the important behaviors or characteristics. Second, add any common errors to the list. Finally, arrange the list so that it is easy to use.

Listing the important behaviors of a performance is not as easy as is listing the important characteristics of a product. That is because when we are good performers, we are often unaware of the things we do that make our performance good. It is especially difficult for a motor-skill performer to verbalize what he or she does when performing. Try to list, for example, the steps you take to balance a bicycle and move it forward. One way to deal with this problem is to watch a good performer and list all the things you observe that person doing. Later, pick out the most important behaviors and include them in your final checklist.

The common errors are most easily listed after you have had opportunity to watch a *beginning* performer or to examine a beginner's early products. Note that a checklist is especially useful as a diagnostic tool when it includes common errors. If you anticipate using a checklist only as a final check on performance, there is no need to include common errors.

A well-designed checklist should meet the following criteria:

1. The list should be relatively short.
2. Each item should be clear.

3. Each item should focus on an observable characteristic or behavior.
4. Only important characteristics or behaviors should be included.
5. The items should be arranged so that the total list is easy to use.

## Developing Rating Scales

Checklists help us determine the presence or absence of a list of behaviors or characteristics. Rating scales help us determine the quality of a behavior or characteristic. It is helpful to know, for example, that a speaker uses gestures. It is even more helpful to be able to judge the quality of those gestures. A rating scale is used to evaluate that quality of performance. It helps you answer the question: "How well does the speaker gesture?"

A rating scale is developed by taking a list of behaviors or characteristics (as one might use in a checklist) and constructing a qualitative scale for evaluating each behavior or characteristic.

### Example: A Rating Scale for Rating Discussion Leaders*

*Directions:* Rate the discussion leader on each of the following characteristics by placing an "x" anywhere along the horizontal line under each item.

1. To what extent does the leader encourage discussion?

| Discourages discussion by negative comments | Neither discourages nor encourages discussion | Encourages discussion by positive comments |

2. How well does the leader keep the discussion on the right track?

| Lets the discussion wander | Only occasionally brings the discussion back on target | Does not let discussants wander from the main topic |

3. How frequently does the leader ask controversial questions?

| Never asks controversial questions | Occasionally asks controversial questions | Continuously asks controversial questions |

4. How does the leader respond to inappropriate comments?

| Ridicules the one who made the comment | Treats inappropriate comments the same as appropriate ones | Discourages inappropriate comments |

* Excerpted from Terry D. TenBrink, *Evaluation: A Practical Guide for Teachers* (New York: McGraw-Hill, 1974), pp. 276–277. © 1974 by McGraw-Hill Book Co. used with the permission of the McGraw-Hill Book Company.

The rating scale above would help an observer focus on specific, observable aspects of each behavior. Each time the scale was used, the same things would be examined. This would help improve the reliability of evaluating a performance and would reduce the errors due to observer bias.

Developing a rating scale involves the same steps used to develop a checklist, plus the step of defining a scale for each characteristic. This added step is sometimes difficult, but it will be easier if you first define the extreme ends of each scale and then describe the midpoints.

Defining the extremes is easiest if you can think of some real-life examples. Suppose, for example, that you are developing a rating scale for evaluating the social development of third graders. Among the many characteristics you feel are important is that of sharing with friends. To define the extreme ends, think first of a child you know who exemplifies this characteristic. This child shares readily with all her friends in a very unselfish manner. Imagine this child as she shares with others. See her in your mind. Write down what you see her do; describe her sharing. That description defines the positive end of your scale. To define the extreme negative or low end of the scale, think of a child who is really poor at sharing and describe that child's behavior; now you have the basis for the description at the low end of the scale. By examining these two extremes, you will be able to imagine fairly easily what someone would be like who would fall in the middle, and the midpoints of the scale should be fairly easy to define. A completed scale for the characteristic of sharing might look something like this:

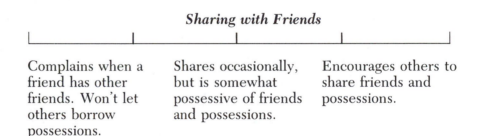

***Sharing with Friends***

| Complains when a friend has other friends. Won't let others borrow possessions. | Shares occasionally, but is somewhat possessive of friends and possessions. | Encourages others to share friends and possessions. |

Note that at this point we have placed no numbers on the scale. For purposes of scoring, one might number the points along the scale. The lowest point could be assigned "1"; the highest, "5." A scale without the numbers is *descriptive;* one with numbers a *numerical-descriptive* scale. Removing the description and simply using numbers would produce a numerical scale. Numerical scales are usually not very helpful unless the characteristic can be easily quantified (e.g., number of times the child shares toys in one day: 0, 1 or 2, 2–4, 4–6, 6 or more).

Following the suggestions above should help you to produce some reasonably good rating scales. However, there are many much more sophisticated techniques for producing scales, which are discussed in some of the references listed at the end of this chapter.

Space does not allow a fuller treatment of the topic of rating-scale development and use. However, several of the questions teachers ask most often about rating scales are listed below, along with brief answers. Read these carefully and ask your instructor for fuller explanations of any that interest you or that you wonder about.

*Questions Teachers Often Ask About Rating Scales*

**Question:** "What advantage is there to using a rating scale? Isn't it easier to construct a checklist that is effective?"

**Answer:** Whenever you simply need to know if a characteristic is present or absent, the checklist is a better tool. However, checklists simply record quantitative information and are not very helpful for judging the quality of a performance or product.

**Question:** "Do I have to have a rating scale in front of me when I evaluate performances? Can't I keep the information in my head that I think is important?"

**Answer:** After you have used a particular rating scale many times, you may be able to evaluate effectively without actually having the scale in front of you. However, even in that situation the scale offers you a convenient way to record the information you have observed. Having an instrument in front of you while you are observing helps you to focus on the really important characteristics and greatly reduces observer bias.

**Question:** "How many points should a rating scale have? Is a five-point scale best? Is a three-point scale O.K.?"

**Answer:** Generally speaking, you will get your most reliable results if you use a five- to seven-point scale. Also, scales with an odd number of points (five or seven) are usually better than those with an even number of points (four or six).

**Question:** "Can students use rating scales to help evaluate each other?"

**Answer:** Definitely. If the scale is well designed and if there are good instructions for the observer, students can rate each other. Student evaluations can be used quite successfully in the performing arts. Well-designed scales can also be used by students to evaluate their own take-home projects, art projects, etc.

# Mastery Test

## Objective 4
To develop checklists and rating scales for evaluating student products and performances.

1. Select one of the following (or similar) student products and develop a checklist that lists the most important criteria for evaluating that product.

|   |   |
|---|---|
| (a) A soap sculpture | (e) A model of a village |
| (b) A relief map | (f) An educational game |
| (c) A pencil sketch | (g) Cursive handwriting |
| (d) A book report | (h) A health poster |

_____

_____

_____

_____

2. Use the format below as a guide to help you develop a rating scale that you might find useful in your own teaching someday.
   (a) Name the performance or social-personal trait to be evaluated:

   _____

   _____

   (b) List the major steps to take or important characteristics to be considered in the evaluation:

   _____

   _____

   _____

   _____

   _____

   (c) Select four or five items from the list above and produce a scale for each item, describing the extremes first and then the midpoints. (You may decide to have more than four or five items in your full scale, but do at least four or five for purposes of this exercise.)

## ANSWER KEY

### Mastery Test, Objective 4

1. *Developing checklists:* Your checklist should be clear, concise, and easy to use. If possible, try using it. Ask someone who is an expert at the performance to check your list to see if you have included only the important behaviors.

2. *Constructing rating scales:* Check your scale against the criteria for a good rating scale. Share your scale with classmates and ask them if they feel that they would be able to use it successfully.

## Objective 5

To describe how to use information to evaluate.

To evaluate is to judge, to place a value on. When we assign grades, we are judging. When we determine that a child is functioning below grade level, we are judging. When we evaluate a child's progress, we are judging. When we evaluate a teacher's effectiveness, we are judging. The basic question we will answer in this last section of this chapter is: "How can one use information that has been obtained (through observation, tests, etc.) to evaluate, to form judgments?" Let's take a look at the process of forming judgments in general and then examine more carefully several specific kinds of classroom judgments (i.e., grading, judging student progress, judging changes in student attitudes, and judging the effectiveness of teaching).

## FORMING JUDGMENTS

The process of forming judgments is really well known to all of us because we use it many times each day. We judge the value of a car we want to buy, the quality of a restaurant, the value of a TV show, the neatness of our classroom, the warmth of our home, the friendliness of our neighbors, etc. Each time we make these judgments, we use the same basic process. We compare information we have about the "thing" we are judging to some referent. For example, we say that a restaurant is bad because the food is not nearly as good as "Mom's." We decide that it's cold in the house because the thermometer reads below 65°. We determine that a car is too expensive because other, similar cars are selling for less. Or, we may feel that it's too expensive because it's $500 more than we can afford to spend. In each case we compare information we have to some referent. The following chart, which illustrates this process for a variety of judgments, breaks each judgment down into two parts: (1) information used, and (2) the referent to which the information is compared.

### COMMON JUDGMENTS

| Judgment | Information | Compared to | Referent |
|---|---|---|---|
| Peter is my best speller. | Peter's spelling test scores | | The spelling scores of his classmates |
| Sally reads above grade level. | Sally's reading achievement score | | The average reading score of students at her grade level |
| This book is the best one I've seen on teaching math. | My perusal of the book | | My perusal of other math books |
| Bobby has an above-average I.Q. | Bobby's I.Q. score | | The average I.Q. test score of students Bobby's age |
| The class is ready to move to the next unit in the math book. | The math achievement scores | | The level of math achievement deemed necessary to do the work in the next unit |
| George is too tall for the Navy. | George's height | | Navy's maximum height limit |
| Elaine has made a great deal of progress on learning to study in her seat. | The number of times Elaine left her seat today | | The number of times Elaine left her seat one day last week |

Note that different kinds of referents are used in the examples above. Frequently, we compare information we have with some reference group (for example, the food in the restaurant compared to food in most other restaurants we have dined in, or the number of problems George got correct compared to the average number correct by the class as a whole). This kind of judgment is based on a norm-referenced approach.

Whenever we want to determine whether the persons or things we are judging meet some minimal criterion or standard, we specify that criterion carefully and use it as our basis for comparison. For example, a car is judged to be too expensive when we compare its price to the amount we can afford to spend. The amount we can afford to spend is our criterion, and the kind of judgment we make using such a standard is called a criterion-referenced judgment. Criterion-referenced judgments allow us to judge a student's work independently of how well or how poorly the other students have done. It is an important type of judgment when using a mastery-learning approach to classroom teaching.

A third type of judgment that is quite useful is called self-referenced judgments. When making this type of judgment, the individual (or thing) being judged serves as his or her own (self) referent. For example, we judge Sam's performance to be very good. Compared to what he was doing yesterday, today's performance was very good. Whenever we are concerned about student progress, we should make self-referenced judgments. Self-referenced judgments should also be used for diagnosing a student's strengths and weaknesses. To answer the question "How are Sarah's math skills compared to her reading skills?" is to make a self-referenced judgment.

Whenever you need to select a few students from among a larger group, you will need to make norm-referenced judgments. Comparing a student to a norm group such as classmates is helpful whenever you need to make comparisons among several individuals in order to judge their relative merit (e.g., who is the best math student). To select one student and not another (as in choosing a class leader) requires you to be able to compare those two students on certain characteristics. That requires norm-referenced judgments. These types of judgments should always be used when you need to compare students.

Criterion-referenced judgments, on the other hand, are most helpful when making decisions about the kind of assignment to give a student or the level of achievement at which to begin a student. In other words, whenever a certain specified standard of performance or achievement is necessary before an action can be taken, criterion-referenced judgments are most useful.

When decisions must be made that rely on information about a student's progress or about his or her relative aptitude in different subjects, self-referenced judgments are in order.

# Your Turn

# TYPES OF JUDGMENTS

Answer the questions below to see how well you understand the basic process of forming judgments of different types.

1. What is at the heart of the *process* of forming judgments?
   (a) information
   (b) comparisons
   (c) people
   (d) statistics

2. To make a judgment is to place a _____ on.
   (a) mark
   (b) number
   (c) value

3–6. For each of the following situations, determine the kind of judgment being made. Use the following key: A, norm-referenced; B, criterion-referenced; C, self-referenced.

_____ 3. A third grade teacher discovers that her class scored above the national average on a math achievement test.

_____ 4. A high school biology teacher selected his best students to help him set up the experiments for the next day.

_____ 5. Mitsy's teacher was really pleased because of her progress in reading. Her gains since last year are obvious.

_____ 6. Four of the students who took the algebra aptitude test failed to get a high enough score, and they were not allowed to take beginning algebra.

---

## ANSWER KEY

### Your Turn: Types of Judgments

1. B   2. C   3. A   4. A   5. C   6. B

---

TYPES OF
JUDGMENTS

### Grading

Assigning grades has forever been a task teachers dislike. There seems to be no "fair" way to do it, and any grading system used seems to be subject to all kinds of interpretation problems. The next few paragraphs will not resolve the problems of grading, but they should help you to better understand the alternatives available to you.

One of the most common questions teachers get from students concerning grading policy is: "Are you going to grade on the curve?" Whether grades are fitted to a normal curve or just "curved" to make a reasonable distribution, the basic idea behind grading "on a curve" is the same: making norm-referenced judgments, a very common form of assigning grades. The class as a whole is used as a norm group, and the class average usually serves as the referent against which all other grades are judged. Usually the average score is assigned a grade of "C," and some proportion of scores on either side of that average are also assigned grades of "C" (the "C" range usually includes 30 percent to 50 percent of the class). After that, grades are assigned by selecting some cut-off points so that a certain (usually smaller) percentage of students fall into the "B" and "D" ranges, respectively. Finally, those left fall into the "A" and "F" ranges, respectively, as their scores deviate above or below "C."

What do you think are the advantages and disadvantages of this form of grading? List them below and then compare your answers later on with the information in the table on page 398.

| *Advantages* | *Disadvantages* |
| --- | --- |
| _____ | _____ |
| _____ | _____ |

_____     _____
_____     _____
_____     _____

Remember that whenever you grade someone's work by comparing it to someone else's (or to the average of some group), you are basically using a norm-referenced approach, and all the disadvantages of that type of approach apply.

Another way to assign grades is to establish certain cut-off points for each grade. These cut-off points serve as criteria against which a given student's performance is judged. A common way in which this approach is used is for a teacher to assign points for every assignment and every test. Next, the teacher determines how many total points a student must get in order to get an "A," how many to get a "B," etc. Each assignment or test can be graded that way, and the total number of points for the marking period can be added together and compared to cut-off totals in the same way to assign report card grades. This could be called criterion-referenced grading. However, true criterion-referenced evaluation is a bit more complex than what we have just described because the cut-off scores should be determined on the basis of some meaningful external criterion.

What do you think are the advantages and disadvantages of this kind of criterion-referenced grading?

| _Advantages_ | _Disadvantages_ |
| --- | --- |
| _____ | _____ |
| _____ | _____ |
| _____ | _____ |
| _____ | _____ |
| _____ | _____ |

Teachers often find themselves wanting to give a student a good grade for having made so much improvement. Grading on the basis of improvement is a popular kind of self-referenced grading. Comparing a student to himself or herself is a desirable, humane way to grade. However, this kind of grading has many disadvantages. Can you think of some of them? After writing down your ideas, study the following table.

| _Advantages_ | _Disadvantages_ |
| --- | --- |
| _____ | _____ |
| _____ | _____ |
| _____ | _____ |
| _____ | _____ |
| _____ | _____ |

## ADVANTAGES AND DISADVANTAGES OF DIFFERENT TYPES OF GRADING

| Type of Grading | Advantages | Disadvantages |
|---|---|---|
| Norm-referenced | 1. Allows for comparisons among students<br>2. Classes can be compared to other classes<br>3. Allows teacher to spot students who are dropping behind the class | 1. If whole class does well, some students still get poor grades<br>2. If class as a whole does poorly, a good grade could be misleading<br>3. Does not allow individual progress or individual circumstances to be considered<br>4. The whole class (or large portions of it) must be evaluated in the same way<br>5. Everyone in class (or norm group) must be evaluated with the same instrument under the same conditions |
| Criterion-referenced | 1. Helps teacher to decide if students are ready to move on<br>2. Criteria are independent of group performance<br>3. Works well in a mastery-learning setting<br>4. Each individual can be evaluated on different material, depending on his or her level of achievement | 1. It is difficult to develop meaningful criteria (therefore arbitrary cut-off scores are often used)<br>2. Presents unique problems in computing the reliability of criterion-referenced tests<br>3. Makes it difficult to make comparisons among students |
| Self-referenced | 1. Allows you to check student progress<br>2. Makes it possible to compare achievement across different subjects for the same individual | 1. All measures taken on an individual must be taken with similar instruments under similar circumstances<br>2. Does not help you to compare an individual with his or her peers |

## Judging Student Progress

Teachers have an ongoing concern about the amount of progress their students are making. If students are making a reasonable amount of progress, the methods, materials, etc., are probably working. If no progress or too little progress is being made, some changes may need to be made somewhere in the instructional program.

A judgment of student progress is, of course, a self-referenced judgment, and thus all the disadvantages of that type of judgment will hold. It is especially important that progress in achievement be measured the same way each time progress is checked. For example, suppose that you were trying to check a student's progress in reading. It would be best if you could use the same type of test each time progress was checked (alternate forms of the same standardized tests; observations of oral reading, using the same type of checklist or rating scale, etc.).

The following suggestions should help you do a good job of evaluating student progress. Study them carefully and then discuss with your classmates ways in which these suggestions could be carried out at various grade levels for different subject matters.

### Suggestions for Evaluating Student Progress

1. Determine ahead of time what student characteristics or skills you are going to keep track of (don't suddenly ask, half way through the semester, "Has any progress been made?").

2. Establish a baseline (achievement level, behavior patterns, etc.) early in the semester.

3. Choose and/or develop instruments (tests, rating scales, etc.) in advance that you can use throughout a student's progress.

4. Describe the changes you expect will occur as your students progress. This description will help you focus your evaluation on appropriate behaviors and achievements.

5. Obtain information often enough so that you can see any progression that might be occurring and so that a single bad sample of information won't throw your evaluation off.

## Evaluating Changes in Attitude

Most psychologists would define an attitude as a predisposition to act in a negative or positive way toward some object or person. Note that the attitude is a *predisposition*, which is not observable or measurable. However, it is a predisposition to *act*, and that *is* observable. This means, then, that in order to measure attitudes, one must focus on the actions or behaviors of students. Of course, the difficult part is discerning what any given action or pattern of actions means (i.e., what the attitude is that is producing the actions).

Usually, a teacher becomes concerned about attitude change when he or she discovers that one or more students have a bad attitude. Common among these are bad attitudes toward a given subject matter, a negative attitude toward the teacher, or feelings of prejudice toward minority students in the class. The important thing to remember when you first become aware of a bad attitude is that there must have been some behaviors that led you to discover that attitude. The student(s) must have said some things (speech is an observable behavior), done some things, or refused to do some things that made you aware of the attitude. Your first step, therefore, is to try to determine what specific behaviors led you to believe that there was an attitude that needed changing.

Once you have determined the behaviors associated with an attitude you think should change, your next step is to systematically obtain information about the frequency of occurrence of those behaviors. These data will serve as the baseline (the referent) against which you will judge any future changes in attitude.

When you are sure that the behaviors you observed are frequent and do indeed represent an inappropriate attitude, you are ready to set down a plan for observing any possible changes in attitude (as they would be reflected in changes in behaviors). There are two very important things to consider at this point. First, be certain that you make frequent observations so that you can feel confident that the behavior you are observing is representative and not isolated. Second, look for the behaviors when the student is in the presence of or thinking about the object of his or her inappropriate attitude (e.g., look for cutting-up behaviors during math if the student dislikes math).

Finally, when the information is obtained, you must judge whether or not the attitude has changed. Remember the disadvantages of making self-referenced judgments. Differences between any two sets of observations may not mean too much. However, if you find over a period of time (and attitudes usually take considerable time to change) that the undesirable behaviors are decreasing and the desirable ones increasing, an attitude change is probably occurring.

You may find it very helpful to use a rating scale to help you summarize the data from your observations. Suppose, for example, that you were trying to see if a student's attitude toward math were improving. You might develop a rating scale that would look something like this:

| *Hates math* | | *Tolerates math* | | *Loves math* |
|---|---|---|---|---|
| 1 | 2 | 3 | 4 | 5 |

| | | |
|---|---|---|
| Complains about math; puts off doing assignments; turns in sloppy math papers | Says, "Don't care about math grade"; does assignment but delays same; never chooses math over other subjects | Says, "I like math"; gets right at assignments; does extra-credit work; chooses math over other subjects |

Note that the behaviors characteristic of different attitudes have been placed under the two end points and the midpoint of the scale. Each time we observed our student react to math, we could determine which set of behaviors his or her actions were most like and mark an "X" on the scale accordingly. Several scales marked each in turn over a semester would give us a picture of any progress the student was making.

In summary, the basic steps involved in evaluating a student's change in attitude are as follows:

1. Determine the behaviors associated with the attitude you think should change.
2. Systematically obtain information about the frequency of occurrence of these attitudes.
3. Decide if the behaviors occur frequently enough and consistently enough to represent an inappropriate attitude.
4. Set down a plan for observing any possible changes in attitude over time.
5. Decide whether the attitude has changed by comparing the information obtained at two or more different times.
6. Record your findings—possibly using a rating scale.

## Evaluating Instruction

Most teachers have a real desire to know whether or not their instruction is effective. They also fear that they, or their principal, will find out that it is not effective. Principals, fellow teachers, students, and parents are all going to be judging the quality of instruction. Therefore it is advantageous for the teacher to have well-documented evidence of his or her teaching effectiveness.

Of course, besides accountability, teachers are concerned about improvement. They are always wanting information to help them upgrade their courses. So let's explore briefly some of the options available to teachers who wish to evaluate their own teaching. The information provided here will help you start thinking about evaluating instruction, but it in no way pretends to make you an excellent evaluator. Several books on program evaluation are cited in the references at the end of this chapter. Later, you may have an opportunity to enroll in a program-evaluation course. In the meantime, here are a few basic suggestions.

There are two primary considerations in evaluating your own instruction. First, you must determine the kind of information you will obtain about the effectiveness of your instruction. Second, you must determine an appropriate referent for judging the effectiveness of your instruction.

There are at least three kinds of information that can be used to determine the effectiveness of your instruction. The first is information about your own behaviors as a teacher. If you feel, for example, that good instruction occurs when teachers do certain things (e.g., provide behavioral objectives for their students, interact a great deal with their students, or ask certain types of questions during instruction), obtaining information about whether or not you do these things is a place to begin in the evaluation of your teaching. Many teacher-effectiveness rating scales do focus on such teacher behaviors. Although this kind of information can be helpful to you as you check your own progress as a teacher, it may be misleading about the *effectiveness* of instruction. A teacher's doing certain things doesn't necessarily ensure either good teaching or improved learning.

A more popular (and slightly better measure) of teaching effectiveness comes from student ratings of teacher effectiveness. There are a number of fairly well-developed instruments that allow the students to evaluate their teachers. If you decide to design one of your own, focus on those characteristics of good teachers which seem to make a difference. Even open-ended questions, e.g., "What did you like best about this class?" or "What could be done to make this class more effective?" can sometimes give the teacher useful information.

Of course, the ultimate test of teaching effectiveness is how well the students learn. There are several problems, however, with using learner achievement as a measure of teaching effectiveness. First, students may learn well despite the teacher. Second, it is difficult to know what would have happened had a teacher used a different approach; even though the students learned well, could they have learned better? Or, suppose that a class does very poorly. Were there extenuating circumstances? Were the textbooks poorly written? Would the students have done that poorly had another teacher taught the lesson? These last questions are not easy to answer, but they do suggest an important solution to the many problems of evaluating instructional effectiveness. That solution is to evaluate the various *components* of the instructional process separately rather than trying to obtain an overall measure. Suppose, for example, that we were developing a rating scale for students to evaluate the instruction in a high school English class. Instead of focusing all our questions on the teacher, we would also ask questions about some of the other components of instruction in that classroom. We might ask the students for their opinions about such things as the textbook, the workbook, the library assignments, the small-group discussions, the tests, etc.

A second major consideration when evaluating instruction is the choice of an appropriate referent. You must decide what you are going to use to compare your teaching to. Will you compare it to other teachers (e.g., by comparing your students' standardized achievement scores to the scores of other classes in your school district)? Or, will you be judging your teaching effectiveness by some predetermined criterion (e.g., "At least 80% of my students should score at or above grade level on the *Iowa Test of Basic Skills*)? Or, will you use a self-referenced approach (e.g., comparing the student ratings from this semester with those of the previous two semesters)? All three of these types of referents are legitimate. You simply need to decide which would be most useful to you in helping you to improve your teaching. A discussion of this issue with your peers may help to clarify your own thinking.

# Mastery Test

## OBJECTIVE 5     To describe how to use information to evaluate.

1. What is the major advantage of grading on a curve?
   (a) Allows comparisons among students
   (b) Produces more accurate judgments
   (c) Allows for differences in individuals
   For each of the following, determine the kind of grading that is involved. Use the following key: A, norm-referenced; B, criterion-referenced; C, self-referenced.
2. A teacher gives George a "D" because his scores were far below the class average.
3. A high school biology teacher promises an "A" to anyone scoring above 90% on the test.
4. Ms. Kelly tells Jane's parents that she reads well above grade level as judged by her scores on a standardized test.
5. "I think your language arts grade will soon be up to the same high level as your math grade."
6. What is the biggest problem in judging student progress?
   (a) Deciding when to measure progress
   (b) Getting similar measurements from one time to the next
7. What type of judgment is being made when a teacher evaluates a student's progress?
   (a) norm-referenced
   (b) criterion-referenced
   (c) self-referenced
8. What is being measured or observed in the evaluation of attitude changes?
   (a) feelings
   (b) ideas
   (c) predispositions
   (d) behaviors
9. What can be used to measure success in teaching?
   (a) student performance
   (b) student ratings of the teacher
   (c) observations of the teacher's behaviors
   (d) all of the above
   (e) none of the above

# Answer Key

## Mastery Test, Objective 5

1. a  2. b  3. c  4. d  5. d  6. A  7. B
8. A  9. C

**Alternative Learning Activities**

Take a poll among your peers, asking them to list for you all the things they dislike about the way they have been graded throughout their educational careers. Find out what they think would be the most equitable way to grade. Share these findings with your classmates and discuss the implications for your own teaching.

Ask as many parents as you can what kind of information they would like to have about their children's progress in school. Get them to be as specific as possible.

Once you have written good test questions, you still need to put a certain number of them together in some format to produce a test. Ask a teacher you know to tell you some of the important things to consider when putting a test together (e.g., make sure the ditto-master produces clear copy).

NOTES

1. See T. D. TenBrink, *Evaluation: A Practical Guide for Teachers* (New York: McGraw-Hill Book Company, 1974) for more details.

ADDITIONAL READINGS

Ahmann, J.S., and M.D. Glock. *Evaluating Student Progress: Principles of Tests and Measurements*, 6th ed. Boston: Allyn and Bacon, 1981.

Bloom, B.S., T.J. Hastings, and G.F. Madaus. *Handbook on Formative and Summative Evaluation of Student Learning*. New York: McGraw-Hill Book Company, 1971.

Gronlund, N.E. *Measurement and Evaluation in Teaching*, 3rd ed. New York: Macmillan Co., 1976.

Lyman, H.B. *Test Scores and What They Mean*, 2nd ed. Englewood Cliffs, N.J.: Prentice-Hall, 1971.

Stufflebeam, D.I., et al. *Educational Evaluation and Decision Making*. Itasca, Illinois: F.E. Peacock Publishers, 1971.

TenBrink, T.D. *Evaluation: A Practical Guide for Teachers*. New York: McGraw-Hill Book Company, 1974.

Terwilliger, J.S. *Assigning Grades to Students*. Glenview, Ill.: Scott, Foresman, and Company, 1971.

Wittrock, M.C., and D.E. Wiley, eds. *The Evaluation of Instruction: Issues and Problems*. New York: Holt, Rinehart and Winston, 1970.

Jerry Short and Tom Lough

# 10. Using

# Microcomputers

# in the Classroom

# Objectives

**1** To describe different ways computers can be used in classrooms.

**2** To introduce students to computer systems and their components.

**3** To describe strategies for helping students operate computers without fear and anxiety.

**4** To describe computer programming.

**5** To describe the evaluation of software and the use of computers for class presentations, demonstrations, and simulations.

**6** To describe the use of computers for individualized instruction.

**7** To describe word processing and several educational applications.

**8** To describe how to use other general purpose software such as data bases, spreadsheets, and graphics programs.

**9** To discuss the future of computers in education.

The overall goal of this chapter is to familiarize you with the use of microcomputers in the classroom. The term *microcomputer* refers to the class of small computers, often called personal computers, that are widely used in education today. These include the Apple IIe, the IBM PC, and the Commodore 64. When the term *computer* is used in this chapter, it refers to a microcomputer.

The emphasis in the chapter is on how microcomputers can be used to teach a wide variety of learning objectives. Over thirty-five different classroom applications of computers are described. As you read these descriptions, try to imagine how you might extend these applications and adapt them for your own classes and your own teaching objectives.

The chapter is written both for those who have never used microcomputers and for those who have had some experience with them. After reading the chapter, you will need "hands-on" training with computers and time to gain experience using them. We hope this chapter will stimulate your interest in computers, encourage you to obtain further training, and help you learn to use computers effectively in your teaching.

# Objective 1

To describe different ways computers can be used in classrooms.

## LEARNING ACTIVITY 1.1

Imagine that you are a new teacher going to your first faculty meeting in your new school. A parent conference has taken longer than you expected and you arrive a few minutes late. As you walk in, everyone is listening attentively to the principal:

> . . . and each one will have 128K RAM, two disk drives, and a color monitor. For peripheral devices, we'll have joy sticks, graphics pads, and dot matrix printers. For programming languages, we'll have BASIC and Logo. There will be software packages for word processing, spread sheets and data bases, and funds for instructional software in math, science, language arts, social studies, art, music, and other areas.

You wonder if you are at the right meeting. You haven't understood much of the details of the principal's presentation, but you recognize the subject: *computers*. You realize that computers are coming into your career.

You have managed to get along without computers until now. You haven't deliberately avoided them, but you haven't sought them out either. Now, however, it looks as if you are going to be using computers *and* teaching students to use them. You are not sure how you feel about this. On the one hand, you're excited; on the other hand, you're worried and a little frightened. Several questions cross your mind.

- Why would anyone want a computer in a classroom?
- What will you use it for?
- Aren't computers fragile and easily damaged?
- What if some of your students know more about them than you do?
- How will you have the time to add one more thing to the already crowded school day?

Suddenly you realize the principal is continuing to talk. You stop worrying and start listening again.

> . . . and we want to do this right. At first we will have ten computers in the computer lab and four computers on rolling stands for you to take into your classrooms. There's a great deal of controversy about the role of computers in education today and there are many unanswered questions. Here are a few: Do we need to teach all our students to write programs for computers, or do they need only to know how to use programs written by others? How will computers improve our teaching? How can we use them in math, English, science, music, and other subjects? Our goal will be to integrate the computer into our classes, but only where there is a good reason to do so . . . only where the computer will help us do something new or do something better.

We'll spend a large part of this year learning to use computers ourselves and teaching each other. We'll start at next week's meeting. Between now and then, I'd like each of us to read about educational uses of computers, talk to other teachers and students, and visit some other schools that are already using computers. In addition, you might want to visit a computer store and interview people who use computers in business or at home. I'd like each of you to come to the next meeting prepared to discuss some ways computers might be used in our school.

As you listen, you feel your level of anxiety decrease and your level of excitement and anticipation rise. The reading, interviewing, and visiting sound interesting. You accept the fact that the computers are coming; you feel you will be ready for them.

## LEARNING ACTIVITY 1.2

In many ways this is a chapter about the future, not the present. Most schools today do not use computers extensively because there are very few computers in the schools, and certainly not enough to provide one computer for each classroom. This condition is, however, changing rapidly: the percentage of U.S. high schools with at least one computer increased from 43 percent to 86 percent from 1981 to 1983.[1] If this trend continues, many classrooms will have computers in the next decade and many teachers will use computers in their own instruction and teach their students to use them.

There are at least three reasons for this rapid change. First, computers have become essential elements in our society because they do so many things so quickly and so accurately. Second, the cost and size of computers have decreased dramatically during the last few years. A computer that fits on a small desk and costs less than $500 today would have occupied an entire office and cost $40,000 twenty years ago. Third, our vision of how computers can be used has expanded; we now use them in many ways that were unanticipated two decades ago.

How can computers be used in classrooms? Taylor has suggested they can be used in three general ways: as *tools, tutors,* and *tutees.*[2] We can use computers as *tools* for thinking and problem solving, in much the same way we use paper, pencils, typewriters, and calculators as tools. In this sense, a computer is just one more tool, although an extremely powerful one, to help us write, plan, calculate, draw, design, and store and analyze information. Computers can also be used as *tutors* to teach us skills and concepts. The computer is an infinitely patient tutor that can help us learn facts and understand concepts. In order to use a computer as either a tool or a tutor, we need *software* prepared by others. For example, to use a computer as a writing tool, we need a type of software called a *word processing program.* In order to use a computer as a tutor for math, we need software that will present demonstrations and problems and analyze our work and our answers. Today, most educational software comes on 5¼-inch diskettes (often called floppy disks). These diskettes are inserted in the computer to direct it to perform different operations. Inserting different diskettes with different software into a computer is comparable to playing different records on a phonograph. Thus, by using different software, we can get a single computer to help us do many different things and teach us many different subjects.

The third way we can use a computer in a classroom is to make it our *tutee* or student. In other words, in this mode, we teach the computer to do something new. We do this by *programming* the computer and teaching it to perform some procedure or task we want it to do. For example, you might write a program to use a computer to help you keep records about your class, or a student might write a program to solve certain types of math problems. In this third mode, you or your students have direct control over the computer because you write the programs that direct the computer to do the tasks you want done.

## LEARNING ACTIVITY 1.3

The idea that computers can be used as tools, tutors, and tutees is a helpful generalization to remind you that there are many different ways that computers can be used in education. Let's imagine that you are the teacher who attended the faculty meeting described at the beginning of this section. During the year you have the opportunity to visit schools in which computers are being used. Here are some of the applications you might see as you observe and talk to teachers and students in different schools.

**FIGURE 10.1**

In a kindergarten, a computer sits on a small low table at the side of the room as shown on p. 405. Students go to the computer individually for about 15 minutes each day. They work a program that familiarizes them with the keyboard and gives them practice recognizing letters of the alphabet. One student is working attentively at the computer and laughing. You ask her what she is doing and she explains it this way.

That's Stickybear. [She points to the cartoon character on the screen.] I push the keys to get him to do different things. I'll push the key with the "C" on it. Watch. He cries and shows me the word "cry." I'll push "B." See, a bee flies around him. Now if I push "K," he'll give me a kiss.

**FIGURE 10.2**  Stickybear ABC Program from Xerox Education Publications.

Your next visit is to a fourth grade classroom. Here the computer is at the front of the room and the screen is turned toward the class so that everyone can see it. The teacher is using the computer as a teaching aid and demonstration for a classroom presentation on writing.

**FIGURE 10.3**   Using the computer as a teaching aid.

The students generate ideas and sentences for a story. The teacher types these into the computer and they appear on the screen for the class to see. The computer software for this lesson is a *word processing program* that allows the teacher and students to edit, correct, and rearrange sentences and paragraphs easily. The teacher describes her use of the computer this way:

> We call this our newsroom period. We write a news story together. It's usually about something that has happened here at school or on a field trip. We write one story every day. I ask different students to start the story, add the next sentence, and suggest revisions. As they tell the story, I type it and it appears on the screen where the students can see it. With the word processing program in the computer, we can move sentences around, correct spelling, insert phrases, and delete the parts we want to eliminate. When we have a fairly good draft of the story, we stop and save it. That's the end of the class part of the lesson. Then I select two students to be the editors for the day. Later in the day, they work on the computer by themselves, editing and polishing the story. When they are satisfied with it, they have the computer print it in a narrow column format with the right margin justified so it will look like a column in a newspaper. At the end of each week, we have five stories. Then the editors for that week get together and paste up a newspaper and put illustrations in it. We make copies of it and each student gets a copy to take home. The parents love to hear what's going on at school. And the students are learning a lot about using a computer as a word processor. More importantly, they are learning that writing is useful and enjoyable.

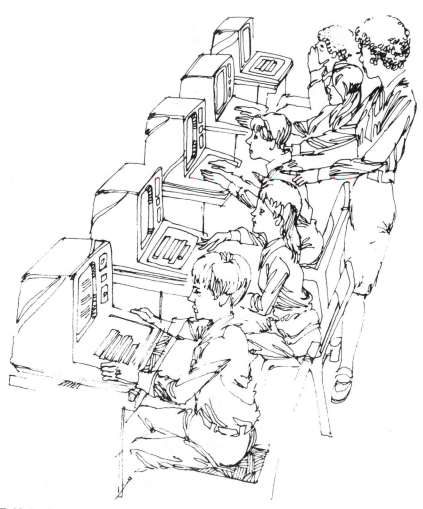

**FIGURE 10.4**   A computer lab.

Your next visit takes you to a middle school. Here fifteen computers are placed in a computer lab. In the morning the lab is used as a computer classroom, where students and teachers meet in class groups to study computer programming. In the afternoon the lab becomes a computer center for individual work. Students go to the lab from their classrooms and study halls just as they would to the library.

You arrive to observe a morning computer programming class. The class is studying Logo, a general purpose computer language that students use to instruct a computer to perform many different tasks such as drawing, designing, solving math problems, and writing poetry. At the beginning of the class, the teacher talks to the entire group for about ten minutes about a new Logo command, REPEAT. To demonstrate the command, she types a program on the computer and has the students watch the results. She answers questions about the command and asks if there is a volunteer who would like to try using the REPEAT command to demonstrate it for the class. Almost everyone volunteers. She chooses one student, who uses the command to produce an interesting design on the screen. When the teacher ends the group presentation, the students begin to work in pairs at the computers. They have their own projects and are quickly absorbed in them. The teacher walks around the lab, answering questions, providing information as needed, and observing student progress. Students are using their knowledge of a programming language to write programs that will instruct the computer to do different things. One student is working on a program that will direct the computer to draw shapes of varying sizes with different numbers of equal sides such as squares, pentagons, and hexagons. Another student is designing a word game. A third is writing a program to help her with math problems. A fourth uses the new REPEAT command to draw the design shown in Figure 10.5.

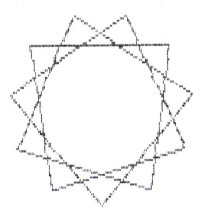

**FIGURE 10.5**  A Logo design.

Your next visit takes you to a high school science class where computers are being used as tools to collect data about experiments. The teacher has obtained a number of instruments that connect the computer to various measuring devices. Using these instruments, the computer reads, records, and analyzes the results of the students' experiments; for example, one instrument measures temperature, and another measures length. Students in the physics lab are using these instruments to study the expansion and contraction of metals as a function of temperature. As the metals are heated and cooled, the instruments read temperature and length, the data are transmitted to the computer, and the computer stores these data and presents them on the screen. The students observe the relationship between changes in temperature and length and use the computer to process the data and present them in graphic and mathematical forms.

Your final visit on the tour takes you to a teacher who is working at a computer by herself — with no students involved. She explains what she is doing this way:

> The computer has really made my work a lot easier. I use a word processing program to prepare all my course materials: lesson plans, handouts, and tests. I save time because it is so easy to revise and improve them. I use other software programs to make up special exercises. For example, one program creates crossword puzzles; I just type in words and definitions; the program arranges the words in a crossword puzzle format and prints out the blank puzzle with the clues ready for me to give to students. I also use a grade book software program. I enter all the students' names at the beginning of the year and then enter their grades for each assignment as I grade it. The computer keeps the record, automatically adds and averages grades, and prints out a complete record of individual and class performance, test scores, grades, and attendance.

In your tour of classes and schools, you have seen computers used in many different ways to achieve many different educational objectives. You have also seen computers in use by students at different grade levels from kindergarten to high school. The tour has illustrated the variety of ways computers can be arranged and used in schools: a single computer in a classroom used by one student at a time; groups of students using a single computer in a classroom; a teacher using a computer to demonstrate concepts to a class; students with access to multiple computers in a computer lab; single computers used to help with science experiments in a science lab. You have seen computers applied to many different objectives:

- Learning the alphabet.
- Writing and editing a newspaper.
- Programming a computer to draw designs.
- Measuring the results of science experiments.
- Designing lesson plans, tests, and class materials.
- Keeping class records.

If you continued the tour through more schools (and into the future), you would realize that you had seen only a few of the ways computers can be used in classroom applications.

# Mastery Test

## OBJECTIVE 1   To describe different ways computers can be used in classrooms.

1. Describe three general ways that computers can be used in classrooms, and give an example of each type of use.

(a) _____

_____

_____

(b) _____

_____

_____

(c) _____

_____

_____

2. Someone says to you, "Computers have little use in education. They can only do routine things like drill and practice in arithmetic." Write a response that would give the person some additional information about the usefulness of computers in schools.

_____

_____

_____

_____

_____

_____

_____

# ANSWER KEY

## Mastery Test, Objective 1

1. In any order: tutor, tool, tutee. Some typical examples are:

*Tutor:* Students use a computer for practice in alphabet recognition, typing skills, math concepts, spelling, or vocabulary.

*Tool:* Students use a computer as a word processor for writing or as an instrument for collecting and analyzing data from science experiments.

*Tutee:* Students program computers to perform specific tasks such as solving math problems and drawing designs.

2. Your answer might include these points:

(a) The computer certainly is good for drill and practice because it is so patient and can work with individual students on specific needs.

(b) However, computers can be used in many other ways: for demonstrations, learning of concepts, writing, math, science, language arts, history, art, and so on.

(c) The computer is new in education, and many innovative applications will be developed in the future.

(d) The computer is so important in our world that students need to learn to use it as a tool for thinking, decision making, and work.

# Objective 2

To introduce students to computer systems and their components.

When you begin to use computers in your classroom, one of your objectives will be to familiarize your students with the computer and with the function of the various parts of the computer system. Students will want to know, "What is that for?" and "How do I use it?" They will also be eager to try the computer themselves.

There are many different types of computers. Each is different in detail but similar in general operation. Your objective will be to teach your students both the specific procedures and the general ones so that they can use the classroom computer and transfer their skills to other computers later.

## LEARNING ACTIVITY 2.1

Imagine that you are planning to introduce your class to a computer for the first time. Some of the students have never used a computer before. You have connected the computer, and it is set up at the front of the room. You conduct the class this way:

> *You:* Here's our new computer. What do you want to know about it?
>
> *Students:* What's it for?
>
> What are we going to do with it?
>
> How do we work it?
>
> Can we use it now?
>
> *You:* Good questions. You want to know what we're going to use it for and how to use it. Those will be our objectives today. What do you think you can use a computer for?
>
> *Students:* To do math.
>
> To teach us.
>
> Play games.
>
> To write on.
>
> Draw picture.
>
> Help us think.
>
> My mother uses one at work.
>
> *You:* What does she use it for?
>
> *Student:* I don't know.
>
> *You:* Can you ask her and tell us tomorrow?
>
> *Student:* Sure.
>
> *You:* You know a lot of different ways we can use a computer. Now, let's see if we can learn what the parts of the computer are used for.

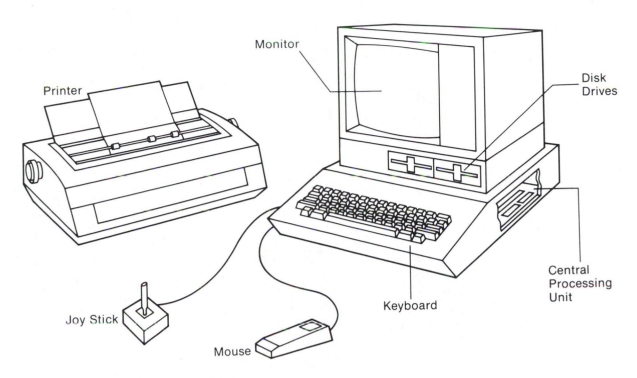

**FIGURE 10.6**   A microcomputer system.

Here's a drawing with the names of the parts of the computer system: the keyboard, central processing unit (CPU) and memory, the monitor screen, the disk drive, printer, joy stick, and mouse. This equipment is called the *hardware*. The diskette, which looks something like a small phonograph record, contains the *software*. In one way, a computer is like a phonograph. A phonograph isn't of much use without records; similarly, a computer isn't of much use without software.

*Student:* Do you have different software diskettes so the computer can do different things?

*You:* That's exactly right. I have two different diskettes here. Let me show you how the diskettes make the computer do different things. Watch me carefully and see if you can discover what each part of the computer does. I'll go step by step.

1. Hold the diskette carefully with your thumb on the label, put it into the disk drive, and close the drive door.

**FIGURE 10.7**   Inserting a diskette into a disk drive.

2. Turn on the computer and the monitor.

3. The warning light on the disk drive comes on, showing that the disk drive is operating. The software program on the diskette is transferred to the working memory of the computer. Do not open the disk drive or remove the diskette when the warning light is on because you will damage the diskette.

4. The software program is now loaded into the computer's memory and ready to use.

*You:* Terry, will you work the computer for us?
*Terry:* I don't know how.
*You:* I'll help you. We'll all help you.
*Terry:* Do I need to know how to type?
*You:* No. If you know touch typing, that makes it easier, but you can look for the letters and keys you need.

Terry works the computer and the class watches and helps. The program presents some math problems in the form of a game. Soon the class begins to call out answers and Terry types them. Both Terry and the class seem to enjoy themselves. After about ten minutes, you interrupt the activity.

> *You:* Now let's load another program and get the computer to do something else. This is a word processing program.

You load the second diskette, repeating the steps for the class. You ask students to tell you the names of their favorite musicians. As they tell you, you type the information, and the students see their list develop on the screen. You show the students a few of the advantages of a word processing program such as the ease of correcting mistakes, moving words and sentences, and reforming the arrangement of material on a page. You also show them how you can use the keyboard, joy stick, or mouse to move the marker (called the cursor) around the screen to place words at different locations. After all the names are listed, you continue the lesson.

> *You:* Now let me show you some other things about the computer. Our list of names is on the screen and also in the memory of the computer, but if we turn the computer off, the list will be lost. The memory is cleared whenever the computer is turned off. However, we can save our list for future use by transferring it to a diskette. Here is a blank file diskette. Just before class I had the computer *format* or *initialize* it so the diskette would be organized to accept and store information. Now I'll save the list on the file diskette. Notice the light on the disk drive comes on while the computer is recording the file on the disk. Our list is now on the diskette and we can load it into the computer tomorrow or any later time to add to it or revise it. Now we can do something else. We can print our list on the printer. Let me show you that. I'll type a command that tells the computer to run the printer and print our list. Watch what happens. (The printer prints the list.)
>
> *You:* O.K. You've seen the computer work. Let's talk about what you observed. What questions do you have?
>
> *Student:* When can we use it?
>
> *You:* Here's one plan. Tomorrow I'll teach two of you to do what I did today. Then, the next day, those two students will each teach two more. We'll continue that way and, in less than a week, everyone will know how to use the computer. Then I'll ask you to sign up to use the computer for thirty minutes a week. While you're using it, the rest of the class will continue with the regular lesson. Each of you will have a partner who will be responsible for making sure you understand what the class is doing while you are working on the computer. For the first month, our objective will be to familiarize you with the computer and help you to become more comfortable using it. After that, we will start using it in our writing and math classes. Are there other questions?
>
> *Student:* Can we hurt it?
>
> *You:* Not unless you're rough and careless. A computer is a piece of fine equipment that could be hurt if you dropped it or mishandled it. We also need to make sure it's away from the dust of the chalkboard. Handle the diskettes carefully too, and make sure you don't touch them through the openings in the protective covers. If you follow those guidelines, you won't hurt anything. You can't break the computer by typing the wrong thing or pushing the wrong keys. Sometimes, if you type the wrong thing, the computer won't understand and will wait for you to try again.
>
> *Student:* What are all those other keys on the keyboard for?

*You:* We'll find that out as we go along. Let me ask you a question. What do you think the keyboard is for?

*Student:* Typing.

*You:* Yes. But when you type, what happens?

*Student:* What you type appears on the screen.

*You:* Right. But what are you doing to the computer when you type?

*Student:* You're telling it what to do.

*You:* Right. You're telling the computer what to do. We call the keyboard an *input device* because it sends information and instructions into the computer. The mouse and the joy stick are also input devices. Did we use any other input device today?

*Student:* We sent information that was on the diskette into the computer from the disk drive.

*You:* Great. The disk drive is also an input device. We call other parts of the computer *output devices*. The computer sends information to them. We've used three output devices today. Can you identify them?

*Student:* The printer.

*Student:* The disk drive. We put the list of our favorite musicians on the diskette to save it.

*You:* Right. The disk drive is both an input and output device. And the third? . . . Well, the monitor is an output device. The computer takes the signal we type, processes it, and displays it on the screen. So the monitor screen is also an output device.

*Student:* Where is the real computer if all those things are input and output devices?

*You:* Great question. The computer is inside. Let me take the cover off and show you the parts.

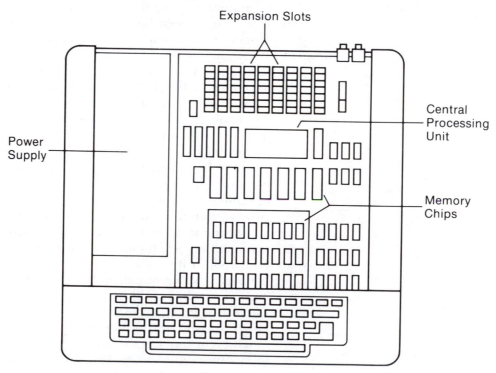

**FIGURE 10.8** Inside a typical microcomputer

The main parts of the computer are units called *chips*. The large chip is the *Central Processing Unit* or *CPU*. It does all the computing. The smaller chips are memory chips.

Student: It's so empty inside. The real computer is a lot smaller than I thought it would be.

You: Computers used to be much larger. But now one chip contains tens of thousands of transistors and circuits.

Student: How do they make them so small?

You: That's a good question. Who would like to look that up and tell the class how these chips are made?

Student: I'll try.

You: Good. Thanks for volunteering. Tomorrow I'll work with you and teach you to operate the computer, and you can teach two others. By the end of the week we should all be able to operate this computer.

# Mastery Test

## OBJECTIVE 2     To introduce students to computer systems and their components.

1. Label the diagram in Figure 10.9 to identify the following components of a microcomputer system.

   Monitor
   Keyboard
   Disk drive
   Printer
   CPU (Central Processing Unit)
   Joy stick
   Mouse

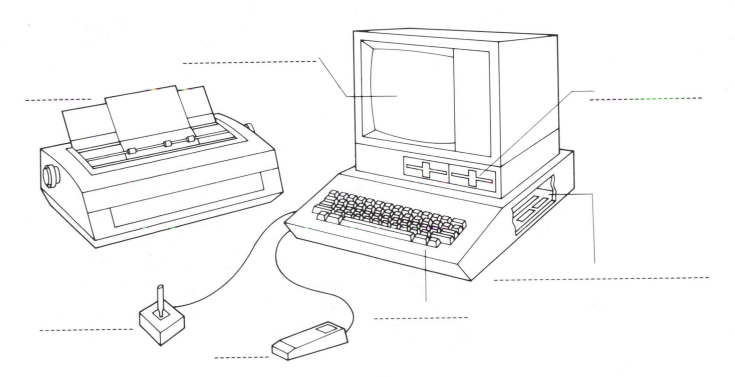

**FIGURE 10.9**

2. You are preparing an initial lesson for your class to demonstrate and explain how a microcomputer works. You plan to begin by asking students to observe you carefully as you use the computer and try to discover the purpose of each part. At the end of the lesson, you plan to summarize by asking them to describe what they think each part is used for. List the concepts you want them to know about each component.

Keyboard _____

Monitor _____

CPU _____

Disk drive _____

Diskette _____

Printer _____

# ANSWER KEY

Mastery Test, Objective 2

1.

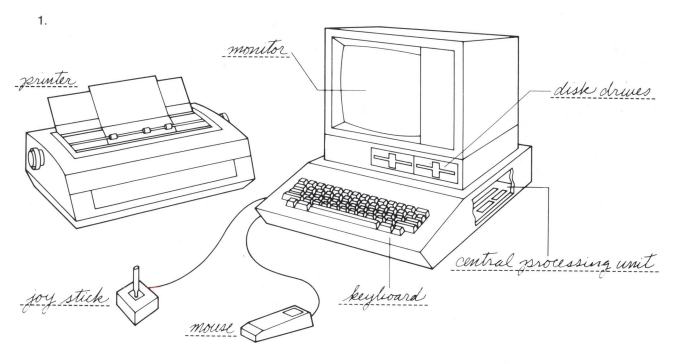

**FIGURE 10.10** A microcomputer system.

2. These are some of the concepts you might want your students to know:

Keyboard: an input device used for entering information into the computer.

Monitor: An output device used to present information on a screen.

CPU: The central processing unit of the computer that calculates and processes data.

Disk drive: An input device that reads diskettes to put information into the computer and an output device that saves information on diskettes.

Diskette: Contains software; a storage place; the place information and programs are stored and saved.

Printer: An output device that produces a printed copy.

# Objective 3

To describe strategies for helping students operate computers without fear and anxiety.

## LEARNING ACTIVITY 3.1

Teachers and students sometimes avoid computers because of fear. A common fear we have when we try something new is the fear of embarrassment: we are afraid that we will make a mistake and that other people will notice our mistake, laugh at us, and think that we are incompetent. Many of us are afraid of computers for this reason. Computers are new and unfamiliar to us; we know we will make mistakes when we start to use them. We therefore stay away from computers and never put ourselves in a position where we can make a mistake. This may be a safe solution, but it is also a limiting one. If we overemphasize the cost of mistakes and embarrassment, we will seldom try anything new.

Mistakes will happen when you work with a computer. There is even a special name for them: *bugs.* When a computer program doesn't work the way you want it to, you say it has a bug in it. *Debugging* is the process of reviewing, revising, and correcting bugs so that a program will work properly.

There are many exact procedures you must follow in working with a computer because the computer understands commands only if they are in the exact form it has been programmed to receive. For example, if the correct form of a command is

```
PRINT "LIST.2
```

the computer will not understand if you type any of these commands:

```
PRINT LIST.2     (No quotation mark before LIST.)
PRINT"LIST.2     (No space before the quotation mark.)
PRINT "LIST . 2  (Too many spaces around the period.)
```

If you type one of these variations by accident, no damage will be done; the computer will simply send a message such as

```
I DON'T RECOGNIZE THE COMMAND PRINT LIST.2
```

or

```
SYNTAX ERROR
```

Then the computer will patiently wait for you to notice the problem and type the command in the exact form it understands. The computer is extremely patient and doesn't criticize you when you make a mistake; it simply tells you it doesn't understand and waits for your next message.

As this example shows, it is easy to make mistakes working with a computer. Everyone makes them, even experts. Most of the time the mistakes are easily corrected and do no damage. Although the computer requires exact instruction, you don't have to feel inadequate if you make mistakes. You have lots of company.

## LEARNING ACTIVITY 3.2

Probably the best thing you can do as a teacher to help your students overcome their fear of being embarrassed about making mistakes on the computer is to make some mistakes yourself and demonstrate how to deal with them. Here is the way an ineffective teacher might deal with mistakes. Later we'll see how an effective teacher would deal with them.

**Ineffective Teacher.**   While working with a computer, the teacher makes a mistake. He thinks to himself:

> Oh, that was dumb. I made a mistake and all the students saw me do it. It's awful. They will lose respect for me and think I don't know what I'm doing. I'll have to hide the mistake so I won't be embarrassed.

The teacher says this to the students:

> This computer isn't working right today. Let's stop using it now. Get out your workbooks and start on page 76.

**Effective Teacher.**   While working with a computer, the teacher makes a mistake. He thinks to himself:

> O.K., I just made a mistake. That's O.K. Mistakes aren't awful. Sometimes they are inconvenient, but they are often good opportunities to learn. Let me see what I can learn from this one.

The teacher says this to the students:

*Teacher:*  I just made a mistake. Hmmm. I wonder what I did wrong. Can any of you help me?
*Student:*  You left out the period in the command.
*Teacher:*  That's right. I did. What can I learn from that?
*Student:*  The computer is dumb in the sense that it can understand commands in only one form.
*Student:*  It can't read your mind and tell what you want it to do.
*Student:*  You have to type things exactly right.
*Teacher:*  Good. Did my mistake hurt anything?
*Student:*  No. Just type it again with the period.
*Teacher:*  So mistakes don't hurt us. In fact, they often give us an opportunity to learn.

The ineffective teacher was embarrassed by his mistake and tried to hide it. Students in his class, following his model, are probably embarrassed to admit mistakes and to learn from them. In contrast, the effective teacher accepted his mistake and took the opportunity to show his class what could be learned from it. Probably the best way to reduce your students' feelings of fear and anxiety about working with computers is to model the effective teacher's thoughts and actions and demonstrate to your class that mistakes are not embarrassing, but rather a natural part of learning.

## LEARNING ACTIVITY 3.3

There are some common computer problems that are annoying and frustrating to students. You can spend a few minutes warning students about them.

1. Diskettes can be damaged by careless handling. When this happens, the programs and information on them can no longer be used. To prevent this, students should follow these two procedures:

    (a) Handle the diskettes only by their protective covers and never touch the actual diskettes through the holes in the covers.

    (b) Never remove a diskette from the disk drive while the drive is running and the drive light is on. This can damage the diskette and make it unusable.

2. While you are working with the computer, the current information is stored in the computer's *Random Access Memory* or *RAM*. If the computer is turned off inadvertently or the power fails, even momentarily, the information will be lost. The solution to this problem is to save your work on your file diskette at frequent intervals, about every fifteen minutes, even if you have not completed a task. Then, if a power failure does occur, most of the information you have been working with will be saved on the diskette and can be reloaded into the computer.

3. Almost everyone who works with microcomputers has at some time erased something from a file diskette by accident or damaged a diskette so that it could no longer be used. If this happens, much work may be lost. The solution is to make a second *backup* copy of your file diskette and keep the copy in a safe place. Then if an accident does occur, you can retrieve the information from the backup copy. Most careful users of computers make backup copies of all their important work at the end of each session at the computer.

# Mastery Test

**OBJECTIVE 3**   To describe strategies for helping students operate computers without fear and anxiety.

1. Describe how you would answer a student who says: "I don't want to use the computer. I'm afraid I might break or damage something."

_____

_____

2. What general strategy can a teacher use to reduce students' anxiety about using computers?

_____

_____

_____

_____

3. You realize you have made a mistake while showing a group of students some procedure for the computer. Describe the best way to handle the situation.

_____

_____

_____

_____

4. What is an easily damaged part of a computer system? How do you prevent damage to it?

_____

_____

_____

5. What happens to the information in a computer's Random Access Memory (RAM) if the power fails or the computer is turned off accidentally?

_____

6. What can you do to prevent the loss of your work?

_____

# ANSWER KEY

## Mastery Test, Objective 3

1. You might say something like this to the student: "If you use reasonable care, you won't damage it. Nothing you type will hurt it. Don't worry about mistakes. We all make them when we are learning new things. Consider mistakes as opportunities to learn something new about computers."

2. Model a positive attitude toward mistakes and refuse to be embarrassed by them. Encourage your students to take the same attitude toward mistakes. Discourage students who make fun of each other's mistakes.

3. Admit the mistake. Indicate you are not embarrassed. Correct the mistake by asking the students to help you. Show that you consider mistakes to be opportunities for learning and a natural part of the learning process.

4. The diskette. Handle the diskette gently by its protective cover; never touch the diskette itself; don't remove a diskette from a disk drive while the drive is running.

5. The information is lost.

6. Save your work on a diskette frequently.

# Objective 4

To describe computer programming.

## LEARNING ACTIVITY 4.1

"I'm not lazy or slow; I just can't do anything until I'm told to do so in a way that I can understand."

If computers could talk, this is probably one of the first things they would say. Such a statement underscores the function of a computer language. It is only through a computer language that a computer receives instructions it can understand. But what is a computer language, and why is it really necessary?

In your study for Objective 2 in this chapter, you learned the various components of a microcomputer. One of the components was the central processing unit, or CPU. The CPU is the element that does all the "computing" in a computer. But the only language it can understand is composed of two words, ON and OFF. These two words are interpreted electrically to mean that an electrical signal is either present or not present in a particular circuit. These two conditions, or *states*, are represented mathematically by the numbers 1 and 0.

In order for a CPU to function, it must receive commands as combinations of 1's and 0's. Needless to say, it is unimaginably difficult for a person to communicate with a computer in such a fashion. Most CPUs are designed to process the 1's and 0's in groups. For example, the CPU in the Apple computer accepts a group of eight 1's and 0's at a time. However, it is still very difficult for us to "talk" to the computer even in groups of 1's and 0's.

What we need is something that allows us to tell the computer "in plain English" what we want it to do, and then to translate our words into the groups of 1's and 0's that the CPU can understand. This is the function of a computer language.

For example, when you tell a computer to print something, the PRINT command of the computer language is translated into a series of 1's and 0's that is received and put into operation by the CPU.

Although individual computer language commands allow us to tell the computer what to do, this is still not very convenient or particularly powerful. It is only when we are able to group these language commands into *programs* that the full power of the computer becomes evident.

There are many different languages available for microcomputers today. The more popular ones in education are BASIC, Logo, and Pascal. Each language has its strengths and weaknesses. Selection of a computer language usually depends on the nature of the task and the availability of the language.

Regardless of the language used, computer programming is seen by many to be an important skill for today's students. Writing effective computer programs demands a logical thought process and seems to help develop the skills of problem solving and decision making. Thus, computer programming is a major focus of the curriculum for many schools, especially high schools.

## LEARNING ACTIVITY 4.2

Let's look briefly at some sample programming tasks and how they might be accomplished using two popular computer languages, BASIC and Logo. This section is not intended to teach you these languages, but to illustrate how they might be used to accomplish simple tasks.

One task to be accomplished is that of accepting two numbers, multiplying them, and displaying the result. Since the task is well defined, we can use a general problem-solving scheme of breaking the task down into smaller subtasks and accomplishing them one at a time. An outline is helpful in this process.

1. Ask for the two numbers.
2. Accept the first number.
3. Accept the second number.
4. Multiply the numbers together.
5. Display the result.

Here is a BASIC program that accomplishes the specified task. Notice how it follows the outline above.

```
10 REM MULTIPLY TWO NUMBERS
20 PRINT "ENTER TWO NUMBERS"
30 INPUT N1
40 INPUT N2
50 LET PR = N1 * N2
60 PRINT PR
70 END
```

Line 10 contains the command REM. This stands for remark, and allows the programmer to include explanations in the program to make it easy to read. Line 20 asks the program user to ENTER TWO NUMBERS. Lines 30 and 40 accept the numbers, calling them N1 and N2 respectively. Line 50 multiplies the numbers together and calls the product PR. The asterisk (*) is used to tell the computer to multiply the two numbers together. Line 60 prints PR, the product of the two numbers. Line 70 indicates the end of the program.

Here is a Logo program that accomplishes the same task. A short Logo program like this is called a *procedure*.

```
TO MULTIPLY.TWO.NUMBERS
PRINT [ENTER TWO NUMBERS]
MAKE "NUMBER1 READWORD
MAKE "NUMBER2 READWORD
MAKE "PRODUCT :NUMBER1 * :NUMBER2
PRINT :PRODUCT
END
```

The word TO indicates that the instructions following it make up a Logo procedure. The name of the procedure, MULTIPLY.TWO.NUMBERS, provides the information about its function. The first line of the procedure asks the user to ENTER TWO NUMBERS. Each READWORD command in the next line accepts a number. The PRINT command prints the result of the first number accepted times the second number accepted. The command END indicates the end of the procedure.

Another programming task is to draw a square on the computer screen. The Logo language is especially suited for this purpose because of its easy-to-use style of graphics. Logo uses a triangular marker called the *turtle* to draw on the screen. The turtle moves about the screen in much the same fashion that you move; that is, you walk FORWARD in the direction you are heading, and you turn LEFT or RIGHT to change your direction. Here is a Logo procedure to draw a square.

```
TO SQUARE
REPEAT 4 [FORWARD 100 RIGHT 90]
END
```

The form of the SQUARE procedure is the same as that of MULTIPLY.TWO.NUMBERS above. Here the statement REPEAT 4 [FORWARD 100 RIGHT 90] tells the turtle to REPEAT 4 times the following instructions: move FORWARD 100 "steps" straight ahead and then turn RIGHT 90 degrees. These correspond to the same instructions you would use to tell a person to walk in a path with the shape of a square.

**FIGURE 10.11**

In contrast, the BASIC language usually needs Cartesian coordinates (horizontal and vertical distances to particular locations) to identify the beginning and ending points of graphics lines. Here is a program to draw a square in Applesoft BASIC, the language provided with the Apple computer.

```
10 REM DRAW A SQUARE
20 HGR
30 HPLOT 0,0 TO 0,100 TO 100,100 TO 100,0 TO 0,0
30 END
```

In comparing the two languages as shown in this section, you can detect certain similarities and differences. Regardless of the computer language you are using, learning to write programs in any computer language enables you to communicate with the computer, as you tell it what to do in ways it can understand.

## LEARNING ACTIVITY 4.3

Just as style is important in writing, so is style important in programming. In order for a computer program to function properly, it must be technically and logically correct. In most instances the outcome of the program demonstrates whether it functions as you intended or not.

For example, let's say you have written a program that accepts two numbers, divides the first by the second, and prints the results. When running the program, you type in 6 for the first number and 2 for the second. The computer prints the answer, 3. Next, you type in 7 for the first number and 0 for the second. Since dividing by 0 is not defined, the computer does not know what to do. It produces an error message, and stops the program. You have encountered a *bug* in the program. In order for the program to function properly, the bug must be eliminated. *Debugging* programs is an important skill, although some computer teachers suggest that, if a computer program is properly planned and written, debugging should not be necessary.

Good programming style goes beyond proper programming function. Is the program organized concisely and efficiently? It is possible to write programs that appear to function properly yet are very slow and poorly organized. A well-organized program proceeds directly from one subtask to the next in a logical manner, taking advantage of the fastest methods for solving a problem.

For example, a program to accept five student grades and then to calculate and display the average grade might use five sets of the same commands to process the five numbers. A more efficient way might be to put the number processing commands into a group and to use the group of commands five times. Such groups of commands are sometimes called *subroutines*.

When a programming task is well defined, as was the multiplication task in the preceding Learning Activity, a *top down* approach is often used to develop the program. With this method the entire task is outlined. Each part of the outline is broken down into smaller and smaller detail until the entire task is described as an outlined series of many small subtasks, each of which can be accomplished by computer commands, operations, or subroutines. In developing the outline, one gains a better understanding of the problem and of the strategy to be used in solving it, before any of the program is written.

There are many ways to develop the outline. One way is to write it as if outlining a composition. Another way is to draw a *flow chart*, to illustrate graphically the sequence of events that produce the desired result. A simple flow chart is shown on p. 427.

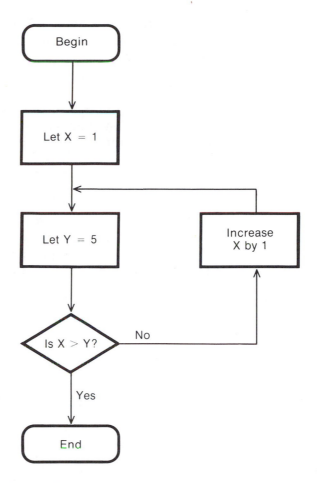

**FIGURE 10.12**   Simple flow chart.

Once the outline is fully developed, the computer program is written to correspond to the various parts, beginning with the main topics.

Sometimes the programming task is not well defined. You may have a vague idea of what you want the program to do, but the exact organization and sequence of events is not firmly fixed in your mind. In such a case you will probably use a *bottom up* programming approach. With this method an outline is helpful but not absolutely necessary. Groups of commands are assembled to perform the subtasks that are identified. These groups are then connected in sequence by other commands. The bottom up approach is characterized by a certain amount of flexibility and sometimes may not produce programs that are as concise and efficient as the top down approach.

Often, neither of these approaches is used in "pure" form; rather, a combination of the two seems to be popular. Sometimes called a "middle out" approach, this combination might consist of a complete outline and the beginnings of a computer program with the main topics, followed by the development of several detailed subtasks, then the commands to connect the two.

Regardless of the approach taken to develop the program, it is important that the program be *readable;* that is, another person should be able to look at the program and understand what you have done. This is accomplished in a variety of ways, including:

1. Organizing the program in a logical manner.
2. Grouping the commands into subroutines clearly.
3. Including in the program labels or remarks that briefly describe the function of each section.

There are a number of reasons you should make your programs readable. A program that is not readable is extremely difficult to debug. As the program author, you must be able to look at the program later and understand what you were doing. You cannot count on being able to remember. In addition, others who use your program may want to look at the commands so that they can learn how you arranged them. Having a readable program will make their work much easier and more enjoyable. Finally, when the program is written and debugged, you have the pleasure of running it and observing its operation. Through the computer language in the program, you tell the computer what you want it to do, and the computer does it.

# Mastery Test

## OBJECTIVE 4    To describe computer programming.

1. Why is a special language needed to tell a computer what to do?

_____

_____

_____

2. Describe a modest programming project you or your students might enjoy.

_____

_____

_____

3. Describe the top down programming approach.

_____

_____

_____

_____

_____

## ANSWER KEY

### Mastery Test, Objective 4

1. A computer language is needed to translate the intentions of the computer user into the groups of 1's and 0's that the computer can understand.
2. Projects might include writing programs to add and subtract various numbers, or to draw various figures, such as triangles and hexagons.

3. The top down programming approach is used when writing a computer program to accomplish a well-defined task. First, a detailed outline is developed. Then the computer program is written in small parts that, when put together in order, correspond directly with the outline.

# Objective 5

To describe the evaluation of software and the use of computers for class presentations, demonstrations, and simulations.

## LEARNING ACTIVITY 5.1

Consider this teaching situation: Mr. Smith, who has a single computer in his classroom, buys a software program called "Our Government." The program consists of pages of text that appear on the screen along with a few multiple-choice questions. The students "turn the pages" by touching keys on the keyboard and answer questions by pressing specified keys. Since only one computer is available, it takes about two weeks for everyone in the class to work the program. When Mr. Smith tries to hold a class discussion about the ideas in the program, many students have forgotten what they read.

This situation illustrates an ineffective use of a computer to teach something that could have been taught more effectively and simply by other methods. When the computer is used for little more than "turning pages," its real potential is wasted. In this particular situation it would have been more effective not to use the computer. Students could have read printed copies of the material. Next, the teacher could have tested them about the relevant concepts and given them feedback about their performance. Then, after only a single day, the entire class would have been prepared for the class discussion.

It is important to remember that a computer provides an additional option for teachers, but it does not replace the other methods the teacher has used in the past. Effective teachers do not use computers simply because they are new and innovative. They use computers for their advantages in teaching certain objectives. Many research studies have shown that moderate improvements in student performance and motivation occur when computers are used as part of a learning environment.[3] Greatest improvement can be expected when instructional objectives are carefully matched to the special capabilities of the computer and the software.

Two examples will illustrate this point. If an objective specifies that students must master facts or skills by repeated practice (e.g., addition, typing, or foreign language vocabulary), the computer can be useful. It is a patient tutor that individualizes practice schedules, encourages students, and makes learning more interesting by providing immediate feedback. On the other hand, if an objective states that students are to deal creatively with a particular content area, the computer can provide the opportunity for students to store information about that area and access it in different ways to provide new insights. For example, a class might create a data base about economic conditions, wars, and inventions during a period of history. They could then use the data base to test hypotheses such as "Periods of economic depression precede wars" or "Wars produce inventions that are later useful in peacetime." Students would use the computer to search the data base for examples that support or contradict these hypotheses. As these examples illustrate, the computer's instructional power will best be utilized when its capabilities and software are carefully matched to instructional objectives.

In this chapter many different applications of computers in education are described. As you read, consider how the special capabilities of computers and the selected software facilitate learning and how they relate to the instructional objectives.

## LEARNING ACTIVITY 5.2

There are thousands of educational software programs on the market today, and thousands more will be available in the future. Although many of these programs are well advertised and attractively packaged, many educators feel that much of the current software is poorly designed from an instructional point of view. For example, some software programs produce much more exciting pictures and sounds for an *incorrect* response than for a correct one. When students work with this software, they sometimes deliberately make mistakes to get the vivid feedback. Other software programs may be poorly designed from a programming point of view. They simply do not run or are so complex to operate that students get lost in the intricacies of the details required to use the program. Finally, the content of programs may be incorrect, incomplete, or inappropriate for a particular student group.

Teachers need to be able to select software wisely. Since software is expensive, mistakes are costly. Most teachers prefer to try a software package themselves if they can get it on an approval basis or borrow it from a software library. By working the program from the point of view of students, teachers can detect bugs and judge the usefulness of the program for their students and their instructional objectives. In doing this, they evaluate the effectiveness of the software in the same way that they would evaluate the effectiveness of any other instructional materials. It is probably wise to keep in mind some general criteria for instructional effectiveness, such as Gagné's Events of Instruction.[4] By using these guidelines while reviewing a software package, the teacher would consider these questions:

Does the program . . .
1. Gain the student's attention?
2. Clearly tell the student the objectives?
3. Recall prerequisite learning for the student?
4. Present the instructional materials effectively?
5. Provide learning guidance?
6. Elicit relevant performance from the student?

7. Provide feedback to the student about performance?
8. Assess performance?
9. Enhance the student's retention and transfer?

Since there are so many different software packages to choose from, teachers need some way to narrow their choices before they actually evaluate programs themselves. Fortunately, there are a number of different sources of evaluative reviews of educational software available; for example, EPIE (Educational Products Information Exchange) publishes continuing reviews of new software and organizes these reviews into different content areas. An hour or so spent with reviews allows the teacher to narrow the choices and select one or two programs to review personally. Since software reviews are such an important source of information for teachers, a list of sources of reviews is included in the reference section at the end of this chapter.

The evaluation process helps focus attention on both the learning objectives and the software being evaluated. In the following activities you will read about computers being used in various ways. Keep in mind that the programs used must be appropriate for the objectives and the methodology.

## LEARNING ACTIVITY 5.3

A computer can be used for class presentations as an electronic blackboard. To do this, it is necessary to arrange the computer monitor so that everyone can see it. This can be done in several ways: (1) by having a small group of students view a single monitor, (2) by connecting multiple monitors to the computer and placing them at different locations in the classroom, or (3) by using a video projector to show the computer output on a large screen at the front of the class.

In one application Mrs. Humphreys prepared charts on a computer using a graphics software program. In class she used a computer with two monitors to display the charts at appropriate times during the lesson. In response to student questions, she used the computer to draw new charts that appeared immediately on the monitors for the class to see. This use of a computer as an electronic blackboard provides a convenient way for teachers to present visual and text materials to a class and to show illustrations that would be too complex and time-consuming to draw on a regular blackboard or overhead projector. More importantly the computer materials can be revised easily in response to student questions.

The computer can be used creatively for classroom presentations by taking advantage of its unique capabilities to demonstrate concepts that would be difficult to present in other ways. For example, students in a math class could write algebraic equations and enter them in the computer. The computer would present drawings of the curves generated by the equations. In another application, a teacher could run a simulation program for the entire class and use the computer to analyze the results of the class's decisions. The simulation can be run again and again to give the class experience with the situation and the variables that affect it. For example, the class might work with an environmental simulation in which students could make decisions about the cost and benefits of various pollution control programs. As the instructor enters decisions in the computer, the students watch the results, noting the effects of their decisions on the simulated environment and economy. In some cases their decisions produce a serious depression with extensive unemployment because they have required too much investment in pollution equipment; in other cases, pollution gets out of control and the environment is damaged. As they work with the simulation, the students become aware of the balance between costs and benefits in social and economic settings.

## LEARNING ACTIVITY 5.4

Imagine that you visit a high school and observe a history class. The teacher has checked out a computer from the audiovisual office and brought it into the classroom for a special project. The class is working together on a computer simulation that asks the students to imagine that they are living in the 1800s and are leading a wagon train of settlers west across the United States. The students must decide how to spend their initial funds on food, oxen, wagons, weapons, ammunition, and other supplies. After the decisions made by the class are entered in the computer, the expedition begins. The computer presents events that simulate the actual events faced by pioneers such as floods, droughts, enemy attacks, and illness. As each event is presented, the class must decide how to respond to it and how to expend their resources to meet it. These decisions are entered in the computer, which reports the results and the new condition of the wagon train.

As you watch the students work with the simulation for the first time, you observe that they exhaust their supplies and equipment too early and the expedition fails. The pioneers die in a snowstorm on a mountain pass. The students review the decisions that led to the disaster and discuss some new strategies that they could use. On the second attempt, they modify their initial decisions about how to use their funds and change the way they react to events. Once again, however, the simulated expedition fails. The class begins to question the computer simulation: "Things couldn't have been that bad." "It couldn't have been that difficult to make the trip." The teacher suggests that the students find out more about the difficulty of the journey.

In class the following day, the students report their findings and share their surprise about the hardships of the journey and the low rate of success. Deciding that the computer simulation is reasonably realistic, they begin a third time to plan and carry out an expedition. Sometimes they seem involved in the simulation simply as a game they want to win. When this happens, the teacher asks questions that lead them to think about the kinds of decisions they are making, the kinds of events they can plan for, and the kind of events that are unpredictable. In a structured way she asks them to think about their thinking.

As the students continue with the simulation, they begin to experience success, and more of the wagon trains reach the final destination. One student, who has become intrigued by the historical period depicted in the simulation, observes that the class's experience matches the pioneers' actual experience: they, too, became more successful over time because the later wagon trains learned from the mistakes of the earlier groups.

## LEARNING OBJECTIVE 5.5

Simulations can be used not only by an entire class but also by small groups and individuals. Here is an example. Ms. Wright's physics students had been studying various aspects of motion, including acceleration, velocity, and movement in one and two dimensions. The usual lectures and laboratory activities had been completed. Now Ms. Wright wanted a final activity that would help her students "put it all together." She decided to use the Logo programming language to simulate the movement of an object in a frictionless environment (e.g., a rocket ship in deep space). Since none of her students had ever experienced such an environment, she hoped that an activity with it would give them more of a basis for an intuitive understanding of the concepts they had just finished studying.

Ms. Wright found a Logo program that converts the Logo *turtle* into a "dynaturtle," which behaves much like a rocket in outer space. It is propelled by brief thrusts in the direction it faces; however, it can be turned to face any direction as it moves.

After properly introducing the activity, Ms. Wright asked her students to work in pairs during the next week to explore how to gain control of the dynaturtle. They were surprised to find that it was not easy to make it go where they wanted it to. After a few minutes, however, they began to discover some techniques for controlling its movements. Ms. Wright helped them make the connection between what they were doing with the simulated frictionless environment and the laws of motion they had just studied. She then challenged them to figure out how to make the dynaturtle move in a circular path, in preparation for the next unit.

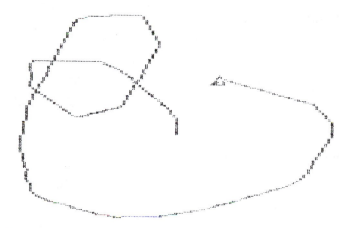

**FIGURE 10.13**   Dynaturtle tracing.

Some of her students knew the Logo language, and they examined the procedures she used to create the simulation. The students made some modifications so that the dynaturtle drew its path in different colors according to how fast it moved across the screen. One advanced student began to work on a program to introduce the effects of gravity into the simulation, to see if the dynaturtle would go into an elliptical orbit around a mass with a large gravitational potential, in the same way that planets orbit around the sun.

A few months later Ms. Wright noticed that her students seemed to have a deeper understanding of motion in a gravitational field and of centripetal force than her students of earlier years. She wondered if the dynaturtle activity had anything to do with it. . . .

By using computer simulations, classes can experience an environment or historical period and become involved in making decisions that affect the outcome of events. In addition, simulations give students the opportunity to practice making decisions in a safe setting where there are no real penalties for mistakes. In the simulated setting the results of decisions are known quickly, and there is the opportunity to profit from the experience and try again.

# Mastery Test

## OBJECTIVE 5
To describe the evaluation of software and the use of computers for class presentations, demonstrations, and simulations.

1. A microcomputer can be used effectively for class presentations, demonstrations, or simulations. Describe an application of this type that you could make in your subject area and grade level. Describe your objective(s), how the computer would be used, how the software would be selected, and why the computer is appropriate.

*Objective(s):*

_____

_____

*How a computer will be used:*

_____

_____

_____

_____

*How the software will be selected:*

_____

_____

_____

_____

_____

*Reasons for using a computer in teaching this objective:*

_____

_____

_____

# ANSWER KEY

Mastery Test, Objective 5

1. Your answer should include your objective(s), the way you would use the computer, how you would select the software, and a rationale for using the computer in preference to other instructional methods. A sample answer follows.

*Objective:* To teach effective sentence construction.

*Use of computer:* The teacher chooses sentences from class papers and enters them in a computer using a word processing program. Some of the sentences are effective; others need improvement. (He chooses at least one type from each student's paper.) Using the computer and a large monitor, he shows a sentence to the class. They decide what type of sentence it is and, if it is ineffective, they suggest revisions. He makes the revisions and the improved sentence appears on the screen.

*Selection of software:* The word processing program selected was recommended by EPIE for class demonstrations because it has the capability to print on the computer screen in large letters, if desired. The most important criterion of the software in this particular teaching situation was that it presents the instructional materials effectively.

*Rationale for using a microcomputer:* Using the computer makes it easy to base lessons on the students' own sentences. The sentences can be entered easily in the computer, stored, and presented. The computer and a word processing program make it possible for the class to make and evaluate alternate revisions.

# Objective 6

To describe the use of computers for individualized instruction.

## LEARNING ACTIVITY 6.1

Many educators feel that the computer is an excellent aid for individual instruction. Computer Assisted Instruction, called CAI for short, is a method in which the computer teaches the individual student. It takes advantage of several strengths of the computer as a medium for the delivery of instruction, including:

1. Speed
2. Patience
3. Individualization
4. Animation, graphics, and text delivery
5. Immediate feedback of results

CAI can be used for drill and practice and as a tutorial.

In drill and practice, the learning objective is the maintenance or mastery of a skill that has already been learned. Drill objectives usually involve associative learning, such as reviewing vocabulary definitions or arithmetic facts. Practice objectives, on the other hand, tend to focus on using procedures such as writing sentences or working arithmetic problems. The essential elements of drill and practice computer programs are the presentation of problems and the evaluation of student responses.

The objective of a tutorial program is to assist the student in learning a new skill; it differs from drill and practice in that it delivers instruction. A typical tutorial program presents information or instruction to the students, asks questions, and then evaluates the responses. Additional information or reinforcement is presented based on the responses. For example, a program to assist a student learning about the Battle of Gettysburg prints some information on the screen, followed by a drawing of the battlefield. Then the student is asked a question based on the information and map. The program evaluates the answer and provides reinforcement or additional information as appropriate.

Although many of the drill and practice and tutorial programs in use are available from commercial vendors, some teachers prefer to develop their own. CAI development systems, such as Pilot, are available to assist teachers in writing tutorials and drill and practice programs for specific classroom situations. Many find that this effort is worthwhile only if the material can be used a number of times; otherwise, the time it takes to develop and test an original program is quite demanding.

Another use of the computer in individualized instruction is called Computer Managed Instruction (CMI). The computer is not necessarily used to deliver instruction; instead, it serves as a record keeper, keeping track of student assessment, feedback, scheduling, and future individualized assignments. With CMI, instructional material is usually divided into modules that can be developed in any format, such as a printed booklet or a laboratory experiment. At the end of each module, the student takes a test that is scored and analyzed by the computer. The results are compared with past performance, and the student receives a computer generated feedback report with suggestions for the next assignment or module. With CMI, the computer takes over much of the routine paper work and record keeping, leaving the teacher more time for conferences with students and individualized instruction with students who are having difficulty.

## LEARNING ACTIVITY 6.2

O.K., everyone, let's settle down and get to work. We can stay in the computer lab only until 10:30. After you have loaded the arithmetic drill program into your computers, type RUN and follow the instructions.

Mr. McDonald has found that his students are having a great deal of difficulty working arithmetic problems such as 12 + 5 * 7. Although they know the rules for precedence of operations, they need more practice with them. His students are willing to work, but the math book has only a few such problems in the chapter. Mr. McDonald has identified a need for more practice, and finds that the computer laboratory has several programs that seem to fill the need. After evaluating them (see Learning Activity 5.2), he finds one designed to give his students the practice they need in an acceptable manner. Since the learning objective is based on practice, the choice of the program is an appropriate one.

A few days later several students approach Mr. McDonald to ask if he will help them write their own practice programs. Three of the students already know BASIC, and four are learning Logo. Mr. McDonald outlines some of the ways drill and practice programs work in enough detail so that the students can begin their program designs.

Mr. McDonald knows that his students will learn much more than just arithmetic by writing and running their own practice programs. They will learn to apply what they have learned about the computer to accomplish their own personal goals.

The next day another group of students comes to Mr. McDonald with an advertisement of a game called *Math Man* (available from Scholastic, Inc.), which has arithmetic exercises similar to those they have been solving. Mr. McDonald is generally reluctant to mix computer games with his instruction, but he sees the potential of this particular game to accomplish his instructional objective. It certainly looks like a more interesting program than the one his students are currently using. He decides to order a copy to evaluate.

## LEARNING ACTIVITY 6.3

When teachers first begin to think about using CAI with their students, they often imagine themselves just placing students in front of computers and leaving them. However, CAI use is much like any other instructional medium; it is necessary for the teacher to pay attention to preparation and objectives, and to maintain an active line of communications with the students. Here is how one teacher used a CAI tutorial in an effective manner.

Mr. Johnson always has to rush at the end of each school year to cover World Wars I and II, and the Korean and Vietnam conflicts in his American History class. This year he decides to use a different teaching strategy . . . one that takes advantage of the computers in his school.

Instead of hurried lectures and frantic tests, he plans to make time available each week for his students to work through tutorial programs on the two World Wars. In this way he might be able to speed the process along a little. He will also be providing more flexibility for students who do not learn as quickly as others.

After carefully introducing the units, he explains to the students that they will be using the World War computer programs in the computer laboratory three times each week, with lectures and other classroom activities on the other two days. Although he did not expect the computers to take over the teaching job completely, several things happen that surprised him.

"Mr. Johnson, would you please explain what the computer says here?"

"Well, Shirley, this paragraph is trying to say that the assassination of the archduke was not necessarily the reason the war began. In a way, it was just the excuse to start it. That is what the computer means by the phrase 'immediate cause' right there. Later in your lesson you will learn some of the underlying causes of the war . . . the real reasons it all began."

"Well, I'm still not sure I understand, but what you said helps."

"Mr. Johnson, there is too much reading. I'm bored."

"With all those airplane drawings you do, James, I expected that you would be interested in learning about how airplanes made such a difference in the war. Have you heard of the Red Baron?"

"You mean this is where the Red Baron fought? Which lesson is that in?"

"Let's see. You are on number 7 now. The aviation information begins to appear in the next four or five lessons. You will begin to see it pretty soon."

"O.K. Thanks!"

"Mr. Johnson, I'm finished."

"Hmmm. You went through those lessons pretty quickly, Laura. Would you like to play this computer game based on what you just learned?"

*(later)*

"Mr. Johnson, may I go through some of the lessons again? I think I went too fast. I forgot some things I need for the game."

"Mr. Johnson, the computer is wrong! Look. See here where it asks for the date of the Pearl Harbor attack? When I put in December 7, 1941, the computer ways 'That is incorrect. The correct date is December 17, 1941.' Why does it do that?"

"I'm not sure, Susan. But, I agree with you that the computer program is wrong."

"I looked up the date in the encyclopedia just to make sure."

"Maybe I'll have our media specialist telephone the company that sold us the program. Perhaps someone there will know what to do."

*(later)*

"Susan, the company said to tell you thanks for showing them where their program was wrong. They sent us a new copy of the corrected program. Would you like to be the first to try it?"

"Mr. Johnson, can Mary, David, and I do an extra credit project?"

"What do you have in mind, Mike?"

"David has a Battle of Midway board game at home that's a lot of fun to play. We would like to write a computer program that lets us play a game like that."

"That's a great idea! Tell me more . . ."

In the final analysis Mr. Johnson's students do not learn much faster than they did with his usual approach, but they seem to be more interested in the information than his classes were in previous years. The combination of class lectures and computer work may be responsible for part of that difference. Mr. Johnson's willingness to try this approach is appreciated by most students. He is now perceived more as a helper and less as an adversary.

## LEARNING ACTIVITY 6.4

Computers can be used effectively with exceptional individuals. In many instances, physical and mental handicaps can be overcome or minimized with a computer.

For example, Jonathan was a fourteen-year-old student who had spastic cerebral palsy and a speech disorder. The muscles of his mouth were partially paralyzed, weak, and uncoordinated. The only sounds he could produce were a few consonants. His self concept was poor, and his writing and spelling were erratic. When he was given access to a computer with a speech synthesizer attached, he quickly learned how to make it talk for him. He used a short Logo program to tell the synthesizer what to say. Soon afterward he delivered his first oral report in class. As a result, his self-image improved dramatically, and his irregular spelling began to stabilize.

Other computer applications include controlling wheelchairs, enlarging text, and stimulating paralyzed leg muscles in sequence to enable walking. The potential of computers and individualized instruction for exceptional individuals is one of the most exciting educational applications of the future.

# Mastery Test

## OBJECTIVE 6    To describe the use of computers for individualized instruction.

1. List two ways that computers can be used for computer assisted instruction (CAI).

   _____

   _____

2. The choice of a drill or a practice CAI program depends on the instructional objectives. In each of the situations below, select either drill or practice as the appropriate software, based on your assessment of the instructional objective.

   _____ (a) Students are having difficulty remembering various parts of speech and their definitions.

   _____ (b) Students know how to work a certain type of word problem in math class but are unsure of themselves.

   _____ (c) Biology students are overwhelmed with the number of muscle names they will need to remember for the final exam.

3. Describe a classroom situation in which a tutorial computer program might be used effectively.

   _____

   _____

   _____

   _____

   _____

4. A student is paralyzed from the neck down but is able to press a switch by a move of the chin. Describe how a computer might benefit this student.

_____

_____

_____

## ANSWER KEY

### Mastery Test, Objective 6

1. Drill and practice, tutorial
2. Skill mastery or maintenance are objectives of both drill programs and practice programs; however, drill programs focus on associative learning, whereas practice programs concentrate on procedures.
    (a) drill
    (b) practice
    (c) drill
3. Since tutorials deliver instruction, they are useful in a variety of situations. For example, in an algebra class, there might be an exceptionally fast learner. A tutorial algebra program would permit this student to work ahead of the class in an individualized manner.
4. The switch could be connected to a computer and used to select answers on a tutorial program or to interact with the computer in many other ways.

# Objective 7

To describe word processing and several educational applications.

There is a package for you in the school office. Opening it, you discover the word processing program that the principal said was coming. The notebook and diskettes seem inviting enough, but questions flood your mind. What can a word processor do that pencil and paper cannot? Why should you invest time learning something new when the old way has worked for a long time? How can you use the word processor in your classes? Is a word processor fun for students to use?

In Section 1 you read about a class that used a word processor program on their computer to produce a newspaper. In this section you will learn more about the specific capabilities of a typical word processor and will consider several additional classroom applications.

## LEARNING ACTIVITY 7.1

Word processors make it possible for you to write and to manage what you write in innovative ways. A word processor can do this because the words you write are not "physical" until they are printed on paper. Instead, what you write is interpreted by the computer as a series of electric and magnetic patterns stored in the computer's memory, on a storage diskette, or perhaps both. The word processor can manipulate these patterns easily, much more easily that you can manipulate words and sentences on pieces of paper.

In general, all actions in word processing can be grouped into the following categories. In order to have a good overview of word processing, it is important for you and your students to know about these categories. Sometimes these categories are called *modes.*

**1. Enter text.**   This refers to the act of writing something into the computer. With most word processors this is accomplished by typing on the keyboard; thus, typing skills are helpful (but not essential) for word processing.

**2. Edit.**   This describes the process of changing anything that has been written previously. Editing tasks can be small or large, depending on the changes being made. For example, it is a small task to change the spelling of a word from "comptuer" to "computer." But to move several paragraphs to new locations is a larger editing task.

**3. Format.**   With a word processor, it is possible to arrange what you write in many configurations, or *formats.* For example, do you want single or double spacing? How wide do you want the side margins? What about the top and bottom margins? Do you want the pages numbered automatically? Some word processors can *justify* what you write, that is, arrange both the left and right vertical edges so they are straight, like the sides of this paragraph. A few word processors can even suggest where hyphens should appear in a justified document.

**4. Store.**   What you write usually can be stored in two ways: on diskette and on paper (sometimes called *hard copy*). Most word processors save what you write by putting it on a file diskette. You need to select a name for each separate document you write and save. (For example, as we prepared this chapter on a word processor, the name used for storing this part of the chapter was called OBJ7, for Objective 7, on our file diskette.) To produce a copy of what you write with a printer, you need to tell your word processor the name of the document to print.

## LEARNING ACTIVITY 7.2

The following modes might suggest some of the things a word processor can do that are not possible with pencil and paper, and give you some ideas for classroom applications. Let's examine some of these modes in more detail.

### Enter Text

To enter text, some word processors require that you specify the document name from the beginning. Others let you begin writing immediately and name the document just before it is stored. Most word processors have what is called *wrap.* This means that, as you finish typing a word near the right side of the screen, it is automatically moved to the next screen line if it is too long. If you have typing experience you know that you must press "carriage return" at the end of each line when using a typewriter. This is not required with most word processors; it's automatic. The only time you need to press "return" is at the end of a paragraph or to make space between paragraphs.

**Edit**

Now let's look at some examples of specific editing capabilities and think about their implications for writing and teaching.

1. *Cursor movement.*   The cursor, a blinking object on the computer screen, marks the location of the next character you type. Before you can enter text or edit it, you must move the cursor to the desired location. Some word processors have several different speeds for cursor movement. You can move the cursor ahead or back one letter at a time. It is also possible to move the cursor ahead to the next paragraph or the next page.

2. *Insert text.*   With a word processor it is possible to insert letters, words, or even whole paragraphs or pages at the cursor location. Thus, you can write an outline with the word processor and then insert more polished sentences beneath each heading of the outline as you develop what you are writing. Also, it is easy to make "wholesale" changes without having to write the entire composition over. Just move the sentences or paragraphs around on the screen until they are in a suitable form.

For example, here is a listing of text before and after editing on a word processor.

*before*

The first rais of the sun hit the tarpaper roof and Glen was the first to the breakfast table. Allen had not selpt well, but was sound asleep at sunup.

*after*

Allen had not slept well, but was sound asleep when the first rays of the sun hit the tar paper roof. As usual, Glen was the first to the breakfast table.

You can also move letters around in creative ways. For example, with a word processor, it is easy to create a "picture" such as the following.

```
     H
    HHH
   OOOOO
   UUUUU
   SS  SS
   EE  EE
```

**FIGURE 10.14**   "Picture" drawn with letters.

With many word processors, it is possible to insert portions of other documents stored on the file diskette into the composition you are working on. For example, in letter writing, you could read in the first four lines of another letter that already has your return address typed. Or you could call in several paragraphs of a letter written previously to Mr. Smith.

3. *Delete text.*   With a word processor, it is easy to delete letters, words, paragraphs, and pages from what you have written. When you do so, the computer automatically "closes up" the holes, leaving your composition in a unified compact form.

4. *Search (and replace).*   Most word processors can search automatically through your document to find certain words or phrases. Of-

ten, search (and replace) is used in conjunction with other operations. For example, if a student wants to edit his history report by inserting the date where he mentions the founding of Jamestown, he tells the word processor to search for "Jamestown." When "Jamestown" is found in the document, the word processor displays that part of the composition on the computer screen, with the cursor at "Jamestown." He makes his final cursor moves, then inserts the date of 1607 at the location he has selected.

The full search and replace capability is a powerful one and is used to make many changes of the same nature. For example, if a student misspells "pilgirm" throughout his report, he could tell the word processor to search for "pilgirm" and automatically replace it with "pilgrim."

Many experienced writers use this capability to streamline their writing. For example, if the word "anthropomorphic" appears often in a composition, the word "anth" might be typed instead. Later, as the writing nears completion, a search and replace operation changes "anth" to "anthropomorphic" quickly and easily.

### Format

The formatting capabilities of a word processor make it possible to arrange what you write in almost any way you want.

```
For   example,
you can make a
narrow column
like this
```

or a wider one. Some word processors, however, cannot show on the screen what the final printed product will look like. For example, one of them shows lowercase letters as capital letters on the screen, and capital letters are highlighted in another color. This sometimes makes it difficult to visualize the final printed form.

One especially useful aspect of formatting is line spacing. Many writers print out their drafts double spaced, make editing marks on the hard copy, then transfer these changes to the word processor document. When the composition is in final form, it is printed in a single-spaced format.

By the way, there are separate programs available to check the spelling of words in the files of most word processors. As students use them to correct spelling errors in their compositions, they become aware of which words they are misspelling most frequently. Most spelling checkers can also count and classify words. This makes it possible to check how often certain words (such as "very") are used. No, a program to check for mistakes in grammar is not yet available for schools! But such programs are being developed.

## LEARNING ACTIVITY 7.3

What are some ways to use a word processor in the classroom? This is like asking for ways to use pencil and paper, in a way! Here are some scenarios that might give you some ideas.

In her fourth grade classroom Mrs. Baker has a pen pal project. Her students use the word processor to write letters to pen pals in a school in another state. She asks them not to send the letters until they have been checked by a friend. The children do not mind having their mistakes identified because errors are so easy to correct. The best part is that they do not have to copy the whole letter over! Sometimes Mrs. Baker sends the letters printed on paper. Other times she simply sends the diskette with the letter files on it. She is currently exploring a way to send the letter files over the telephone line to the pen pals' computer.

Ms. Garcia has a word processor available for her chemistry students to use for writing their laboratory reports. She has observed that, once the report is written into the computer, the group members print it, look it over, suggest corrections, edit the report, then print an improved version. This never happened before when reports were written by hand.

Mr. Tatum's English students use a word processor regularly for their research papers and essays. They store all their notes and outlines in word processor diskette files and arrange them into a logical order. Then they develop more of the narrative as the first draft takes shape. After rewriting, they polish their composition using a system of peer review, make their final corrections and changes, and then print a professional looking report to turn in. Mr. Tatum has noticed that his students show much less reluctance to make significant changes in what they have written than previously, when no word processor was available.

Mr. Ngo's gifted students are exploring more innovative ways to use word processors. Julio is designing crossword puzzles. Anita is trying to set up a household budget for her father. Maurice writes song lyrics on his word processor and uses hyphens to space the syllables so they align with the notes on a sheet of music he has written separately. Regina is writing a Latin-English dictionary, using the search function to "look up" a desired word.

In all the examples above, the teachers recognize that the word processor is another tool available for classroom use. They integrate the use of this tool into their teaching by matching its capabilities with their learning objectives.

A final example shows Mrs. O'Neil, a history teacher, designing her final examination with a word processor. Since she had her syllabus and most of her lesson plans and objectives stored as word processor files on her diskette, she brings into the exam document the important parts of these other files. Then she moves them around into a logical order, formulates her exam questions, deletes her notes, and prints her final examination, all in record time.

# Mastery Test

## OBJECTIVE 7     To describe word processing and several educational applications.

1. List several of the general capabilities of a word processor.

_____

_____

2. A student comes to you with a draft of a report in which several paragraphs are out of order. Describe how a word processor would be of value.

_____

_____

_____

3. Briefly describe a specific teaching activity in your area and grade level that takes advantage of the word processor's capabilities. Or describe specifically how a word processor could help with your teaching and administrative work.

_____

_____

_____

_____

## ANSWER KEY

### Mastery Test, Objective 7

1. Enter text, edit, format, store.
2. A word processor could be used to arrange the paragraphs into any desired order if the document was stored in a word processor file on a diskette. Perhaps several arrangements could be set up, and the best one selected for final printing.

3. Various responses are appropriate. Here is a possible response by a sixth grade language arts teacher: In order to encourage the use of descriptive words when writing, students are asked to use the word processor to replace certain mundane words in a sample composition with more descriptive ones.

# Objective 8

To describe how to use other general purpose software such as data bases, spreadsheets, and graphics programs.

General purpose software consists of programs that are not necessarily designed for specific instructional objectives. You have already learned a little about word processing programs, perhaps the most widely used general purpose software. In this section you will learn about three additional programs and explore several ways that they might be applied in the classroom.

## LEARNING ACTIVITY 8.1

### Data Base

A *data base* program gives the computer the capability of storing and retrieving information.

If you look into several classrooms, you will see many common items. One such item is a small box for $3 \times 5$ index cards. Teachers use these boxes to catalog and store all kinds of information, such as lunch money records, emergency telephone numbers of parents, favorite books, and student progress on class projects.

In order to look up some information in such a system, a teacher must first find the correct card and then scan it for the specific information being sought. Usually this is not too great a chore; however, when there are a great many cards, or when time is short, a teacher may wish for a faster method.

The computer can become such a box of index cards. That is, the computer can store information in much the same fashion as the index card box, but the computer can look up information much faster than most people can. Moreover, the computer is capable of more sophisticated searching than many people are.

When a computer is used in this manner, it establishes a *data base;* that is, it stores information in a manner that makes it easy for you to search for what you want. In addition, the information can be manipulated in many ways not possible with an index card system.

## Spreadsheet

A *spreadsheet* program changes the computer into an electronic ledger page that performs calculations automatically.

High school business courses, such as bookkeeping, use paper ledger pages for student work. As the problems are posed, solutions must be worked out in pencil or pen on the ledger pages, with the proper entries made in the correct column and on the correct row. Moreover, the correct totals must appear on the "bottom line." This is laborious work, especially for projects of any magnitude.

The computer is capable of becoming an electronic ledger page laid out in labeled rows and columns, just like the ledger pages in the student workbooks. But the computer can do something else that the workbook cannot. Each place a number goes can "come alive," in the sense that a mathematical operation can be defined for it. Thus, when the entry for February in a column labeled "Net Income" is changed from $110.00 to $150.00, the number appearing at the place for the Total Net Income is changed automatically to a figure $40.00 higher. Thus, a computer *spreadsheet* is an extremely powerful tool for use in business classes. Also, many teachers find a spreadsheet helpful in tabulating and calculating grades and performing item analyses of tests.

## Graphics Programs

*Graphics* programs that draw graphs and charts are useful when it is necessary to display and analyze information. Often, information available in tabular form is not easy to understand; however, when the information is graphed, it is much easier to see relationships. There are a number of programs available that accept tabular information and draw graphic displays of the information on the screen or on a printer. These *graphics* programs are helpful in science classes, business classes, math classes, and others that make use of tabulated information. For example, a government class might use such a program to draw a pie chart to show how the federal budget is apportioned. A biology class would draw bar graphs to illustrate the growth rate of various bacteria under study.

## LEARNING ACTIVITY 8.2

A data base can be used in a variety of classroom settings. Here is one teacher's story.

Each year Mr. Winkler has the students in his music class write research reports on the lives of various composers. The assignment is never greeted with enthusiasm. This year he has decided to do it differently. During the summer, one of his colleagues taught him to use a data base program that the school purchased. This program will be the foundation of the research assignment.

> . . . and instead of writing a report, I want you to put the information about your composer into the computer data base. Make sure that you have a year for each item of information or action you type. After all of you have entered at least a dozen items for your composers, we will have the computer print them out in several different ways.

Mr. Winkler shows his students that the data base stores information in a manner similar to the way that they write facts on $3 \times 5$ index cards. Each "index card" in the computer is called a *record*. Just as each index card has a particular spot for specific information, so does each record in the computer. Each record has several *fields*. For example, in the composer data base, each record might have a field for the composer's name, the date of the reported action, and the action itself. Perhaps a field for the country in which the action took place might be included. The entire assembly of records is called a *file*, corresponding to all the index cards in a file box.

Here is a sample record entered by one of Mr. Winkler's students. The field names appear inside the $< >$ marks.

```
<Composer name> Handel
<Year> 1742
<Action> Conducted first public performance of Messiah
<Country> Ireland
<Student researcher> Louis Smith
<Source> World Book Encyclopedia
```

After all the student entries are placed into the computer data base, Mr. Winkler shows his class how to search for particular items of information. First, he has the computer print all the items for each composer. Next, he instructs the computer to print all items for all composers in chronological order. The students are surprised to learn that, at the time Handel's *Messiah* was being performed for the first time, Johann Sebastian Bach was fifty-seven years old and already going blind, and that young Joseph Haydn was a twelve-year-old singer in the Austrian emperor's court school.

Students begin to think of other ways to search for information on the computer. For example, they ask the computer to print the actions that took place in England between the years 1750 and 1800. They also search the data base for clues to see if Bach and Handel ever met.

After the project is finished, several students ask if they can add information on contemporary composers to the data base. They also ask if the computer will be available during Parents' Night so that they can show their parents what they have learned. Others begin work on a rock-group data base.

From observing his students, Mr. Winkler concludes that they are much more interested in the composer research project than were his students of previous years. Moreover, they are able to view the history of music from a time perspective not readily available to his earlier students. Although the quality of the student research work is no better or worse than in earlier years, Mr. Winkler feels that the affective learning that took place is worthwhile; and he begins to work on ways to improve this project for next year.

He is interested in using the data base program to create a "test bank" of music questions that his students might use for individual study or that he might use for making up examinations. Perhaps the students will be interested in helping to establish the bank . . . .

## LEARNING ACTIVITY 8.3

The spreadsheet program is one of the most popular in the general business community. There are many educational uses of this program as well. Here is how a business teacher integrated the use of a spread-sheet program into her classes.

Ms. Allen's students are excited. They are going to be using computers in this year's accounting class for the first time! Having learned to use a spreadsheet program, Ms. Allen wants to show her students how to take advantage of it to remove some of the drudgery of the accounting exercises. Besides, she reasons, most of them will be using computers in their jobs after graduation. Why not start now?

Tax preparation is always an important accounting function. Ms. Allen teaches her students the fundamentals of setting up and using the spreadsheet program and then assigns a tax preparation project.

Here are the year's financial records for three part-time businesses, and some information about the owners. Set up the spreadsheet program so that it becomes a tax form that accepts your entries for each business and calculates the tax. Use the spreadsheet to find the most advantageous way for each tax report to be filed. For example, would Ann Johnson pay less tax with an individual return or with a joint return?

Ms. Allen helps her students review the fundamentals of spread-sheet use. The computer screen is arranged like a ledger sheet, with rows and columns. The rows and columns divide the screen into *cells*. Each cell is identified by the row and the column in which it is located; for example, the cell in column C and row 2 is called C2.

|   | A | B | C | D |
|---|---|---|---|---|
| 1 |   |   |   |   |
| 2 |   |   | cell C2 |   |
| 3 |   |   |   |   |

**FIGURE 10.15**   Electronic spreadsheet showing cell C2.

The particular spreadsheet Ms. Allen is using has 63 columns and 254 rows. Larger ones are available. Needless to say, it would take a rather large piece of paper for this many rows and columns. The entire spreadsheet is not visible at one time; it is much too big to fit on the computer screen. Instead, only a small section can be seen. In Ms. Allen's spreadsheet this section is 8 columns wide and 21 rows long. This 8 by 21 "window" can be moved to look at the entries anywhere on the spreadsheet. For example, you could view the values in the cells in columns H through O and rows 17 through 37 just as easily as those in columns A through D and rows 1 through 21.

Ms. Allen reviews with her students how to place both labels (words) and values (numbers) in the spreadsheet cells. She uses as an example a situation in which expenses are categorized and totaled. Here is what part of it looks like.

|    | K        | L        | M      |
|----|----------|----------|--------|
| 17 |          |          |        |
| 18 |          |          |        |
| 19 | EXPENSES | CATEGORY | AMOUNT |
| 20 |          |          |        |
| 21 |          | POSTAGE  | 73.45  |
| 22 |          | SUPPLIES | 115.59 |
| 23 |          | PHONE    | 35.67  |
| 24 |          |          |        |
| 25 |          | TOTAL    | 224.71 |
| 26 |          |          |        |
| 27 |          |          |        |

**FIGURE 10.16**  Part of a spreadsheet project.

The amounts 73.45, 115.59, and 35.67 are entered by the students. Cell M25 is programmed to add all the numbers in cells M21 through M23 automatically and to display the total there. Any change in the numbers in cells M21, M22, or M23 is immediately reflected in the total in cell M25. Thus, the spreadsheet can be used to explore questions such as, "What would the total be if . . . ?" In fact, Ms. Allen's students will explore a similar question when they determine the most advantageous way to file each tax on the project.

While Ms. Allen is helping her students with the spreadsheet program, another teacher in a room down the hall is setting up a way to turn the spreadsheet into a grade book. He establishes a column for student names, and columns for test scores. He then programs the cells at the end of the rows to calculate and display the average of all the scores in their respective rows. He plans to make a one-row version of this spreadsheet available to students so they can check the calculation of their individual averages privately.

In still another classroom, a third teacher is setting up a spreadsheet to help her students study statistics. She establishes rows and columns for data, and she programs certain cells to calculate and display statistical information such as the mean and standard deviation. With such a setup her students will be able not only to calculate the mean and standard deviation of a set of numbers quickly, but also to explore the effect of changes in individual numbers in the sets.

Later in the year Ms. Allen contacts a company representative to find out if it is possible to program the spreadsheet to accept information from the data base program. She finds that it can be done; however, the representative mentions a much more fascinating idea. He tells Ms. Allen about a new program ready for release that includes a data base, a spreadsheet, and a word processor all together. Immediately she begins to get ideas for class projects that might use such a program. She also thinks of uses for classes other than hers, so that other teachers might be willing to share in the cost of the program.

# Mastery Test

## OBJECTIVE 8
To describe how to use other general purpose software such as data bases, spreadsheets, and graphics programs.

1. Briefly describe the function of a data base, a spreadsheet, and a graphics program.

_____
_____
_____
_____
_____
_____

2. Devise a project in a subject of your choice that might take advantage of a data base program.

_____
_____
_____
_____

3. How could a spreadsheet program be used in other than business classes?

_____
_____
_____

## ANSWER KEY

Mastery Test, Objective 8

1. A data base program stores information in fields. The information can be searched in various ways. A spreadsheet program turns the computer screen into a ledger sheet that can accept both labels and values. Individual locations in the sheet can be programmed with mathematical functions. A graphics program accepts data and displays it graphically. Pie charts, bar graphs, and other pictorial representations can be produced.

2. As an example, a data base containing information about the United States might be an interesting project for a geography class to establish. Fields for each state might include the capital, major agricultural products, industries, population, date of admission, and per capita income.

3. A spreadsheet might be useful in a mathematics class, giving the students another vehicle for exploring numerical relationships.

# Objective 9

To discuss the future of computers in education.

## LEARNING ACTIVITY 9.1

A major goal of this chapter has been to illustrate the variety of ways microcomputers can be used in the classroom. One purpose for doing this was to stimulate your interest in integrating computers into your own classroom teaching. A second reason was to illustrate that computers can be important tools for teachers. They can help teachers become more effective and efficient in designing and managing instruction, and they offer possibilities for teaching new concepts and skills that have not been taught before.

This chapter has emphasized the positive aspects and the potentials of computers in education. Not all people view computers this way. They raise a number of important concerns about the computer revolution in education. First, they question whether we can afford computers in education when there are so many other financial needs. In this sense they question whether the money spent on computers would not be spent more effectively on other educational priorities. Second, they question whether learning time should be diverted from other basic subject areas and used to teach about computers. Again, this is an issue of priorities: which educational objectives are most important and relevant in our society? Some people have warned about the dehumanizing aspects of computers, about the artificiality of pictures shown on the computer screen, and about the social isolation that occurs when a student works alone for long periods of time at a computer. These warnings usually relate to using computers as replacements for traditional classrooms rather than as tools for teachers and students to use in the classroom.

Another important issue involves equality of opportunity for access to computers. There is the possibility that computers may further stratify society and divide those who can use a computer effectively as a tool from those who cannot. Surveys of the usage of computers in schools suggest that this concern is valid. Schools in poorer communities have fewer computers than do schools in wealthier communities. Students in the poorer schools use computers for drill and practice of basic skills; students in wealthier schools learn computer programming and develop competency in controlling computers for their own purposes. It is easy to see how this unequal access to computers can harm disadvantaged students in terms of their access to good jobs and high-level careers. If computers are truly tools for problem solving and decision making, as necessary to education in the future as pencils and books are now, equal access is an important goal for educators to achieve.

Another issue related to equality of opportunity is the different expectations and experiences of boys and girls in using computers. Surveys have indicated that girls in school spend less time working with computers than boys. Our knowledge of sex differences in parental expectations and teacher behavior suggest that computers would be seen as more appropriate for boys than for girls. Where access time to computers is limited, teachers will probably have to take some specific steps to encourage girls to use computers and ensure they have equal time to work on them. For example, one study identified a situation in which the teacher posted a sign-up sheet for computer time at the beginning of each week. Male students were aggressive in getting to the sign-up sheet and quickly reserved most of the computer time. Female students waited at the end of the line and found most of the time already reserved when they got to the sign-up sheet.[5] The teacher in this case could foster equal access by using separate sign-up sheets for boys and girls, making the time assignments herself, or passing the sign-up sheet around the class in a different order each week. The important thing for any teacher to realize is that this problem may occur and that active steps will be needed to ensure equal access.

## LEARNING ACTIVITY 9.2

A Chinese proverb warns, "It is extremely difficult to prophesy, especially about the future." Yet some trends in the classroom use of microcomputers seem inevitable. The number of computers being placed in schools will increase. The cost of microcomputers will decrease and, at the same time, their power and memory will increase. In other words, more computer power will be available to more students at lower cost.

One author believes that providing a personal computer for every student is an attainable goal.[6] At a cost of $250 per computer, the expense of providing one computer to each student in the U.S. would represent only 1 percent of the $25,000 currently spent on a student's education from kindergarten through high school. If we think of a computer as a learning and thinking tool, it may be as necessary to provide all students with ready access to a computer in the future as it is to provide them with pencils and paper today.

A few years ago computers were used in school mainly to teach students about computers. Even today, the major use of computers in high schools is to teach students to write computer programs. There is serious debate today about whether this is the best use of computers in education. Do we need to teach students to program computers or simply to use the programs and software packages developed by others? Or do students need to learn both? The answer is uncertain. The trend seems to be toward the development of general purpose software packages, such as word processing, graphics, and spreadsheet programs, which can be used in many different applications without the user's knowing how to write programs or to develop software. In the future both computer hardware and software will become "friendlier" (i.e., easier to use), and this trend may further reduce the number of people who need to know how to write computer programs. In the near future, both writing programs and using software will continue to be appropriate educational objectives in schools; however, the emphasis will probably shift to assuring that all students can use general purpose software packages.

## LEARNING ACTIVITY 9.3

Today the typical educational computer has a keyboard for input and a monitor screen and printer for output; however, other ways of communicating with computers are already available. These suggest that in the future we will be much more flexible in communicating with computers than we are now. Input devices like *light pens, touch tablets,* and *touch sensitive monitor screens* allow users to bypass the keyboard by simply touching a tablet or screen to choose an answer or direct the computer to begin a new operation. Various types of sensors can be connected to the computer as input devices to measure temperature, pressure, speed, light, and other variables for science experiments. Through the use of voice synthesizers, computers can speak words and sentences rather than display them or print them. A few software programs in reading already use this feature. With them, a student can select a word on the screen and the computer will pronounce it. Computers can also output to plotters to draw graphs, charts, and illustrations in multiple colors. Computers can be used to control video disk and video tape players in *interactive video systems* so that televised pictures can be integrated into computer assisted instruction. In such a system, the student might observe a televised lab experiment and then use the computer to analyze data and write a lab report. Using appropriate computer controls, the student could watch a part of the experiment again and observe it in slow motion. Finally, a computer can be used in *robotics* to study movement and manipulation.

These input and output devices are now available in specialized applications in schools; they will be used much more frequently in the future. In addition, other innovations are now being developed in laboratories. Someday we may communicate with computers by talking to them rather than by typing information at a keyboard. Even more exciting is the prospect that we may be able to program computers by using natural language instructions such as conversational English, rather than special formal computer languages like BASIC and Logo. For example, the programs you saw earlier written in BASIC and Logo, might be replaced by saying to the computer:

Ask me for two numbers.
Multiply them.
Tell me the answer.

In summary, the future will bring changes in hardware, software, and programming languages that will make computers friendlier and easier to use. Many of the specific operational details you must teach students today will be different and perhaps unnecessary in the future. For this reason the appropriate emphasis in educational computing should be on the functions of computers rather than on the specific mechanics of operation. Whenever possible, provide students with lists of instructions and operational aids for these procedures rather than insisting on memorization and unaided performance. In this way students will be able to concentrate on the function and uses of the computer rather than becoming bogged down in current operating problems that are likely to be solved by improved hardware and software in the future. In this chapter we have emphasized what computers can do and how they can be used rather than the step-by-step procedures needed to run currently available computers and software. You and your students need to be able to find and follow these procedures, but they are not the essence of the effective use of computers in the classroom.

Unlike many educational innovations, the computer has appealed to many different groups of educators. For educators who emphasize the importance of basic skills, the computer offers an effective way for students to achieve mastery skills in reading, writing, and mathematics. For educators who emphasize the importance of exploration and discovery in learning, the computer offers the opportunity to create new environments or "microworlds" through simulations so that students can explore concepts, discover relationships, practice decision making, and develop competence and self-confidence in controlling a part of their world. For educators interested in improving the education of the handicapped, the computer offers many opportunities to help these students gain new control of important skills and concepts. As the examples in this chapter have shown, teachers can use computers for many different purposes. For the future it is important for teachers to remember the range of instructional options that computers make available to them.

# Mastery Test

## OBJECTIVE 9    To discuss the future of computers in education.

1. One author has estimated that the cost of providing a microcomputer to every U.S. student in grades K–12 would be only about _____ percent of the total cost of educating a student in grades K–12.

2. Briefly describe the "computer access issue" as it affects the following groups:

boys vs. girls:

_____

_____

poor vs. wealthy:

_____

_____

3. A teacher observes that girls in his class do not assert themselves to get to the computer sign-up sheet on Monday morning and consequently get less computer time than the boys in his class do. Describe one

change he could make in the sign-up procedure to provide equal computer time to students in both groups.

_____

_____

4. Studies have shown that students in school in wealthier areas usually use computers for _____.

_____

   Students in schools in poorer areas usually use computers for _____.

5. Place a check mark before the predictions that are made in the chapter.

   _____ (a) The number of computers in schools will not increase much in the next decade.
   _____ (b) The cost of computers will continue to decline.
   _____ (c) The power of computers will continue to increase.
   _____ (d) There will be many new ways of interacting with computers in addition to typing at the computer keyboard.
   _____ (e) Software programs will become friendlier and easier to use.
   _____ (f ) Most of us will be users of computer software rather than authors of computer programs.
   _____ (g) Computers will become much easier to use.
   _____ (h) Computers will make it possible to teach new things that we have never taught or never taught well to many students.
   _____ (i ) Computers are a passing fad in education and probably will not change schools much in the next decade.

## ANSWER KEY

### Mastery Test, Objective 9

1. 1 percent.
2. Studies show that boys and girls have unequal access to computers, with boys having greater access and being encouraged to use computers for more applications. Since the computer is a powerful tool for problem solving and decision making, girls may thus have unequal opportunity for higher-level jobs and careers.

   Studies show that schools in poor communities have fewer computers than schools in wealthier communities. Again, a group of stu-dents already economically disadvantaged may fall farther behind in an area that is closely related to their future jobs and career opportunities.
3. Make up separate sign-up sheets for boys and girls so that equal time is allotted to students regardless of sex.
4. Learning to program; drill and practice of basic skills.
5. b, c, d, e, f, g, h.

NOTES

1. James Hassett, "Computers in the Classroom," *Psychology Today*, September 1984, pp. 22–29.

2. Robert P. Taylor, *The Computer in the School: Tutor, Tool, Tutee* (New York: Teachers College Press, 1980).

3. Gerald W. Bracey, "Computers in Education, What the Research Shows," *Electronic Learning*, November/December 1982, pp. 51–54.

4. Robert M. Gagné, *The Conditions of Learning*, 3rd ed. (New York: Holt, Rinehart, and Winston, 1977).

5. Jane G. Shubert and Thomas W. Bakke, "Practical Solutions to Over-

coming Equity in Computer Use," *The Computing Teacher*, April 1984, pp. 28–30.

6. Seymour Papert, "The Computer as Mudpie," *Classroom Computer Learning*, January 1984, pp. 37–38, 40.

SOURCES OF REVIEWS
OF EDUCATIONAL
SOFTWARE

EPIE Evaluations, Educational Products Information Exchange, Box 18, Teacher's College, Columbia University, New York, NY 10027.

microSIFT Reviews, microSIFT, NWREL, 300 S.W. Sixth Avenue, Portland, OR 97204.

ADDITIONAL READINGS

*Books*

Bennett, R. E., and C. A. Maher, eds. *Microcomputers and Exceptional Children*. New York: The Haworth Press, 1984.

Browning, Philip, ed. *Computer Technology for the Handicapped in Special Education and Rehabilitation: Resource Vol. II*. ICCE Publications (1787 Agate, University of Oregon, Eugene, OR 97403), 1985.

Bull, Glen, et al. *Nudges: Apple Logo Projects*. New York: Holt, Rinehart and Winston, 1985.

Dennis, J. Richard, and Robert J. Kansky. *Instructional Computing: An Action Guide for Educators*. Glenview, Illinois: Scott, Foresman and Company, 1984.

Hagen, Dolores. *Microcomputer Resource Book for Special Education*. Reston, Virginia: Reston Publishing Co., 1984.

Harlowe, Steven, ed. *Humanistic Perspectives on Computers in the Schools*. New York: The Haworth Press, 1985.

Harper, Dennis, and James Stewart, eds. *Run: Computer Education*, Monterey, California: Brooks/Cole Publishing Co., 1985.

Heck, William P., et al. *Guidelines for Evaluating Computerized Instructional Materials*. Reston, Virginia: National Council of Teachers of Mathematics, 1981.

Hunter, Beverly. *My Children Use Computers*. Reston, Virginia: Reston Publishing Co., 1984.

Leggett, Stanton, ed. *Microcomputers Go to School: Where and How to Get the Most from Them*. Chicago: Teach 'em, Inc., 1984.

Moursund, David. *Introduction to Computers in Education for Elementary and Middle School Teachers*. Eugene, Oregon: International Council for Computers in Education, 1981.

Papert, Seymour. *Mindstorms: Children, Computers, and Powerful Ideas*. New York: Basic Books, Inc., 1980.

Peterson, Dale, ed. *Intelligent Schoolhouse: Readings on Computers & Learning*. Reston, Virginia: Reston Publishing Co., 1984.

Taffee, Stephen J., ed. *Computers in Education 85/86*. Guilford, Connecticut: The Dushkin Publishing Group, 1985.

Taylor, Robert P. *The Computer in the School: Tutor, Tool, Tutee*. New York: Teachers College Press, 1980.

Tobias, Joyce, et al. *Beyond Mindstorms: Teaching with Logo*. New York: Holt, Rinehart and Winston, 1986.

Turkle, Sherry. *The Second Self: Computer and the Human Spirit*. New York: Simon and Schuster, 1984.

Yazdani, Masoud. *New Horizons in Educational Computing.* New York: John Wiley & Sons, 1984.

*Periodicals*

*Classroom Computer Learning,* 19 Davis Drive, Belmont, CA 94002.

*Closing the Gap: Microcomputers for the Handicapped,* Post Office Box 68, Henderson, MN 56014.

*Educational Technology,* Educational Technology Publications, 140 Sylvan Ave., Englewood Cliffs, NJ 07632.

*Electronic Learning,* Scholastic, Inc., 730 Broadway, New York, NY 10003.

*Teaching and Computers,* Scholastic Inc., 730 Broadway, New York, NY 10003.

*The Computing Teacher,* University of Oregon, 1787 Agate Street, Eugene, OR 97403.

*The International Logo Exchange Newsletter,* Post Office Box 5686, Charlottesville, VA 22905.

*The National Logo Exchange Newsletter,* Post Office Box 5341, Charlottesville, VA 22905.

# Appendix A

## The Question Master Game

PREPARATION FOR THE GAME

1. Cut out the cards on the following pages and stack them in three piles: Chance Cards, Question About Questions Cards, and Classification Cards.
2. Read the directions.
3. Turn to the game board and begin.

**THE QUESTION MASTER**

DIRECTIONS

*Object:* The object of the game is to become the first teacher in your neighborhood to reach that magic circle of the select few (to wit, the Question Master Circle).

*Players:* 2 to 6

*Moves:* You move along the board from the space marked "Start" by rolling a die. If you don't have any dice, then simply make and cut out cards numbered from 1 to 6, and each player can select a card from the pile on his or her turn. If you are a professional game player, use your spinner.

*Pieces:* Use anything that fits on the spaces (different coins, buttons, small pieces of paper with your initials, chess pieces, etc.).

*Spaces:*

*Classification.* When you land on a space marked with a C, *another* player selects a card from the pile of Classification Cards and reads the question to you. You must then classify the question on the appropriate level of Bloom's *Taxonomy*. The correct answer is printed on the card. If you are correct, you can stay on that space. If you are *incorrect*, you must go back *three spaces*.

*Question.* When you land on a space marked with a Q, *another* player selects a card from the pile of Question About Questions Cards. If you answer the question correctly (correct answers are also written on the card), you stay on that space. If you answer incorrectly, you must go back *three spaces*.

Ah, the whims of fortune. If you land on this space, select a card from the Chance pile and follow the instructions.

An arrow signifies a different route that must be followed when you land on this space. The first of these is a shorter route; the second is a longer route.

You lose one turn if you land on this space.

If you land on a space marked Gym, Principal's Office, Lunch Room, or Detention Hall, then you have no questions to answer or classify. You may also be sent to these locations by a Chance Card.

   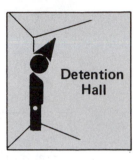

The Question Master:    You need *not* land on the last space (Question Master) by exact count.

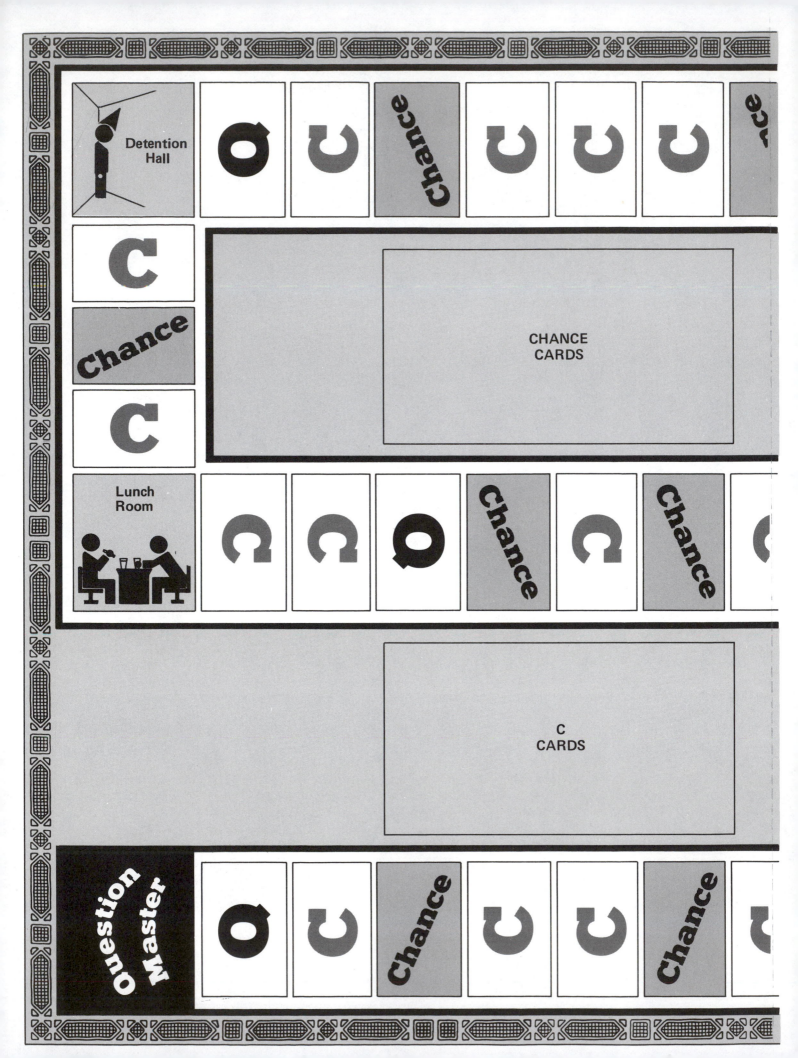

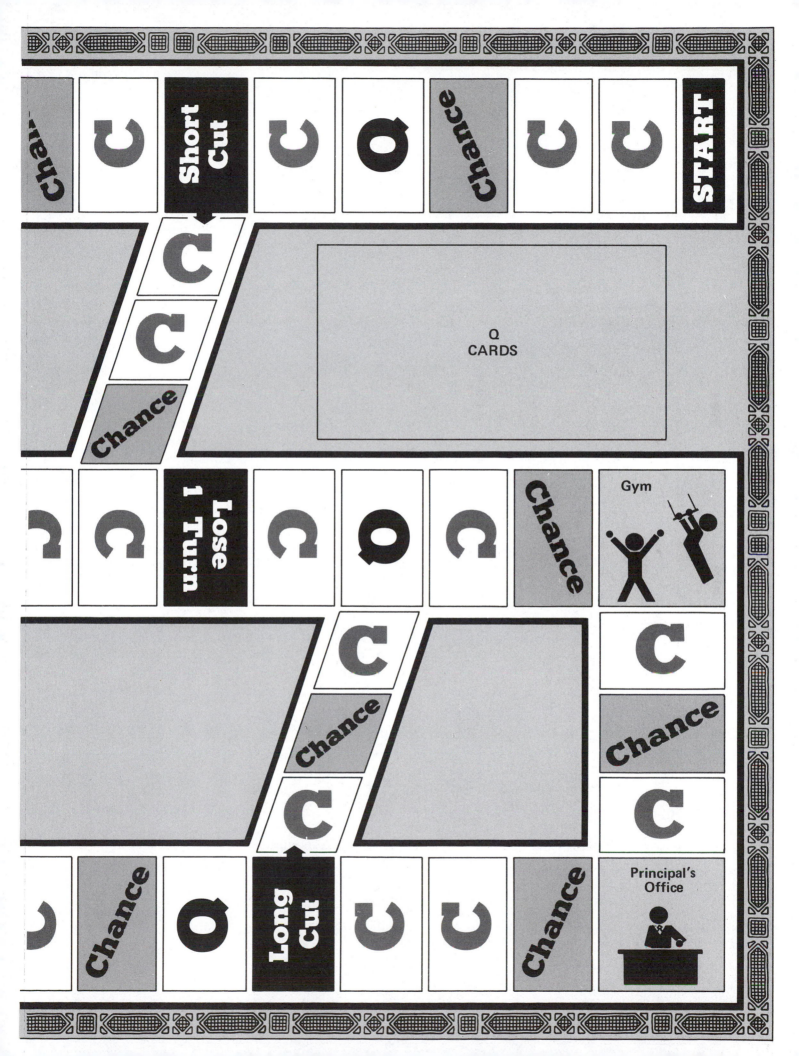

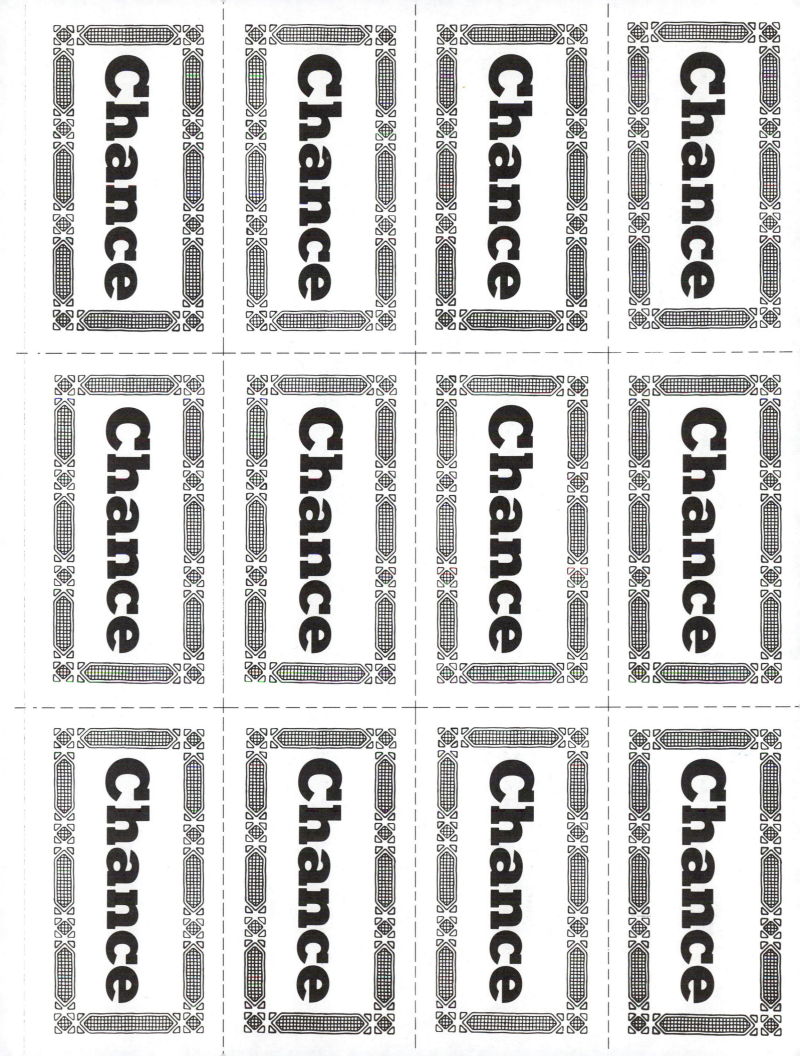

**Chance Card**

Students just selected you as their best teacher. Roll the dice to determine how many spaces you can move ahead.

---

**Chance Card**

Two more students fell asleep when you asked a question. Move back 2 spaces.

---

**Chance Card**

You've just been assigned to stay after school with kids who were behavior problems. Go to detention hall.

---

**Chance Card**

The principal is coming to observe you and you forgot your lesson plans. Go back 3 spaces.

---

**Chance Card**

You forgot to lock your cabinet, and your prize Hopi Indian Kit is gone. Go back 3 spaces.

---

**Chance Card**

You have been using only memory questions in class and your students do not really understand the material. Go back 3 spaces.

---

**Chance Card**

Your evaluation report just came back and you will be getting tenure. Live it up. Take another turn.

---

**Chance Card**

Your car ran out of gas on your way to work. Lose one turn.

---

**Chance Card**

*Promotion.* Move ahead six spaces if you can re-cite the 6 levels of Bloom's *Taxonomy* backwards within ten seconds. GO.

---

**Chance Card**

Teacher of the Year Award. Move ahead 4 spaces.

---

**Chance Card**

You've just been passed by for merit. Move back 3 spaces.

---

**Chance Card**

The principal smiled at you and said you were doing a fine job. Stay where you are.

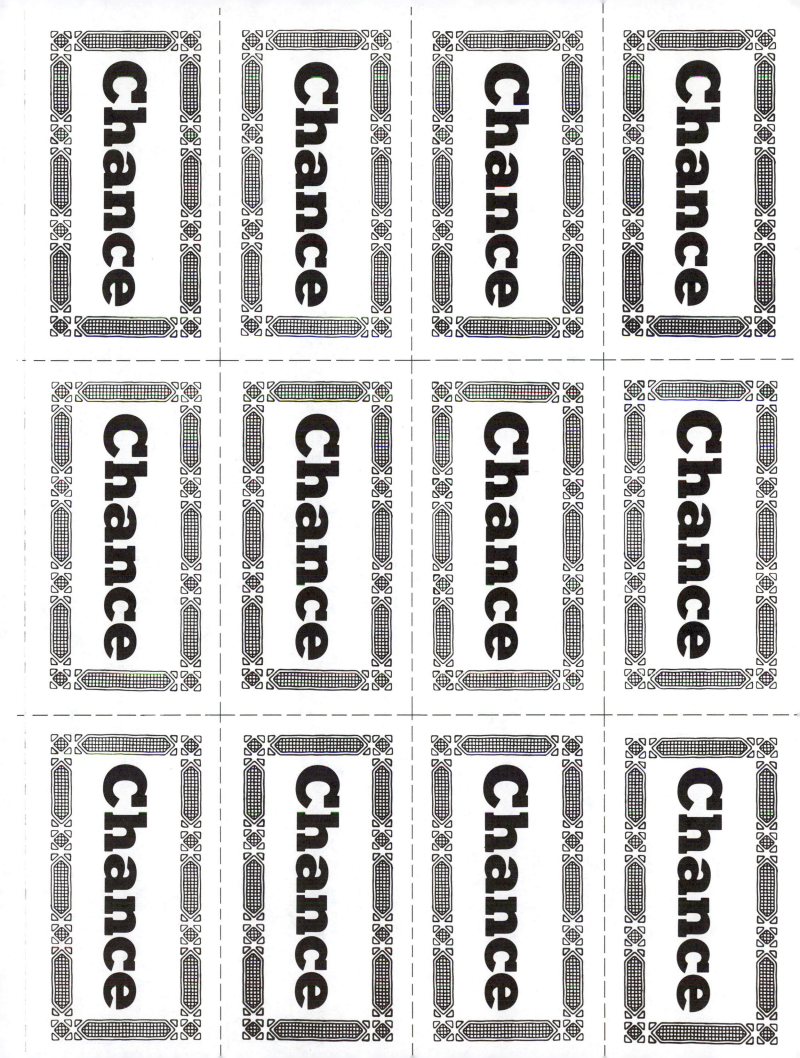

**Chance Card**

TGIF (Thank God It's Friday). You made it to Friday. Move ahead one space.

**Chance Card**

You've just been assigned lunch room duty. Move directly to the lunch room.

**Chance Card**

Christmas Vacation — get your battery recharged. Move ahead 5 spaces.

**Chance Card**

June is here and everyone has spring fever. Lose one turn.

**Chance Card**

You are being considered for assistant principal. Go directly to the principal's office and wait — for three turns before going on.

**Chance Card**

Congratulations! You are now the new basketball coach. Go directly to the gym.

**Chance Card**

Your attendance reports are missing and the principal would like you to recall who was absent during the last week. Go to the principal's office. Lose two turns.

**Chance Card**

Your higher order questions are really making a difference and student grades are improving. Go ahead five spaces.

**Chance Card**

Faculty meeting this afternoon. Lose one turn.

**Chance Card**

Inservice workshop this afternoon. Go ahead 4 spaces.

**Chance Card**

The parents of your students are so pleased with your effective classroom questions that they have taken an ad out in the local newspaper thanking you. Take another turn.

**Chance Card**

You stayed up last night until 2:00 a.m. grading student papers, and you forgot to take them to school this morning. Lose one turn.

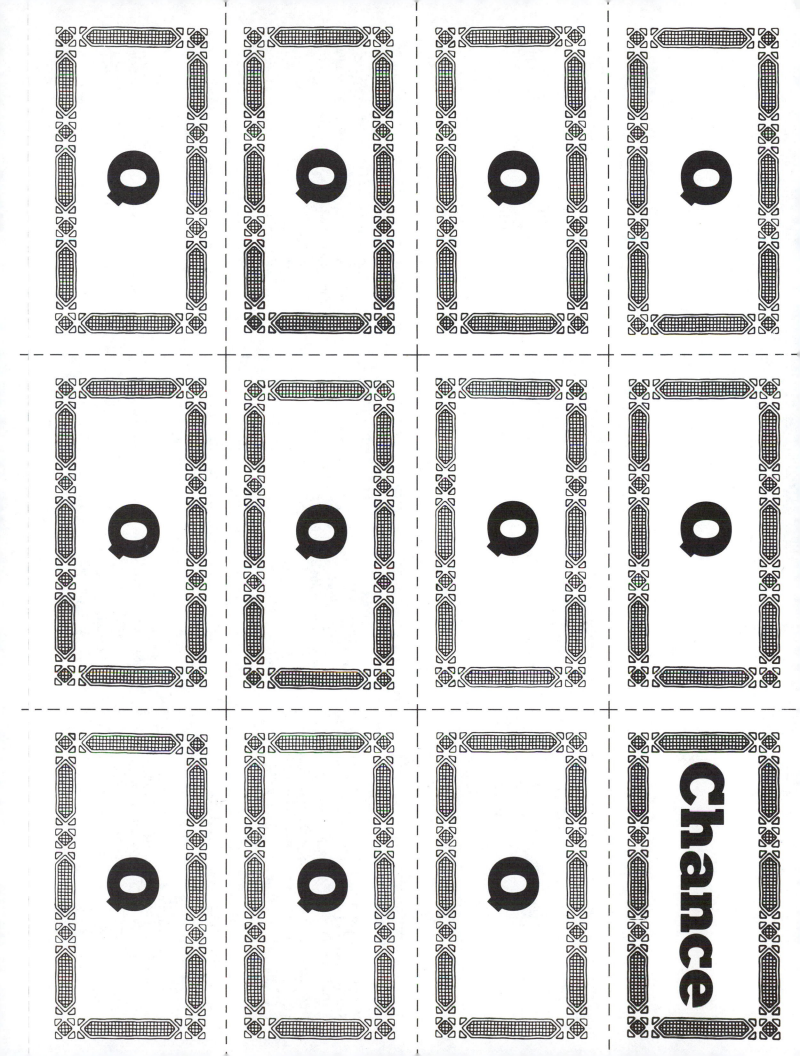

## Question About Questions Cards

Analysis questions call for higher order thinking. True or false?

*Answer:* True

---

## Question About Questions Cards

Which of the following is *not* a process required by analysis questions? (a) identifying evidence to support a statement (b) making a statement based on evidence (c) explaining motives or causes (d) making predictions.

*Answer:* (d)

---

## Question About Questions Cards

A "why" question suggests a question asked on the analysis level. True or false?

*Answer:* True

---

## Question About Questions Cards

Synthesis questions require students to do all of the following *except* (a) make predictions (b) solve problems (c) construct original communications (d) evaluate ideas, solutions to problems, and aesthetic works.

*Answer:* (d)

---

## Question About Questions Cards

A student who is asked to interpret a cartoon is functioning on a (a) knowledge (b) comprehension (c) application (d) analysis level

*Answer:* (b)

---

## Question About Questions Cards

Application level questions generally have more than one possible answer. True or false?

*Answer:* False

---

## Question About Questions Cards

If you were asked to use a particular process in order to solve a problem, what level of the *Taxonomy* would you be operating on?

*Answer:* application

---

## Question About Questions Cards

When you are asked to solve mathematical problems, you are usually working at what level of the *Taxonomy?*

*Answer:* application

---

## Chance Card

Your use of higher order questions has made this your best year of teaching. Take an extra turn.

---

## Question About Questions Cards

Most of the questions asked by teachers are on what level of thinking?

*Answer:* Lower order or memory or knowledge level

---

## Question About Questions Card

Memory questions are lower order and not useful. Teachers would be better off if they did not use them. True or false?

*Answer:* False. Although overused, they are essential for other levels of thinking to occur.

---

## Question About Questions Card

Comprehension questions require students to (a) repeat information exactly (b) make comparisons (c) make judgments (d) offer opinions, beliefs, and values.

*Answer:* (b)

**Classification Card**

Who wrote *Romeo and Juliet?*

*Answer:* knowledge

---

**Classification Card**

What did King John say in the next chapter?

*Answer:* knowledge

---

**Classification Card**

How are these two solutions similar?

*Answer:* comprehension

---

**Classification Card**

How would you state the main idea of this poem?

*Answer:* comprehension

---

**Classification Card**

What is the capital of Maryland?

*Answer:* knowledge

---

**Classification Card**

Who is the governor of Wisconsin?

*Answer:* knowledge

---

**Classification Card**

Who wrote *Pollution: The Last Chapter?*

*Answer:* knowledge

---

**Classification Card**

When was the charter written?

*Answer:* knowledge

---

**Question About Questions Cards**

Synthesis questions require original and creative thought from students. True or false?

*Answer:* True

---

**Question About Questions Cards**

Which level of the *Taxonomy* would you be functioning at if you drew a self-portrait?

*Answer:* synthesis

---

**Question About Questions Cards**

What level of the *Taxonomy* is a question that asks you to describe what you think the United States will be like in the year 2000?

*Answer:* synthesis

---

**Question About Questions Cards**

Your new assignment is to judge an all-male beauty contest. You will be asked to decide on a winner. What level of the *Taxonomy* will you be working on?

*Answer:* evaluation

**Classification Card**

What is the meaning of democracy? (The students have previously been given the definition.)

*Answer:* knowledge

---

**Classification Card**

How is ecology defined? (The students have previously been given the definition.)

*Answer:* knowledge

---

**Classification Card**

What was the topic of yesterday's discussion?

*Answer:* knowledge

---

**Classification Card**

Give the textbook definition of the feminist movement.

*Answer:* knowledge

---

**Classification Card**

How does the geography of Maine compare with the geography of Mexico?

*Answer:* comprehension

---

**Classification Card**

Considering your two reading assignments, what characteristics do Vietnam and Thailand have in common?

*Answer:* comprehension

---

**Classification Card**

In your own words, what were the main ideas in your homework assignment?

*Answer:* comprehension

---

**Classification Card**

Describe yesterday's discussion in your own words.

*Answer:* comprehension

---

**Classification Card**

What does this chart mean?

*Answer:* comprehension

---

**Classification Card**

What is the message of this political cartoon?

*Answer:* comprehension

---

**Classification Card**

How does yesterday's class discussion compare with your textbook account of the American Revolution?

*Answer:* comprehension

---

**Classification Card**

Using the process we discussed yesterday, solve this problem.

*Answer:* application

**Classification Card**

Who was our greatest President?

*Answer:* evaluation

---

**Classification Card**

Do you believe that he's telling the truth?

*Answer:* evaluation

---

**Classification Card**

Locate Memphis by latitude and longitude on a map.

*Answer:* application

---

**Classification Card**

If Harry takes two hours to mow a lawn and Harriet takes one hour, how long would it take if they both mowed the lawn?

*Answer:* application

---

**Classification Card**

Should the United States stop foreign aid?

*Answer:* evaluation

---

**Classification Card**

Which solution is best?

*Answer:* evaluation

---

**Classification Card**

Who is your favorite movie star?

*Answer:* evaluation

---

**Classification Card**

Which party do you prefer: Democrats or Republicans?

*Answer:* evaluation

---

**Classification Card**

What would society be like if marriage were against the law?

*Answer:* synthesis

---

**Classification Card**

How would people respond if Congress enacted a law that forced people to wear seat belts?

*Answer:* synthesis

---

**Classification Card**

Which song do you prefer?

*Answer:* evaluation

---

**Classification Card**

Should people be allowed to marry at any age?

*Answer:* evaluation

## Classification Card

Do you like modern art?

*Answer:* evaluation

## Classification Code

Why is New York called "The Empire State"?

*Answer:* analysis

## Classification Card

Using any land area in the world, choose a site you consider an ideal location for a city.

*Answer:* synthesis

## Classification Card

Do you prefer Picasso, Chagall, or Miro?

*Answer:* evaluation

## Classification Card

Why did Myra refuse to give her diary to the publisher?

*Answer:* analysis

## Classification Card

What would be the effects of a woman being elected President?

*Answer:* synthesis

## Classification Card

Solve $x^2 + 14 = 18$.

*Answer:* application

## Classification Card

What evidence can you cite to support your argument?

*Answer:* analysis

## Classification Card

How many answers to this problem can you think of?

*Answer:* synthesis

## Classification Card

Using the rules of punctuation that we have learned, find the error in the following sentence.

*Answer:* application

## Classification Card

What is the tone of the article?

*Answer:* analysis

## Classification Card

Compose a letter to a friend who is having problems in his studies.

*Answer:* synthesis

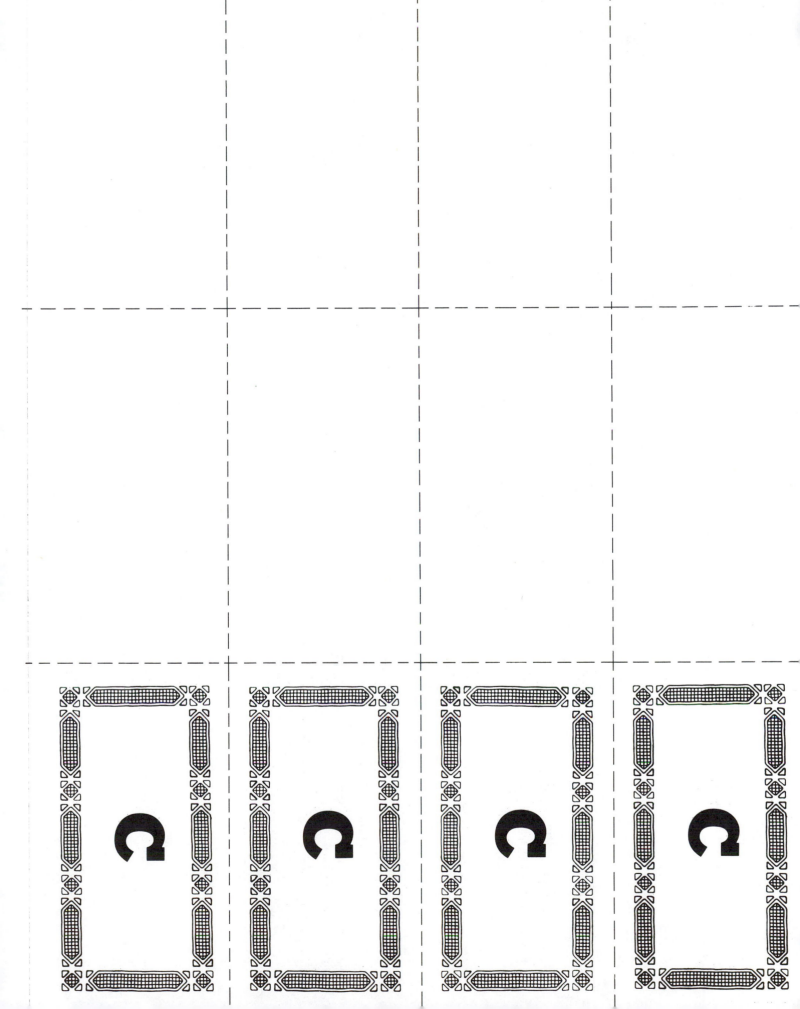

**Classification Card**

Draw a picture of your favorite building.

*Answer:* synthesis

---

**Classification Card**

How can we make foreign aid more effective?

*Answer:* synthesis

---

**Classification Card**

How can we determine the weight of this object without a standard scale?

*Answer:* synthesis

---

**Classification Card**

What should we call our pet?

*Answer:* synthesis

# Appendix B

## Concept Cards

| | | |
|---|---|---|
| soldier | rhythm | haiku |
| family | translation | set (in mathematics) |
| love | intensity (in color) | distance |
| justice | well done (in cooking) | direction |
| vertebrae | coordination | melody |
| amoeba | transportation | accent |
| vowel | heredity | waste |
| mass media | photosynthesis | airplane |

| cloud | map | hypotenuse |
|---|---|---|
| polygon | symmetry | square feet |
| moisture | counterpoint | preposition |
| gravity | hue | adverb |
| wood | resource | debate |
| mass | personality | idiomatic phrase |
| vapor | off key | exercise |
| democracy | harmony | sprint |
| slavery | exponent | curve ball |
| | | pocket (in football) |

# Glossary

**Abstract concepts.** Those concepts that can be acquired only indirectly through the senses or cannot be perceived directly through the senses.

**Active listening.** Differentiating between the intellectual and emotional content of a message, and making inferences regarding the feelings experienced by the speaker.

**Advance organizers.** Informing students of the way in which new information is organized.

**Affective objectives.** Objectives that deal primarily with emotion and feeling.

**Analysis questions.** Questions that require the student to break down a communication into its constituent parts such that the relative hierarchy of ideas is made clear and/or the relations between the ideas expressed are made explicit.

**Application questions.** Questions requiring the student to apply a rule or process to a problem in order to determine the correct answer.

**Attending behavior.** Use of verbal and nonverbal cues by the listener that demonstrate he or she is listening with care and empathy to what is being said.

**Attitude.** A predisposition to act in a positive or negative way toward persons, ideas, or events.

**Attraction.** Friendship patterns in the classroom group.

**BASIC.** A computer language that is widely used on microcomputers. The name is an acronym for Beginner's All-purpose Symbolic Instruction Code.

**Bug.** The special name for a mistake in a computer program. When a program does not do what it was intended to do, it is said to have a bug in it.

**Central processing unit (CPU).** The part of a computer that calculates and processes data.

**Checklist.** A list of criteria, or things to look for, for evaluating some performance or end product.

**Classroom management.** That set of teacher behaviors by which the teacher establishes and maintains conditions that facilitate effective and efficient instruction—conditions that promote on-task behavior.

**Closure.** Actions and statements by teachers that are designed to bring a lesson presentation to an appropriate conclusion.

**Cohesiveness.** The collective feeling that the class members have about the classroom group; the sum of the individual members' feelings about the group.

**Comprehension questions.** Questions requiring the student to select, organize, and arrange mentally the materials pertinent to answering the question.

**Computer assisted instruction (CAI).** An instructional method in which the computer presents instructional material to the individual student.

**Computer language.** A set of instructions that can be carried out by a computer, and that can be arranged by a user to cause the computer to accomplish particular tasks.

**Computer managed instruction (CMI).** Use of the computer for instructional management purposes. For example, the computer might serve as a record keeper by keeping track of student assessment, feedback, scheduling, and future individualized assignments.

**Computer memory.** A part of the computer that can store information. The Read Only Memory (ROM) section is permanent memory, while information stored in the Random Access Memory (RAM) is lost when the computer is turned off.

**Concepts.** Categories into which our experiences are organized, and the larger network of intellectual relationships brought about through categorization.

**Concrete concepts.** Those concepts that can be perceived directly through one of the five senses.

**Conditional reinforcers.** Reinforcers that are learned.

**Conjunctive concepts.** Concepts that have only a single set of qualities or characteristics to learn.

**Convergent thinking.** Thinking that occurs when the task, or question, is so structured that several people will arrive at similar conclusions or answers, and the number of possible appropriate conclusions is very limited (usually one conclusion).

**Criterial attributes.** The basic characteristics of a concept.

**Criterion-referenced judgments.** Judgments made by comparing the information you have about an individual with some performance criterion, that is, some description of expected behavior.

**Data base.** An arrangement of information or data stored in a computer in such a way that it can be manipulated.

**Debugging.** The process of eliminating mistakes from a computer program. (See also **Bug.**)

**Decision.** A choice among alternative courses of action.

**Desist behaviors.** Behaviors the teacher uses in an effort to stop student misbehavior.

**Diagnostic procedures.** Procedures to determine what

pupils are capable of doing with respect to given learning tasks.

**Disjunctive concepts.** Concepts that have two or more sets of alternative conditions under which the concept appears.

**Disk drive.** A device that can read information from a diskette into the computer, or store information from the computer on a diskette.

**Diskette.** A thin sheet of magnetic material protected by an outer covering. Information is stored magnetically on the diskette material.

**Divergent thinking.** Thinking that occurs when the task, or question, is so open that several people will arrive at very different conclusions or answers, and the number of possible appropriate conclusions is fairly large.

**Effective teacher.** One who is able to bring about intended learning outcomes.

**Enactive medium.** A representational medium for acquiring concepts by enacting or doing the concept.

**Evaluation.** The process of obtaining information and using it to form judgments which, in turn, are to be used in decision making.

**Evaluation questions.** Questions requiring students to use criteria or standards to form a judgment about the value of the topic or phenomena being considered.

**Expectations.** Those perceptions that the teacher and the students hold regarding their relationships to one another.

**Explaining behavior.** Planned teacher talk designed to clarify any idea, procedure, or process not understood by a student.

**Extinction.** Withholding of an anticipated reward in an instance where that behavior was previously rewarded; results in the decreased frequency of the previously rewarded behavior.

**Facts.** Well-grounded, clearly established pieces of information.

**Feedback.** Information about the effects or consequences of actions taken.

**Fine-tuning.** Making small adjustments in the planned procedures for a lesson during actual teaching of the lesson.

**Goals.** General statements of purpose.

**Group-focus behaviors.** Those behaviors teachers use to maintain a focus on the group, rather than on an individual student, during individual recitations.

**Hardware.** Any tangible portion of a computer or related accessories.

**Iconic medium.** A representational medium for acquiring concepts by viewing a picture or image of the concept.

**Inference.** A conclusion derived from, and bearing some relation to, assumed premises.

**Input device.** A mechanism that permits the computer to accept information; for example, the keyboard is an input device.

**Inquiry.** Obtaining information by asking.

**Instructional grouping.** Dividing a class of pupils into small subunits for purposes of teaching. Groups can be formed according to achievement or interest, depending on instructional purpose.

**Instructional objectives.** Statements of desired changes in students' thoughts, actions, or feelings that a particular course or educational program should bring about.

**Instructional strategies.** Plans for managing the learning environment in order to provide learning opportunities and meet objectives. Strategies involve the methods used, along with concerns for motivating, sequencing, pacing, and grouping.

**Interval schedule.** A type of intermittent reinforcement in which the teacher reinforces the student after a specified period of time.

**Inventory questions.** Questions asking individuals to describe their thoughts, feelings, and manifested actions.

**Judgment.** Estimate of present conditions or prediction of future conditions. Involves comparing information to some referent.

**Knowledge questions.** Questions requiring the student to recognize or recall information.

**Leadership.** Those behaviors that help the group move toward the accomplishment of its objectives.

**Logo.** A high-level computer language designed for educational purposes.

**Memory.** See **Computer memory.**

**Microcomputer.** The class of small computers, often called personal computers, that are widely used in education today. These include the Apple IIe and the Commodore 64 computers.

**Monitor.** An output device used to display computer information on a screen. Most monitors resemble television sets.

**Movement management behaviors.** Those behaviors that the teacher uses to initiate, sustain, or terminate a classroom activity.

**Noncriterial attributes.** Features that are frequently present in concept illustrations, though they are not an essential part of the concept.

**Norm-referenced judgments.** Judgments made by comparing the information you have about an individual with information you have about a group of similar individuals.

**Norms.** Shared expectations of how group members should think, feel, and behave.

**Observation.** The process of looking and listening, noticing the important elements of a performance or a product.

**On-task behavior.** Student behavior that is appropriate to the task.

**Output device.** A mechanism that permits the computer to send information; for example, a printer is a widely used output device.

**Overlapping behaviors.** Those behaviors by which the teacher indicates that he or she is attending to more than one issue when there is more than one issue to deal with at a particular time.

**Pascal.** A high-level computer language used in computer science.

**Primary reinforcers.** Reinforcers that are unlearned and that are necessary to sustain life.

**Probing questions.** Questions following a response that require the respondent to provide more support, to be clearer or more accurate, or to offer greater specificity or originality.

**Program.** An arrangement of computer commands in a particular language that causes the computer to perform a specified task.

**Punishment.** Use of an unpleasant stimulus to eliminate an undesirable behavior.

**Questionnaire.** A list of written questions that can be read and responded to by the student or other respondent.

**RAM.** See **Computer memory.**

**Rating scales.** Instruments that provide a scale of values describing someone or something being evaluated.

**Ratio schedule.** A type of intermittent reinforcement in which the teacher reinforces the student after the behavior has occurred a certain number of times.

**Referent.** That to which you compare the information you have about an individual in order to form a judgment.

**Reflection.** Giving direct feedback to individuals about the way their verbal and nonverbal messages are being received.

**Reinforcement.** The process of using reinforcers; in general, any event that increases the strength of a response. A reward for the purpose of maintaining an already acquired behavior is called *positive reinforcement*. Strengthening a behavior through the removal of an unpleasant stimulus is called *negative reinforcement*.

**Relational concepts.** Concepts that describe relationships between items.

**Review closure.** A type of closure technique whose main characteristic is an attempt to summarize the major points of a presentation or discussion.

**ROM.** See **Computer memory.**

**Self-referenced judgments.** Judgments made by comparing information you have about an individual to some other information you have about that same individual.

**Set induction.** Actions and statements by the teacher that are designed to relate the experiences of the students to the objectives of the lesson.

**Simulation, computer.** A computer program that establishes a model or working representation of a particular situation.

**Software.** A computer program.

**Spreadsheet.** A program that establishes a ledger-like page in the computer. Entries in this ledger may be linked by mathematical relationships.

**Steering group.** A group of pupils within the class who are carefully observed by the teacher to determine whether the class is understanding the content being discussed in the lesson.

**Symbolic medium.** A representational medium for acquiring concepts through symbols such as language.

**Synthesis questions.** Questions requiring the student to put together elements and parts so as to form a whole. Include producing original communications, making predictions, and solving problems for which a variety of answers are possible.

**Systems design.** A self-correcting and logical methodology of decision making to be used for the design and development of constructed entities; particularly in this book, instructional systems.

**Target mistakes.** The teacher stopping the wrong student or desisting a less serious deviancy.

**Taxonomy.** A classification system; used here in reference to a classification system of educational objectives or skills.

**Teaching skill.** A distinct set of identifiable behaviors needed to perform teaching functions.

**Terminal goals.** Goals one can expect to reach at the end of a given learning experience.

**Test.** An instrument that presents a common situation to which all students respond, a common set of instructions, and a common set of rules for scanning the students' responses. Used primarily for determining aptitude and achievement.

**Theoretical knowledge.** Concepts, facts, and propositions that make up much of the content of the disciplines.

**Time out.** The removal of a reward from the student or the removal of the student from the reward.

**Unit Plan.** A plan for a sequence of several lessons dealing with the same general topic.

**Wait time.** The amount of time the teacher waits after asking a question before calling for the answer.

**Withitness behaviors.** Behaviors by which the teacher communicates to students that he or she knows what is going on.

**Word processing.** A method of writing or composing text assisted by a computer.

# Index